Life Drawing

Life Drawing

A Deleuzean Aesthetics of Existence

Gordon C. F. Bearn

FORDHAM UNIVERSITY PRESS

NEW YORK 2013

Copyright © 2013 Fordham University Press

All rights reserved. No part of this publication may be reproduced, stored in a retrieval system, or transmitted in any form or
by any means—electronic, mechanical, photocopy, recording, or
any other—except for brief quotations in printed reviews,
without the prior permission of the publisher.

Fordham University Press has no responsibility for the persistence or accuracy of URLs for external or third-party Internet
websites referred to in this publication and does not guarantee
that any content on such websites is, or will remain, accurate or
appropriate.

Fordham University Press also publishes its books in a variety of
electronic formats. Some content that appears in print may not
be available in electronic books.

Library of Congress Cataloging-in-Publication Data is available
from the publisher.

Printed in the United States of America

15 14 13   5 4 3 2 1

First edition

CONTENTS

A special word for careless is caress.

—GERTRUDE STEIN

The two of us wrote *Anti-Oedipus* together. Since each of us was several, that was already quite a crowd. Here we have made use of everything that came within range, what was closest as well as farthest away. We have assigned clever pseudonyms to prevent recognition. Why have we kept our own names? Out of habit, purely out of habit. To make ourselves unrecognizable in turn. To render imperceptible, not ourselves, but what makes us act, feel, and think. Also because it's nice to talk like everybody else, to say the sun rises, when everybody knows it's only a manner of speaking. To reach, not the point where one no longer says I, but the point where it is no longer of any importance whether one says I. We are no longer ourselves. Each will know his own. We have been aided, inspired, multiplied.

—GILLES DELEUZE AND FÉLIX GUATTARI, *A Thousand Plateaus: Capitalism and Schizophrenia*

I did not write this book alone. I couldn't have. True enough, my fingers wrote or typed its various chapters in various drafts, but I didn't write or type alone. I couldn't have. Nothing is written alone. Writing is folding heterogeneous materials together, egg whites into pancake batter. True enough, it may be your fingers around the wooden spoon, but your fingers are not alone; with them always there is the family recipe and the irreplaceable Sunday breakfasts still alive in your affections. Nothing is written alone. Writing is writing together.

Often the roman-numeraled pages of a book are the only place we can feel the heterogeneity of the materials folded into its pages. I still remember when my student hands anxiously opened a very large and heavy book on

Frege to find myself suddenly put at ease by the opening words of Dummett's preface.

> I am always disappointed when a book lacks a preface: it is like arriving at someone's house for dinner, and being conducted straight into the dining-room. A preface is personal, the body of the book is impersonal: the preface tells you the author's feelings about his book, or some of them. A reader who wishes to remain aloof can skip the preface without loss; but one who wants to be personally introduced has, I feel, the right to be. (Dummett [1973] 1981, ix)

In prefaces we learn of the heterogeneous materials buffeting the author's writing. In Dummett's case, among other buffetings, we learn of the importance of his working against racism, of his gratitude to his favorite conversational partners, and of his shock at discovering Frege's anti-Semitism. My skepticism about the category of the personal, the concept of the person, also moves me to be skeptical of the distinction between the personal preface and the impersonal body of the book. The body of the book is traversed by many material energies. Some of these will be connected to everything; some will be as nearly discrete as the gift of a quotation from *Ecce Homo*. But only nearly. The most discrete of gifts harbors connections in all directions, and it is no indiscretion to enjoy them.

I do not, therefore, think it unusual that I wrote this book in the exciting winds of places, friends, and conversations enjoyed. But I have not tried to hide that fact, and that may take some readers by surprise. Even if every author writes with the voices of others echoing on the accumulating pages, still one mostly conceals this fact from one's readers, thus maintaining the pretense of organized personal authorship. But part of the joy of writing this book has been the space it provided for enjoying, once again, so much of the past almost ten years. The joys of continuing conversations otherwise. As I have not tried to hide this fact from my readers, you will find irregular references to persons and places the winds of whose philosophical energies drew my writing on. I think of this as a way of making manifest the dispersed origins of thinking which are disguised by the usual practice of pretending the author's voice and the voices of others can be kept separate. Separated by the convention of numbering the voices of others in roman numerals and of the author's own in arabic. But the separation is only pretense. Writing is writing together.

Some of the material energy of this book, which it has drawn from the togetherness of others, appears in the text to follow explicitly in its continuing lines, and some of it appears more quietly in footnotes appended to stretches that owe their excitement to what becomes of thinking together. For a while there were so many footnotes expressing our writing together that it almost got in the way of the onward energy of the text itself. Sometimes I heard that there was no almost about it; it did. So succumbing to tradition, I find myself listing the names of those with whom this writing was written together, and allowing the more or less sequential writing of these chapters to order these names, I provide the traditional list.

Michael Mendelson
Alison Freeman, now Alison Valish
Norman Melchert
Roslyn Weiss
Michael Raposa
Paul Standish
Tony and Renzo Viscardi
Maria Gandolfo
Joe Lucia
Michelle De Mooy
Chris Hagel
Jessica Glomb
Mark Bickhard
Joe Volpe
Barbara Flanagan
Adriana Novoa
Alex Levine
Yossi Berlow
Kristen Todeschini
Bobby George
Seth Moglen
Simten Gurac
Flore Chevalier
Johan Thomas

Steve Goldman
Don Jackson
Roy Miller
Sarah Zurat
John Pettegrew
Richard Matthews
David Eck
Hannah Behrman
Colin Gore
Tony Ferrizzi

At the very end of this project the generosity of a Faculty Research Grant from Lehigh University and the administrative finesse of Jessica Morgan made it possible to include the images scattered among the following chapters.

Throughout there have been voices and places shared with my family, Ellen and Cary and Alice, and these three, and school, college, field hockey, Japan, Islay Pod, and more are affectionately woven into the text as a whole. But there are two others without whom this writing would never have become the becoming it became. Without the friendship and prodding of Russel Wiebe, I would never have read *A Thousand Plateaus* and so this writing would never have begun. And without the friendship and affectionate editorial attention of Erin Seeba, this writing would never have found its way to print. I dedicate this book, therefore, to the living memory of Russel Wiebe, whose life is over (June 19, 1953–May 30, 2009), and to the open future of Erin Seeba, whose academic life is now enjoying its brilliant spring.

Thank you all, for allofit.

Overture

So, you see, there is hope.

   —GILLES DELEUZE AND FÉLIX GUATTARI, "On Capitalism and Desire"

We must invent our lines of flight, if we are able, and the only way we can invent them is by effectively drawing them, in our lives.

   —GILLES DELEUZE AND FÉLIX GUATTARI, *A Thousand Plateaus: Capitalism and Schizophrenia*

This book was such fun to write. There were difficult moments, of course, but mostly this book gave me all the inordinate joy of discovery and creation, the surest way to joy.

   There is no unhappy creation, it is always a *vis comica*. (Deleuze 1967b, 134)

And it is a personal book. By the end you will know how much I enjoy sticks, for example, but it's not just sticks, and it's not just rust. And the book teems with the affection of others, already listed by name; there would be no book at all if their affectionate attention to our conversations, scrappy and tender, had not drawn this book out of me. In a way, we were drawing out these discoveries and creations together, none of us alone, an author, all of us together, not merely an author. Mostly we were, each with the other, excitedly together. And it was such fun. But what does it do?

It might help to be told that this will be an existential philosophy inspired by Gilles Deleuze, especially by his *A Thousand Plateaus* (1980), which he wrote with Félix Guattari. It is thus existential in the spirit of their book. Unfortunately, "existentialism" has come to refer to a certain voluntaristic way of responding to the threat of nihilism. This is roughly the way existentialism is conceived by the encyclopedias, and it comfortably includes the three towering existentialist philosophers: Kierkegaard, Heidegger, and Sartre. But unfortunately this way of conceiving existentialism leaves out Nietzsche, because he never believed in free will, let alone voluntarism. Moreover, the only one of those favored three who ever actually called himself an existentialist was Sartre, and even Sartre's association with existentialism came to an end when he espoused his version of Marxism in 1960. Existentialism, as standardly conceived, is no longer alive. But what if existential philosophers were not just the familiar ones, with their more or less voluntaristic philosophies, what if rather more generously, existentialism included all those philosophers who took the threat of nihilism seriously. That is the sense in which this book describes an existential philosophy inspired by *A Thousand Plateaus*. But what is the threat of nihilism?

The threat of nihilism is not simply the concern that we are not living the good life. As old as that concern is, it was always protected, fenced in by the presumption that there was a good life, a good way to organize your life. Perhaps your life is not organized that way now, but rest assured, there is a good way to organize your life, to lead a meaningful life. Nihilism is a deeper anxiety than that. Nihilism is the anxiety that there may be no way to lead a meaningful life, at all, that there is nothing of value, anywhere, period. And since reason, itself, is one of the things that nihilism renders valueless, it is clear that nihilism is not so much the result of rational argument as the discovery of a dreadful mood you feel you will never escape.

The threat of nihilism may be familiar in religious traditions that speak of a dark night of the soul, the long and dreadful night that one passes through as one turns from the self to god. But I suspect this may still be a fenced-in form of dreadfulness, since there is always the self to return to and god to come nearer. Nevertheless, nothing at this point turns on deciding whether or not those religious traditions fenced in the dark night of the soul. Nor does much turn on whether the threat of nihilism began its crawl over Europe some time around 1800. I am tempted by the suggestion that industrial capitalism was born at about the same time as the threat of nihilism, but I will not defend that suggestion here. Nevertheless, something I do care about did happen around 1800, or to be precise, March 22, 1801. That was the day Heinrich von Kleist wrote a patronizing letter to Wilhelmine von Zenge in which he told her that his acquaintance with Kantian philosophy had shattered his world. Here is a cutting from Kleist's letter:

> If people all had green lenses instead of eyes they would be bound to think that the things they see through them *are* green—and they would never be able to decide whether the eye shows them things as they are or whether it isn't adding something to them belonging not to them but to the eye. It is the same with our minds. We cannot decide whether what we call truth is truly truth or whether it only seems so to us. . . . Since this conviction—that no truth is discoverable here on earth—appeared before my soul, I have given up reading. I have paced my room in idleness, sat down at the open window, run out of the house, in the end by the unrest in me I was driven to the cafés and tobacco houses, I went to plays and concerts to distract myself, I even, to blot everything out, did a very silly thing that I would rather Carl told you about than me; and still in all this outer tumult the one thought working and burning in my anxious soul was this: your *highest* and *only* goal in life has sunk. (Kleist 1801, 421–22)

Kleist's letter informs Wilhelmine that Kant's philosophy had shattered his world and delivered him to the cold arms of irredeemable pointlessness. I would like to draw Kleist out a little farther and equate the threat of nihilism with the threat of pointlessness. And I suggest that we characterize as an existentialist any philosopher who writes in response to the threat of irredeemable pointlessness.

Conceived as a response to the threat of pointlessness and meaninglessness, existentialism opens its doors to Nietzsche and those other two great thinkers of alienation and anxiety, Marx and Freud. Moreover, so conceived, existentialism did not die when voluntarism lost its attractions. It lived on in the writings, for example, of Bataille, Baudrillard, Derrida, Lyotard, Badiou, and indeed the pair who inspired this book: Deleuze and Guattari. Nor is it just the postwar French. No matter what the encyclopedias say, Wittgenstein, too, was an existential philosopher.

In my first book, *Waking to Wonder*, I offered an interpretation of Wittgenstein's philosophical development along existential lines I derived from Nietzsche (Bearn 1997a). And although there is a nice connection to this new book in that Nietzsche himself, in his essay "Schopenhauer as Educator"

(Nietzsche [1874] 1995), cites the letter from Kleist to similar effect, I had not then read either Nietzsche's essay or Kleist's letter. However, I had read *The Claim of Reason* by Stanley Cavell (Cavell 1979).

Like many students in the 1970s, I had been introduced to Wittgenstein by a few scraps about privacy and experience ripped from the torso of the *Investigations*, and I wasn't really sure what to do with them. I remember feeling that it didn't matter whether or not there could be a private language; there might still be private experience. It is not an uncommon reaction. The *Investigations* is an unusual philosophical text, if only because its author has such a negative view of professionalized philosophy. When it was published in 1953, just about the only stretch of Wittgenstein's book that seemed relevant to the concerns of the professors was precisely that stretch of remarks on privacy and experience; mostly those remarks were felt to be inconclusive or worse. But it turns out that one of the ways the professors mangled the reception of Wittgenstein's writings was by being blind to their existential dimension, even in those putatively professional remarks on the possibility of a private language (Baker 1988).

Although the author of the *Investigations* writes with unmistakable passion for the importance of the topics he considers, the actual topics he writes about can easily seem unworthy of the passion he devotes to them. Why does he wonder whether he can say "bububu" and mean "if it doesn't rain I shall go for a walk"? (Wittgenstein [1953] 1976, p. 18e). Why is it so important to remember the platitude that tables with three legs don't wobble, while those with four do, sometimes? (Wittgenstein [1953] 1976, §79). It is not hard to understand why its first readers overlooked the existential passion of Wittgenstein's *Investigations*.

This blindness to the existential is less excusable with his first book, because the author of the *Tractatus Logico-Philosophicus* tells us explicitly that the importance of his book does not lie in the logical and ontological discussions that fill its pages. Rather, its importance consists in its contribution to the vanishing of the riddle of existence and the problem of life, to our coming to see the world aright; in a word: the importance of that book was its mysticism (Wittgenstein [1921] 1961, 6.44–6.54). But since the existential trajectory of the *Tractatus* had already been overlooked, it was easy to miss it in the more obscure surroundings of the *Investigations*. The general situation, even today, is well described by Cavell:

Even when the acceptance of Wittgenstein as one of the major philosophical voices of the West since Kant may be taken for granted, it is apt to be controversial to find that his reception by professional philosophy is insufficient, that the spiritual fervor or seriousness of his writing is internal to his teaching, say its manner (or method) to its substance, and that something in the very professionalization of philosophy debars professional philosophers from taking his seriousness seriously. (Cavell 1989, 30)

My initially unsympathetic response to the *Investigations* was partially corrected by my falling for the mysticism of the *Tractatus*, but I was still floundering for a way to receive Wittgenstein's existential investigations when I read *The Claim of Reason* (Cavell 1979).

At first, I was not convinced. I knew the *Investigations* was not as easy to place and parry as most people were telling me, but I found it hard to believe that it was as difficult as Cavell insisted. A while later, helped by a teacher and a friend, both of whom knew Cavell personally, the book opened up. It presented Wittgenstein as an author whose writing is everywhere a response to the threat of skepticism. When Cavell got wind that there were those who would like him to say something more directly about Wittgenstein's relation to what Nietzsche called nihilism, he explained why he would not: "I persist, as indicated, in calling the issue by its, or its ancestor's, older name of skepticism" (Cavell [1987] 1990a, 94). Almost alone, especially at that time, Cavell did not think that Wittgenstein had an answer to the skeptic. The existence of another's pain or of the world itself are not, according to Cavell, known with certainty. There is thus a puckish sense in which the skeptic is actually correct. But only puckish, for on this account, that correctness reveals not an intellectual lack but our metaphysical finitude (Cavell [1969] 1976, 263). A parenthetical paragraph in an essay Cavell wrote on Emerson puts it this way: "It is true that we do not know the existence of the world with certainty; our relation to its existence is deeper— one in which it is accepted, that is to say, received. My favorite way of putting this is to say that existence is to be acknowledged" (Cavell 1981, 133). What Wittgenstein made possible for Cavell was to interpret this acceptance, reception, or acknowledgment in terms of our meaning what we say, seriously. It was a question of authenticity.

Cavell is more likely to write of skepticism than of nihilism and more likely to write about seriousness than about authenticity, but just as he confesses to calling nihilism by its older name, skepticism, so he persists in discussing authenticity under cover of seriousness. For example, he interprets J. L. Austin's occasional criticisms of A. J. Ayer for not writing seriously as a criticism of Ayer's having written "inauthentically" (Cavell [1969] 1976, 109). And in a paper that he declined to reprint in his first book of essays, thus a paper that he may have had misgivings about, Cavell puts it about as directly as he ever did: "In Wittgenstein's work 'ordinary' or 'everyday' contexts and examples are, I suggest, meant to carry the force of 'authentic' examples authentically responded to in language" (Cavell [1964] 1984, 217). Quite naturally, then, Cavell pointed me in the direction of an existential interpretation of Wittgenstein's *Investigations* which kept its sights on authenticity.

The threat of pointlessness surfaces in Wittgenstein as not knowing how to describe or think about those aspects of our lives that mean the most to us. Whether we love someone, or are simply hungry for sex. Whether we are enjoying our way of life, or have simply become busy. We wonder whether we love him, and so we find ourselves thinking about love, and so we find ourselves thinking about the word *love*. The trouble is that we are not sure whether to call *this* love, or *this* envy, or *this* happiness. So Wittgenstein's turn to the language in which we express our troubles is not a trivialization of those troubles, but their continuation. And he thinks he has found a way to still them, for a spell (Wittgenstein [1953] 1976, §§111, 133; see Wittgenstein [1921] 1961, 4.002).

According to Wittgenstein, the trouble comes from our trying to spiff up our language. We take the ragged use of the words *love* or *true* and try to make one aspect of their uses do all the work, as if that one aspect were the essence of love or of truth. Sometimes Wittgenstein calls this subliming the logic of our language, turning the solid materiality of our life with some word, all at once, into gas (Wittgenstein [1953] 1976, §89). Sometimes he describes this as losing control of our language, following our words away from their natural, authentic homes out onto slippery metaphysical ice, where there is no friction, where it seems there is no constraint at all on what we can say, where we seem to be able to get away with saying anything (§107). It can leave us feeling our lives are entirely arbitrary, that there is nothing secure, not love, not justice, not meaning, not even the very point of living, itself. Wittgenstein's solution is to lead our words back from the slippery metaphysical ice, to the everyday, to the "rough ground" (§107). Here he is:

> When philosophers use a word—"knowledge", "being", "object", "I", "proposition", "name"—and try to grasp the *essence* of the thing, one must always ask oneself: is the word ever actually used in this way in the language which is its original home?
>
> What *we* do is to bring words back from their metaphysical to their everyday use. (Wittgenstein [1953] 1976, §116)

By reminding us of the special circumstances in which a sentence such as "I am here" is used, the philosopher will be revealed to have been using it in circumstances where it cannot be meant seriously, that is to say, authentically. Cavell insists that as it is in the power of words to wander onto slippery ice, so it is in their power to return, to be recalled to the everyday which is their authentic home (Cavell 1989, 47). This double power means that the quieting of our troubled lives will not be accomplished once and for all time, but only "momentarily" (Cavell 1994, 153). The task of becoming authentic is never completed, but always repeated.

By the time I was completing my interpretation of Wittgenstein's existential investigations, I had come more and more under the influence of Derrida. Typically, philosophers influenced by Wittgenstein dismiss Derrida. Searle held the line against Derrida with nine (professionalized) necessary and sufficient conditions for the performance of a sincere and nondefective promise (Searle [1969] 1970, 57). And Searle is not above reprimanding Derrida for knowing next to nothing about philosophy of language and for his commitment to a "traditional pre-Wittgensteinian conception of language" (Searle 1994, 639, 664). Even Cavell has his (unprofessionalizable) momentary, Wittgensteinian peace, which seems to insulate him from the disseminating powers of Derrida's iterability. And for a while Cavell's dismissal of Derrida was mine too. As I moved out from Wittgenstein into French philosophy of the 1960s, it was Foucault who first seemed congenial, even congenial to the grammatical investigations that Cavell had taught me to pursue. Foucault seemed to be offering grammatical investigations of the human sciences, much as Kuhn was offering a grammar or structure of revolutions in the physical sciences. Moreover, while Kuhn was discovering that scientific life was held together by judgments deeper than rules, he was enjoying conversations with Cavell, whose reading of Wittgenstein was issuing in the thought that our linguistic life was held together by attunements deeper than rules. Derrida seemed to be doing something altogether different: denying that our linguistic life was held together at all. So I spurned his results. But not his writings.

Thinking it important to say precisely what was wrong with Derrida's approach to philosophy, I continued to read him; in particular I read him as part of the last chapter of a story about twentieth-century architecture that began with Loos and Carnap, Le Corbusier and Wittgenstein (see Bearn 1992). But there is something about Derrida's writing that is attractive; it has a wonderful sound. I enjoyed the way Derrida's line,

> This (therefore) will not have been a book. (Derrida [1972a] 1981, 3)

which is the first sentence of his *Dissemination*, might have been an equally good way to begin the *Tractatus*, or indeed the *Investigations*. Naturally, I began to wonder whether Derrida's and Wittgenstein's (mature) writings were more deeply congruent, and one natural place to think about that was repetition.

"Iterability" is Derrida's word for the fact that it is a condition for being a word, spoken or written, that it be able to function in contexts other than the one in which it actually appeared. If it were not able to function in different contexts, then it would not be a significant mark. It would be a smudge (Derrida 1971). Cavell agrees: "That a word can recur is analytic of 'word'" (Cavell 1979, 78, 192). Where then is the disagreement? It concerns the consequences of iterability, of its being analytic that a word can recur. According to Derrida what iterability entails is that a significant mark can never be fully present in any single appearance. Wherever it appears, it must always retain the ability, even there, to mean something other than what it was meant to mean. Derrida concludes that since every linguistic expression can be used in contexts that are unusual or out of the ordinary, no linguistic act can ever be successful. This means that according to Derrida there can be no Wittgensteinian peace, even momentarily. When we bring our words back to their everyday homes where we were hoping to mean what we said, seriously, authentically, we must fail. And so on this account there is no hope for peace, no hope for an escape from the threat of pointlessness to authenticity. Not even momentarily.

Learning to read *The Claim of Reason* was the most important event in my philosophical life. And I am not the first to have fallen for the voice of Cavell's writing; there is something about the liquid line of his prose, meandering without break, continuous intensities; there is something about Cavell's prose that feels like friendship. And the man is generosity itself. Although I began to take Derrida's side against Cavell, I was careful to acknowledge the real attractions of Cavell's philosophy. And I still wince when I read those first reviews of *The Claim of Reason* that admonish Cavell for his self-indulgence while, with a grudge, admitting that "Cavell's self-indulgence does not obliterate his talent and intelligence" (Mounce 1981; see Kenny 1980). The attractions of Cavell's writing are not the attractions of professionalism; they are the palpable attractions of what Emerson, in the language of 1837, italicized as *Man Thinking*.

The rewards of the turn to Derrida have been enormous, but not at first. At first, trading Wittgenstein's momentary peace for Derrida's endless iterations left me with nothing to say to the threat of pointlessness. No way to mean what I said, authentically, seriously. Derrida himself, although mocked for his playfulness, describes the trajectory of all significant action in almost tragic terms: "Plenitude is the end (the goal), but were it attained, it would be the end (death)" (Derrida 1988a, 129). Perhaps the best we could hope for would be the absurdist comedy of *Waiting for Godot*, the smiles of Estragon. It wasn't much. And then some time in February 1993, Russel Wiebe wanted to see whether there were fires hidden in the fuss just beginning to surround *A Thousand Plateaus*. John Madritch, Joe Lucia, and I joined in, and nothing's been the same since.

Something strange was going on. It wasn't just that I had to burrow into books from my botanical past to hang on to "Introduction: Rhizome." Derrida had once already sent me to the internal anatomy of the ear (Derrida 1972c). It was perhaps the metaphysical abandon with which Deleuze and Guattari announced: "There are only lines" (Deleuze and Guattari [1980] 1987, 8). Or perhaps it was their laconic, "We're tired of trees," or their comic "Grass is the only way out" (15, 19). It certainly had something to do with their rejection of both Foucault's genealogy and Derrida's dissemination (11, 24). But in the midst of all that unsettling, it didn't really help to be told that the magic formula we all sought was "PLURALISM = MONISM" (20).

Their translator suggested that their book be read the way records were played, not straight through, but jumping around, skipping from track to track. Since no one in our little group had yet read *Anti-Oedipus* or *The Logic of Sense*, the concept that seemed most preposterous to us was that there could be a body without organs, so figuring we were giving the book a test of fire, we read "November 28, 1947: How Do You Make Yourself a Body without Organs?"

That particular plateau attempts a description of how to live a life that is "full of gaiety, ecstasy, and dance" (Deleuze and Guattari [1980] 1987, 150). This is what making yourself a body without organs promised, and it was also the hope that Nietzsche's affirmative philosophy had offered to the threat of nihilism, of pointlessness. There was no doubt, then, that this book had an existential dimension in just the Nietzschean sense that I had found in Wittgenstein. But with a difference. Where Wittgenstein had been concerned with stopping, with finding peace, this new pair seemed interested in going on. This was very different from Derrida. Derrida, just like Wittgenstein, is concerned with stopping, the difference is only that Derrida argues that it is not possible to stop, to really and authentically stop. But Deleuze and Guattari were not trying to stop at all; they were trying to go on. Here they are:

> Where psychoanalysis says, "Stop, find yourself again," we should say instead, "Let's go further still, we haven't found our BwO [body without organs] yet, we haven't sufficiently dismantled our self." Substitute forgetting for anamnesis, experimentation for interpretation. Find your body without organs. Find out how to make it. It's a question of life and death, youth and old age, sadness and joy. It is where everything is played out. (Deleuze and Guattari [1980] 1987, 151)

As it turns out, it wasn't the organs that were the problem; it was the organization. (Deleuze and Guattari [1980] 1987, 158).[1] So the program for making yourself a body without organs is a program of disorganization. A program designed to disorganize the three great strata of organization: organism, significance, and subjectification (159). The hope of making yourself a body without organs is not to find peace and security, but risking the worst, to excite "becomings, becomings-animal, becomings-molecular" (162).

And it had a lot to do with desire. "The BwO is desire" (Deleuze and Guattari [1980] 1987, 165). But Deleuze and Guattari do not conceive of desiring something in negative terms. For a very long time, at least since Plato, philosophers have tended to think of desire as a lack, an absence: Walking along the tracks, I notice the train company has herbicided all the wineberries to death, and mourning their absence, I want some. And for just as long philosophers have been inclined to think of the satisfaction of desire as filling that absence. Turning off the tracks toward a pond, in the sun and out of the herbicide's reach, I find a thicket of wineberry vines, loaded with fruit. It is a pleasure to satisfy my desire, gorging my fingers red. But it doesn't last: Walking back home I wish I had brought some berries with me in my handkerchief. Desire hollowing out again.

It should sound familiar. This traditional account of desire and its temporary satisfaction has precisely the structure of Wittgenstein's quest for quietude and peace. And the connection to desire is made by Derrida's featuring the phrase "wanting to say," which is a way of saying what you meant. Suppose meaning what we say is saying precisely what, there and then, we wanted to say, then if the traditional account of desire is right, satisfaction will never be complete, never be more than momentary. It does sound a little familiar. All that that could be hoped for would be the smiles of Estragon. But while telling us how to make ourselves bodies without organs, Deleuze and Guattari also sketch an understanding of desire more or less entirely opposed to the traditional one.

Not negative, they sketch a fully affirmative conception of desire. Desiring is defined not as a static absence, but as a process, a way of becoming. Harking back to *Anti-Oedipus*, they slip a definition of desire into a parenthesis: "(with desire defined as a process of production without reference to any exterior agency, whether it be a lack that hollows it out or a pleasure that fills it)" (Deleuze and Guattari [1980] 1987, 154). And with this new account of desire there is a new account of what desire desires. No longer is it pleasure, satisfaction, the stopping of desire, temporarily. What the process of desire desires is immanent to desire, desire's continuation. They put it this way:

> There is, in fact, a joy that is immanent to desire as though desire were filled by itself and its contemplations, a joy that implies no lack or impossibility and is not measured by pleasure since it is what distributes intensities of pleasure and prevents them from being suffused by anxiety, shame and guilt. (Deleuze and Guattari [1980] 1987, 155)

It is too soon, and these few notes, are only an overture, but perhaps you can sense how even these few sketchy ideas might have seemed just the bridge to take us beyond what Derrida had left of Wittgenstein: wry smiles. And the name of this bridge was not authenticity, not even momentary authenticity. The name of this bridge was pointlessness, a disorganized pointlessness not to be escaped but to be achieved.

Delicious becoming delirious, the joy promised by making yourself a disorganized body without organs is amazing. Deleuze and Guattari tell us that one avenue to this joy could be an analog of the medieval practice of courtly love, the very *gaya scienza* praised by Nietzsche (Nietzsche [1882] 1974; Nietzsche [1886] 1966, §260). Courtly love is sometimes introduced as the practice of placing external constraints on the satisfaction of desire, a woman granting erotic favors to her lover only after her lover performs specified deeds of valor. But Deleuze and Guattari warn us that "it would be an error to interpret courtly love in terms of a law of lack" (Deleuze and Guattari [1980] 1987, 156). It would be an error to suppose that courtly love consisted in postponing pleasure, thus increasing the aching desire as the final silencing of that desire comes desperately to be sought. Postponement, a way of making the pain of desiring worse. This is not how Deleuze and Guattari interpret courtly love. On their account, the practice of courtly love releases desire more intensely to be enjoyed, not to be quelled but to be continued. Their shoulders touch, floating dizzy, enjoying desiring.

> "Joy" in courtly love, the exchange of hearts, the test or "assay": everything is allowed, as long as it is not external to desire or transcendent to its plane or internal to persons. The slightest caress may be as strong as an orgasm; orgasm is a mere fact, a rather deplorable one, in relation to desire in pursuit of its principle. Everything is allowed: all that counts is for pleasure to be the flow of desire itself. (Deleuze and Guattari [1980] 1987, 156)

Wandering caresses not organized by any climactic goal are a model of the risky joy on offer here. And by featuring disorganization Deleuze and Guattari have already set themselves against the exquisite authenticity for which both Wittgenstein and Derrida yearn. In a discussion of architecture, Derrida had once used the expression "beyond authenticity and inauthenticity" (Derrida 1991), and although he gave this his usual wry

twist, it now seemed that Deleuze and Guattari might have a way of returning this happy expression to its Yes-saying Nietzschean roots.

And then there was Kundera, in particular the 1997 paperback edition of
Kundera's *Slowness* (Kundera 1995). Living with *A Thousand Plateaus* seemed
to offer a way into the existential dimensions of that strangely metaphysical
book. *Slowness* eased all doubt. Kundera's little book crystallized a dualism
between the sensual enjoyments of slow wandering caresses and the des-
perate teleological speed of what he calls the religion of orgasm. And there
was a way in which a number of concepts that had seemed univocal were
doubled by what Kundera wrote. It was as if there were an affirmative slow
version of art, of desire, of enjoyment, of repetition, of theater, of a life
lived in the present, and then on the other side negative fast versions of all
those concepts. Perhaps there were affirmative and negative versions of the
notion of a concept, itself. *Slowness* made me see that there would be a way
of bringing it all together in an aesthetics of existence inspired by Deleuze,
especially by his *A Thousand Plateaus* which he wrote with Guattari. It pre-
cipitated this book.

I wanted to write something that would be more than a representation of
what others have thought, and I wanted it to be more than a representation
of what I thought. I wanted it to do something. So much of academia is involved in providing representations of things. Representations of reconstruction in America. Of utilitarian themes in Melville. Of children in the
drawings of Mary Cassatt. Of the life cycles of various ticks. Of the truth
conditions for subjunctive conditionals. Of the various uses of *Achtung* in
the writings of Kant. Of the origin of species by means of natural selection.
Enormous learning goes into and comes out of such representational projects, but in philosophy, if not everywhere else, those representations have
drained the blood from the powerful texts themselves. Bottled and displayed, there is much to learn, but the rooms reek of formaldehyde. And yet
it is difficult to imagine what an alternative to this diet of representations
would be, and it can feel presumptuous to attempt something else.

> My ideal, when I write about an author, would be to write nothing that could
> cause him sadness, or if he is dead, that might make him weep in his grave.
> Think of the author you are writing about. Think of him so hard that he can
> no longer be an object, and equally so that you cannot identify with him. Avoid
> the double shame of the scholar and the familiar. Give back to an author a little

of the joy, the energy, the life of love and politics that he knew how to give and invent. So many dead writers must have wept over what has been written about them. (Deleuze and Parnet [1977] 1987, 119)

One alternative to bloodless representationalism would be writing that brings the reader the experiences described. Some of Plato's *Dialogues* head this way; Descartes's *Meditations* do too, and so do Wittgenstein's *Investigations*. You could think of this as pornographic philosophy, for pornographic writing, by describing excitement, excites. At least that is the intention. Mine too. I have tried to clear the moral and conceptual ground of obstacles standing in the way of making our lives beautiful, but I have also tried to make the ride itself exemplary and enjoyable. By representing excitement, I have tried to excite, to excite becoming.

At first I was quite taken by a remark Foucault made while distinguishing his work from Sartre's: "From the idea that the self is not given to us, I think that there is only one practical consequence: we have to create ourselves as a work of art" (Foucault 1983, 351). My intention in this book was therefore to show how we could create our lives as works of art. I called the project *Life Drawing*, the name given to classes in which art students are taught to draw the human figure from life, often naked. I came gradually to think, however, that it might be misleading to follow Foucault by making my guiding idea the work of art. Making your life a work of art is too much like carving a statue, subtraction not addition, and besides there are so many more beautiful things than there are works of art. Art seemed too particular a notion. My guiding idea was becoming the far more generous idea of beauty. And now the title *Life Drawing* unveiled additional enjoyments. As we are drawn to sit down by the stream just here, or to pause at just this painting along the gallery wall, so too anomalous individuals, people and things, draw our lives out, exciting movement, becoming. And letting yourself be drawn requires that you not be focused on any point. It will be active, for you have to prepare yourself, but it is not intentional. Being drawn in by the music or the smell is a way of losing yourself as you dissolve into scent's sensuality. I wanted us to be drawn to beauty by beauty, not simply by art. And though there is plenty of art, there is beauty everywhere. Every stick, for example, but it's not just sticks, and it's not just the Pollock glory of bird droppings splashed on the sidewalk: It's allofit. Yes, as Cage knew, "Beauty is . . . underfoot wherever we take the trouble to look" (Cage [1961] 1973, 98).

But how was I to write this wilder book? How was I even to begin? Alison Freeman quietly suggested that I try beginning in the middle, and I did. I had always been intrigued by the middle, the middle, for example, of walking to the store, when the walk's being simply an errand disappears in wandering enjoyments. Deleuze and Guattari's rhizomes were always in the middle. The rhizomatic middle was the answer.

> A rhizome has no beginning or end; it is always in the middle, between things, interbeing, *intermezzo*. The tree is filiation, but the rhizome is alliance, uniquely alliance. The tree imposes the verb "to be," but the fabric of the rhizome is the conjunction, "and . . . and . . . and . . ." Where are you going? Where are you coming from? What are you heading for? These are totally useless questions. . . . Kleist, Lenz, and Büchner have another way of traveling and moving: proceeding from the middle, through the middle, coming and going rather than starting and finishing. (Deleuze and Guattari [1980] 1987, 25)

I found a large piece of cardboard, sat down on the floor, drew a circle in the middle, and all that was left was to find a middle from which I could make alliances with desire, authenticity, beauty, and so on, enjoying. Since its negative senses were the root of nihilism and its affirmative Nietzschean senses were nihilism's overcoming, I wrote pointlessness in the middle of the circle, and hoping to use *Slowness* to precipitate an aesthetics of existence from the affirmative dimensions of pointlessness, I was beginning.

Once, while I was working on these things, I found myself on the beach being asked whether, given my focus on aesthetics, there were not a work of art that I thought powerfully embodied the hope of life drawing.[2] There is. I have known it for a long time.[3] Once I even performed it. It is a 1970 piece by Alvin Lucier called *I Am Sitting in a Room*. The score explains itself.

> I am sitting in a room different from the one you are in now.
>   I am recording the sound of my speaking voice and I am going to play it back into the room again and again until the resonant frequencies of the room

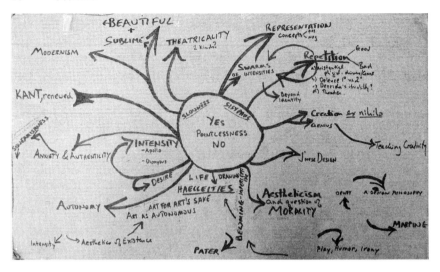

Figure 0-1. Cardboard drawing.

reinforce themselves so that any semblance of my speech, with perhaps the exception of rhythm, is destroyed.

What you will hear, then, are the natural resonant frequencies of the room articulated by speech.

I regard this activity not so much as a demonstration of a physical fact, but more as a way to smooth out any irregularities my speech might have. (Lucier 1980, 30)[4]

It is all there. We think repetition is a bad thing, that it deprives our words of their power, making them thin, unable to be meant seriously, authentically. But it is not so. As these repetitions are repeatedly recorded, the sounding words resound, cohering continuously, rhythm liquefying their senses. We are normally more practically inclined, using words to get things done, to achieve our ends. Reaching out to the lettuce, the words become invisible. But words are material things too; it is we in our practical living who disappear their singular specificities. We cannot feel the beauty that is underfoot, wherever we take the trouble to look. In the rushing of our living, there isn't time to look. But when we release ourselves and our life with language from these teleological constraints, singularities slip away from the working world, becoming aerial, becoming beautiful. Of course,

Gertrude Stein knew this. Gertrude Stein knew this, intimately. And soon you will find that I think becoming beautiful means breaking through to the other side of representation, and that I think becoming itself is beyond representation, so that by invoking an older use of the word becoming, I enjoy saying that becoming beautiful is becoming becoming.

Yes and No

> While every noble morality develops from a triumphant affirmation of itself, slave morality from the outset says No to what is "outside," what is "different," what is "not itself"; and *this* No is its creative deed. This inversion of the value-positing eye—this need to direct one's view outward instead of back to oneself—is of the essence of *ressentiment:* in order to exist, slave morality always first needs a hostile external world; it needs, physiologically speaking, external stimuli in order to act at all—its action is fundamentally reaction.
>
> —FRIEDRICH NIETZSCHE, *On the Genealogy of Morals*

> The child is innocence and forgetfulness, a new beginning, a game, a self-propelling wheel, a first motion, a sacred Yes-saying.
>
> —FRIEDRICH NIETZSCHE, *Thus Spoke Zarathustra*

No

Yes. Surprising as it seems, Western philosophy is afraid of Yes. In the wake of his early fascination with Schopenhauer's dark pessimism, Nietzsche discovered in ancient Greek tragedy the energizing and terrifying power of Yes. Tragedy as dangerous affirmation, like wine. This was not, nor is it today, the standard approach to tragedy.

Slice one thin feature from the haunches of human tragedy: Tragedies disrupt our projects. Using all one's intellectual energy to avoid sleeping with your mother, you find yourself siring siblings. Flying to an important meeting, the plane explodes. Called from a budding theatrical career to war, imprisoned, fortunate to return alive, you find you have not really survived. Tragedy, negatively construed, names the eruption of brute fact, dumb luck, in the middle of our well-planned lives. We struggle to give our lives significance, meaning, a point, and then tragedy discovers all our planning pointless. Unless there is another way.

Death itself shares this feature of tragedy: a disruption of our projects none can avoid. The arbitrariness or contingency of death scars existence as a whole, for since death can come at any moment, there is no moment of human life that is not already marked by the possibility of death, that is not, already, in its way, mourning mortality.[1] If tragedy is as unavoidable as death, then the lesson of tragedy is the final pointlessness of human existence. Death and tragedy, negatively construed, sound a despairing No to our projects. Unless there is another way.

In Camus's *The Myth of Sisyphus* (1942), the pointlessness of existence, the call of suicide, is driven home by repetition. Repeatedly rolling his rock to the top of a mountain, the rock rolls back again, Sisyphus is trailing it to the bottom, where he begins to roll it to the top, again. Even children know that it is an extreme form of punishment to be made to dig a hole and fill it in, again. Such action comes to no end, no conclusion. It has no point. And those who punish by enforcing pointless activity are, however stone faced, mocking those they punish. Pointless action is barely action at all, so that to be compelled to act repetitiously is to be punished physically, and at the same time, metaphysically.

Worse. Repetition is not confined to punishment. There is repetition, also, in the lives of those who have escaped this kind of explicit punishment. Every morning on the train to the big city, or the trail to the barn, every evening on the train, or the trail, back. Every human life confronts repetition (Camus [1942a] 1991, 12–13). Ecclesiastes finds it in the rising and setting of the sun, the birth and death of generations; its author forced to conclude that there is no escape from this pointless repetition: "That which hath been is that which shall be, and that which hath been done is that which shall be done; and there is nothing new under the sun" (Ecclesiastes 1.9). It is one of the paradoxes of repetition that although life's repetitions seem to demonstrate the inevitability of change, each repetition, in a repetitiousness of men and flies, seems to demonstrate that nothing ever changes. Unless in smug self-satisfaction we think tragedy could never touch our own lives, tragedy reminds us of the fundamental pointlessness of human existence. Or is there another way?

Insofar as action is motivated by desire, action aims at satisfying a desire. If the desire were satisfied, the action would stop. It would have reached its end, telos, and it would be over, satisfied (see Derrida 1988a, 129). So the pointlessness of existence exposes desire as unsatisfiable: "The eye is not satisfied with seeing, nor the ear filled with hearing" (Ecclesiastes 1.7). This depressing discovery depends on construing desire in negative terms. Negatively construed, desire is a lack which our actions try to fill, but which the inescapable repetitiousness of our lives reveals to be beyond satisfaction, for truly to satisfy a desire, would that not be the impossible filling beyond all possible emptying?

In speech, as children know, repetition can separate the sound of a word from its meaning, and as a bon mot becomes a cliché, its impact. In writing, what gets separated is the shape of the word from its meaning:

cup
cup
cup
cup
cup
cup
cup.

One point of using a word is to call out some feature of its meaning that answers to the demands of our use of the word, the way a cup of coffee answers to our desire for coffee. But repetition deprives the use of a word of the point of its use in just the way that digging and refilling a hole deprives the shovel, and the shoveling, of their point. Words so construed are construed negatively, as containers, vessels, which when filled are meaningful, and when empty are meaningless. The repeated use of a word is like filling a cup with water, emptying it, refilling it, emptying it. A pointless, meaningless use of the cup. And so too of the word *cup*. Emptied of meaning.

Here again there is no escaping repetition, no more than there was any hope of escaping the interruption of our projects by death. In this case, the very significance of a linguistic mark depends on its being usable, again. To be meaningful, a mark must repeat a pattern with a use in the language. So the disruptive power of repetition is at the heart of linguistic meaning itself, whatever the tough realistic philosophers say, linguistic meaning is riddled with repetition. So the meaninglessness of existence, which arrives in the wake of a realization of the repetitious repetitions of human life, is complete. Nor is it as if the realm of linguistic meaning could survive the loss of existential meaning. In their twinned repetitiousness, linguistic meaning and existential meaning become pointless together, at once.

It is a bleak picture, black on black. The repetitiousness of our lives reveals those lives to be without meaning, without significance. Pointless. What is the meaning of life? It has none. A Sophoclean catechism:

—The best thing?—*Never to be born.*
—Second best?—*To die soon.*

Or is there perhaps another way?

If pointlessness is unavoidable, then life will be worth something only if pointlessness is worth something. Only if we can discover a positive construal no less of repetition than of pointlessness itself. Only if there is a way from No to Yes. And there is. Its name is beauty. Its being is becoming. But we are only just beginning.

Double Negation and Ressentiment

I have said that Western philosophy is afraid of Yes, that it is a philosophy of negation. But there is an obvious sense in which this is wrong; philosophers have constructed one positive philosophical system after another. Isn't this constructive work affirmative? Of course it is. This makes my assertion wrong, but that should not stop us. It is not a good thing for a philosopher to be afraid of being wrong. It promotes cagey "maybe"'s, "for the most part"'s, "one aspect"'s; it promotes, in a word, scholarship, and it is, itself, an example of the negative bent of philosophy. Descartes's philosophy is a perfect example of a philosophy motivated by this fear of error, and his was, nevertheless, a constructive philosophy. But it was constructive in the very weakest sense: affirmation by double negation. If we stick to clear and distinct ideas, then at least we will *not* be *wrong*, or weaker still, we will have *no* reason to *doubt*. Double negation. "When stepped on, a worm doubles up. That is clever. In that way he lessens the probability of being stepped on again" (Nietzsche [1888a] 1982, 1.31).[2] Philosophers have too often wormed their way to affirmation by multiplying negations. But double negation offers no joy. The postponed interview you had been dreading does not release joy. You may be relieved, glad, unburdened, but not joyful.

Driving in anger, speeding through an intersection, you miss disaster by inches. Exhaling, you feel relieved, thankful, not joyful. And so too philosophy's double negation is unsatisfying. Affirmation without joy. A fake affirmation.

Hegel made double negation the center of his philosophy, but the example of Descartes, and the excruciating timidity of the footnotes into which philosophy disappears, are sufficient to demonstrate that philosophy's dominant color has always been the color of the worm, *vermis*, vermilion. As with so much else, we owe the discovery of philosophy's habitual pseudo-affirmation to Nietzsche. *On the Genealogy of Morals* (1887) finds behind the positive ideals of goodness and truth, the twisted work of revengeful men and women. Think again of Descartes, at first glance, you will think he is in love with certainty. When pragmatists say you are being "too Cartesian," it always means you are evincing too much interest in epistemological certitude, an interest pragmatists take evident pride in having overcome. But, as we soon learn, Descartes's meditations are motivated more by the desire to avoid error than by any interest in truth itself. It is fear of epistemic disaster which motivates his constructive project. Descartes backs his way into certainty. Nietzsche's *Genealogy* discovers the same vermilion motivations behind philosophy's concern with the good: fear of disaster, existential disaster. We have backed our way into the good. Painted ourselves into a vermilion corner.

They tell us that moral philosophy is about the good life. What we ought to do. The course catalogs all agree. But the minute you open the books, you find that moral philosophy has wormed its way into those apparently positive values. It spends its time trying to show what we should *not* do. Where it speaks in positive terms at all, it is often motivated by a partisan ethics, correcting the injustices done to one's favorite group, which is normally, even including defenders of animal rights, a group to which one belongs, oneself. Not that this is an entirely bad thing. If you can walk, then spending only one afternoon with someone confined to a wheel chair is more than enough to realize that there is still much that could be done to accommodate our cities to life in a chair. But partisan ethics are essentially reactive ethics; they begin, and often end, with the schoolyard shriek: stop it! Moral philosophy, even that dominated by apparently affirmative partisan ethics, concentrates its cross eyes on its No's.[3]

The moral good is, in fact, a No. In Kant's moral philosophy, for instance, the requirement that the maxim of one's action be able to be conceived and willed as a universal law is negative. It doesn't tell us what to do, but only that if the maxim of our action cannot be conceived or willed as a universal law, then it is prohibited by the moral law. Kant says his moral law is a compass, but unlike a compass it doesn't point north: it tells us all the directions which are not-north. We find our way to the north, the good, once again, by double negation. Kant has many defenders today, and there is currently a great deal of interest in discovering that Kant was not as inflexible or inhuman as he at first appears. So I expect to be told that my two sentence account of Kant's moral philosophy is not only brutally brief, but viciously partial, for I have not mentioned Kant's apparently positive requirement that we are to treat others as ends in themselves. But this too is merely pseudo-affirmation. This too is painted vermilion: *"Act in such a way that you always treat humanity, whether in your own person or in the person of any other*, never simply as a means, *but always at the same time as an end"* (Kant [1785] 1956, 96, my emphasis in roman type). Listen carefully, here again negation is worming its way by duplicity to affirmation. First negation: it is evil to use another merely as a means; second negation: stop it.

Utilitarianism's interest in maximizing pleasure, over all, might seem to be an exception to this haste to imitate the worm. Pleasure, after all, seems something positive, and there is a sharp distinction between the consequences of an ethics that maximizes pleasure and one that minimizes pain, for human extinction would extinguish human pain. But there is still a vermilion tone to utilitarian ethics: both in its original versions sketched in terms of an admittedly unanalyzed notion of pleasure and in its more professional versions that eliminate all talk of pleasure, replacing it with the intentionally empty notion of desire satisfaction. We are told that this professionalization is a significant advance because we no longer need to duck the demand that we provide an analysis of pleasure. But the old and the new ways of framing utilitarianism are one in their acceptance of a conception of desire as rather like a pain that satisfaction would remove. And this conception of desire is, once again, conceived in negative terms as a painful lack. The apparently positive professionalization of utilitarianism as maximizing desire satisfaction thus turns out, once again, to be the pseudo-affirmation of double negation. What does maximizing desire satisfaction come to? Minimizing the painful lack that is desire, so long as you do not increase a like pain in others. However surprisingly, utilitarians, too, worm their way to affirmation.

Kant and Mill are only two, but two is the beginning of infinity, and these two examples could be multiplied many times over, reaching back to Plato on desire and forward to Derrida on wanting to say. I used to think that the seed of all these double negations was the Platonic conception of desire as lack. If desire is what motivates human action, and if desire were a painful lack, then all of human action would be motivated by the desire to supplement that lack, or in other words, to negate that negation, to remove that pain.[4] The importance of desire to human life is such that this account of the origin of philosophy's vermilion colors might actually be defensible, and in chapter 6, I will articulate a different affirmative account of desire. But this genealogy doesn't go deep enough, for as I shall there try to show, wide stretches of human experience, particularly those having to do with the enjoyment of certain kinds of pain, must be pinched and squeezed if they are ever to fit into the negative conception of desire as lack. So what we need is not just an alternative conception of desire, but also an explanation of the attractiveness of the negative conception of desire. Nietzsche has a suggestion.

Nietzsche accepts a distinction between two broad kinds of person, on the one hand those he calls, more or less equivalently, nobles or powerful or masters or rulers or knightly aristocrats or blond beasts, and on the other hand, those he calls quite consistently slaves but also the weak, the impotent, the Jews (Nietzsche [1887] 1967a, e.g., 1.7, 1.10). When Nietzsche asks his dangerous question about the value of values, the value of truth or the value of morality, he is asking for whom these values are valuable: the nobles or the slaves. Philosophers since Socrates have been spellbound by the question *What is . . . ?* What is courage? What is justice? What is knowledge? But Deleuze tells us that what distinguished Nietzsche's genealogy was that he never asked *What?* but always *For whom?* (Deleuze [1962] 1983, 77). And in each case Nietzsche's *For whom?* is asked with respect to the nobles and the slaves. Told that pity is a virtue, ask "For whom is pity a virtue?" Nietzsche approaches a philosophical question as if he were casting it, staging it. Who's talking? It is a "method of dramatization" (Deleuze [1962] 1983, 79; Deleuze 1967a, 89–90).

From Nietzsche's perspective, any account of the origin of philosophy's vermilion constructions in terms of what desire is, for example a lack, would persist in the traditional philosophical gambit of asking *What?* It would content itself with the question *what is*, when the meaning or sense of anything is best viewed from the side of *For whom?* So the real question ought to be: What kind of person would think of desire as a lack? A noble or a slave? If it is slaves who naturally conceive of desire in terms of what they lack, then the fact that we are each of us slavish some of the time would contribute to an explanation of the power of the picture of desire as lack.

To help dramatize this question, Nietzsche imagines that these two kinds of person, slaves and nobles, are living in relatively natural conditions, that is, without the hindrances of human society. This dramatization has obvious resonances with the fiction of a state of nature, but unlike the use to which that fiction is normally put, Nietzsche is not concerned with the justification of moral values whose value or importance is taken for granted. He appeals to these two types of person to help understand the value of moral values: genealogy, not as apologetics, but as critique. Sometimes Nietzsche puts nobles and slaves outside of humanity altogether, imagining them as animals: birds of prey and lambs, lions and cows (Nietzsche [1887] 1967a, 1.13). Loosed from human society, these two kinds of person, nobles and slaves, would fall into the relation of predator and prey, and Nietzsche's criticism of moral value is that many of the moral values we unhesitatingly endorse are the values of those who find themselves as prey, praying for deliverance.

The life of the nobles is an idealized form of the life of predatory lions or the life of medieval knights and warriors.[5] A life which

> presupposed a powerful physicality, a flourishing, abundant, even overflowing health, together with that which serves to preserve it: war, adventure, hunting, dancing, war games, and in general all that involves vigorous, free, joyful, activity. (Nietzsche [1887] 1967a, 1.7)

The life of the slaves is quite different. They live in constant fear of their predators, and so have very good memories of the evil they have suffered in the past and of hiding places where they might avoid evil in the future. Thus the slave, the lamb, the cow is neither upright nor naïve nor honest and straightforward with himself. His soul *squints;* his spirit loves hiding places, secret paths and back doors, everything covert entices him as *his* world, *his* security, *his* refreshment; he understands how to keep silent, how not to forget, how to wait, how to be provisionally self-deprecating and humble. A race of such men of *ressentiment* is bound to become eventually cleverer than any noble race; it will also honor cleverness to a far higher degree: namely as a condition of existence of the first importance; while with noble men cleverness can easily acquire a subtle flavor of luxury. (Nietzsche [1887] 1967a, 1.10)

Nietzsche's general philosophical stance is so familiar that it takes little effort to see that the slaves will take to humility and hiding, but it is a mark of Nietzsche's continuing power to provoke that we remain, or I remain, surprised to discover that nobles do not have much call for a good memory and that it is the slaves who emphasize the importance of cleverness, who know all about high IQ clubs.

Noble minds don't remember offenses against them; they have taken physical revenge at the time the offenses occurred, and bruised or not, nothing is left to remember: "To be incapable of taking one's enemies, one's accidents, even one's misdeeds seriously for very long—that is the sign of strong, full natures" (Nietzsche [1887] 1967a, 1.10). The nobles actively forget the past and move on: "There could be no happiness, no cheerfulness, no hope, no pride, no *present* without forgetfulness" (2.1). Nietzsche speaks of this noble assemblage as one in which the digestive activities of the stomach, here figuring as the traces of the past on the noble body, do not enter consciousness. Quietly digested. Thus the slavish assemblage, in which memory is held for ever, is figured in almost bovine terms as constant regurgitation: The "dyspeptic . . . cannot 'have done' with anything" (2.1).

This noble "active forgetting" which is the key to living in the "present" must not be construed as yet another form of double negation (Nietzsche [1887] 1967a, 2.1). It is a sign of how close even Nietzsche remains to the vermilion worm that this active forgetting, the key to living cheerfully in the present, can seem negative. In time we will have to distinguish two forms of the traditional ideal of living in the present. According to the negative version of this ideal, to live in the present is to cut one's ties to the past and to the future. This is the ideal that comes under attack in Derrida's

Speech and Phenomena (1967c). In that book, Derrida argues that Husserl's attempt to carve out a domain of the present, free from the traces of the past and the projects of the future, will deliver a domain without meaning. Derrida's argument is cousin to Wittgenstein's argument against the possibility of a logically private language. Life in the isolated present is impossible, and even were it possible, it would be without meaning (Wittgenstein 1986).

There is another way of living in the present, and that is by bringing it all in. In this way the present is inhabited and eluded at once. What is eluded is a present construed as an unchanging infinitesimal slice of being (Deleuze [1969] 1990, 1). Suppose the present were a house. On the one hand you could try to live in a house with nothing in it, a negative conception of the present; close out the past and the future; close out the whole world. But then even you could not be in the house. So you cannot live in the present, construed negatively. On the other hand, you could try to bring everything into the house, the past and the future, even the barn, even the cow, warm and fragrant. This would be to live in the present, positively; open all the windows; and that is the way we should understand the active forgetting of the nobles. An openness that permits the present to be drawn at once out of the past and into the future, an openness that reveals the becoming of the present as beyond representation. Beyond egg-sliced being. Like Alice growing: "She is larger now; she was smaller before. But it is at the same moment that one becomes larger than one was and smaller than one becomes" (Deleuze [1969] 1990, 1). It pertains to the essence of becoming that it is beyond being identified as this or that. And becoming is another way of saying beautiful.

Active forgetting should *not* be construed as "I really must stop thinking about the great friendship I have lost or the ugly treatment I barely endured." That first way tangles us in thinking about what we lost or endured in order *not* to think about it. Precisely the impossibility Sartre confronts as our flight from anguish (Sartre [1943] 1992, 83). A second way: We could try to forget the past by throwing ourselves into some project or other, but here again, when the momentum of the project in which we are burying our pain subsides, then the familiar aching will rise again. Of course, with this familiarity can come a certain affection, as when the lingering pain is the only real thing left of a friendship lost, or when even the ugliness we were forced to suffer is *ours*, our past, our distinction, the focus of our concern. It is so hard to forget because our vermilion souls thrive on recollection.

If it is neither of these two, what should active forgetting be? An aerial double affirmation. Both of the previous tacks sought for something new whose primary characterization was that it was *not* the painful old thing. Double negation. But the new should be aerial, lifting the weight of the past up into a new Yes. A new Yes to the past. A double affirmation of the past in the present. It was always here (Bergson [1896] 1991). If you hurt, you do hurt. The hurt too deserves its Yes. Not as if we were addicted to what is lost, but if it hurts, it hurts. The fact that we cry when our friends die does not mean either that we should cry all the time or that we should rig our existence so that we never ever cried. We should say Yes to a present, a present into which can be folded the past and up into whose future we can lift a new song. An aerial air.

may i be gay

like every lark

who lifts his life

from all the dark

who wings his why

beyond because

and sings an if

of day to yes

—E. E. CUMMINGS, *73 Poems* (1963) in cummings 1991, 815

Active forgetting puts the past in service of the present, opens the windows, crafting new intensities, not copying the beauty now past, not carping on the ugliness endured, but crafting a new Yes, including the past. Yes. Active forgetting is a double affirmation. That is what makes it active. "It wills now not exactly what occurs, but something *in* that which occurs, something yet to come which would be consistent with what occurs, in accordance with the laws of an obscure, humorous conformity: the Event" (Deleuze [1969] 1990, 149). Active forgetting forces nothing from consciousness, not even past pain; that would be the way of double negation. Active forgetting brings to consciousness more and more life. Not subtraction, addition. The old, limp carrot is not tossed in the garbage; it is added to the soup.

It is a shock to read Deleuze's uncompromising announcement that "either ethics makes no sense at all, or this is what it means and has nothing else to say: not to be unworthy of what happens to us" (Deleuze [1969] 1990, 149). To be unworthy of what happens to you is to be stuck, trapped, mired in the past. *Ressentiment.* To be worthy of what happens to you is to be more than what happened to you. It is to use what happened, without *ressentiment*, in creation, in becoming.[6] Not to survive but to live. Double affirmation. (See chapter 9, "An Ethics of Affection.")

Memory is a characteristic of slaves. Cleverness is another. A predator's prey is unable to take physical revenge on the more powerful predator; so to avoid being eaten, the prey must outwit its predator. The predator's power allows it the luxury of being naive and straightforward. Predators can even court "a certain imprudence . . . a recklessness whether in the face of danger or of the enemy . . . [an] enthusiastic impulsiveness in anger, love, reverence, gratitude, and revenge" (Nietzsche [1887] 1967a, 1.11). Their prey do not behave this way, and so it is the slaves, not the nobles, for whom being clever is a necessity of existence.

Someone is sure to "discover" that actually cows can be less intelligent than those who prey upon them under cover of darkness or grass. A quick refutation of Nietzsche's point, but is it? This constant attempt to refute is, itself, an expression of the obsession with negation that this chapter is trying to understand and move beyond. On its face, it is serious and clever, but also willfully obtuse, not unlike people whose thinking runs aground on every metaphor, who are deaf to all but the most predictable humor and irony. The reply to this defiant, dwarfish objection is simply that human slaves have an ability to retreat to cleverness that cows do not have. But the objection puts us face to face with the spiritual form of revenge that paints philosophy the vermilion colors of double negation.

Speaking of the slaves as Jews, Nietzsche writes: "The Jews, that priestly people, who in opposing their enemies and conquerors were ultimately satisfied with nothing less than a radical revaluation of their enemies' values, that is to say, an act of the *most spiritual revenge*" (Nietzsche [1887] 1967a, 1.7).

The most spiritual act of revenge thrives on the bad air in the swamps of *ressentiment* (1.12, 2.7). *Ressentiment* was already introduced in the first epigraph to this chapter:

> While every noble morality develops from a triumphant affirmation of itself, slave morality from the outset says No to what is "outside," what is "different," what is "not itself"; and *this* No is its creative deed. This inversion of the value-positing eye—this need to direct one's view outward instead of back to oneself—is of the essence of *ressentiment:* in order to exist, slave morality always first needs a hostile external world; it needs, physiologically speaking, external stimuli in order to act at all—its action is fundamentally reaction. (Nietzsche [1887] 1967a, 1.10)

Ressentiment puts the blame outside oneself.[7] It is familiar to almost everyone. Finally, you arrange to meet Joe at the Burger King, but letting your departure be delayed, you arrive late and are furious at the *god damn traffic.* Or you fail to complete a project on time, and lash out at those who are trying to help: Driven by *ressentiment,* we "make evil-doers out of friends" (Nietzsche [1887] 1967a, 3.15). The whole world seems to be conspiring against us; we aren't paid enough, or respected enough, or appreciated enough, or helped enough, or left alone enough. It is not that we hate everything; hate is too honest, too exposed. The color of *ressentiment* is not the honest red of fire and heat; its color is vermilion, the color of poisonous toadstools. And it reeks of rot. Vermilion worms, ready to double up, crawl around the dank, rotting grasses. Those filled with *ressentiment* despise the whole, fetid world, but they can still love; they love their contempt, feeding themselves on the secondhand contents of their dyspeptic stomachs.

> They enjoy being mistrustful and dwelling on nasty deeds and imaginary slights; they scour the entrails of their past and present for obscure and questionable occurrences that offer them the opportunity to revel in tormenting suspicions and to intoxicate themselves with the poison of their own malice: they tear open their oldest wounds, they bleed from long healed scars. (Nietzsche [1887] 1967a, 3.15)

Why? Why do we exaggerate the negative? Why do we never exaggerate the positive? (Nietzsche [1882] 1974, 326). Why is our first move always to persist in complaining, devoting our mental powers to proving that we really have been wronged? There is always time for contempt and complaint, even self-contempt, but we have to set aside special time—we have to plan ahead—to enjoy ourselves. What is going on? Why are we so fond of complaining?

Ressentiment exercises its spiritual revenge by reversing the values of the nobles. In a well-known passage, Nietzsche accounts for this reversal in terms of the predator-prey relationship.

> That lambs dislike great birds of prey does not seem strange: only it gives no ground for reproaching these birds of prey for bearing off little lambs. And if the lambs say among themselves: "these birds of prey are evil; and whoever is least like a bird of prey, but rather its opposite, a lamb—would he not be good?" there is no reason to find fault with this institution of an ideal. (Nietzsche [1887] 1967a, 1.13)

The primary existential fact presents the first negation: the pointlessness of existence—you graze and graze, and then they swoop down and take you to dinner. So it is easy to see why the lambs would want to put an end to all this carnivorousness: the second negation. The slave morality of good and evil defends virtues that are virtues for slaves, naturally. Nietzsche voices the slave's thoughts:

> "He is good who does not outrage, who harms nobody, who does not attack, who does not require, who leaves revenge to God, who keeps himself hidden as we do, who avoids evil and desires little from life, like us, the patient, humble, and just." (Nietzsche [1887] 1967a, 1.13)

Slave virtues serve the interests of the slaves, and the fundamental one, the double negation at the heart of this ideal of the good, is not to cause slaves any trouble. The victim's shriek: "Stop it!"

All by itself this would give slave morality no purchase on the nobles, for they don't need slavish validation; they may not need validation at all. But the finest invention of *ressentiment*, the invention that will justify the criticism by the slaves of the nobles, is still to come. The finest invention of *ressentiment* is freedom, the free soul, the blank self.

> This type of man *needs* to believe in a neutral independent "subject," prompted by an instinct for self-preservation and self-affirmation in which every lie is sanctified. The subject . . . has perhaps been believed in hitherto more firmly than anything else on earth because it makes possible to the majority of

mortals, the weak and oppressed of every kind, the sublime self-deception that interprets weakness as freedom, and their being thus-and-thus as a *merit*. (Nietzsche [1887] 1967a, 1.13)

Weakness as freedom. Freedom takes its best cases from those circumstances where we are able to do more than one thing but are unable to decide, stuck in front of an open refrigerator unable to decide. With the freedom of the soul atom in place, the lambs can turn their ideals against the eagles; the weak can turn against the strong. Their spiritual revenge is complete: Eagles should not be eagles; they should be lambs.

Nietzsche objects to the spiritual revenge of the weak not because he cannot understand the motivation of the weak, but because it is metaphysically absurd. He thinks it is absurd to expect strength to express itself as anything but strength. As Nietzsche sees it, there is no more to lightning than the lightning flash, and there is no more to being powerful than expressing one's power. Under pressure from the "misleading influence of language," the misleading influence of subject-predicate constructions, we suppose that there is a blank "doer" behind every deed, a "doer" who could have behaved in very different ways (Nietzsche [1887] 1967a, 1.13).[8] As Nietzsche sees it, the slave revolt is metaphysically absurd, but that has not made it any less victorious. In this conception, it is the rare, the powerful, who lose out in the struggle for existence, and it is the common, the average, who survive (Nietzsche [1882] 1974, 5.351).

Nietzsche was ready to give up the soul or the self, but only to turn us in the direction of possible reconceptions of the soul: "The way is open for new versions and refinements of the soul-hypothesis; and such conceptions as 'mortal soul,' and 'soul as subjective multiplicity' and 'soul as social structure of drives and affects'" (Nietzsche [1886] 1966, #12).[9] The denial that the self is one thing, the idea of the self as an inordinate multiplicity, a haecceity,[10] will play a role in pages to come, but at this point I am only seeking an explanation of philosophy's obsession with double negation. That obsession may perhaps be explained by appeal to Nietzsche's account of *ressentiment*.

The first thing to clear away is the smug assertion that if there were two clearly defined types of person, nobles and slaves, then perhaps Nietzsche's account of *ressentiment* might work, but as it is, when people do not instantiate either of these pure types, his story can get no grip on reality. The fact is, that from a certain point of view, we are already slaves. Faced with the repetitiousness of our lives, faced with the pointlessness of human existence, we are all slaves, stuck in hopeless situations, waiting for death. Moreover, even if you do not occupy that dark viewpoint, we all react occasionally in slavish ways, if not all the time then at any time taking spiritual revenge on others. This is the way I would like to answer the question I raised a few paragraphs ago, namely, why is it that we are so fond of complaining? Slavish *ressentiment* is at the root of all our complaining.

Obviously, we like to complain; we really like it, almost more than we like anything else. Yesterday was a fine fall day, a great wind had blown the steamy humidity out of the valley, the sky was blue, everything seemed precise, the wind was strong and crisp and blew its energy right into us, sharing its power. It was good. Then I overhear someone complaining. "Oh this *wind*. And it's so *cold* now. It was warmer in the morning." I know. It's nothing. We hear it all the time. But if yesterday was not good enough for this person, what would make it better? Isn't it obvious? This person is longing for a day that is not too cold, and not too hot, and not too wet, and not too snowy. And not too close to the busy holidays or too close to the busy workweek. Or too close to the yawning morning or yawning night, the overfull midday or the lonely midnight. What do we want? What are we waiting for? What would ever satisfy our complaining souls? I would like to say that our constant willingness to complain shows that what we are really longing for, more than for the weekend and more even than for the holidays, is the end of life itself. Death. I know this is an overstatement. In truth, such vermilion souls do not want death. Death takes too much strength. Too much life. What such a person, often enough ourselves, really wants is not death but bland, zestless existence. Climate control. Shut the windows. Settle back for some beige food. Listen again to the voice of *ressentiment* describing a good character: "He is good who does not outrage, who harms nobody, who does not attack . . . who keeps himself hidden as we do, who avoids evil and desires little from life, like us, the patient, humble and just" (Nietzsche [1887] 1967a, 1.13). Quiet desperation seeking a quiet spot. And they blink. Lizards.

What do we get out of complaining? They will say it is to let off steam, but this is the slave speaking again. Why let off steam? To keep the container from exploding. Perhaps to lower the temperature, to keep our lives from heating up, to restore the tepid temperatures we crave. It is double negation, again, the explosion is bad; stop it. The heat is dangerous; stop it. We are still in the schoolyard. Get off my toe!

In the pages that follow, I try to rekindle the flames, risking danger.[11] Complaining does more than simply release the pressure. When we complain together, we gain that group feeling that comes from having a common enemy. Complaining is a public act. Most of the time I share my complaints with others who have or might have the same complaint, and this brings us together. Like sheep on a rainy night, we huddle together for warmth. Nietzsche too understands the importance of huddling: "a kind of concentration and organization of the sick . . . (the word 'church' is the most popular name for it)" (Nietzsche [1887] 1967a, 3.16). Precisely this huddling together can sometimes be stifling, but there is often no place to go to escape. At those times, Nietzsche suggests that if you want to get away from swamp gases, it would help to wear a mask, the mask of conformism: "We, too, associate with 'people'; we, too, modestly don the dress in which (*as* which) others know us, respect us, look for us. . . . We, too, do what all prudent masks do, and in response to every curiosity that does not concern our 'dress' we politely place a chair against the door" (Nietzsche [1882] 1974, 5.365).

Complaining can release pressure and bring us companionship, but there is more. Complaining makes us feel morally superior to those we are complaining about. It lifts us up and puts them down. Feeling bad is bad. And venting our complaints will release some energy and bring us together with others who are feeling the same way. But better than all of this is to be indignant at the way we have been treated; we deserved better. We were worthy of better treatment, and that is why we are indignant, disgusted. In my own experience, this is the best kind of complaining. It makes me feel much better to see myself as a victim of injustice than simply to feel rotten. It is not me. I am not really rotten at all. It is those *rotten bastards* who did it to me, them; they're the ones who don't deserve to be enjoying their salaries, their prestige, their power, their pleasure. And this is our spiritual revenge; we don't actually take their prestige from them, but narrowing our indignant eyes, we overpower their *right* to that prestige. Of course this makes us feel powerful. In spite of raised eyebrows in the conservative press, it should be no surprise that movements of empowerment can be spread by spreading the awareness of being a victim, for precisely by seeing oneself as a victim one can become empowered. The easiest, cheapest, empowerment possible is spiritual revenge; absent any change in our material circumstances, we can overpower our enemies with our endless supply of moral disgust, the mean hinge that opens the doors of *ressentiment*, complaints, and pity.

Nietzsche refers to something he calls "stilts of 'noble indignation' for the aid of the spiritually flatfooted" (Nietzsche [1887] 1967a, 3.26). Indignant at not receiving the recognition or respect we deserve, we can, in this mood, become readier and readier to force that respect out of those who are refusing it to us. Dignity, respect, recognition: These are sharp, violent concepts. In the good-hearted, amusement park nihilism of our times, we have forgotten, but Hegel knew. Nevertheless, blinded by the Enlightenment ideal of mutual recognition, mutual respect, Hegel did not realize that what we need is not *more* respect, but less. We need an ethics without respect, an ethics of affection (chapter 9).

Four Ways to Avoid Pointlessness by Double Negation

The bleak opening story of this chapter, revealing the pointlessness of existence, is a story told by *ressentiment*. It is story motored by the desire to find some reason for living, or failing that, to find some way to hide or to understand our suffering. At its best this produces the fake Yes of double negation. The vermilion worm.

Recall the pointlessness of existence as it surfaced in the opening story. Tragedy interrupts our projects. It reveals all our hurrying to and fro as simply so much pointless effort. But it is worse. Although some of us do avoid tragedy, death is inevitable. We bury our friends or they bury us. And death interrupts our projects in just the way tragedy does. We struggle and struggle, and then we die, every single one. Even our struggles on behalf of others, and their projects, are struggles on behalf of those who will also die. What is the point? Power? Who remembers Ozymandias? Wealth? Your bloated bank account won't mean much when, late one night, you awake, alone, dying in your fouled sheets. Life is pointless. This was the first negation. It is answered, in various ways, by a second negation. Nietzsche isolates four. These four strategies of double negation don't have to be kept separate; they can overlap; and we need not keep to Nietzsche's tendency to give religious examples of their use. They remain in use even among those proud of their secular moral security.

One way of negating the pointlessness of life is to deny life. These are the ascetic self-sacrificers that appear all over the world, in many philosophical and religious traditions. These ascetics take the honest direct route: Rather than live a pointless life, they would, as nearly as possible, continue to survive, but without life (see Vaneigem 1979).

> If possible, will and desire are abolished altogether; all that produces
> affects and "blood" is avoided (abstinence from salt: the hygienic regimen of
> the fakirs); no love; no hate; indifference; no revenge; no wealth; no work;
> one begs; if possible, no women, or as little as possible. (Nietzsche [1887]
> 1967a, 3.17)

This strategy, on Nietzsche's own account, works. It frees those who practice it from the deep despair of a pointless life. These techniques can produce hallucinations, for example, in Saint Teresa of Avila, but their final state is one of "total hypnotization and repose," which Nietzsche finds to be the final state of virtually all the self-sacrificial traditions. It is at its clearest in the praise of dreamless sleep in the Upanishads (Nietzsche [1887] 1967a, 3.17). Although, at the slightest provocation, Nietzsche will smear what he thinks of as the lies of religious traditions, Nietzsche praises this first strategy for its recognition that moral virtue is *not* the way to this state of dreamless sleep, the final redemption. So he praises this first form of the second negation for moving, in its own life-denying way, beyond good and evil (3.17). This strategy does, however, present in Nietzsche's eyes one serious difficulty, namely, its difficulty. To pull it off, to attain the state of total hypnosis, dreamless sleep, requires "rare energy and above all courage, contempt for opinion, 'intellectual stoicism'" (3.18). Although Nietzsche rejects the resentful presuppositions of this strategy, it seems clear that he respects its practitioners.

Rather than directly sacrificing our desiring selves, rather than cutting out our own hearts, pointlessness can be negated by losing the self in mechanical activity. Nietzsche is thinking of the regimented life of those whose lives display "absolute regularity, punctilious and unthinking obedience, a mode of life fixed once and for all, fully occupied time, a certain permission, indeed training for 'impersonality,' self-forgetfulness," for not caring about one's self (Nietzsche [1887] 1967a, 3.18). These might be monks or nuns, but in our busy world, these could also be those secular sorts who smother the fire of life by blanketing their lives with scheduled activities, employment or leisure, probably both. No play here; one is either working for a salary or working on one's backhand. Scheduled to exhaustion, this person finds no time to reflect on the pointlessness of all this hurrying. It may seem at first as though such a person has a full life and many interests, but it soon appears that such a person has only one interest: avoiding the empty chronological time that makes self-reflection unavoidable. If this overcomes pointlessness, it is not by facing it, but by hiding from it. It is no honest Yes; rather, under cover of a commitment to tennis or yoga or the Mets, it is simply the fake Yes of double negation.

In the same genre as the second strategy for negating pointlessness is the attempt to fill up time not with anything at all, mechanical activity itself, but with *easy* pleasures, especially (in Nietzsche's telling) the pleasure of giving pleasure: "doing good, relieving, helping, encouraging, consoling, praising, rewarding" (Nietzsche [1887] 1967a, 3.18). Here the pleasure comes from the slight, minimal, increase in the feeling of power that comes from helping another who needs something you have to give. Once as I was struggling along a snowy sidewalk, sweating my way to Lehigh in too many sweaters, I found myself passing a car stuck in the snow. I just started pushing it, and as the car drove away, the driver noticed out his window that I had pushed him. Easy pleasure, cheap power. Those who enjoy this kind of helping others often form communities and help each other. And Nietzsche observes that within herds of these people, within communities, within congregations, even more pleasure can be milked from these deeds of goodness: "The *formation of a herd* is a significant victory and advance in the struggle against depression" (3.18).

This herd formation need have nothing to do with the traditional religious groups that are appear on Nietzsche's pages. It may be groups of almost any sort: men's groups, women's groups, political groups, activist groups deploying partisan ethics, or support groups specific to endless varieties of trauma. In each case, these groups, which do deliver some relief, are stimulated by nothing positive, but only by something negative. Their activism is reactivism. They are each invented to oppose whatever that group finds most oppressive, whether it be social, political, moral, or physiological. There is no denying that these groups do some good, but from the perspective of my concern with an honest Yes, this good work is mostly the good work of the worm.

The fourth way of negating the pointlessness of existence is by far the most clever, for in this strategy, the pointlessness is not diminished or denied or blocked from view; it is simply reinterpreted as having a point: a moral point. The pain of life is given moral significance, and life itself is given meaning, a painful meaning perhaps, but meaning nevertheless. In Nietzsche's favorite Christian version of this strategy, human pain and depression are reinterpreted as suffering caused by sin. Much better than not being able to understand existence, much better than enduring pointlessness, each sinner now understands that he or she is the reason they are suffering. Each sinner must therefore seek the reason for his or her suffering in themselves, "in some *guilt*, in a piece of the past, he must understand his suffering as a punishment" (Nietzsche [1887] 1967a, 3.20). And whereas before one had wished for the pain or emptiness to end, now one wishes for it all the more, for one's suffering is a proof that existence has meaning, as punishment for sin. So one wallows in punishment: " '*more* pain, *more* pain' " (3.20). Hair shirts. Self-flagellation. One comes to love rooting out the sins of one's past, to dwell on the impossibility of one's ever recovering innocence. This is not fun, but at least it makes sense: Pointless pain is redeemed in an orgy of punishment.

There is a secular version of this negation too. Where the religious version reinterpreted our suffering as our *justified* punishment by the Deity, the secular version reinterprets our suffering as our *un*-justified oppression by some hated terrestrial enemy. This is the same cherished moral indignation that surfaced when I was discussing complaining. In this secular version, pointlessness is not removed by discovering *our own* sinfulness but by discovering the sinfulness *of others*. In particular, our oppressors. Here we glory in the global oppressiveness of *white supremacy*, which will never understand us, or *patriarchy*, which perverts our being. Or on the other side of the same two issues, we glory in the pain we suffer at the hands of *African Americans* too lazy to climb the economic ladder without unfair advantages, or at the hands of *women* who should never have left the kitchen to take jobs from the men who really deserved them. Whether minorities oppressed by majorities or majorities resenting each minuscule gain made by the minorities, this manner of adding a second No to the pointlessness of existence, the hopelessness of our situation, can work for anyone. The enemies elevated to the position of unjustified metaphysical oppressor come in every sex, every color, every nationality, every religion, and we can all be reassured. There is an oppressor for everyone, and thus no one need fear that the universe has no moral order. It does. I don't deserve my fate.

The pointlessness of the world thus acquires moral significance not as our justified punishment for sinning but as our unjustified oppression by sinners. Indignant, we rise a little above that oppression, even if only spiritually. Thank heavens, we are not just suffering. We are oppressed. Our pointless pain is here given a point, a meaning, by being interpreted as our unjustified oppression by those who don't deserve the power they enjoy.

I have tried to emphasize that each of these four strategies for evading or drowning the pointlessness of existence remains dominated by the enemy, pointlessness, which in their various ways, these strategies evade. In this way they are all reactive. What I will be attempting, here, is to go back a stage. To find a way to an innocent Yes. Moving. Rather than accepting the pointlessness of existence as a problem to be solved, I will attempt to embrace that pointlessness. That is the attempt of this entire project. To ride an affirmative wave of pointlessness. Becoming beautiful.

Philosophizing without Ressentiment

Nietzsche invented his concept of *ressentiment*, first of all, to account for the slave revolt against the nobles, but he also knew of the deep bond between *ressentiment* and philosophy, philosophy itself. Thus Nietzsche's opposition to *ressentiment* projects a new image of life, a new image of philosophy. Neither scientific nor manifest: an innocent image.

For too long, Deleuze reminds us, we have permitted philosophical thought, if not thought in general, to be ruled by *ressentiment* (Deleuze [1962] 1983, 35, 103). Philosophy as traditionally practiced is caught in the whirlpool formed by the currents of *ressentiment* and bad conscience. *Ressentiment* turns philosophy against existence, the pointless repetitiousness of our lives. But ever upbeat, philosophers have never, ever, suspected that life might be pointlessness and horror, all the way down.[12] In spite of everything, philosophers tell a story about the real possibility of philosophical knowledge. They are, each one, committed to the possibility of acquiring philosophical wisdom, even if that wisdom must be skeptical, or Pyrrhonian. Inevitably we are told that we have wrongly permitted our thinking to be influenced by the attractions of what is outside the realm of thought: the passionate body. Always, we are scolded for having succumbed to easy temptations, and these temptations are described in every possible way: the attractions of materiality that Augustine warned against, the attractions of spirituality that Wittgenstein warned against, the attractions of poetry that Carnap warned against, the attractions of literality that Derrida warned against, the attractions of the other invisible world that Nietzsche warned against, the attractions of this visible world that Descartes warned against. There are even philosophers who warn against the temptations of truth; don't worry, they say, this is good enough for the time being: pragmatists. But in every case, the fault is really ours. We succumbed. We shouldn't have. We should have known better. Bad conscience.

Always the same enemy, eroticism; always the same cure, asceticism. We must discipline our selves, control the desires of our body, resist easy rewards, take on the serious and difficult task of becoming wise. Don't even start philosophy until you are past middle age. The worst is not that we suffer; no, we all suffer from existence. Our suffering is the first negation; everyone can see that. The worst crime is to think that the way beyond suffering need not detour through a second negation, through the whip, through asceticism. Earnest voices have already scolded me. Don't let the children hear you saying redemption is possible without the whip. Stick to the script: The way out of suffering requires the practice of a difficult method, a discipline; philosophical wisdom can be ours, but only if we discipline the passionate body (Deleuze [1962] 1983, 103). The worst crime is to think that there is a way to affirmation that is not the way of double negation, a way to affirmation that could say, simply, Yes, and not rather No, No.

Philosophical method, so we are told, is a pharmakon in service of what is taken to be the natural functioning of thinking, the natural attractions between thinking and truth. In philosophy, the ascetic ideal works its magic by a method that reverses the misleading effects of the body, or the will, returning us to the natural beginning from which we have strayed. And always the ascetic return is difficult, disciplining our desires until we find ourselves at the limits of the body, leaning out of a window overlooking a garden, enjoying the pure experience of god, or the good, or crisp positive facts. Religion, philosophy, and science, companions in asceticism, companions in double negation. The natural way to truth is unnaturally blocked by the desiring body. Remove the block. Find the way back. Philosophizing out of *ressentiment*.

Perhaps if we could get thought moving again, if we could give up the resentful image of philosophical thought as naturally ready for the truth (but blocked), perhaps then, philosophy could find its way to Yes. Innocence. Not a second innocence, not the world redeemed, not even *resignation*: innocence here and now.[13] Yes. These were Nietzsche's glad tidings (Nietzsche [1888b] 1982, #32). They announce an "affirmative thought, a thought which affirms life and the will to life, a thought which finally expels the whole of the negative; to believe in the *innocence* of the future and the past, to believe in the eternal return" (Deleuze [1962] 1983, 35, my emphasis).

We should not think of thought as naturally attracted to the truth, blocked by a body that simply needs to be moved out of the way in order for truth to enter our souls. Thinking requires provocation. It needs to be put in motion, but the provocation that thought requires is not extrinsic to thinking itself (Deleuze [1962] 1983, 108).[14] Thought itself is movement, and what it wants is to move. Thought seeks intensification.[15] In a certain sense thought does not want to avoid error and seek truth. There is even something faintly ridiculous about using "wrong" or "false" as a term of criticism in philosophy. Yes, they say, it is always fun to read an author like Kierkegaard, who can write, but you realize that he is wrong about the nature of time, that he simply didn't know enough physics. Plato too, they say, can be enjoyable, but you do realize, don't you, that learning is not recollection, that philosophy is not practicing to die. Wittgenstein is spellbinding, yes he is, but the private-language argument is awful, either invalid or unsound, probably both. Sometimes it seems that professionals see the history of the great philosophers as the history of those without any special gift for their own subject. How else could it be so obvious that they were all so terribly wrong? And thus philosophers sometimes divide their subject with a sneer: You can be interested in philosophy or the history of philosophy, or whatever it is the new guy does.

I am heading for a contradiction. On the one hand, I am saying that traditional philosophy has been dominated by double negation, driven by *ressentiment* and bad conscience. On the other hand, I seem to think more of the dead philosophers than those who write the history of philosophy with embalming fluid. This is not really a problem, for as Nietzsche knew, *ressentiment* makes us inventive, gets thought moving. The only problem is that *ressentiment* moves thought to ideals, moves thought out of this world. The great dead philosophers ride a wave of *ressentiment*, but they do ride a wave. Thought in motion. Scholarship may not fit the model, but Plato and Plotinus surely do (Nietzsche [1882] 1974, 5.366). Philosophy is an *adventure*. Philosophy is a feast, not a collection of guidebooks and cookbooks. It is not even as if the adventure were described in the guidebooks. If you stick to the book, the adventure dies. Follow the recipe perfectly, and the food will be as good as store-bought. Thinking, like adventure, requires provocation. Risk.

In the past century, it has not been so unusual to think about the relation of truth to philosophy in novel terms. Pragmatists tell us that we should give up truth and settle for what works, or else they tell us that truth is what works and anything that looks like a truth that transcends the efficient is beyond understanding. But pragmatism is more opposed to movement, than even those botanists of error, philosophers who wander the world identifying falsehoods. For falsehoods might be prods to activity. The pragmatist wanders the world saying, stop worrying, this is good enough; the pragmatist preaches resignation with the smile that comes from knowing one is defending common sense, confident that no one, except the philosophers, will be shocked.[16] Heidegger, too, is concerned with something more than truth as correspondence. According to Heidegger, the correspondence between assertions and reality presupposes the disclosure of a world within which such assertions might be true or false. And it is with this deeper notion of truth as disclosure that he hopes to overcome the limitations of our energetic pursuit of pragmatic efficiency. Heidegger is certainly concerned to move us from our comfortable acceptance of the technological age, but this is motion in service of something secure and peaceful, non-willing, *Gelassenheit* (Heidegger [1959] 1966, 54, 59). Willing is bad. Stop it. Receive. *Gelassenheit.* Double negation.

Neither of these ways of relinquishing the question "True or False?" is what I meant to point to with the word adventure. If thought were only interested in the truth, who would bother? It is too difficult. (A genealogy of pragmatism.) Thought wants adventure, intensity.[17] An image of thought as adventure, an innocent, affirmative image of thinking, is an image of thought in motion, active.[18] And it takes two. To set itself in motion, thinking requires provocation, a kick start, or else it will remain in the deep ruts that confine it to the paths of the traditional resentful image of thinking. Philosophy, like everything else, begins with strife. Traditional philosophy responds with double negations: No, No. How would an adventurous philosophy respond? By saying Yes, but what does it mean to say Yes to strife? What is the strife that calls for philosophy? *The strife which provokes philosophy is the strife of concepts.* The strife of conceptual representation.

The dogmas of the quiet past, are inadequate to the stormy present.

—ABRAHAM LINCOLN, December 1, 1862

Dividing the world into this and that, the dogmas of the past ensure the quietude of common sense, which has seen everything and understands everything. Good and evil. True and false. Essence and accident. Internal and external. The majoritarian white males and the minoritarian others, whatever their relative numbers. The quietude of common sense need not be silent; there may be noises everywhere, but they all fit. None of the noises surprises anyone. Raising money to help treat drug addicts, which a moralistic culture refuses to see as needing medical attention. Raising awareness of the needs of those confined to wheelchairs. This can produce much noise. But it is quiet nevertheless, philosophically quiet. Requiring no thinking. What requires thought is what doesn't fit, what common sense is not ready for. What doesn't make sense. The inordinate. The inordinate that provokes strife. Conceptual strife. Like what? A beautiful bruise received at the hands of a drunken lover. A Norwegian omelet. Like what?

It is not be possible to give a tidy conceptual representation of what kind of thing calls for thinking, for it is precisely our inability to represent what calls for thinking that calls for thinking. Deleuze and Guattari will say that what we are talking about is an anomalous individual,[19] or a sign,[20] or an event.[21] It must be a singular individual, because when we can't conceptualize some thing, that thing is not a representative of a type; it is rather singular, a sensual singularity. A haecceity (Deleuze and Guattari [1980] 1987, 260–65). I fear this is becoming difficult to follow, out as we are beyond where the conceptual security of common sense can be of any help. So let's move to a more experiential dimension.

Try to recall those times when you were really thinking. This is never adversarial. It is never when an enemy says: But aren't you saying this and isn't that immoral or too close to Kant or something or somebody else. Those are times when your heart sinks, and you struggle to find the thing to say in reply. Inevitably there is a reply. Usually these little replies to the little objections don't help anyone.

> The simpleminded use of the notions "right" or "wrong" is one of the chief
> obstacles to the progress of understanding. (Whitehead [1938] 1968, 11)

Occasionally one of those critical questions will linger long enough to become your own, and then perhaps you will be able to move with it, instead of simply parrying it. The times when you were really thinking are often with someone else, and if there were adversarial elements, these will have been playful. Like child's play. Most of the time such joint thinkings are not adversarial, at all, but people tumbling together in thought, incomplete sentences, urging this, trying that, doesn't that remind you of this, and suddenly a line from a song you have loved since forever comes clear and you are moving. It is particularly important that this be conducted in incomplete sentences.[22] Not because the conversationalists know each other so well they can finish the sentences for one another. In that case the incompletion would be accidental, but in living thinking the incompletion is essential. Nobody knows where they are going or if they are even making sense. With any luck, they aren't. It requires trust, or better, if trust is between two, this doesn't even require trust. It requires that two are thinking together on their own but together.

Braque described the years in which he and Picasso were creating cubism as a time when he and Picasso were like mountaineers roped together, not two forming a unity (double negation), but two folded together into a new assemblage of their separate parts. Like certain cubist still lifes. Disorganized together. Caressing thought.

Figure 1-1. Pablo Picasso. *Still Life with Chair Caning.* 1912. Réunion des Musées Nationaux/Art Resource, N.Y.

Figure 1-2. Jasper Johns. *Untitled.* 1972. Photo: © Rheinisches Bildarchiv (rba_c000558).

How does this work? Who are these two, roped together? Sometimes it deliciously is, but it doesn't have to be, another person. It can be the light, or the wind, or a stick, or a thing, or an artwork. I was alone with Jasper Johns's *Untitled*, 1972, a puzzling work by a puzzling artist. I knew that Johns sometimes organized his so-called crosshatch paintings from the '70s by repeating patterns, sometimes straight and sometimes as in a mirror. I suddenly thought that these four panels might only be two from two directions. The ones on the left seemed to be the originals, front view, and the ones on the right, the originals again, back view, depicted the way they would look if the two left panels had been looked at from the other side of the wall they were hanging on, as if the two on the right had been folded out from behind the two on the left. On the panel farthest to the right, there are pieces of wood that remind one of the wood used behind canvases to stretch them, and attached to the wood are plaster casts of various parts of human bodies. The wood made me more sure that it was the deepest layer of the work behind the canvas, and then suddenly, I thought that perhaps this was one panel disassembled layer by layer, from left to right, with the bottom layer the one farthest to the right with the wood and attached body parts. And in this frame of mind it became important that the two middle panels were of different intensities, the one on the right the paler of the two as if it were hidden or farther from the viewer's eye than the one on the middle left. My mind was racing, thinking of repetition, of iterability, and of art trying to be authentic in an age of inauthenticity. I was trying out various ways of reorienting the panels so that they would fit together, with the body parts underneath, as if the foundation of this very abstract and incorporeal work was perhaps in the disassembled parts of the passionate body, as if the purity of art were grounded in the disorganized body that the surfaces of the painting hide. Was this a way of saying that artistic purity was unavoidably inauthentic, inevitably ruined by the artist's erotic body? But the movement had stopped.

As it turns out, this interpretation of the *Untitled* (1972) isn't going to work. Although the piece might be about the body and art, the hypothesis that this piece is the one panel, the leftmost one, dismantled layer by layer moving right, doesn't fit entirely with the patterns painted. But two things remain. The first is that this flight of thought was terrific. One of those times when you wish you could just grab a stranger—I was alone that day—and start talking it through as two. Times when you find yourself looking

into people's eyes for just a little too long and then chickening out, returning to your own thoughts, again. This thought flight was kick started by
the inordinate anomalousness of *Untitled* (1972). The untamed sensations of
this work got me going, and the thoughts just tumbled turbulent together.
Moving. Joining. Derrida. Iterability. Austin. Authenticity. The body. Art.
Eroticism. A small little whirlwind of ideas that somehow was carrying me
along with it. That is the first thing. I had caught this breeze and was sail-
ing this way and that, carried by the wind, thrilled at the speed and the
distance I was covering. It doesn't matter that this was, from some art historical point of view, not correct. What I experienced that afternoon was the
reason we think. Not to find the answer, but to fly.

The second thing that remains is that when I finally put this flight of
thought into a thesis about the hidden role of the body in painting or in
art, the flight stopped. I was back on the ground again. The singular, anomalous individuals that kick us up into thinking can, I admit, be conceived
simply as puzzles to be solved: Find the children hidden in the bark of the
tree, you can see the girl but can you see the old woman too?

But received as puzzles, these anomalous individuals do *not* provoke
thinking. They do not let us fly. We fly only if we allow ourselves to follow
the contingent breezes, only if we allow ourselves to ride the waves of these
affectionate feelings. I have only bodysurfed, but I imagine that to ride a
wave, you have to catch it at the right moment and let it direct your motions,
even as you try to remain in control, sometimes changing direction suddenly, sometimes riding it all the way up the beach, and there is always risk,
always the possibility of disaster. When my flight came to rest with its little
thesis about the body and art, then the ocean's wave was reduced to a garden
hose, watering some intellectual project or other. Without a project, when
the flight was *pointless*, that was thinking at its best. An innocent image of
thought, the *adventure* of thought in motion.

This is an innocent image of thought in the specific sense that it says
Yes to wherever the thought moves. Not quite "wherever" of course,
because this thought is interested in motion, not stasis, not truth. What
makes innocent thoughts so attractive is that they are interesting, where
the interesting is that in which we have no particular interest, no *particular* interest (see Wilde 1889, 915–16). Innocent thinking seeks motion,
not rest. So innocent thinking will say No to what arrests the motion of

Figure 1-3. Pavel Tchelitchew. *Hide and Seek (Cache-Cache).* 1942. Digital Image ©
The Museum of Modern Art/Licensed by SCALA / Art Resource, N.Y.

the thought. If, nevertheless, this kind of thinking is to be fully affirmative, then this No, once again will have to be the ersatz No of double
affirmation. It can be made more approachable if we remember the platitude that the attractive beauty of a girl, or a boy, or a stream sparkling
down the hill on the other side of the gully can be intensified by veiling the
girl, or the boy, or arranging the garden so that the stream's sunlit sparkle
surprises. We say Yes to the sparkle and also Yes to its tantalizing appearance, Yes to her breast and Yes to the power of the glimpsed curve. The
ersatz No of double affirmation. Disorganization in service of intensification, a delight in disorder.

A sweet disorder in the dress
Kindles in clothes a wantonness:
A lawn about the shoulders thrown
Into a fine distraction:

MY WIFE AND MY MOTHER-IN-LAW
They are both in this picture — Find them

Figure 1-4. *Old Woman, Young Girl.* Image Courtesy of the Library of Congress.

An erring lace, which here and there
Enthrals the crimson stomacher:
A cuff neglectful, and thereby
Ribbands to flow confusedly:
A winning wave, deserving note,
In the tempestuous petticoat:
A careless shoe-string, in whose tie
I see a wild civility:
Do more bewitch me than when art
is too precise in every part.

——ROBERT HERRICK (1591–1674), from Gardner 1972, 240

If the path to inordinate beauty is by indirection, then this indirection says
No to the direct approach, but it is an ersatz No. The power of Yes comes
not from *ressentiment*'s repeated No's but from Yes, repeated in innocence.

I am using the word *innocence* much as it is in Zarathustra's announcement: "The child is innocence and forgetfulness, a new beginning, a game, a self-propelling wheel, a first motion, a sacred Yes-saying" (Nietzsche [1883–85] 1980, 1.1). This is not the use of *innocence* that contrasts it with being guilty, the way a trial can find some person guilty or innocent. In those circumstances innocence remains part of the realm of good and evil. But sometimes *innocence* is used in a way that doesn't contrast with being guilty, but with being either-guilty-or-not-guilty. That is the way I am using *innocence* when I contrast it with the attitude of *ressentiment*. For *ressentiment* is expressed in the contrast between good and evil. Innocence is expressed in the vision of a world beyond good and evil. Adam and Eve, before they ate the fruit of the tree of the knowledge of good and evil, were innocent, naked.[23] Think of it this way. If you wear clothes, then you can sometimes be improperly attired and sometimes properly, but if you do not wear clothes at all, ever, then there is never any question of proper or improper attire. Sometimes I think children are innocent in this sense. Today, children are being treated more and more like adults, but imagine a scene such as one in Hitchcock's *Spellbound*: A three-year-old girl, trying to play with her five-year-old brother, sneaks up and pushes him while he is sitting on the iron railing outside their house. Unfortunately the brother loses his grip and impales himself on the spikes at the bottom of the railing. Dead, assuredly dead, but I am still inclined to say that the child might be neither guilty nor not-guilty. This is like the innocence that is one of the conditions for saying Yes. The child is accepted as innocent, as deserving neither punishment nor revenge. What I am concerned with is an analogous acceptance of the world as innocent, not characterized by good and evil, which are moral categories born of *ressentiment*. If there were no definite qualities, there would be no death, no tragedy, nothing to atone for. A world in which there was neither justice nor injustice. An innocent world. A world in which there were no genuine opposites (Nietzsche [1873] 1962, #6; Nietzsche [1888b] 1982, #32). A world of continuous variations. An inordinate, beautiful world. But that is by way of anticipation; some of it will surface if we turn to Nietzsche's early reading of Heraclitus.

Pointlessness and Aionic Time

Nietzsche mentions, of course, that for Heraclitus everything is made of fire, and everything changes, but it is not at the center of the story he weaves around Heraclitus's fragments. For Nietzsche, and then again for Deleuze, the central fragments concern neither fire nor change, but play. Fragment 52: "Time [Aion] is a child playing a game of draughts [sometimes translated as knucklebones]; kingship is in the hands of the child" (K. Freeman 1948, 28). Nietzsche, and then again Deleuze, will interpret this as a game in which there is no room for injustice, nor we may add, justice. An innocent game, beyond good and evil. Here is Nietzsche:

> Before his [that is, Heraclitus's] fire-gaze not a drop of injustice remains in the world poured all around him. . . . In this world only play, play as artists and children engage in it, exhibits coming-to-be and passing away, structuring and destroying, without any moral additive, in forever equal *innocence*. And as children and artists play, so plays the ever-living fire. It constructs and destroys, all in *innocence*. Such is the game that aeon plays with itself. (Nietzsche [1873] 1962, #7, my emphases)

And here is Deleuze: "We must understand the secret of Heraclitus' interpretation . . . not a theodicy but a cosmodicy, not a sum of injustices to be expiated but justice as the law of this world; not hubris but play, *innocence*" (Deleuze [1962] 1983, 25, my emphasis). But what is the connection between this innocence beyond good and evil and the game a child plays, and what is the connection between that game and time (Aion)? Suppose the game is a dice game, a game of knucklebones. Diogenes tells us that Heraclitus would sometimes "retire to the temple of Artemis and play at knucklebones with the boys; and when the Ephesians stood round him and looked on, he said 'Why you rascals, are you astonished? Is it not better to do this than to take part in your civil life?'" (Diogenes [c. 225] 1995, 9.3). Let us try to construct a distinction between the time of games, dice games, call this Aion, and the time of productive (civil or uncivil) life, call this Chronos (see Deleuze [1969] 1990, 162–68).

Chronos first. When we are engaged in a purposive project, say getting a piece of legislation passed, or reaching a verdict in a trial, or building a canoe, then time shakes itself out into different moments of various durations, the moment of planning the canoe, the moment of constructing the canoe, and the moment of completion, setting it in the water to paddle. These purposive projects encourage the division of time as Chronos into past, present, and future. This division itself produces its own difficulties. We know, for instance, that once this division of time is in place it can easily come to seem, as it did to Augustine, that the only thing that is, is the present. It can seem that the present is the only real moment and the past, which is no longer, and the future, which is not yet, have what must be a second-class being dependent, in some way, on the present which alone truly is. It is almost as if the world as a whole died in each moment only to be born again in each succeeding moment. Something similar to this was Descartes's account of endurance: God creates the world again and again. But this idea was not original with Descartes; it has a long medieval tradition. How long are these moments of momentary present existence? In the wake of the infinitesimal calculus, it is easy to think that these moments could be infinitesimally brief, enduring for $1/\infty$ units of time. So we have a steady series of present moments, each one static and unchanging, whose successive perishing gives us a sense of temporal change. Becoming egg-sliced into units of being. It is in this frame of mind that one can feel the attraction of the desire to live in the only reality there really is, in the present. But likely enough, this approach to living in the present will be negative, eliminating the past and the future. Living in a house with nothing in it.

If this is the way to think about time as Chronos, what is the time of god's constant creation of the chronological world? God's time could not also be Chronological. That would institute a regress, for the infinitesimal moments of Chronological time would themselves be divisible into even smaller moments. And during these smaller moments god would create the chronological moments of the world. But then the perpetual perishing of these smaller moments would set the same problems, and we would need god to create these smaller moments during even tinier moments. God would thereby become so infinitely busy creating a single moment that the original moment could never get going (Zeno). Whitehead's epochal theory of time is a response to a version of this problem, what he thinks of as the valid argument that remains in Zeno once the invalid bits revealed by nineteenth-century limit theory are removed.[24] What Whitehead calls physical time (our Chronos) is the result of dividing the concrete entity in its completion (Whitehead [1929] 1978, 283). But the genesis of that entity, a concrescence that is analogous to the time of god in the creation of each moment, is something else altogether. Whitehead puts the epochal nature of time in these terms: "In every act of becoming there is the becoming of something with temporal extension; but . . . the act itself is not extensive, in the sense that it is divisible into earlier and later acts of becoming" (69). I think of Whitehead for a number of reasons, and raise it to the surface not to defend the epochal theory in any detail (in fact, so baldy stated it is little better than an appeal to god); my intention was only to give a taste of the problem that Heraclitus's Aion might be addressing. Aion might be God's time, the time of concrescence. Chronos, the egg-sliced time of being. Aion, the liquid time of becoming.

Aion. What is the time of a game, a dice game, for example? I am feeling around for a distinction between chronological time and another kind of time, so I will not permit myself to say that there is no such distinction; I will not permit myself to say that in a game, as in the building of a canoe, there is the same division into planning, execution, and completion, so that there is no difference between the time of games and the chronological time of purposive activity. This means that I am committed to finding some feature of gaming that is not purposive. Right off, this will seem wrong. Gaming has an obvious purpose: winning. True. But it is not the whole story. It is true that when I play a game, say the card game P-I-G, I do try to win. Actually in this game, we aim simply not to lose, rather than to win. But the fun of playing P-I-G is not in not losing; it is in the playing. It is one of those games that almost always gets tedious before it reaches its end, but in the middle it can be fun. The same is true of the board game Monopoly. This long-winded game also becomes something of a grind when it moves in on its end. But somewhere in the middle it too can be fun. Much as I like to win, and even as I am not eager to sound again the platitudes of Edwardian England, I want to say that the point of games is not to win but to reach the time in the middle where the point of the game floats away leaving us just playing. Pointlessly. And I want to consider the possibility that the time in the middle might be the time of a child playing a game of dice, not the time of succession, the succession of concrete moments, but the time of creation. Yes.

It has to be a child. When grown-ups play with dice, they want to win, to win money, and the time of the middle is therefore made inaccessible. Grown-ups play what Deleuze calls "human games" (Deleuze [1968] 1994, 282). Human games are boxed in by four walls on four sides: (i) by the rules presupposed by the game, (ii) by the way these rules separate winning situations from losing ones, (iii) by the way individual moves in the game bring us incrementally closer or farther from the winning situations, and finally, (iv) human games are walled in by the immobile, "sedentary" form of play—we do move but only on a board carefully etched with the distinction between good and evil (Deleuze [1968] 1994, 282).

> This false and human manner of playing does not hide its presuppositions, which are moral presuppositions, the hypothesis here being that of Good and Evil, and the game an apprenticeship in morality. (Deleuze [1968] 1994, 282)

To get to the middle of time you would have to give up caring about the end, the point of the game. The middle of time is pointless, beyond good and evil.

> There is no other ethic than the *amor fati* of philosophy. (Deleuze and Guattari [1991] 1994, 159)

The middle of time is rhizomatic: "A rhizome has no beginning or end; it is always in the middle, between things, interbeing, *intermezzo*" (Deleuze and Guattari [1980] 1987, 25).[25]

Deleuze introduces his account of the "divine game" he contrasts with this human game by remarking that it was perhaps of this divine game that Heraclitus spoke (Deleuze [1968] 1994, 283). In the human dice game, we do affirm chance; we accept the role of the dice, but only conditionally, only within the framework of winning and losing, good and evil. In the divine game spoken of by Heraclitus, "every time, the whole of chance is affirmed in a necessarily winning throw" (283). Bad players, grown-ups, want to roll a 4, for example, and they will be able to win if they roll the bones enough to turn up 4 (Deleuze [1962] 1983, 26–27). How could you roll in such a way that you always won? Not by aiming for a 4, because in that case you would not be able to throw a *necessarily* winning throw. But neither could it be that you resigned yourself to your fate, as when one is willing to accept the punishment of a court, however unjust. What is required to play well? Pointlessness. Deleuze: "That the universe has no purpose, that it has no end to hope for any more than it has causes to be known—this is the certainty necessary to play well. . . . The dice throw fails because chance has not been affirmed enough in one throw" (27). In order to play well we have to release the divine time of creation from the grip of purposive chronological time. If Aion is the time of a child playing with knucklebones, then Aion is time unstructured by human projects that divide Chronological time into past, present, and future.

In Descartes's story each Chronological moment is created by god. And we can now answer the question about god's time. God's time is Aion: purposeless, pointless, affirmative time. Innocent time. For when we release ourselves from all purposes, we release ourselves from all negation, all differentiation of dice-states into winning and not winning. We escape the checkerboard of good and evil. *Pointlessness, which we thought was the source of all our despair, turns out to have been the answer.* Aionic time is pointless time. Emptied full (Ammons 1981). Emptied of projects and purposes that divided one thing from another, the many are now together. "In fact, the one is now many" (Nietzsche [1873] 1962, #6; see Deleuze and Guattari [1980] 1987, 21). But the many are not many self-identical individuals: persons, goats, organs. When we release the purposes that control the human game, we release all the purposes that control the game of life: the species-specific surrounding world, the *Umwelt*, of the goat is organized by what is serviceable, or not, to the goat; within the goat, the organs serve to ovulate or to pump or to oxygenate. Heidegger tells us that a carpenter's workshop would be organized similarly. Each environment, each *Umwelt*, organized like those grown-ups hoping to roll a 4. The Chronological world is a world of overlapping *Umwelten*. But the Aionic world is not a world of *Umwelten*. The Aionic world is one that is many, but not many self-identical individuals and their surrounding worlds. It is a world of *individuals without identity*. An inordinate multiplicity. Swarms of processes like the molecular composition of ocean currents. These currents are distinguishable, from a certain point of view, as currents, but they are not fundamentally individuals. Fundamentally they are swarms of particles with various trajectories, velocities, and so on. At a molar level there are currents but not at a molecular level. I do not think there is any need to make this molar-molecular distinction into a version of Kant's distinction between the empirical and the transcendental, as if we could say reidentifiable particulars were empirically molar (real) but transcendentally molecular (ideal). For a while I was tempted by this, but it is better to see this molecular-molar distinction not as absolute but as relative. At any level of analysis we can find a molar and a molecular plane (Deleuze and Guattari [1980] 1987, 40–41).

This metaphysic of swarms will be discussed in a bit more detail later, but even at this stage we can see that the distinction between Chronological and Aionic time is analogous to this distinction between the molar and molecular. I picture it like the complexly interlaced designs on medieval manuscripts, both Hiberno-Saxon and Islamic; from afar these are stars or crosses, but from up close to the surface, it is clear that these lines are tangled in ways that do not resemble stars or crosses at all. The Aionic time of creation is the time of these lines. We think that we are fundamentally reidentifiable individuals, but this is not so. I do not think it an accident that in the Islamic case, at least, this artistic commitment to running lines of continuous variations was part of a religious package that forbade certain sorts of representational designs. These designs are therefore very fortunate examples of the *subrepresentational* lines that move without purpose, pointlessly, the time of Aion: the child playing dice. Aion: thought on the move, innocence. What the child innocently affirms are these lines that are hidden in the surfaces of purposive Chronological time as reidentifiable objects.

Deleuze does not say that humans can experience the world Aionically. What he says is that we can come close to this in the work of art. "A pure idea of play—in other words, of a game which would be nothing else but play instead of being fragmented, limited, intercut with the work of men. (What is the human game closest to the solitary divine game? As Rimbaud said: look for H, the work of art.)" (Deleuze [1968] 1994, 283). This was already Nietzsche's interpretation of Heraclitus Fragment 52.

> Only aesthetic man can look thus at the world, a man who has experienced
> in artists and in the birth of art objects how the struggle of the many can yet
> carry rules and laws inherent in itself, how the artist stands contemplatively
> above and at the same time actively within his work, how necessity and random
> play, oppositional tension and harmony must pair to create a work of art.
> (Nietzsche [1873] 1962, #7)

Figure 1-5. The Dunfallandy Knot. Stone. Tayside, Scotland. © Courtesy of
RCAHMS. Licensor www.rchams.gov.uk.

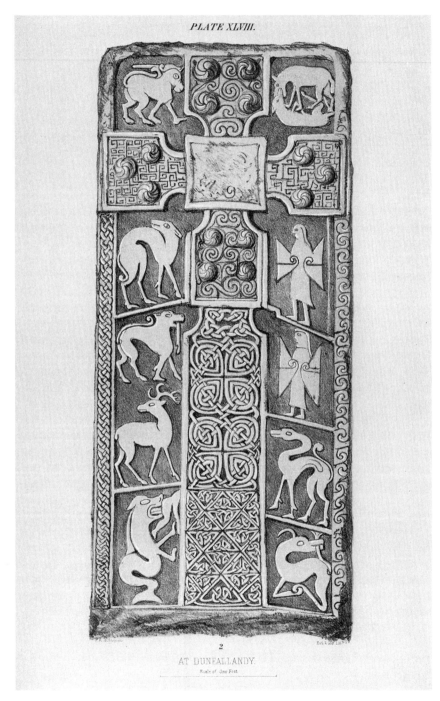

AT DUNFALLANDY.

Scale of One Foot

Figure 1-6. The Dunfallandy Knot. Drawing. © Courtesy of RCAHMS. Licensor www.rchams.gov.uk.

Figure 1-7. Leaf from Qur'an. Bayerische Staatsbibliothek München. Cod.arab. 1, fol. 2r resp.

To look at the world aesthetically is to be alert to beauty. Alert to becoming. To become sensitive to the surface effects of the reidentifiable objects we covet, wash, and wear, to become sensitive to the lines animating what to all the world looks like a mere star or a cross, to learn to live on the surfaces of things. On the surface, our categories lose their grip. Look: It is a patch of ground. Nothing special. Sit down and accustom your eyes to its surfaces: They teem. "You only need sit still long enough in some attractive spot in the woods that all its inhabitants may exhibit themselves to you by turns" (Thoreau [1854] 1984, 275). Ants crawling up leaves of grass, the struggle of an inchworm to bridge the gap between blades, old acorns soft with rot, pebbles and stones in casual abandon, spots of light and darkness moving with the wind in the leaves over head; move closer; the rich smell of dirt recalls the first smells of spring when the ground thaws.

Figure 1-8. Leaf from Qur'an. Spain. Almohad period, 1226/7. Bayerische Staats-bibliothek München. Cod.arab. 1, fol. 2v.

The Aionic present is accessible by releasing the play of these surfaces. This cannot happen unless we are willing to accept the world uncontrolled by our projects. It is an accepting, affirmative, innocent attitude to the world, and it is linked to uselessness, pointlessness. It is linked to beauty through the traditional Kantian account of beauty as purposiveness without a purpose. " 'Play,' the useless—as the ideal of him who is overfull of strength, as 'childlike.' The 'childlikeness' of God, *pais paizon*"[26] (Nietzsche [1901] 1967b, #797). The middle time of beauty is the time of purposeless play, and this is also the time of innocence, the innocence of the artist who can accept the fortunate accident. Every artist welcomes accidents, affirms chance, but it is the rare artist who affirms chance completely. Perhaps John Cage was such an artist. The way to innocence is, ridding purpose, entering the Aionic middle time of pointless play. This is the way to affirmation and intensity in both life and art, and that is why I am here describing an aesthetics of existence. Not because I think art is what we ought to emulate, but because art and life, at their best, are beyond good and evil, innocent, affirmative, intense. Yes. Beautiful.

Yes

I can appreciate the reader's skepticism. It has taken some time for me not to find this idea incredible. After all the suggestion is that we have been completely wrong about existence. Pointlessness and repetitiousness are good. How is it possible to turn our evaluation of pointlessness entirely around?

For many years I have, enjoyed Wittgenstein's acceptance or acknowledgment of our human finitude, especially as these appear in the Wittgensteinian work of Stanley Cavell (see Cavell 1979 and 1989). But Wittgenstein's "acceptance" does not move toward pointlessness. For Wittgenstein, the form of a philosophical problem is not knowing one's way about, being lost, away from home, and the form of an answer is finding our way home (Wittgenstein [1953] 1976, §§11, 116, 123). That is why I was inspired by Cavell to see Wittgenstein's mature philosophy as oscillating between uncanniness and peace (Bearn 1993, 1997a). An oscillation induced by the double negation at the heart of Wittgensteinian acceptance. I confront Wittgenstein directly in chapter 4. What I am attempting, here, is to philosophize without nostalgia, without aching for home. To look on the world with innocent, joyful eyes, not out of the deep disquietude of being lost, unable to find the trail home. And the clue to innocence was the Aionic time of the child playing knucklebones, a time accessible by giving up purposes, by moving in the realm of pointlessness. Pointlessness: a fine thing, a beautiful becoming.

Briefly, the idea is that if we are looking for a point, pointlessness is terrible, inciting one or more of the four double negations enumerated above. But if we are not looking for a point, then pointlessness can be so much more than simply bearable. It opens us to the most intense joy. This Heraclitean alternative to the philosophy of double negation does not make pointlessness bearable, neither does it resign itself to it; it affirms pointlessness as it enters the Aionic time of beauty, of becoming.

When I introduced the pointlessness of life, I suggested that the repetitiousness of our lives made their pointlessness unavoidable. This spells failure for each of the four ways of avoiding pointlessness by double negation which I have canvassed. Repetition. Repetition. But perhaps repetition is actually a good thing?

Think of cheers at football games. De-fense. De-fense. Or at pep rallies before the game. The animal energy released by chanting: Beat Groton. Beat Groton. Or the mock chanting of students heading out on Saturday night: Get-Drunk. Get-Drunk. Par-ty. Par-ty. Or more staid, the refraining alleluias of Christian hymns at Easter. In music there is sometimes a powerful repeated note. As I write this chapter, I am still in the glow of the discovery of a section of the Prelude of Bach's suite in C major for unaccompanied Cello (BWV 1009) during which we hear a G pedal, the same open G string, repeated, at regular intervals, again and again, forty-nine times, for what amounts, in Yo-Yo Ma's 1983 recording, to a section lasting more than thirty seconds.[27] Again, when a composer uses a leitmotif in association with a certain character in an opera, the emotional contours of that character fill out the leitmotif which begins as something like a code, but ends as something more like a concentrated poem, or coda. As Nehamas reminds us, even in TV soap operas, we have seen the characters in so many different situations that small gestures or expressions become, through repetition, loaded with significance (Nehamas 1988). What is going on here? Is repetition not, after all, the place our lives and our words empty themselves of meaning?

Perhaps the answer is that repetition is death to univocality but the life force of linguistic energy. Repetition breaks the spell of goal-directed practicality. In the resentful image of thinking, the repetitions of a word can seem to confuse and disturb the use of language, and one will feel inclined to eliminate all but the single, serious, central semantic content of any word. The repetitions of a word bring more and more of the semantic energy of the word into play. Like the innocent child with the knucklebones, repetition flattens the field of play, removing the boundaries between winning and losing, between one significance and another. Energizing our language, charging our words with meaning to the utmost degree (Pound [1934] 1987, 36). According to Frege, for example, it is precisely this utmost degree of charged meaning that gets in the way of speaking the truth, for in this case it is never clear what meaning is meant, so it is never clear whether we have spoken the true or the false (Frege [1918] 1968, 514–15). On Frege's account it may be very well for the damp fields of poetry or the humanities to put up with this muddle of meanings, but it will not do for the "exact sciences which are drier the more exact they are, for exact science is directed toward truth and only the truth" (514). There is a complex dispute between Searle and Derrida over the question of whether any such Fregean purification or dehydration of moist, muddled meanings can ever be accomplished (see Glendinning 1998; Bearn 1995b). Here I want to observe only that if one is attempting innocence, as I am here, then the very idea that there is one thing that a sentence aims at is not something that can remain unchallenged, whether that one thing is Frege's narrow truth or the more open arms of Austin's felicity (Austin 1976). I am trying to move in such a way that the very idea of having a point, whether of a sentence or of a life, is overcome.

Repetition doesn't only invigorate words. Take another example I started with. The commuter life, day in day out, into the city, back out to the suburbs, again and again. I was trying to make it seem pointless. But turning back on myself now, when I was living in Connecticut, I led the Conrail commuter life for two years. But it wasn't the repetitiousness of this life that made it hard; it was the long hours that commuting forces one to keep. The repetitions actually increase one's fondness for the train station, for the rolling stock, the platforms one passes, the news agents, and the passengers who seem to be exactly on your schedule. All of these you come to know like family, or at least they become comfortably familiar. Familiar, like a family. We see family again and again. Is that good or bad? Would it be better if I found different girls in the beds each morning when I woke them up? What makes it possible to get to know someone like family? Repetition. Repetition and innocence. Innocent acceptance of the person. The same kind of overall acceptance that gives repetitions of words their power, their intensified energy. Not one meaning. Not seven. Words disseminating unruly significances endlessly. An inordinate multiplicity. (See Derrida 1972a.)

Once we start thinking of the positive role of pointlessness in our lives, we will discover that many of our favorite activities are pointless. Consider driving a car. All but a very few US adults can drive. They drive to work.

They drive to shop. They drive to drop off the kids. They drive to pick them up. Many of us complain about all this driving, but when it comes to the weekend, you find many of these same people, who complained through the week about all their driving, doing what? Going for drives. And if they like drives, there may develop a number of drives that they go on, around the lake or out past the cows or the scary tree house. It is the same with walks. Some walks have a point. You can walk to Wawa's for milk, or down the street to the playground. But the best walks, like the best drives, are pointless. Not walking to class or to school, but just walking. And as with driving, walks can be repeated: Let's go on the walk to the first lookout, or to the giraffe tree, or as Alice and I did yesterday, to the F bridge.

Someone is sure to be thinking that if you are going to the F bridge, then there *is* a point to your walk, getting to the bridge, so it isn't pointless. But that will not be the point of the walk the way milk is the point of the trip to Wawa. The bridge is where we sit or turn around, but we don't walk to the bridge to sit down. Someone might. You might be walking with someone who thought the point was to get to the bridge and turn around, like tagging first on the way to second. But such a person wouldn't yet have figured out what it was to take a walk; their actions would even begin to smell of the escape into mechanical activity that we just met in those lives that were scheduled to exhaustion. Actually, when Alice and I came back from the F bridge, we came back with some apples bought at Scholl's Orchard, so it might look like there was a point to this walk. But it was rather as if you decided to bake with your mother; this will produce a cake, and the cake may be good and enjoyable, but it is, so to speak, a gift of the time together, an Aionic gift, not the point of the chronological time together. Since Alice and I were pointlessly walking, the apples we bought were as much a gift of Aion as the windfallen ones we ate off the ground as we walked through the orchard to the fruit stand up by the road. We could, perhaps, make sense of all sorts of climactic pleasures according to this model of pointless baking and the gift of cake.

It is just like Monopoly. The Aionic middle time, overcoming the craving for a single point, can surface in the middle of an otherwise purposive undertaking. But there are conditions. Not just any purposive walk can open us to Aionic time. They have to be long enough. How long? Long enough to have a middle. "A rhizome has no beginning or end; it is always

beautiful by unleashing the subrepresentational lines tangled in the representational frame of our lives. And becoming beautiful is becoming alive,
becoming a child. "The child is innocence and forgetfulness, a new beginning, a game, a self-propelling wheel, a first motion, a sacred Yes-saying"
(Nietzsche [1883–85] 1980, 1.1).

TWO

Learning to Swim

> But to want to have cognition *before* we have any is as absurd as the
> wise resolution of Scholasticus to learn to swim *before he ventured into
> the water.*
>
> —G. W. F. HEGEL, *The Encyclopedia Logic*

Is that the point? Pointlessness. Is that us, pulling on our boots, preparing
to trudge off in pursuit of pointlessness, in pursuit of no longer being in
pursuit of anything? The suggestion that we may solve the problem of life's
point by embracing pointlessness is an easy mark, maybe even self-defeating:
the paradox of trudging boots. But consider swimming.

Hegel mocked the pseudo wise resolution to learn to swim before going
into the water. In the right frame of mind, it can appear that learning to
swim is simply impossible. Either you can swim, or you can't. If you can
swim, you can. If you can't swim, you'll drown. So learning to swim is impossible. And yet all over the world, children return from their swimming
lessons alive, and better swimmers too. Hegel was counting on our recog-
nizing the obvious mistake: Between swimming and drowning there is a
space within which the children play, and learn to swim. With any luck, the
easy assault on pointlessness will succumb to a similar sort of critique. And
so it is: Between life's having a single point, and life's having no point, there

is a positive conception of pointlessness that evades the paradox of trudging boots.

We are already familiar with the negative conception of pointlessness that delivers us to nihilism. Here, from the middle of the 1880s, is how Nietzsche characterizes it:

> From time immemorial we have ascribed the value of an action, a character, an existence, to the *intention*, the *purpose* for the sake of which one has acted or lived: this age-old idiosyncrasy finally takes a dangerous turn—provided, that is, that the absence of intention and purpose in events comes more and more to the forefront of consciousness. Thus there seems to be in preparation a universal disvaluation: "Nothing has any meaning"—this melancholy sentence means "All meaning lies in intention, and if intention is altogether lacking, then meaning is altogether lacking, too." (Nietzsche [1901] 1967b, #666)

Nietzsche is providing one genealogy of nihilism. So long as our life in this world had a purpose, a meaning, a point, there was a reason to go on living. But if our life were without purpose, meaning, point, there would be no reason to go on living, not even to help those who come after us. If our life is without purpose, there is no reason to feel good about working for our children or our children's children, for if existence is pointless, then it is pointless, and not just pointless for us. If existence is pointless, then working for the good of others is spending one's pointless time on earth pointlessly stockpiling canned goods so our children will be able to spend their point-less lives pointlessly stockpiling canned goods for their children, and so on. This is the full-fledged negative version of pointlessness. In the face of such pointlessness, dying soon is only second best.

However, in the same paragraph, Nietzsche observes that what is needed is a "more rigorous critique" of the concept of purpose. The negative result I just recited presupposes that if existence were to have any value it would have to have a purpose. But this leaves the notion of purpose untouched. If we came to see purposes themselves as artificial segmentations of the continuous process of existence, then this melancholy, negative version of pointlessness would evaporate. Nietzsche continues:

> "One must understand that an action is never caused by a purpose; that purpose and means are interpretations whereby certain points in an event are emphasized and selected at the expense of other points, which indeed, form the

> majority, that every single time something is done with a purpose in view, something fundamentally different and other occurs;[1] that every purposive action is like the supposed purposiveness of the heat the sun gives off: the enormously greater part is squandered; a part hardly worth considering serves a "purpose," has "meaning"; that a "purpose" and its "means" provide an indescribably imprecise description, which can, indeed, issue commands as a prescription, as a "will," but which . . . in place of indefinite entities posit nothing but fixed magnitudes. (Nietzsche [1901] 1967b, #666)

When we talk about the purposes of action we are disciplining the energy of our lives. Our lives move continuously into the future, and the attribution of intentions to our actions is an effort to control our lives, to force definite magnitudes out of the flux of experience. Aromas of Bergson. Our lives do not have *one* point. But neither do they have *many* points, for example, seven. Nor is it that they point in *all* directions. Nor do they have *no* point at all. Not one. Not none. Not many. Not all. Our lives have inordinately many points. I might have said innumerably or uncountably many points, but I like the excessive feeling of inordinate. They are moving in such *indefinite* directions that they are positively pointless. This is not the resentful attempt to deny all of the energy of the sun except that which supplies energy to the vegetables in my garden. It is the innocent acceptance of the sun's energy as a whole, heating so much more than my tomatoes, with the energy of a star, given without reserve, received in innocence.

This positive account of pointlessness already surfaced during my discussion of Aionic time, but now, I want to peg it to two passages of Nietzsche's *Genealogy.* Here is the first passage, a cutting from a thicket I am leaving behind.[2]

> What, then, is the meaning of ascetic ideals? In the case of an artist, as we see, *nothing whatever! . . . Or so many things it amounts to nothing whatever!* (Nietzsche [1887] 1967a, 3.5, second emphasis mine)

All I want from this passage is Nietzsche's endorsement of the logic of pointlessness, positively construed. There can, it is true, be pointlessness from the side of negation when there is *no* point. But there can also be pointlessness from the other side, from the side of affirmation when there are so inordinately many indefinite points that there might as well be none. Beyond the one and the many: an inordinate multiplicity: aromas of Bergson, again. This is the key logical move of life drawing. There is a traditional smoothness that comes by subtraction. Derrideans know that this traditional smoothness is inaccessible. But there is another smoothness that comes from addition. And this positive version is accessible, as accessible as Yes. As accessible as And.

And the second passage from the *Genealogy* that confirms the essential logic of life drawing is a well-known passage in which Nietzsche is writing against "pure reason" and "knowledge in itself." He insists that these represent unthinkable possibilities, because they seem to demand an eye that looks from no particular place, which has no particular view. Precisely the unthinkable notion of a god's-eye point of view. It is god's eye, so it is impartial. But it is also a point of view, so it is paradoxically also partial. Against this, Nietzsche offers the view that impartiality should be approached not by negation (tear out your eyes and look at the object *directly*)[3] but by affirmation:

> There is *only* perspective seeing, *only* a perspective "knowing"; and the *more* affects we allow to speak about one thing, the *more* eyes, different *eyes*, we can use to observe one thing, the more complete will our "concept" of this thing, our "objectivity," be. (Nietzsche [1887] 1967a, 3.12)

In this context, too, Nietzsche approaches impartial objectivity by innocent affirmation, Yes, and again, Yes (Nietzsche [1883–85] 1980, 4.19.12; Nietzsche [1886] 1966, 3.56). All that concerns me here is the logic of impartiality that Nietzsche presupposes. Impartiality is normally construed as *not* being partial, but in this passage Nietzsche suggests that we think of impartiality in terms of an inordinate multiplicity of indefinite views. The negative form of impartiality, like the negative form of pointlessness, is marooned on *ressentiment*. The positive notion of impartiality, like the positive from of pointlessness, moves with the waves, innocently Yes.[4]

And so the paradox of trudging boots is no problem. Although the point is pointlessness, pointlessness positively construed is not the negation of the traditional yearning for a point; it is its inordinate fruition, Yes. Lofting affirmation, we can slip the paradox of trudging boots.

The problem now changes shape: How can we say No to *ressentiment* while still saying Yes to everything? It is another logical obstacle to any serious consideration of Life Drawing, an obstacle, once again, already known to Nietzsche.

> The psychological problem of the type of Zarathustra is how he that says No and *does* No to an unheard-of degree, to everything to which one has so far said Yes, can nevertheless be the opposite of a No-saying spirit. (Nietzsche [1888c] 1967a, 3.6.6)

The logic of this Yes and No is not the familiar logic taught in the schools. I have already argued that the existential logic of double negation provides only an imitation of Yes, a vermilion No to a No. Perhaps the existential logic of double affirmation is the route to an ersatz No, the leisurely No that derives from double affirmation. Not the struggling No of *ressentiment*. It puts one in mind of Oscar Wilde's dialogue on the decay of lying.

The central voice in that dialogue is a man, probably young and attractive, who's very name is alive, Vivian. Many of us, like Vivian's interlocutor, Cyril, may not see the problem here: How could lying possibly be decaying since politicians, and many others, show no sign of losing their taste for lying? Apparently we have too low an opinion of lying. Vivian tells us that politicians

> never rise beyond the level of misrepresentation, and actually condescend to prove, to discuss, to argue. How different from the temper of the true liar, with his frank, fearless statements, his superb irresponsibility, his healthy, natural disdain for proof of any kind! After all, what is a fine lie? Simply that which is its own evidence. If a man is sufficiently unimaginative to produce evidence in support of a lie, he might just as well speak the truth at once. (Wilde 1889, 910)

Those who merely misrepresent show their commitment to truth by their efforts to get others to believe that their lies are true. They would like to be able to speak the truth, but for reasons of their own, they do not. They have not yet escaped what Vivian calls "our monstrous worship of facts" (Wilde 1889, 912). In contrast, the true liar is beyond representation and also beyond misrepresentation.

Invoking Théophile Gautier, Vivian tells us that the true art of lying, like every art, requires the complete indifference to practical matters that is the condition of enjoying beauty.

The only beautiful things, as somebody once said, are things that do not
concern us. As long as a thing is useful or necessary to us, or affects us in any
way, either for pain or for pleasure, or appeals strongly to our sympathies, or is
a vital part of the environment in which we live, it is outside the proper sphere
of art. To art's subject matter we should be more or less indifferent. We should,
at any rate have no preferences, no prejudices, no partisan feeling of any kind.
(Wilde 1889, 915–16)

This is the passage that makes me give Wilde credit for the thought that
the interesting is that in which we have no *particular* interest, but the passage is really about beauty. The true art of lying aims at beauty; it is unconcerned with representation and misrepresentation; it is equally unconcerned
with the practical and the impractical. Fine lying aims at intensifying our
enjoyment of beauty, and if along the way it shows an unconcern with representing the facts, well, at least it is not merely a misrepresentation of them.
It neither represents something else, nor does it fall under another representation. A fine lie makes us feel that there is more to everything than
what is required to be the thing that it is; it intensifies our experience of what
it calls to our attention. It draws us into the thing itself. As Vivian puts it,
"Art never expresses anything but itself," and "lying, the telling of beautiful
untrue things, is the proper aim of Art" (Wilde 1889, 930–31).

The art of lying, by being beyond practicality and impracticality, might
even be said to aim at a positive sense of pointlessness, and so Wilde may
already have shown us how double affirmation can produce an imitation
negation. We are not used to thinking of negation by double affirmation,
but we should be. It is a common phenomenon, as common as it is to intensify both of two different things by keeping them separate: "the pathos of
distance" (Nietzsche [1886] 1966, §257). Enjoying dinner, saying Yes to both
courses, we intensify them together, not by rushing on through, but by paus-
ing between, lingering.

It is difficult to imagine anyone more innocent, more accepting of chance
than Cage, but even he prepares his piano. Even Cage decides to sit down
with his dog-eared *I Ching* and compose. Even Cage decides not to eat mush-
rooms if they are poisonous. But there is no other goal here than saying
Yes. According to Cage, nothing is *accomplished* by writing or hearing
or playing a piece of music (Cage [1961] 1973, xii). He tells us: "Give up
the desire to control sound, clear [your minds] . . . of music, and set about

discovering means to let sounds be themselves rather than vehicles for man-made theories or expressions of human sentiments" (10). He understands that this brings his work closer and closer to theater. And we will be concerned, soon enough, with dancing and theatricality. But let me end with Cage's ode to Kant.

> And what is the purpose of writing music? One is, of course, not dealing with purposes but dealing with sounds. Or the answer must take the form of paradox: a purposeful purposelessness or a purposeless play. This play, however, is an affirmation of life—not an attempt to bring order out of chaos nor to suggest improvements in creation, but simply a way of waking up to the very life we're living, which is so excellent once one gets one's mind and one's desires out of its way and lets it act of its own accord. (Cage [1961] 1973, 12)[5]

Beauty. Pointlessness. Affirmation. Life. Purposefully purposeless. "When one moves toward a goal it seems impossible that 'goal-lessness as such' is the principle of our faith" (Nietzsche [1901] 1967b, #25; Nietzsche [1887] 1967a). But it is.

What about the apparent absurdity of making pointlessness the point? Crafting pointlessness is like walking down the beach to sea. Walking to the sea is not swimming, and crafting is not pointlessness. But there is no problem. Walk on down to the water. It will be fine. I have seen the sea. I have enjoyed it. I have felt it on my flesh. In my mouth. Fresh and salty.

THREE

Andante Vivace

> *Quand la crainte est bannie, les caresses cherchent les caresses.*
> —VIVANT DENON, *Point de lendemain*

Kundera's short novel *Slowness* (1995) approaches, in its own way, the same territory that I have moved toward under the word Yes.[1] So, roughly speaking, Kundera's Speed is my No, and his Slowness is my Yes. But there will be differences; for one, Kundera doesn't share my determination to turn back from double negation to an original Yes, and this difference may explain the central puzzle or paradox of *Slowness*: its speed.

Grave ma non troppo tratto (*Beethoven, op. 135*)

Kundera's brief novel in defense of moving slowly moves very fast. This is not, as some might think, a trivial matter, as if it were nothing more than a small joke at the author's expense. The story's narrator (whose mother called him Milanku [91], but whom I will refer to, less familiarly, as Milan) presents himself as a would-be Epicurean. And he tells us (correctly) that for Epicurus pleasure was nothing positive but only the absence of suffering, the absence of pain (7). I am convinced that any approach to Yes by double negation will never get closer than a fake Yes; thus from my point of view, Milan's Epicurean project, like the existential projects of most philosophers, is doomed from the start.

Although this is not precisely Milan's evaluation of the Epicurean project, he too has doubts about its realizability. His suggestion is that the way to achieve the absence of pain is to go slow, to take your time, but Milan is not optimistic about the chances for success. He even tells us that the sort of life Epicurus had in mind "may not be compatible with human nature" (8). It turns out that Milan thinks going slow requires quiet, secrecy, privacy, but that in the contemporary world, there is no longer any privacy. We are all always, one way or another, on stage. This is certainly true for the famous; their worldwide fame saps their liberty (40–41). But even those of us without fame are always aware of the possibility of becoming famous; so Milan says, the possibility of fame "shadows" every one of us, all the time (41). Thus, even when we are alone, and ostensibly private, we will be playing to the crowd, especially when what we are playing to the crowd is our authenticity, staging sincerity. Milan adopts his friend Pontevin's figure for the theatricality of modern life; he refers to it as dancing (18), and it is a condition of going slow that you are *not* a dancer (10). But in the terms of the novel, it is not at all clear that one can leave the stage without dancing off stage, in which case one could never really leave, never really go slow, so never really live the Epicurean dream of a slow life without suffering. And if one can never really go slow, then the melancholy (7) conclusion of this novel may be the discovery that the best we can hope for is not really slowness, at all, but a kind of instant slowness. Like instant potatoes. The paradoxical speed of *Slowness* is at the heart of its melancholy conclusion. "The chaise has vanished in the mist, and I start the car" (156).

Adagio molto e cantabile *(Beethoven op. 125)*

In the opening paragraphs of the novel, Milan describes the difference between Speed and Slowness in terms of sex. Milan recalls a conversation—but it was really, he says, more like a lecture—a conversation he had with an

American woman in about 1965 (2). She was expounding sexual liberation and returned again and again to the word, and the occurrence, of orgasm. Milan says that, by his count, she used the word forty-three times (3).

> The religion of orgasm: utilitarianism projected into sex life; efficiency versus indolency; coition reduced to an obstacle to be got past as quickly as possible in order to reach an ecstatic explosion, the only true goal of love-making and of the universe. (3)

Speed and Slowness. This lecture articulated "(chillingly theoretically)" the speedy pleasures of sex, orgasm (2). The traditional picture of desire as lack is one source of this worship of speed. Sexual desire can be construed as the painful lack of sexual pleasure, what men crudely describe as getting their rocks off, getting laid, or simply getting some. This is sexual pleasure as double negation. It is uncomfortable to be horny, and the way to eliminate this discomfort is to achieve climax, sexual delight reduced to a burden to be overcome. Diogenes the Cynic, pleasuring himself in public, "wished 'it were as easy to banish hunger by rubbing the belly'" (Diogenes Laertius [c. 225 CE] 1995, 6.69).

There is little doubt that these speedy sexual pleasures, however real, offer pleasures of less intensity than sex can offer. I don't mean to be moralizing against one-night adventures. Milan will be retelling one such adventure as an ideal to be followed. Everything depends on what happens during the night. We already know that the intensity of sexual pleasure is increased by slowing down, not by racing to completion, but by learning the "art of staying as long as possible in a state of arousal" (36). The light touch of her fingers on your collarbone, arms wrapping around shoulders, tracing the furrow down your back . . . *accelerando* . . . squeezing closer, *allegro* . . . pelvis pressing hard into hers . . . hungry for the feel of his body . . . closer than skin can imagine . . . *presto* . . . tearing off clothes . . . naked . . . tasting sweat . . . inhaling sex . . . legs wrapped around face . . . pressing closer . . . there . . . closer . . . yes . . . . . . yes . . . . slow . . . . Slow . . . . *ritardando*. . . . slower . . . feel his tongue . . . . salty in your mouth . . . . moist lips brushing the curve of your breasts . . . firm on his hard nipples . . . *stringendo* . . . her hand . . . *lento* . . . caressing its way along your thighs . . . *ritardando* . . . across your stomach . . . your hands in her hair . . . down his back . . . *stringendo* . . . gasping for air . . . rocking deliriously delicious ... slowly ..... yes ..... slowly and alive, more alive, more amazingly alive than you had ever dreamed. *Andante Vivace.*

At one place listing Epicurean pleasures, Milan mentions caresses (8). And it is caresses that are missing from sexual activity aimed only, as in the case of Diogenes, at removing the discomfort of lusting loins. The caress aims at nothing, or allofit. Sartre helps us understand the nature of the caress. The hand is famous for its opposable thumb. It is a fine instrument, able to type, to drive, to perform the minute maneuverings required for up-to-date laparoscopic surgery. But if it is to caress, all of this must be left behind. The hand must be deprived of its glorious instrumentality, which was of such importance to Diogenes.[2] To caress is not to beat, nor to rub, nor to clutch, nor to hold, nor even to pet, as we pet a dog. The hand, as Sartre puts it, must be turned back into mere flesh by "stripping the body of its action, by cutting it off from the possibilities which surround it" (Sartre [1943] 1992, 507). The fingers of the hand are made to dangle, like things, and these dangling things are turned around, fingers caress not with the fingertips, their business side, but with the backs of the fingers, their useless pointless side, and these dangling things, turned backwards against their design, are dragged by their arm against the wrist of your lover. How fast? What is the tempo of a caress, it intensifies, *stringendo*, but not by quickening. It stretches out and slows down, all the while, tightening up. *Andante Vivace.* The caress is pointless. Sartre moves from here in another direction, because he never leaves the land of double negation. But as I look at it, the caress is Yes. Every sensation counts, the senses say only Yes (Bergson [1889] 1960, 88). On the side of the fingertips while we are typing, only some of the world gets in. QWERTY. Typing, like all instrumental action, says No. No to what is not intended. But the caress receives and enjoys it all. It is not pointlessness as in nihilism; it is the pointlessness of Aionic time, the pointlessness of joy. Though I would rather speak of enjoyments, for the moment I will join Milan and Epicurus in speaking of pleasure, and here Milan is introducing us to the pleasure of uselessness. It is not open to one intended thing, because it is open to so much: It has no single point; it has no sum of single points; it has an inordinate multiplicity of points. Beyond one and many. Yes.

Milan is in mourning not only for the terrifying sacrifice of pleasure to sexual liberation in the speech of that American years ago in 1965. He mourns the general loss of slow pleasures. It is a platitude to observe that life moves faster now than it used to. Letters that used to travel at the speed of mail boats now travel at the speed of light. A lively person, vivacious, will be bubbly, excited, moving fast.[3] Even in musical notations, the word *vivace* has come to mean something quite speedy, as if being alive just were being speedy. But it was not always so. Beethoven, himself, used the notation *Andante Vivace*, and more generally in the eighteenth century *vivace* appears to have indicated a slower tempo than today.[4] This slips delightfully into Milan's claim in *Slowness* that the eighteeth century was a time, the last time perhaps, when the pleasures of slowness could be achieved. Indeed the one-night adventure he retells as a paradigm of slow delight was written in eighteenth-century France (Denon [1777] 1914). Milan sings his song mourning the decline of slow pleasures *Adagio molto e cantabile*.

> Ah, where have they gone, the amblers of yesteryear? Where have they gone, those loafing heroes of folk song, those vagabonds who roam from one mill to another and bed down under the stars? Have they vanished along with footpaths, with grasslands and clearings, with nature? There is a Czech proverb that describes their easy indolence by a metaphor: "They are gazing at God's windows." A person gazing at God's windows is not bored; he is happy. In our world, indolence has turned into having nothing to do, which is a completely different thing: a person with nothing to do is frustrated, bored, is constantly searching for the activity he lacks. (3)

Indolence means painlessness, and so it is a good term for Milan, who is trying to remain faithful to the double negation of the Epicurean project of achieving pleasure construed as the absence of suffering. But it is not a good word for my project, aiming at a multiplied Yes. Nevertheless, I like what Milan has to say about indolence, for he is very close to discovering a positive sense of boredom.[5]

When you are bored, you wish there was something to interest you, but there is nothing; so seeking diversion, you turn from one thing to another, trying to find the thing that would slake your thirst for something, anything, of interest. It is, as Milan, notes, frustrating. Thoreau will call the lives of those in search of anything to stop the boredom, lives of quiet desperation. If there is a positive sense of boredom, it may be what Milan, unfortunately, refers to as indolence. Gazing at God's windows. Apart from indicating that to gaze at God's windows is to look up at the sky, Milan doesn't tell us how he understands this image. Try this Bachelardian thought. In the evening, driving or walking past houses in the town—some of them are cold and dark; others are lit up with a light that is always—it can't be always, but that is the way I recall it—always yellow, warm, the color of a glowing fireplace. Sometimes it actually is firelight, and the windows flicker. Through the windows you can see the life of the house; my friends and I call this snooping, and sometimes it is, but sometimes it is more innocent, enjoying the warm glow of light warming other people. It needn't be a home or a house, I have felt this way looking at a campfire up ahead in the distance or at an old oil drum stuffed with dismantled pallets blazing in the alleys of cities too busy to notice. Gazing at God's windows might be taking the same kind of interest in the sky, the footpaths, and the anarchic plastic garbage heaping up between bridge and bank, gallon containers of milk, coffee cups, soda bottles, coffee cups, a few balls, one old tire, more coffee cups. To gaze at God's windows could be to treat the whole world, in every discarded detail, as the work of God, and so it would be as cheering to our souls as the human glow of houses passed by in the evening. To gaze at God's windows would be to accept the world, completely, needing nothing more. Yes. If this is boredom, it must be a positive sense of the word, indicating not that there is nothing of interest, but that everything is interesting, well beyond my little parochial interests. Yes.

The affirmative sense of boredom will also be positively pointless, like caresses. There is not one point to looking fondly at that tangled undergrowth dropping away before you as the hill goes down. There is not one point. There are not seventeen points. There is an inordinate multiplicity of points, and in this mood they are all activated, all in motion, all in play, pulling our attention this way, and that, not letting our thoughts and emotions settle down, always on the move. Always becoming. Like a caressing hand, it is the movement that is the caress. When we gaze at the world in this way, we are caressing it. Caressing the world. And the tempo of this gazing, what is its tempo? The multiple directions our interests take will keep us absorbed in what to most people is nothing of interest; it will keep us absorbed in such nothing for some time. The tempo is slow but filled with intensity. *Andante Vivace.*

I want to resist Milan's marking these experiences with the word *indolence*. This Epicurean doctrine virtually demands that its ideal be called indolence, but we need not follow. Apart from the general logical betrayal of Yes that this doctrine encourages, this doctrine puts a roof on joy. Since the absence of suffering is what Epicureans call pleasure, they will have reached the maximum personal pleasure by eliminating their suffering. Cicero reports that for Epicurus "complete absence of pain marks the limit of the greatest pleasure, so that thereafter pleasure can be varied and differentiated but not increased" (Long and Sedley 1987, 21.A). In this system, there is only so much pleasure one can have: no suffering. And between the various ways of achieving no suffering, there is nothing, with regard to pleasure (= no suffering), to make one prefer one over the other. As I am thinking about boredom positively construed, caressing the world, the basic value is not pleasure, certainly not pleasure construed negatively, the basic value is not pleasure so much as intensity, *stringendo*.

Tightening the string of a cello increases its tension, raises its pitch, from a zero point where it makes no sound at all, because it has no tension on it, as if it were still in its package. A life may be thought of in similar terms, a life of great intensity pulled tight, but think of it as being able to be pulled not just in two opposing directions, the limitations of the cello string, but in all directions like the skin of a kettle drum. It shouldn't have taken Yo-Yo Ma's amazing performance of Bach's six suites, two days ago at the Moravian church, to remind me that the tremendous intensity of the sound of a cello has something to do with the *bow*. It is the bow pulling against the tension of the tuned string that liberates further intensities, various volumes, of course, but various emotional intensities too. And caressing may not be an inappropriate figure for the bow's involvement with the string, although we should remember that bows can attack strings and that lips can caress, and teeth. An intense life is more than a string tuned, but it is hard to see how it could be more intense than a cello singing, or shrieking. Not one point, not one timbre, tone, pitch, mood, but multiple, continuously varying. Pulled not along one dimension but all possible linear dimensions. Affirmatively pointless. Yes.

The basic value is not pleasure so much as intensity, *stringendo*. This has a number of consequences. I will mention two. The first is that since intensity is in part a function of the inordinate multiplicity of interests or points that are of concern to one affirmatively bored, gazing at God's windows, since intensity is partly a function of this multiplicity of interests: The more interests, the more intensity. Those amblers of yesteryear can live lives along a continuous scale of intensive magnitude, just like the continuous scale of light intensity that is visible through windows in the evening. On this scale of intensive quantity, there is a zero point of no intensity, but there is no upper bound; the sky itself is no limit (Deleuze and Guattari [1980] 1987, 153, 31). The second is that since intensity is the basic value, slowness is only important insofar as it is associated with intensity. Intensity can be slow, as we have seen when considering the caress, but intensity can also travel at a different speed. The speed not of the caress, but the speed at which we dance for joy.

With Kundera's little novel in mind, we will have to approach this speedier intensity, dancing for joy, with some delicacy, because as Milan tells the story, dancing is as much the enemy as slowness is the hero.

Minuet

Milan's attempt at recovering the lost pleasures of slowness will finish in melancholy, for he suspects that these slow Epicurean pleasures—"a gulp of cool water, a look at the sky (at God's windows), a caress" (8)—he suspects that these slow pleasures are not "compatible with human nature" (8). At the breakneck speed of logical argument, what he suspects is this:

(i) Dancing is incompatible with the enjoyment of slow pleasures.
(ii) Dancing is unavoidable.
So (iii) Slow pleasures are unattainable.

fine

I will look at each of these in turn, but first: Why dancing? I have said that this is the way Milan's friend Pontevin refers to the theatricality of modern life. But why dancing? Many of us love to dance, so it is a bit surprising that Pontevin uses dancing as the paradigm of inauthenticity and theatricality.

Ballet might be what he has in mind. Here we do have an extremely theatricalized form of human movement. It is not just the tutus, the toe shoes, the stage, and the intermissions. Even when dancers, as in some of what is called modern dance, attempt to move in ordinary ways, the movements are isolated from their ordinary contexts, and up there on the stage, the movements look exaggerated, occasionally burlesqued. Staged dancing is never just there, the dancers are always aware of themselves and of how they appear to others. But it is not just staged dancing. Ballroom dancing where one is performing a named dance with difficulty, or with luck and practiced grace, is equally concerned with how one appears to others. Even when you and your friends go out dancing just for fun, not to dance the *this* or the *that*, but just to dance, even then, one is aware of how one looks and whether one is dancing gracefully, or like a turkey. This kind of dancing might even be more exposed than when you are dancing a named dance with steps; because it is possible to pretend that the gracelessness of your tango is not *your* gracelessness, but just your inability to tango. When we are just dancing, our ineptitude is ours, and we will therefore be that much more concerned with how we look to the crowd on the dance floor. This is one reason pre-teens, and grown-ups, love to go to dances but don't always have the courage to dance. In sum, even without canvassing every possible kind of dancing, it does begin to look as if Pontevin did not blunder when he made his figure for inauthenticity and theatricality dancing.

Why is dancing incompatible with the enjoyment of slow pleasures? Milan doesn't exactly say this. He says that Epicurus "commanded his disciples: 'You shall live hidden!'" (10). That is, they should live hidden away from the gaze of an audience. But since to dance is to be aware of your impact on an actual or possible audience, it follows that dancers cannot obey the Epicurean command to live hidden. So dancing is incompatible with the enjoyment of slow pleasures.

This speedy little defense of the incompatibility of enjoyment and slow pleasures doesn't actually address the question of why publicity is incompatible with slow pleasures. This is simply assumed in Epicurus's command. So I will supplement the argument, but I will have to be a little circumspect. I want to articulate both Milan's sense that dancing is incompatible with indolence, and my own sense, which will come out more clearly later in this chapter, that the trajectory of Milan's thinking properly leads in a much less melancholy direction. In this way you may be able to feel how, against the trajectory of Kundera's book itself, reading *Slowness* gave me confidence that an existential philosophy, an aesthetics of existence, could be drawn from Deleuze. The difficulty is the difficulty of reconciling Yes and No. Slow pleasures are the pleasures of acceptance; caressing fingers accept the smooth, sensual feel of a lover's shoulder, without reserve. Gazing up into the night sky, our eyes caress the sprinkled stars. Identifying constellations is different. Identification says No. Aquarius is not Ares. The morning star is not the evening star. Gazing into the stars is only Yes. The problem that dancing poses for caressing your lover's shoulder or the stars in the night sky is that dancing introduces a No. The ideal would be to lie on your back in the cool of a summer night playing with the stars, sinking up into the sky. "Gordon, is that you out there? What are you doing?! Come back inside to the party." And you feel that you are being watched, disturbed from your reveries just as if the evening's gnats, flies, and mosquitoes were still biting you back to the earth. Returning to the sky you find your star wanderings now mixed with thoughts about how you look, out there on the grass, to that shape up on the porch: Does this prove I am just too shy to make conversation with the guests at the party I just left, or is this really a sign of being a reflective, philosophical person? What do they think a philosopher is, anyway? And so, not wanting to look unsocialized, with the reverie already broken, you go back to the guests. And the open bar. Dancing draws us in the direction the audience wants us to go. Dancers play to the audience and so dancing converges with kitsch (Bearn 1998a).

Dancers are concerned with how they look to others. All by itself, this would inauthenticate the words and deeds of the dancer. Dancers have become actors in a play written by a generalized public, so dancers cannot take the risk of flouting the good, offending the audience, emptying the living theater. But neither can a dancer bear to share the stage with another dancer battling for the attention of the audience. The dancer's problem is, therefore, how to drive others off the stage without seeming to flout the human good. The solution to this problem is what my friend Pontevin calls "moral judo," one of the wiliest, inventions of the dancer (19). Dancers turn the good into a weapon; by appearing supremely moral, they force everyone else to appear less moral than they, and when their challengers have slunk off the stage, the dancer most expert in moral judo can be found, alone on the stage, radiating goodness without qualification to the whole world. So dancing converges with kitsch, vapid goodness, approved by everybody.[6] A kitsch world is a world in which good triumphs without difficulty over those who are simply evil. It is a creepy, Disney world, and it is so tenaciously good that it is hard to see why there is anything wrong with it, at all, but every night Walt Disney World clouds its entertainment heaven with insecticide.

I love the way Pontevin tells the story of Berck's Missed Kiss. Berck is a public intellectual whom Pontevin despises for his never-ending dance of self-promotion, however incompetent. The story involves the way Berck was taken down by another dancer, an expert in moral judo. It happened during the beginning of the AIDS crisis when with much fear and anxiety; we were just learning about the disease. Berck was lunching with a politician, a competitor for the spotlight at center stage, and some people with AIDS. After dessert was brought in, Berck was surprised by the sudden appearance of a camera crew. The politician got up, abruptly, walked over and kissed one of the people with AIDS, on the lips. This dramatic act of daring goodness threw Berck right off the stage. He had lost the spotlight. What could he do? If he overcame his fear, and kissed that man or another one, he would just be copying the politician, and they, the audience, would see that immediately. He could do nothing except watch the politician steal the show. That is moral judo: the aggressive use of moral virtue to stand superior to one's opponents.

When Berck picked himself up, he knew that to reclaim the spotlight, he had to do that AIDS scene one better, so he flew to Africa to have his picture taken with the one thing on earth more heartrending than a dying man, a dying child (16). It was a fine recovery and a nice move of moral judo on its own. But it was only temporary. The politician came back with religion, at night, in candlelight, in a grand march; and Berck, floundering for another good cause, landed in a country he had thought was in leftist revolt, but which was, to his terrible surprise, peaceful. Pontevin tells it much better, much. He says the incompetent Berck is the "martyr-king of the dancers" (18).

Dancers dance for the audience. This draws dancers in the direction of kitsch to precisely the extent to which they are drawn away from slow pleasures. Milan appears to believe that if slow pleasures are ever to be accessible we must be able, somehow, to stop dancing.

Why is dancing unavoidable? Slow pleasures are Yes. Dancing introduces a No. And the difficulty with escaping from the dance to the slow
pleasures of Yes is the difficulty with every attempt to approach Yes by
double negation. The only Yes it can access is an inauthentic Yes. Would it
help if we lived hidden? Is hiding the answer? When Sartre is discussing
shame, he implies that hiding would do the trick. Imagine you are driving
along in your car, absentmindedly picking your nose. Turning your head,
you find you are being watched by the driver to your right. Sartre thinks
there is a complete difference between the way you lived your actions before and after you were seen. Before you were seen you lived your actions
beyond good and evil, the minute you saw yourself seen, the vulgarity of
your actions descended on you. Sartre tells us: "Nobody can be vulgar all
alone!" (Sartre [1943] 1992, 302). If Sartre were correct, we could live hidden and experience the slow pleasures of Yes. But Milan despairs of ever
being able to hide, to escape dancing. The problem is that the audience
follows you into your hermitage. Your hermitage is but a dressing room.

Backstage there is a wardrobe department. It is where they keep tutus
for the swans of Swan Lake, suitcases for Willy Loman, and jeans for the
Jets. It is a costume department. There are wardrobes, too, in our homes,
and the question of whether it is possible to escape dancing can be thought
through in terms of whether it is possible to dress without thinking about
how you will look to an audience. If you follow the directions of some *Dress
for Success* guide to climbing the corporate ladder, then of course you are
playing to the crowd, of course you are dancing. But many people climbing
that ladder know, without even thinking, how to dress for the corporate
office; they know they should not appear in the office wearing a white tie
with their black shirt, and certainly not in that tight little black dress,
which Vincent spent all last Saturday night trying to look up. It is not just
because it's work, and you have to please your boss. If anything, it's worse
when you go out, and have to please your date. It may be worse because what
you are dancing in the office is The Dedicated Talented Employee Going
Somewhere, but when you go out, what you are dancing is more like, You. I
used to think that I didn't care what I wore. My friends were all wearing
this and that, but I just wore what I wanted to. Then I realized that I was
taking my time, maybe not a lot, perhaps three seconds, but I was deciding,
each morning, which shirt to wear. I was deciding on my look. And it came

out more or less the same every day. For a while Malcolm even thought all philosophers wore baggy green pants; because for reasons I have now forgotten, I then thought I couldn't be Gordon in jeans. The point was vividly brought home to me at a performance at the Touchstone Theater a few weeks ago when I was reminded that some women spend a good hour in the morning fixing themselves so they look all made up, and others spend just as long fixing themselves so they *don't* look all made up.[7] When it comes to dancing, it is always a dead heat. And Milan has been trying to get us to admit that what dies in that dead heat is Yes, the slow pleasures of caresses.

You might think it would be different with caresses. After all, unless turned on by the eyes of strangers, most of our caressing takes place pretty well hidden. What could be easier? Close the door, take off your clothes, and the dance has stopped. But it hasn't. Sometimes even the music is still playing. If this is the first time, and even if you are not following that other guidebook, *How to strip for your mate*, you will not want to get stuck getting out of your pants, and if this is not the first time, you will still not want to look ridiculous in some way or other. And then with your clothes off, and your intimate behavior beginning, consider your secret, hidden, erotic desires and fantasies. Are they really characteristic of You? Are they not just ready-to-wear fantasies, off the shelf? At most there are a few little adjustments that need to be made to the length of this or the breadth of that, fitting the fabric of a familiar fantasy to your physical frame. You can pick it up later today; it should be ready this afternoon. Our wardrobes are scripted twenty-four hours a day, seven days a week. We don't all look alike, but we are all in costume.

This is the first negation. We are always already on stage, dancing. Perhaps we can escape, depart, hide away in some garden hermitage just as Epicurus commanded.[8] But that is just it. Just as Epicurus commanded. Even the departure from the stage is scripted. If we leave the stage, we have no choice but to dance off to our hermitage. Walking alone along the beach, we are still "walking alone along the beach." There is no escape. Vincent, an entomologist friend of both Milan and Pontevin, is staying at the same *château* turned hotel where Milan and his wife, Véra, are spending the night. At one point while trying to seduce a typist named Julie, Vincent booms out a critique of dancing in general and a critique of Berck in particular (by a surprising coincidence, Berck was in the same hotel). Vincent is shocked to find a spectacled man in a three-piece suit rising to the challenge, defending dancing (83–84). Vincent is shocked and speechless that this spectacled man didn't seem to know the script. Nobody ever questioned Pontevin; we all just laughed and agreed. But this man in the three-piece suit, dressed for success, insisted that there was no escape from dancing, that dancing was going to be "part of the human condition from now on" (84). I have been trying to make this conclusion seem plausible too. It is a melancholy conclusion. There is nothing left of authenticity. Everything is simulated.

This sad comedy reaches its apotheosis when Vincent and Julie, before a real audience of strangers, race naked around the swimming pool, shouting their sexual desires at each other. Vincent, finally falling on Julie, discovers, at the point of penetration, that his member is limp. Does that stop them? No. They proceed with the script and simulate the most intimate and intense of human pleasures before an audience of French entomologists and one Czech, aghast (121–23). It is a ridiculous demonstration that when you begin with No, the only attainable Yes is fast and fake.

Da capo, al fine

Molto Adagio, Mit innigster Empfindung (*Beethoven, op. 132*)

There is melancholy in the concluding words of *Slowness.*

> No tomorrow.
>> No audience.
>> I beg you, friend, be happy. I have the vague sense that on your capacity to be happy hangs our only hope.
>> The chaise has vanished in the mist, and I start the car. (156)

The chaise is slow; the car is fast. If this is hope, it is slight. Milan has been worming his way to a simulated Yes. The audience can get in the way of slow pleasures; so naturally he says: "No audience" (156). He says No to No. But double negation is not the way to Yes; it is, at best, the way to the heavy, overripe, sweetness of melancholy. But there is another way, the caress. Milan already understands Yes. Pontevin doesn't. Pontevin, the brilliant poser in the Café Gascon, has dominated the thinking of our crowd for too long. Look what he has done to Vincent, "plural cock" (149); Pontevin is with him, even *there*, forcing him back into his helmet, on his way to his motorcycle, racing away from his poolside debacle. But there is another way; the conclusion doesn't have to be melancholy. Even Milan has fallen under the influence of Pontevin.

Milan's "existential mathematics" is a clue: "There is a secret bond between slowness and memory, between speed and forgetting. . . . The degree of slowness is directly proportional to the intensity of memory; the degree of speed is directly proportional to the intensity of forgetting" (39; also see Bergson [1896] 1991). He's right. When we are angry, we step on the gas and drive as fast as we can. Vincent "hunched over his motorcycle can focus only on the present instant of his flight; he is caught in a fragment of time cut off from both the past and the future; he is wrenched from the continuity of time; he is outside time; in other words he is in a state of ecstasy" (1–2). He is experiencing the ecstasy of living in the present, approached by negation, "cut off," with the help of technology. Speeding on his motorcycle, this man has escaped from his body in a way that would have been inconceivable if he were, for example, rowing. "Ecstasy speed" is like bad sex: "You want to, I want to, let's not waste time!" (2, 33). Forget caresses; forget kisses; forget everything except the organ you crave.

We had such fun two nights ago, when Pontevin wasn't there, we were trading stories around Milan's delightful observation that when you are walking and start trying to remember something, you find yourself slowing down, in order to remember (39). Someone said that Socrates often stopped cold in his tracks, until he had worked out some philosophical problem, and Milan suddenly remembered that, in Plato's terms, philosophical discovery itself would have been a matter of memory. Going slow does not cut off; it brings together. It gathers. The pleasures of going slow, caresses, gazing at god's windows, also bring together, also gather. There are two kinds of ecstasy too. Yes and No: Slow and Fast.

Fast ecstasy lives in the present moment. It says No to the past, which remains there. It says No to the future, which remains to come. So like a horse's blinkers, fast ecstasy denies what it acknowledges, nevertheless, to be there. Sitting quietly on the bench, it is hard not to notice her bare arms over the top of the screen as she changes out of her shirt.[9] The ecstasy of No, fast ecstasy, is a form of dance, theater, machine ecstasy, deus ex machina. This is why it is never pure, its pleasures never robust. The best this fast ecstasy could deliver would be the absence of suffering. Indolence. Ersatz ecstasy. Diogenes in the street.

There is another kind of ecstasy. Milan loves the eighteenth century, like Vincent. But whereas Vincent is in love with the theater of the Marquis de Sade (8), the theater of conquest, Milan is always telling us about the slow pleasures enjoyed one night between a woman and a man whose names are now forgotten. It was first published in June 1777 in a periodical sold by subscription, and its author was indicated only as M.D.G.O.D.R., but we now know the author as the improbably named Vivant Denon (Nowinski 1970, 188). It was a short novel, *un conte*, entitled *Point de lendemain* (*No Tomorrow*), and it is this "no tomorrow" that suggests we are here being treated to a kind of ecstasy. A departure from time as we normally experience it. Ecstasy, again, but this time, slow ecstasy. The story takes place in a "world of secrecy" (5), precisely the secrecy that Epicurus insists is a precondition for the enjoyment of slow pleasures. A twenty-year-old gentleman whom Milan always refers to as the Chevalier, currently the lover of a certain Comtesse, finds himself alone at the theater next to a married woman, Madame de T***, currently the extramarital lover of a man we know only as the Marquis (5). We learn no names. Madame de T*** invites the Chevalier to a château outside Paris, along the Seine. In and around this château, which became in our century a hotel, the very hotel in which Milan and Véra are spending the night, the very night during which, by a third coincidence, Vincent and Julie simulated sex, poolside. In and around this château, the Chevalier and Madame de T*** experienced pleasures of the flesh, slowly, slowly, but incredibly alive, tense with contained energy. *Andante Vivace.*

Often, late at night, after Pontevin has left the café with his more devoted young friends, Vincent almost always among them, Milan will tell those of us who remain the story of the Chevalier and Madame de T***. He always divides it into three stages, but the soft, sexual details with which he stimulates his audience seem endlessly various. When he has finished, we walk back to our separate cars, slowly, holding hands, or further intertwined. In the first stage, the Chevalier and Madame de T*** walk in the garden, sitting on a bench, enjoying a few kisses that become just a little self-propelling. Then a return to the château, or almost, because at the last moment she invents a question that permits them, in a second stage, to return to the garden. This time they find a pavilion to which, she says, it is too bad she has no key, but then to her feigned surprise they discover it is open. Inside, the kisses and caresses come closer to lovemaking. It is here that they find their caresses seeking caresses (Denon [1777] 1914, 48). But Madame de T*** had "planned the interlude in the pavilion as a *ritardando* to brake, to moderate, the foreseeable and foreseen swiftness of events" (37). The time in the pavilion is broken off. In the third and final stage, they return to the château, first to an astonishing room of mirrors in which they spend almost no time and all, and then, finally, to a grotto where they remain until dawn.

No tomorrow. This evening was not to be enjoyed again. The Chevalier, as Milan tells it, is not sure why the night ever happened. What was the point? Madame de T***'s lover the Marquis arrives in the morning and, laughing cynically, tells our Chevalier that his services had been required to cover for the arrival of the real lover, the Marquis himself. So our Chevalier, like Vincent, has been a fake lover (6). Naturally, the Chevalier feels confused, was this night a filthy lie or a night of slow intensities? "He pictures Madame de T*** and is suddenly overcome by a wave of gratitude. My God, how could he pay such mind to the Marquis's laughter? As if the most important thing were not the beauty of the night he had just spent, the beauty that still grips him in such intoxication" (151). Their night together didn't have one point, or no point at all; it had a continuous multiplicity of points. It was affirmatively pointless. Slow ecstasy, burning with a hard gem-like flame (Pater [1873] 1990, 152).

When Milan has told his story, and we are still sitting, still lost in the sensuality of our imaginations, he will tell us that Madame de T*** is "the true disciple of Epicurus. Lovable lover of pleasure. Gentle protective liar. Guardian of happiness" (141). But Madame de T*** is a rare creature, in the end, perhaps, only literary. Milan at these times, late at night, when her story has been told, again, is never very far from the thick, sweet melancholy demeanor that is so familiar to his friends. It is not hard to see why. Milan, even Milan, sitting quietly at the back of our group, disappearing for days at a time with Véra, even Milan has come too close to Pontevin. Even Milan thinks that the key to happiness is escaping the dance, and though he loves the tale of Madame de T*** and her Chevalier, he knows too well that during that night of slow pleasures, they never stopped dancing. He

knows too well that with Madame de T*** "everything is composed, confected, artificial, everything is staged, nothing is straightforward, or in
other words, everything is art; in this case; the art of prolonging the sus-
pense, better yet: the art of staying as long as possible in a state of arousal"
(36). That perfect night with the Chevalier was therefore imperfect. Milan
is melancholy because he does not think there is any way to escape dancing,
to escape artificiality, theatricality, inauthenticity. He would like to enjoy
his life, directly, without the artifice of the imagination, a pure plain kiss,
but he knows too well that even the absence of imagination has itself to be
imagined.[10] Perhaps in the end there is only one kind of ecstasy, the fast
kind, only one possible tempo, presto. Perhaps that is why *Slowness* goes so
very fast. It is as if it took no time at all. Is there any way to slow down? Is
there anyway to enjoy the intensities of Yes?

Vivace

Sometimes when he remains during Milan's telling of his favorite story,
I think I have noticed Pontevin become self-conscious, fidgety, crossing
and uncrossing his legs, not bound by the spell of Milan's tale. Once, the
moment Milan got to the end, Pontevin rose, suddenly, and with mock
solemnity placed his hands on Milan's head and intoned a Latin blessing;
then with the same tone of simulated seriousness, he returned to French:
"We Knights of the Café, we *Gasconiers*, what would we be if we had not
Milan who recalls us to religion, and to the God who makes simple truths
possible, the God without whom we could never stop dancing. For you
know, it is the supernatural power of a God that helps Madame de T***
discover the slow ecstasies of that night. Tonight, therefore, let us thank
Milan for bringing us back to the Church, and the one true God, the Fucking God, the God of Fucking." Milan's story was lost in the laughter that
greeted Pontevin's performance, drowned in the suddenly courageous voice
of Vincent telling tales about his favorite Marquis de Sade and adventures
of a "plural cock" in a different château (146, 149). That night it was Milan
who left before the rest of us "(without being really heard)," quietly, slowly
and alone (8). The crowd at the Café Gascon was happy to be led back, by
Pontevin, to their arrogant irony. If Milan was right, then any escape from

melancholy would require supernatural help, but there is no supernatural being, and Pontevin is not melancholy, so Milan must be wrong. Reason is more violent than they say; here it hurt Milan.

And yet I keep thinking that Milan has given us the answer, a way beyond melancholy, without supernatural support. A terrestrial answer. Caresses. Continuous variations. Beauty. Art. It all seems right, until I wonder if that wasn't just the problem, art, that there was no way to evade dancing, to evade artificiality? It is true, as Milan says, that Madame de T*** is a dancer. And she cannot be separated from other dancers by observing that while she is making her life a beautiful work of art, a good thing, dancers like Berck make their lives merely artificial, a bad thing. Pontevin tells us again and again,

> Dancing is an art! That obsession with seeing his own life as containing the stuff of art is where you find the true essence of the dancer; he doesn't preach morality, he dances it! He hopes to move and dazzle the world with the beauty of his life! He is in love with his life the way a sculptor might be in love with the statue he is carving. (22)

So the dancer and Madame de T*** are both constructing their lives as works of art. But I think it matters that dancers are here said to *carve*, to sculpt their lives. Madame de T*** is not a sculptor; what she practices is the art of *drawing*. Life Drawing.

Sculpting is the art form that Plotinus refers to when he tells us that we should never stop working at making our lives beautiful.[11] Marble sculpture is carved, smoothed, buffed, and polished. Each of these is a negative act. Carving removes all that is excessive, all of what doesn't belong, and the rest of these sculptural activities do so too. Sculpting is therefore double negation. Knowing some of my readers, I rush to include the concession that not all sculpture is put together by subtraction; some is literally put together; some of the sculpture of the twentieth century is put together in this way. But traditionally sculpture operated by subtracting what didn't belong, by double negation, and this seems pretty clearly to be what Plotinus meant. You can tell where I am going. I want to say that dancers sculpt by double negation, but that Madame de T*** does not. We have already seen that there is a convergence between dancing and kitsch, and so it is clear what the dancer sculpts away: whatever gets in the way of the easy sweetness of kitsch. And in Kundera's universe, where kitsch is defined as "the absolute denial of shit," it is clear that what is being sculpted out of our lives is shit (Kundera 1984, 248). What remains is the unadulterated goodness of the dancer, expert in moral judo. Dancing is an art, a sculptural art.

Madame de T*** does not practice a sculptural art. She does not sculpt her adventures with the Chevalier by subtraction. She draws them, assembles them, composes them, by addition. Drawing is fundamentally a process of addition, adding lines to lines. And music, too, is additive, starting with what Cage tells us is mistaken for silence, musical composition fills this silence with sounds, more or less regimented by tradition and keys. When Pater insisted, in italics, that *all art constantly aspires towards the condition of music,* he was insisting on a fundamentally affirmative conception of art (Pater [1873] 1990, 86). It is an affirmative conception of art that would also apply to the life drawing practiced by Madame de T***.

Unlike a devotee of the religion of orgasm, she gathers together all the kinds of sensual, erotic excitement she and the Chevalier can imagine together. In their time together, especially their time in the pavilion during what Milan calls the second stage of the evening, their caresses do *not* seem to seek climactic pleasures; during the middle of the evening, their caresses seek only caresses (Denon [1777] 1914, 48). Since I think of the caress as positively pointless, as open to sensuality from any and all directions, unlimited by devotion to any single goal, the art of life drawing that Madame de T*** practices may indeed present us with an affirmative form of ecstasy. Hers is not the negative ecstasy of Vincent on his motorcycle, escaping, by technological means, both the past and the future. Hers is the affirmative ecstasy of the child playing dice: Aionic ecstasy. She and the Chevalier were living in the present not because there was nothing going on except *just this one thing*; rather they were living in the present because every facet of their sensual being was drawn into their sensual enjoyment. The past and the future, isolated from the present by particular goals, are not isolated by the sensual enjoyments of the Chevalier and Madame de T***. She practices an art of life drawing that brings Aionic ecstasy. Milan's thought, from which he himself turned, was correct: There are two kinds of ecstasy, but they may better be described not as fast and slow but as Chronological and Aionic.

I keep losing the thread. Now I remember. When Milan tried to sketch this distinction in terms of fast and slow, the distinction collapsed, leaving just the fast form of ecstasy, because with Madame de T*** "everything is composed, confected, artificial, everything is staged, nothing is straight-forward, or in other words everything is an art, the art of staying as long as possible in a state of arousal" (36). But if this is why slow ecstasy collapsed into fast ecstasy, then, since I have done nothing to recuperate dancing, Aionic ecstasy must collapse into Chronological ecstasy. Why did we ever turn from dancing?

Pontevin. His corrosive intellect has spilled on everything. Vincent is still young and he may recover; I do not begrudge Pontevin that little con-quest, but with Milan he has burned a hole right through the brightest mind in our group. Pontevin is so good at grabbing the stage, that his ac-count of dancing seems beyond question. He says he is not critical of danc-ers (21). But he knows what his effect is—on Vincent it is clear, and one hopes temporary, but even on Milan, where it seems more permanent. But dancing is a problem only if you approach the world in the resentful spirit of double negation. First negation, we live our lives inauthentically; we are dancers. So we want to say, "No audience" (156) and live our lives directly, confronting the plain sense of things. But once on the stage, the perfor-mance already in progress, there is no way off stage that is not theatrical-ized, danced. There is no way off stage that is not an "Exeunt." And so if we are fated to live our lives as dancers, there is no way out. Milan taught me to see this. He is the only one at the Café Gascon who has realized this melancholy result of Pontevin's arrogant posing. And this made it rela-tively easy for Pontevin to laugh him home alone, that night he blessed him and snidely thanked him for returning all of us to the good god, the Fucking God.

But there is nothing, in principle, wrong with dancing.

Milan's Epicureanism, which equates pleasure with the absence of suffering, makes him conceive of his ideal by double negation, as a form of indolence. But Milan's understanding of slow pleasures is better than that; his deeper understanding is one of the main reasons I was able to say that the primary value, here, is not indolence (= no suffering = pleasure), but in-tensity, like the intensity of a bowed cello string. I already brought this out when thinking about what positive boredom might be, and intensity is, in-deed, the important thing. Dancing should be criticized, not in principle, but only insofar as it decreases the intensity of life. So Pontevin may be quite correct to criticize the convergence of dancing and kitsch, especially in the form it takes as moral judo. Insipid goodness. Kitsch is on a continuum with the highest art, not different in kind as the inauthentic from the authentic; kitsch and the highest art differ as a matter of degree, degree of intensity (Bearn 1998a). So the trick is not, fruitlessly, to try to dress without caring how you look; the trick is not fruitlessly to try to act without acting. The point is to intensify. And here the theatrical flirtatiousness of one's clothes need not be a melancholy sign of failing to achieve authenticity; it may be a joyful sign that one is drawing a tinge of trampiness into one's friendships, the intensities of seduction and reversed power. Of course this can be overdone, but that is just to say that life drawing can be dangerous. This is true.

That is it. Its pretty simple. Life drawing doesn't have to square the circle, as Milan suspected, and as Pontevin conceded that night he brought the supernatural power of god back in. It is not easy to intensify your lives; it needs to be undertaken carefully, but it is possible. Yes. Madame de T*** knew that, so finally, did the Chevalier. Milan felt they had to know, but he couldn't free himself enough from Pontevin to see it himself. The problem of life is to intensify our lives by drawing in more and more of the world, placing the different sides of our lives in tension with each other, all in an effort to help draw out the life lines knotted in our being like the cords of a Hiberno-Saxon knot. Life drawing is intensification by multiplication. Our lives do not have one point, nor do they have no point, or many separable points; they have inordinately many points. The one you think of as central is de-centered but not destroyed; it continues to live in the positive pointlessness of an intensified life. The model here is the caress and, even more, that form of lovemaking in which the caress rules the orgasm, not the other way around. It isn't that climactic pleasures are to be shunned; that would be to try, once again, to sculpt them into oblivion. It is rather like a walk with a lookout along the way—enjoy it when it arrives—but the walk would be worse if we walked it with that enjoyment as its only point. The walk is better and more pointless than that. Climactic sexual enjoyment may be construed on analogy with that lookout or as I have already said on analogy with baking for fun, just to spend the afternoon with your friend or your mother or your father; the cake or cookies that you have baked, are a gift of the Aionic ecstasy that we greet in the middle of baking. Intensity is directly proportional to pointlessness.

Pointlessness is the way to Aionic intensity, Aionic ecstasy, but Aionic ecstasy is not Chronological, so it is neither fast nor slow. How, then, are we to explain the insight of Milan's existential mathematics? Perhaps what he has thought of as slow pleasures are simply one way of entering Aionic time, Aionic ecstasy. Perhaps Aionic time can be entered either by slowing down or speeding up. Milan is a champion of the caress, slow pleasures, gazing at god's windows, a gulp of cool water. As these pleasures open ourselves to many more than one point, to an inordinate multiplicity of points, these slow pleasures will bring us from the Chronological to the Aionic. Absent his melancholy, this is precisely the story Milan, himself, wants to tell. *Andante Vivace.* Now we can see further. Since the primary thing is not velocity but intensity, we can see that it might be possible to find Aionic ecstasy along faster pleasures. These will be the intense moments when we feel like jumping up and running around, or as they say, dancing for joy. In such moments so much is being drawn into and out of our minds and bodies that we are propelled from our seats, but for no particular reason; these are thoughts or feelings that one rides, as one rides a wave, or a kiss. These speedier activities are not goal-oriented activities; they are positively pointless, and so they may be able, as much as Milan's slow pleasures can, to open the door to Aionic ecstasy.[12] There are two ways to enter Aionic time, two ways to intensify your lives. So perhaps it would be better to think of there being two doors to Aionic time, one labeled fast: centrifugal connection. And the other labeled slow: centripetal compression.

Milan taught me that slow pleasures are some of the most intense pleasures. He made me realize how much life drawing can be performed *Andante Vivace.* But once we realize that what is distinctive about these pleasures is not their speed but their intensity, then we are ready to enjoy life drawing also performed *Allegro Vivace.* And the common element is clear.

Life: flourishing, multifaceted, affirmative life. Life exciting Yes. *Vivace.*

derrida is the reason wittgenstein fails
deleuze is the reason derrida is only a messenger

FOUR

Again and Again

> You know the day destroys the night
> Night divides the day
> Tried to run
> Tried to hide
> Break on through to the other side
> Break on through to the other side
> Break on through to the other side, yeah
>
> —JIM MORRISON, "Break on Through (to the Other Side)," 1967

It was never an issue. Nobody ever even suggested that I become a gigolo. So I was never really forced to decide why it would be a bad life. Why would it be a bad life? Set aside all those features of a gigolo's life that won't sufficiently discriminate that life from being a mathematician or a gymnast, features such as that all three of these occupations favor the young. The easiest answers come with no thought at all, thoughtless answers, such as that some things should not be sold. I take this answer seriously, but then the question is *why* those things should not be sold? And why *only* those things, and not rather all things?

The Authenticity Sweepstakes

A number of years ago, I saw a performance of *Da Vinci and the New Cadillac* created and performed by a three-member theatrical troupe calling themselves Luftkugel.[1] At one point in the performance, a member of the troupe was prancing around the stage like a deer. A Luftkugel went up to a person in the audience and asked them to throw one of their shoes at the deer. No? Then taking out a big wad of money, he asked if they would do it for $5. Still No? How about $10? Off it comes, and the shoe is hurled. Then, still holding the tremendous roll of bills, the Luftkugel turned to a man and a woman sitting next to each other and asked them if they knew each other. When they said they did not, he asked the woman if she would hold hands with the stranger for $5? Sure? Okay, will you hug him for $5? No? How about $20? And she hugs him. But now he wants her to kiss him, on the cheek, on the lips, then deeper, wet, with her powerful tongue. He didn't have to go that far. Soon enough, she stopped. And then, all over the audience, a feeling of discomfort, as if we had just been witness to something unsettling. But what? Someone had been paid to hug somebody. What is unsettling about that? Perhaps intimacy and aggression (remember the deer) are so personal, so powerful, that we think of them as inevitably alive, not wooden, not merely the performance of actions, for cash. Was the exchange of cash sufficient to prevent the volunteers from actually performing, reducing their behavior to the performance of scripted, wooden actions? It was worse when she was paid to kiss the stranger, but wouldn't it have been bad enough if she had just been paid to take off her left shoe and put it under her seat? The questions are still, if money ruins intimacy, *how* does it do it? And why doesn't it ruin *everything*?

It might help to imagine the gigolo in a little more detail. A call from a stranger who has seen my ad, finds me knocking on the door of a house I have never seen before. Often enough, as I walk in, I pocket the cash that has been left for me by the door. There is the usual awkwardness at the door, but I am prepared for that, and as the door closes behind me, I pop the cork on the half-bottle of domestic champagne that I always carry for this purpose. Deeper into the house, on the couch or standing in the hallway, still tasting champagne, I place my hand on the small of her back, and urge her gently closer to my body, kissing her cheek in sweet simulation of that innocence which my clients enjoy, or now, since money has exchanged hands, need. A few more caressing fondles and we are unbuttoning in preparation for the kind of sex that pleases my client, usually soft, slow, and long, but I do my best to perform in whatever way is pleasing to them.

There is a certain woodenness, and lack of life. No matter how loud we get, there is not much *vivace*. And there is repetition. I have done it all before. If it looks like this gigolo is following a script, that is because I am, either the generic script I take with me whenever I go out on call, or the more personal script that I follow at the suggestion of my client's gestures. My sexual activities will be the *performance of actions*, not, I want to say, an *actual performance*.[2] Sometimes this is true even when money doesn't change hands.

We all know, or know of, people who are tired of their lonely lives, craving a friend like the ones they imagined they had when they were younger, lonely men and women, who have managed to distribute an active sex life around so many people that for almost a year they have never slept, so to speak, with the same person long enough to learn whether they like rye toast. But the sex, so they say, has been great. Again, this has never been my life, although, in my lonelier youth, it had a certain James Bond attractiveness. But they say the sex was great. Lots of sex. And it was good. As the time lengthens since the last time, hunger and their loneliness grows, until the hunger becomes a craving, and they dream of finding a man or a woman equally eager to satisfy this craving. And then like the gigolo, they will kiss, momentarily. Fondle or caress, a bit. But the point of this coupling is to couple. The religion of orgasm. The preparatory caresses will be present only *symbolically*; they serve to mark the beginning of their coupling, they are not pursued for their own sake but only as symbols of what is to come. And come it does. Soon enough, the hasty couple is laughing to discover they can't walk with their pants at their knees.

A certain element of woodenness is shared with the case of the gigolo; here again our coupling couple seems to be following a script, a script they have followed before, many times. Again, the back room may be loud with moans, but there will not be much *vivace*. And again, as with the gigolo, there is repetition. Repetition in a sense adjacent to the French *répétition*, which can mean rehearsal, repetition as representation. In this case, our hungry couple, painting by numbers, is painting a representation of sexual love. Performing actions, rather than *riding an actual performance*.

It would be more usual to mark this distinction in terms of authenticity. It would be more usual to mark the distinction by saying that the staged or scripted sexual activities were inauthentic; whereas if those activities were unstaged and unscripted, they would be authentic. I will argue against this way of marking what I take to be a real distinction. Seeking to live authentically is like seeking to square a circle. It is impossible. Already in the last chapter, Milan gave us a first taste of this result: There is no way off stage that is not an "Exeunt." Every action is theatrical. Every action, acting (Bearn 1995b). In the authenticity sweepstakes it's inauthenticity all around. Nevertheless, there is a real distinction here that the language of authenticity is unable to make. Even though every action is a performance, we can still distinguish between different kinds of performances. Strong. Intense. Powerful. And their opposites. We make these distinctions when the performances are literally staged. We should make them as well on the stage of daily life. That is why I am marking the distinction normally drawn between theater and authentic life *within* the realm of performance, not between performance and something else. It is a distinction between our gigolo's dehydrated *performance of an action* and the intensity and strength of an *actual performance.*

Sometimes I think that even the best things in life have to begin with the mere performance of an action, a little formal, wooden, as if painting by numbers (see Deleuze and Guattari [1980] 1987, 295). We all know people who are more than our friends; they are the ones who excite movement, body and mind, the ones whose briefest glance is the promise of intimacy to come, beyond constraint. Often, even such friendships beyond friendship begin by *representing* their time together *as* a friendship. There was a first time you went out for dinner, to eat of course, the eating need not be a pretense, but hoping that something might happen, that some shining smile might light the way through dining, to life. So we sit there, waiting for our menus, looking for conversation, changing subjects, nervous laughter. Performing actions. Why do we go through this? Aren't we hoping that something will break free of the representational performance of actions, releasing an actual performance. In the laughter that breaks over the actions we were just performing, an actual performance is breaking into seafoam joy, floating here and there on the surface of the water, unscarred by the rocks, floating, pointlessly, deliriously, seafoam.

I have been thinking of seafoam ever since I read about rising ground in *Difference and Repetition.* Deleuze writes: "Difference is the state in which we can speak of determination *as such.* The difference 'between' two things is only empirical, and the corresponding determinations are only extrinsic. However, instead of something distinguished from something else, imagine something which distinguishes itself—and yet that from which it distinguishes itself does not distinguish itself from it. . . . It is as if the ground rose to the surface, without ceasing to be a ground" (Deleuze [1968] 1994, 28). Seafoam distinguishes itself from the sea, but the sea does not distinguish itself from the foam. And foam, though delicacy itself, survives in the breaking waves. Born in the breaking waves, seafoam is unbreakable. As resilient as rhizomatic crabgrass.

When nothing breaks through the performance of actions, then attention may focus on how bad the restaurant service is, or the food, which was lost in a nameless brown sauce, but these things were not really why you entered the restaurant in the first place. The food is not the primary thing. After all, we are not imagining a sly restaurant critic eating incognito. The critic's eyes must always be on the representation, the form of formal dining. The critic is representation's under laborer. We are simply imagining two people hoping to become more than friends. When attention focuses on the service, then what was to have been secondary has become primary, and the chance of releasing something actual, an actual performance, is gone. The possibility of a joy beyond representation is trapped in the chains of complaint, complaint not driven by the hope of escaping representation, but driven by a wooden interest in correct representation.

Even when things end with an actual performance, they begin by performing actions. So sexual love, even at its best, always has a moment, when your faces move closer for the first kiss of the evening, unbuttoning a shirt, unbuckling a belt. Sexual love, even at its best, begins by performing actions. With luck you will soon find yourselves in motion beyond representation, riding your passionate sexual line not *directly* to the well-known climax, though this may come, pointlessly, as a gift. Seafoam joy, moving here and there, vivace, has many gifts to give.

It may seem, at this point, that we are about to move not only beyond representation, but also beyond repetition, beyond the script repeated, but this is a familiar illusion. They apologize for telling us the way the story ends, but a story not worth reading twice is barely worth reading once (Wilde 1889). What could it have to offer, but information. And they worry that since they went to the restaurant or museum or on the walk once before, and with some individual italicized in their heart, they should never go there again, and especially not with a new italicized individual. Why this worship of the first time? Why this fear of repetition? Our view of repetition is too timid. We will not, therefore, leave repetition, itself, behind, but only a certain kind of repetition.

I shall be invoking, again and again, a distinction between two kinds of repetition to which I was introduced by Deleuze. In the following passage, Deleuze distinguishes two kinds of repetition along an amazing number of dimensions, including representation. I cite the whole passage hoping that, even in the absence of seeing why Deleuze is characterizing the distinction in precisely these terms, the passage as a whole might have a cumulative effect. Don't struggle with it; just let it move through your system.

> The first repetition is repetition of the Same, explained by the identity of the concept or representation; the second includes difference, and includes itself in the alterity of the Idea, in the heterogeneity of an "a-presentation". One is negative, occurring by default in the concept; the other affirmative, occurring by excess in the Idea. One is conjectural the other categorical. One is static, the other dynamic. One is repetition in the effect, the other in the cause. One is extensive, the other intensive. One is ordinary, the other distinctive and singular. One is horizontal, the other vertical. One is developed and explicated, the other enveloped and in need of interpretation. One is revolving, the other evolving. One involves equality, commensurability and symmetry, the other is grounded in inequality, incommensurability and dissymmetry. One is material, the other spiritual, even in nature and in the earth. One is inanimate, the other carries the secret of our deaths and our lives, of our enchainments and our liberations, the demonic and the divine. One is "naked" repetition, the other a clothed repetition, which forms itself in clothing itself, in masking and disguising itself. One concerns accuracy, the other has authenticity as its criterion. (Deleuze [1968] 1994, 24)

I will return to this distinction later, but one feature of this long series of contrasting characterizations that I will *not* be endorsing, without qualification, is the last. For I think that when we move beyond representation, we move, at the same time, beyond both authenticity and inauthenticity.

Concede to those who despair of inevitable inauthenticity that there is only theater. But there are two kinds of theater. A theater of representation and a theater of repetition. This is not a difference like that between street theater and grand opera, for the theater of repetition could just as easily appear on the street as at the Met. It is a difference between two ways of taking or inhabiting the goal of a theatrical performance. Theater of representation takes the goal to be a fine, or at the limit, a *perfect* representation of the pieces of life characterized by the written play, the script. This is how we normally or unthinkingly take theater. In contrast, a theater of repetition takes the goal of a theatrical performance as escaping the script, as breaking through the representations scripted into the play. The goal is rather beauty than perfection. Whereas the theater of representation thinks theater as subservient to the concept, theater of repetition thinks theater as escaping from under the thumb of the concept, as breaking through the frame of conceptual representation. As breaking through (to the other side), beyond authenticity and inauthenticity. I am getting ahead of myself, but when Artaud, for example, wrote that the theater of cruelty hoped "to break through language in order to touch life," he was describing the goal of a theater of repetition. To break through language, or more generally to break through the plane of linguistic and nonlinguistic representations, in order to touch life. To touch life (Artaud [1938] 1968, 13).

What about the role of money? The case of the gigolo may sort itself out if we turn to something, unlike sex, which is not often thought to be ruined by money. Art. Benjamin did not explicitly address the relation between the art market and art's power, but he is well known for the claim that in the age of mechanical reproduction the powerful "aura" of art begins to disappear (Benjamin [1936] 1968, 223). Aura is the umbrella term that Benjamin uses to cover the various ways in which an original art object stands apart from us, in its own time and place. However near or far, an original art work holds itself back from us, demanding our respect for its authority, its aura, a "unique phenomenon of distance, however close it may be" (Benjamin [1936] 1968, 224). All this is meant to change in the age of mechanical reproduction. Benjamin hoped that the cheap availability of near perfect reproductions of art would deprive art of its aura and save us from the irrational pedestal on which we put both art and *der Führer* (Benjamin [1936] 1968, 226, 244). The last of art's aura, the last of art's authority, was meant to wither away when the widespread availability of excellent mechanical reproductions would allow us to exhibit art in our own home, in a form that cries out for our disrespect, our tape, tacks, and scissors. Reproductions do not hold themselves back from us. The Vermeer on the dish towel cleans the spilled spaghetti sauce. But however prescient he was about film and photography, Benjamin's general claim is wrong: The museum and the museum store are not in competition; they are symbiotic.

The motor of Benjamin's considerations is not visual reproduction, narrowly construed, but representation in general. Representation itself: one thing standing for another. And this can bring us back to the start of our discussion, that is, to the power of money to ruin what it helps us buy. Money is, after all, a representational medium, a representational medium with pretensions, in particular the pretension to be able to represent anything and everything. There are other values besides monetary value, but money's ability to represent everything, to be a medium in which any value can be measured against any other, makes money the absolute value. Within the representational domain of money, there are no incommensurable values, indeed there is no *real* value except price. "Under their money-form all commodities look alike" (Marx [1867] 1977, 111).

Just as we saw in the case of mechanical reproduction, it would be wrong to say that the money-form of artworks deprives them of their energy and power. The moment the painting is represented as $100, it has become no different, in market value, from $100 of anything else. The market ensures that the artwork, whatever else it does, has an exchange value, and this secures the ruination of the idea that art possesses an unutterable purity and perfection. But this does not deprive art works of their energy, even in a certain sense, their autonomy. I suspect that Benjamin would be happy to be rid of any autonomous power of artworks, leaving as a remainder only their propositional content, fully amenable to rational critique, and available at the museum store. But artworks have a powerful, impure autonomy that derives not from the absence of any connection with the world, the negative theology of art which Benjamin mocks, but from an inordinate multiplicity of connections with the world (Benjamin [1936] 1968, 226). *Aionic autonomy.* The good kind of pointlessness. But unless something can be done about representation's ruin, the Aionic autonomy I want to defend will be vulnerable to the ruin worked by representation. Aionic autonomy must therefore break on through (to the other side) of representation, or it will be lost.

Now the case of the gigolo, with his half-bottle of domestic champagne and his satisfied clients, takes care of itself. The gigolo performs for a fee; his intimacy is not an actual performance; the exchange of money reduces his actual caresses to the performance of actions. It is a reduction to a kind of theater, theater of representation. Money turns what might have been an actual performance into an action performed for cash. How? By representing it. But how does that make our caresses merely actions. The seafoam joy of the best kind of intimacy is not aimed at any particular climactic goal. Its ecstasy is Aionic. It serves no particular purpose, nor any sum of such purposes. But when we introduce the representational medium of money, these pointlessly caressing fingers return to Chronological time, for they start serving a goal, the earning of $100. So these caressing fingers merely perform an action for cash, no different from anything else that you can exchange for $100. Commodification is Chronological. Notice, even if my client wants to enjoy the kind of pointless Aionic lovemaking I was describing in the last chapter, even that kind of lovemaking will be reduced, ruined by money. An actual performance, vivace, enjoying the ecstasy of Aionic time will have become a mere action, preformed within an hour, for a reasonable fee.

The hasty lovers, pants by their knees, can now fall into place too. Here it is not a question of money, but it remains a matter of representation. These two hungry people, crave more than climactic explosions, or else they would be happy enough to pleasure themselves. They want sexual love. But however much they might enjoy Aionic love, they crave climactic explosions too much to break on through (to the other side) of representation. Their craving dictates the kinds of actions they will engage in; so although they do not eliminate all intimacy except the climactic events themselves, all their other activities are directed by and toward that point. Everything serves the goal of performing that action. So any anticipatory caressing is, as I said, only symbolic; it is there so that their actions will meet the criteria for being sexual love and not simply, you want it, I want it, lets get it over with. So these two, still shod, are staking their actions to a representation of sexual love. They are following a script, as much as the gigolo. There is no breaking through to Aionic ecstasy here, there is only painting by numbers, and quickly, too, before the others notice that our hasty two are not in the living room and come back looking for them. Representational sex is

Chronological. Whether we are trying to get it over with quickly, before we are caught, or whether we are trying to make it last a respectable period of time, representational sex is always Chronological. This answers my first question about how money ruins sexual love, but what of the second question: Why just these two? Why not rather everything?

No one needs to be told that sex is very important, linked to very powerful emotions. So important and so valuable to us that we resist the discovery of the market value of a kiss on the hand, the arm, the cheek, the ear, and so on. The money-form of the kiss is no different from the money-form of canned tuna fish, regularly $1.19 on sale for 99 cents. And for those who care about art, art can play a role in a person's life as important as sex. Sometimes more. And so the reductive representational power of money is a threat to artistic significance too. But why do we not generalize the destructive power of this representational medium to include the whole of life? Perhaps the reason some of us are willing to draw the line at sex, or sex and art, is that everything else is *already ruined*. Since everything is already reduced to the performance of an action, it can look as if sex and art were particularly vulnerable to representation. But they are not. The threat of representation is quite general, and it has already done its work. There may be nothing left of doctoring except the performance of actions for a fee and an interest in performing them more *efficiently*. There may be no more to being a college teacher, than the performance of one's classroom duties and one's research duties, and an interest in performing them more efficiently. Efficiency in this sense means performing more of the actions one is being paid for, in each unit of time. Thus an interest in efficiency presupposes that we are performing actions in Chronological time and only asks that we perform as many of those actions, as well as we can, in as brief a stretch of Chronological time as possible. Everything else is already ruined.

It is easy to see how an interest in efficiency can develop into an interest in doing more than one thing at the same time. Brooms with headlights, mocked in Jacques Tati's *Play Time* (1967), are now a familiar "feature" of many vacuum cleaners. This impetus is parodied by Kwakami's category of the unuseless inventions. These are inventions that look like they might help but don't. Little dust mops to attach to your cat's four feet so that it can dust the floor as it walks. And soon enough, they are through, our hasty

Duster Slippers For Cats

✳ For feline assistance with tedious housework

Ｎow the most boring job around the house becomes hours of fun. Not for you, but for your cat! With these dust-dislodging foot socks, cats can play their part in easing the pressure of domestic chores. Lazy cats are of course much less productive than excitable ones, but this problem may be overcome if you introduce a dog into the house.

13

Figure 4-1. Duster slippers for cats. K. Kawakami. *101 Unuseless Japanese Inventions: The Art of Chindogu.* New York: W. W. Norton.

couple noticing, when it is over, that they now want to leave their brief together, to disappear, again, into anonymous crowds.

In the United States the place this dream of efficiency is realized most regularly is in the car. Fearing that when we are driving we are not really accomplishing anything, we think, if only I could drink my coffee in the car, I would not be wasting this time. Use the drive-thru lane and you can eat lunch in there too. A BlackBerry turns it into an office, and our empty time has been given a point, filled with efficiency. Now, at last, we are not wasting our time behind the wheel.

But we all know, as well, that time behind the wheel, like the time in the middle of a walk, can be anything but a waste, it can be a way of entering Aionic pointlessness, one's thoughts arriving more or less on their own, untutored by any goal, joining forces with the beauty in the trees, the cows, the fields of gold. This positive sense of pointlessness does not cling to one inaccessible point, nor does it add one point to another in some crazy sum of cat and dust mop. Rather to enjoy this Aionic ecstasy we will have to forgo dividing our lives into actions—this is not that—the negativity of concepts. We will have to break on through (to the other side) of these conceptual representations, and in the seafoam thus released, discover the Aionic ecstasy of caressing the world, Yes.[3]

Authenticity and Grace: Kleist

The distinction between performing an action and an actual performance smacks of a number of more or less familiar distinctions, for example, the Aristotelian or Heideggerian distinction between activities explicitly guided by rules and expert practice that leaves rules behind (see, e.g., Dreyfus and Dreyfus 1999, and Dreyfus 2005). The familiar distinction presupposes that our actions are organized by goals, and this sets it apart from the pointlessness we are drawing toward. Or putting the same thing another way, I am insisting that performing an action takes place within the plane of representation, while an actual performance has broken through to touch life.

The performance of an action is always scripted. The symbolical foreplay of our hasty couple was scripted. It took orders from the concept of sexual love which they were using to veil the thinness or desperation of the quest for climax. I was relying on this scripted feature of their coupling to turn us against their activities, however momentarily exciting. But this strategy sets us on a trajectory toward unscripted actions. These would be authentic actions, actions that took no orders from any script. But authentic action, so construed, is an impossible attempt to square the circle. Although this was not his intended lesson, I learned this from the writings of Stanley Cavell.

The difficulty is that simply to be an action, a kick or a kiss requires that the action exhibit the criteria for being a kick or a kiss, for not just anything can be a kick or a kiss. Not just any contact between my shoe and your leg will be a kick. If I throw my shoe at you, or if I stumble into you, this will not be a kick even if the bruises I leave are indistinguishable from those left by kicks. It is not as easy as you might think to articulate the criteria for being a kick; it requires what Wittgenstein would have called a grammatical investigation of our use of the word *kick*. Such an investigation will lead us out of words into the world, for example to the amount of force required to distinguish a kick from a tap. The grammar of our words merges seamlessly with the grammar of our lives. And once the criteria for being a kick or a kiss have been articulated, it may seem as if our difficulties would be solved, authenticity ours; we would only have to hone our actions, perfectly, to those criteria. The true kiss. But it won't work. Even a fake kiss, even betrayal by a kiss, requires that the kiss be a *kiss*. That is to say, if you were to fake a kiss, you would do well to respect precisely the criteria which you would respect if you attempted an authentic kiss.

What we would like to find are criteria not for being a kiss, which are shared by kisses that betray, but criteria for being an *authentic* kiss, which could not possibly be shared by kisses that betray. But what would criteria for authenticity be? If they were specific to kisses or kicks, then they would be a part of the ordinary criteria for being a kiss, and so they would not help. But if they were not specific to kicks and kisses, we would be in no better position. For imagine that the criterion for being an *authentic* kiss was to make some sort of noise, like humming, while you were kissing. It is clear that this sound is not the recipe for an authentic kiss, for it too could be faked. Were some such humming the criterion for being an *authentic* kiss, then the best way to fake a kiss would be to accompany your performance of the action by humming. What we had wanted was a criterion of authenticity which could not be faked. Is this not what we might think of as a *recipe for authenticity*: the very idea contradictory. You can clap your hands; you can recite the prayers; but you can't make the gods listen.

Criteria make faking possible. Cavell summarizes this disappointing situation: "There are no criteria for a thing's *being* so, over and above the criteria for its being *so*" (Cavell 1979, 51, 45). There are no criteria for *being* a kiss over and above the criteria for being a *kiss*. Authentic kisses thus begin to look just as scripted as inauthentic ones. Authenticity remains trapped in the frame of representation. The ideal of authenticity is always to be an authentic *something*, lover or lawyer. An authentic action, of whatever sort, has got to respect the criteria for being an action *of that sort*. This means that it will be *scripted* by the criteria for being an instance of that sort of action. It should sound familiar. Existence is not a predicate. We want criteria by which to exit from the frame of representation, to exit from the grammatical schematism of a kiss, finally landing on the world itself (Cavell 1979, 79). But if these exit criteria were still criteria, they would be part of the frame of representation and not the way out, not the way to exit from it to the world but simply another expression of our being trapped in the frame of representation.[4]

The application or use of criteria faces a dilemma. The application of a criterion is either mediated by another criterion (regress) or it is a matter of choice (arbitrary). That is why Cavell, when considering what gives criteria their strength, tells us that the key thing is *us*, we have to "accept them use them" (Cavell 1979, 83). It begins to seem that since we are trapped in the frame of representation, we are also trapped in inauthenticity, every action, an act.

We have all met them. The jaded. Their veins flowing with thick vermilion poison, confident that there is no way out, that we are fated to failure, fated to inauthenticity. Café Nihilists. We would like to kiss, to *really* kiss, but, so the jaded insist, everything we do seems scripted. "Don't tell me that you love me, 'cause the words just don't ring true."[5] It is hard *not* to feel this discovery as a loss; have we never kissed? Ever? Did "I love you" ever ring true? We feel as if there must have been a time, a time before, when it was all more than an act. When it was *really* true. How could we bear it, all fake. Is there no way to return to this lost innocence, to return to the earth. It is a romantic inflection of innocence and of children that I associate with Wittgenstein, with Wittgenstein's groundless approach to authenticity. Once, not long ago, I loved the sound of that inflection, but it never worked (Bearn 1997a, 203–6). It is hard not to feel the urge to go back, and barring return, we seem to be driven into the cold stony arms of the jaded. This illusion is not just Wittgenstein's; it is common enough. Kleist shared it.

Kleist's "On the Marionette Theater" is not explicitly about authenticity, but it is about dancing, dancing gracefully as opposed to affectedly, and so it is as close to our topic as inauthenticity is to affectation, which is to say, quite close (Kleist [1810] 1982, 240).[6] In Kleist's story, a certain Herr C., principal dancer at the Opera in M., observes to the narrator of our story that the dancing puppets at the marionette theater could help a dancer "perfect his art" (Kleist [1810] 1982, 238). The difference between human dancers and marionettes is their relation to the earth. Humans are terrestrial creatures and need to rest, to catch their breath. A wooden marionette needs no such rest; it has no breath to catch; it is of the air, not the earth. Herr C. insists that "puppets, like elves, need the ground only so that they can touch it lightly and renew the momentum of their limbs through this momentary delay" (Kleist [1810] 1982, 241).[7] Herr C.'s description is striking, and it resonates with Deleuze and Guattari's description of nomadic movement which, unlike migratory movement, doesn't move from point to point; rather, for the nomad, "Every point is a relay and exists only as a relay . . . the life of the nomad is the intermezzo" (Deleuze and Guattari [1980] 1987, 380). Graceful dancing is a becoming-aerial, Herr C. is right, but I do not share his account of how this comes about. According to Herr C., "It would be impossible for a man to come anywhere near the puppet [in terms of gracefulness]. Only a god could equal inanimate matter in this respect; and here is the place where the two ends of the circular world meet" (Kleist [1810] 1982, 241). The idea is that there are two ways to become graceful, either by reducing human consciousness and intellect to zero (the way of the marionette) or by increasing them to infinity (the way of god).

The narrator of Kleist's story is, initially, confused, but finally takes a step in Herr C.'s direction when he realizes, or remembers, that self-consciousness can destroy grace. He himself once knew a fifteen-year-old boy whom he describes as just beginning to attract the attention of women, yet without showing any clear signs of vanity. That is to say, this fifteen-year-old boy was not yet conscious of his graceful air. As it happens, the narrator was with the young boy when the boy became conscious of his grace and beauty. They were together, at the baths, and while the smooth, young boy was drying his foot on a stool, *both* the narrator *and* the boy suddenly realized that the boy was inadvertently inhabiting the pose of a well-known statue in Paris. Nevertheless, when asked by the boy if he had seen the similarity, the narrator, for reasons which remain unclear even to him, denies with a laugh that he had noticed the similarity. The boy, as you might imagine, proceeds to try to inhabit the pose again. But fails. And again. But fails. At this moment, suddenly, all the grace began to drain from the boy. "He stood in front of the mirror for days. One attraction after another left him. Like an iron net, an invisible and incomprehensible power enveloped the free play of his gestures" (Kleist [1810] 1982, 242). Consciousness, or rather self-consciousness, destroyed the boy's grace and beauty.

C. adds a story of his own which shows that the privilege of the young boy, before he acquired self-consciousness, was the privilege of an animal. He tells of the time he was in Russia at the estate of a Herr von G. whose sons were excellent fencers, especially the older one. C., no mean fencer himself, overpowered the elder son without much difficulty. But then the two sons took him out to a bear, which was being raised on the estate by the boys' father. He was told to fence with the bear. He did, but the bear avoided every thrust. The real ones he dodged with a small movement; the fakes, the feinted thrusts, he saw right through and stayed calm and still. The bear's power lay in something Herr C. refers to as seriousness (*der Ernst*) (Kleist [1810] 1982, 243). It was the bear's seriousness that made it impossible to fool the bear with feinted thrusts, and since it is the irregular combination of feints and thrusts that throw one's opponent off balance, the bear was never off balance. "He stood, his paw raised for battle, his eye fixed on mine as if he could read my soul in it, and when my thrusts were not meant seriously, he didn't move" (Kleist [1810] 1982, 243). Nothing fooled the bear. He was completely serious. All point and no play. All point and no pointlessness.[8]

Herr C. concludes: "Grace appears purest in that human form which has either no consciousness or an infinite one, that is, in a puppet or in a god"

(Kleist [1810] 1982, 244). It is a problem of meaning and a problem of anxiety. The young boy was smooth and graceful beyond imagination, but only so long as he was unaware of his grace as *one possible appearance among others.* So long as he was unaware of his grace, his grace was simply there, apparent, and wonderful. The whole of his being was, we are tempted to say, filled with grace. Complete and pure. But the moment the boy became aware of his grace, from that moment on, the space of his appearance opened up with many possibilities. From that moment, it became a live question whether he was being graceful, really graceful, authentically graceful, or just seeming to be so, only simulating grace. Once aware that his grace was simply one possible point in a space of possibilities, the boy was unable, confidently, to distinguish what was seriously graceful from what was only aping grace. Grace shatters at the first sign of consciousness, and proceeding by double negation, Herr C. suggests that the way back to grace will be by negating the negative effects of consciousness. There are no surprises here. It is the same philosophical fixation on double negation that I discussed in chapter 1.

The only innovation is that C. believes infinite consciousness might be another way of recovering grace. I have no doubt that one could present the smooth continuous variations of a graceful movement as a sum of carefully adjusted infinitesimally small moments, much as a digital recording or a filmstrip gives the appearance of smooth transitions by summing discrete bits of sound or light. But that this is a deceptive feature of infinite consciousness can be demonstrated by another story.

There is a more or less true story that Herr H., a German professor who spent a number of years in Japan, tells of his learning the Zen art of archery (Herrigel [1948] 1999). Four years into his training, he was brought to the point of releasing the arrow; until that time his master's attention, and his, had been focused on other aspects of archery, especially breathing. Now it was a question of loosing the arrow toward the target, and in the tradition of double negation, his master told him to release the bow without thinking: "You mustn't open the right hand on purpose" (Herrigel [1948] 1999, 44).[9] Indeed, as in Kleist's tale, the master told Herr H. to release the bow the way a child lets go of a clenched finger, smoothly, with no jerking of the hand, arm, or body. And the master asked: "Do you know why [there is not the slightest jerk when the child lets go]? Because the child doesn't think:

I will now let go of the finger in order to grasp this other thing. Completely un-self-conscious, without purpose, it turns from one to the other" (Herrigel [1948] 1999, 45).

Herr H. found this unusually difficult, but while he was on vacation, trying to analyze his difficulties, he decided that the problem was not really what his master said: It was not really a problem of "lack of purposelessness and egolessness"; it was only a matter of releasing his right thumb as gradually as possible (Herrigel [1948] 1999, 69). Like learning how to release a clutch. So Herr H. focused all of his attention on his right hand. It was demanding, but he was soon releasing the arrow more smoothly than he had ever been able to before. Excited to show his master this step forward, he took his new technique to the next lesson.

> The very first shot I let off after the recommencement of the lessons was, to my mind, a brilliant success. The loose was smooth, unexpected. The Master looked at me for a while and then said hesitantly, like one who can scarcely believe his eyes: "Once again, please!" My second shot seemed to me even better than the first. The Master stepped up to me without a word, took the bow from my hand, and sat down on a cushion, his back toward me. I knew what that meant, and withdrew. (Herrigel [1948] 1999, 71)

Herr H. is Herr C.'s god. By focusing all his intellectual attention on his right hand, Herr H. thought to simulate the thoughtlessness of a child, but it was an obvious deception. And I like to think that even the Buddha himself would not have been able to fool Herr H.'s master. If the idea is to move with the grace of an animal unconscious of his body, then the way of the gods must be a fake. Even if it could fool all the people all the time, it would still be smoke and mirrors.

The gods gone, we are left with the child and the animal. Herr C. construes these in doubly negative terms, as *stopping* the *play* of possible appearances, in particular stopping the anxiety of deciding whether we are faced with or manifesting true[10] gracefulness or merely the imitation of gracefulness. This leaves the actual life of animals and children blank. The redemptive value of being a child is presented as consisting solely in *not* being *conscious*. But this means that Herr C.'s approach to childhood will only ever be able to produce an ersatz child: No No, never Yes. If we are conscious, then any attempt to pretend that we are not, to play the role of the animal or the child, construed in terms of the absence of consciousness, will be a failure. Innocent gracefulness would require *denying* that we are aware that graceful movements are but one point in a space of other possibilities whose proximity to gracefulness puts grace ungracefully off balance. More than simply self-deceptive, this project takes self-deception to infinity. If one is reaching for grace by closing one's eyes, then if one does not *also* close one's eyes to the fact that one is closing one's eyes, one's eyes will not be fully, completely, closed. And then this second closing of the eyes must, for precisely the same reasons, also be hidden from us. This forces a third self-deception, and that is just the beginning. This series of deceptions will never end; Herr C.'s graceful dancing is necessarily inaccessible. No wonder Herr. C. haunts the marionette theater; his twisted dream of authentic grace could only be realized if he were not alive at all, but wooden. It is a disaster.

Herr C. gives childhood and animality a romantic inflection that I associate with Wittgenstein, but there is another inflection. We don't have to think of a child in merely negative terms as *not* an *adult*. Children teem with playful energy that can hardly be tamed by their parents, playful positive energy, driving them up trees and into caves, goading their torture of toads, and each other. And we don't have to think of animals in merely negative terms as *not* being *human*, either. Animals swarm with energy that is lost when they become family pets or zoo attractions; they swarm with positive energy that reveals lives that don't respect the neat conceptual boundaries humans construct for themselves and animals.[11] Animality and childhood are both screened from us by Herr C.'s negative conception of them. I will treat animality and childhood as living Yes, on the other side of representation, not as caged on this side. But, for now, let's return to Wittgenstein's approach to authenticity.

Something Animal: Wittgenstein

We had been wondering about authenticity because it seemed to be a traditional place where the distinction between performing an action and an actual performance might surface; it seemed that what I was calling an actual performance might simply be what others have called authenticity or authentic action. But authentic action is trapped in the frame of representation, trapped in the performance of an action. I repeat.

An authentic kiss would have to be a *kiss*, and so it would have to respect the criteria for being a kiss. The authentic kiss would therefore be just as scripted as the inauthentic kiss. Worse still: The authentic and the inauthentic kiss both have to respect the very same criteria, follow the same script, for both are, after all, *kisses*. What we needed, so it seemed, were not criteria for being a kiss but criteria for being an *authentic* kiss. Letting it stand for other *external* criteria, I considered whether humming while you kissed might not be what the authenticity of an authentic kiss consisted in. But it took little thought to realize that no sooner would we have instituted such a practice than all the hasty couples in all the back rooms of all the old hotels would start humming in unison. The same fate awaits any other suggested external criterion, so we might have decided to turn *inside*. Perhaps the authenticity of a kiss consists in having the right internal thoughts while you are kissing. But what thoughts do you have while you are kissing? Are they always the same whenever you are kissing someone authentically? Isn't it the case that in the midst of what you think of as an authentic kiss your mind could find itself thinking about anything from the wet feel of a tongue to a cramp in your foot? So there doesn't seem to be one internal thing that authentic kissing consists in. Moreover, even if there were one thing that was going on in your mind whenever you supposed you were authentically kissing, it would be a separate question whether that one thing was what the authenticity of an authentic kiss *consisted in*, and not rather, some sort of mental tickle that always accompanied authenticity, the way, for some people, embarrassment is always accompanied by blushing (Wittgenstein [1953] 1976, §153).

So it begins to look not only as if authenticity is trapped in the frame of representation, but that the very idea of authenticity is an illusion. It begins to seem that there is no way to distinguish an authentic kiss from an inauthentic kiss; perhaps there are some authentic kisses, but there is no way of knowing whether *this* kiss is, or is not, authentic. So there is no way to calm the anxiety that what we think of as authentic is not, really, inauthentic. Thus anxiety is always with us, authenticity never certain, peace never ours. The jaded conclude that every action is inauthentic. Scripted. Every action an act.

There we were, and I realized that Wittgenstein would agree with this line of thought but not with the conclusion of the jaded. Wittgenstein still thinks it is possible to achieve authenticity, relief from anxiety about what is or is not a *real* kiss. If his story could be made to work, then we would have achieved what seems at first impossible, the performance of an unscripted action, an authentic action. Such a notion would make my invention of the concept of an actual performance unnecessary. And it was there that I wandered off into Kleist.

Herr C.'s idea was that to become truly graceful we would have to become like the totally serious bear, or a piece of wood. It fails, because, short of self-deception, there is no way back from humanity to something animal.[12] Like Herr C., Wittgenstein thinks of authenticity as the return from human anxiety to what he calls "something animal" (Wittgenstein 1969, §359). And this means that Wittgenstein's approach to authenticity will fail for precisely the same reasons that ruined Herr C.'s approach to gracefulness. This, not Kripke's, is the Wittgensteinian paradox (Kripke 1982). Planets and squirrels don't obey rules. We do. But Wittgenstein would like to treat our obedience as something animal, so he both wants and does not want us to be animals. There is thus a strong similarity to one of the authors that we know Wittgenstein read and respected, Kierkegaard. Kierkegaard's Johannes Climacus puts the paradox of the god-man at the center of religious faith, and thinking about the result of Wittgenstein's dream of a rule-following animal, we could christen the Wittgensteinian paradox: the human-animal (Kierkegaard 1844b). Paradoxical as it is, it is no surprise that it will never work. Approached with Wittgenstein, there can be no peace, no security. Only anxiety. Only inauthenticity.

Lest you enter the ranks of the jaded, let me, for now, simply *assert* that the failure of these two projects, both that of Kleist's Herr C. and that of Wittgenstein himself, does not mean that Aionic ecstasy, the seafoam joy of an actual performance, is impossible. These results only look jaded to those who refuse to break on through (to the other side) of representation. So strap yourself to the mast and sail on.

Wittgenstein's story about attaining authenticity can be described in three stages that have a solid Christian background: innocence, fall, redemption. From the innocence of children and animals, to the anxiety of humans, back to the innocence of animals, second childhood. It can be diagramed,

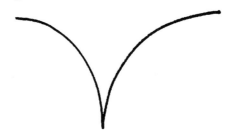

Figure 4-2. Two strokes.

as all strategies of double negation can be diagramed, in two strokes: down and up.

Wittgenstein's story is not a story about authentic action in general. It is, first of all, about authentic *linguistic* action. But the two are closer than you might think (Wittgenstein [1953] 1976, §111). Wittgenstein is motivated by something troubling, the slippery seeming-meaning of some linguistic utterances, forcing us, if we care about what is said, into anxiety about the meaning of our words, and hence, if we are also concerned with what our words are about, into anxiety about the world and ourselves within it. Existential and linguistic anxiety here come together (Bearn 1997a). By avoiding inauthenticity, he hopes with one stroke to calm, but only momentarily, both our philosophical and our existential anxieties, to bring us peace (*Ruhe*) (Wittgenstein [1953] 1976, §133). Animals are the answer for Wittgenstein because animals don't experience anxiety about the meaning of their actions, even animals as humanized as dogs don't stay up late worrying about what he meant when, all of a sudden, he told her to go away from the desk and lie down. And perhaps it is true that nonhuman animals don't experience such anxieties, but it might be even better. It might be that nonhuman animals are actually *unable* to experience such things. This seems to be Wittgenstein's thought.[13] That is why Wittgenstein conceives of peaceful security, free, if only for a moment, from all possible anxiety as "something that lies beyond being justified and unjustified; as it were, as something animal" (Wittgenstein 1969, §359). Let's see how it was meant to work.

Stage 1: Innocence. Wittgenstein stages innocence not in a garden, but on a building site. A builder A is working with an assistant B. A is building with four kinds of building stones: cubic blocks, round pillars, flat slabs, and rectangular beams. Maybe they are working for Cézanne. There are only four words in their language: block, pillar, slab, and beam. As A needs a building stone, of whatever type, he calls out one of the words and B brings it to him. And that is it. That is the whole story of their linguistic lives. The practice of their language extends only as far as orders, or requests, or whatever A's calls are. At this stage, with only this much language, they are probably still indeterminate. Moreover, A and B can have no anxiety about whether they *know* that this is a building stone; they don't even have the concept of knowledge. So these two enjoy authentic linguistic action, beyond the *possibility* of competing meanings, beyond the *possibility* of anxiety about the inauthenticity of their actions. B responds to A's calls very much the way some dogs respond to the command: Sit! Or, perhaps the way the hive picks up the directional dance from the bees returning from the languid land of nectar.

Wittgenstein commands us: "Conceive this as a complete primitive language" (Wittgenstein [1953] 1976, §2). But it is pretty clear that if this were a complete language, then the lives of A and B would, by comparison with our lives, be extraordinarily impoverished.[14] Like Herr von G.'s bear, A and B are restricted to the serious; they can't even make jokes. This may not seem quite right, but that is because we are imagining ourselves as A and B. That, however, is not the story Wittgenstein is telling. Imagining that we ourselves, as we are now constituted, were restricted to the language of A and B, is to imagine people who *can* joke: Such an A might call for a block and then hide behind a pile of building stones; such a B might comply with the call "slab," by bringing a sandwich. But actual A and B are not like that; it is not clear that those kinds of behaviors would mean anything at all to A and B. This is the poverty of their authenticity. Their calls cannot yet be lured from their functional homes; each call can only be used to perform the one linguistic action that it performs naturally, almost by reflex.

The whole Wittgensteinian trick of keeping authenticity from being fingered to death by the jaded will be to add more and more flexibility to the language of A and B without adding the possibility of anxiety about the authenticity of their linguistic life. But the trick won't work.

Wittgenstein faces two problems. The first problem will sound a little peculiar; it is that the sounds of the linguistic behavior of A and B must be further distinguished from the sounds made by raindrops on a tin roof. [15] The raindrops obey the laws of physics, and humans obey the rules for the use of words. But raindrops falling on the tin don't, and *cannot*, make mistakes, whereas humans voicing words sometimes do, and therefore definitely *can*, make mistakes. Mark this distinction by saying that the obedience of drops of rain is causal, but the obedience of drops of meaning is normative. The first problem is to add just enough complexity to the linguistic lives of A and B that they come to resemble ours, both in terms of complexity and in terms of becoming more fully normative than either raindrops, certainly, or bees.

The second problem is really a constraint Wittgenstein places on any acceptable resolution of the first problem. The constraint is simply that the first problem must be solved without destroying all hope of authentic linguistic action, or in terms Wittgenstein would actually use, without destroying all hope of enjoying a peaceful security (Wittgenstein [1953] 1976, §133; 1969, §357).But Wittgenstein solves the first problem in a way that makes authentic linguistic action impossible.

Stage 2: The Fall. If we think of linguistic life as guided by norms, not merely causes, then it is not even clear that A and B have a linguistic life. If they do not have a real linguistic life, that would mean that Wittgenstein conceives of the fall not as a fall into knowledge, the way the other story has it, but as a fall into language.[16] But I am conceiving of the fall into language as initiating the possibility of *mistake*. And since a mistake is something like a nonmoral, secular equivalent of sin, this makes the fall into language not, after all, so very untraditional.[17] And now, already, we can see how Wittgenstein's project will end: If language is essentially linked to the possibility of mistake, then it is essentially linked to precisely that anxiety about meaning which authentic linguistic action was meant to set aside. The ever present possibility of mistake is the dehydrated philosopher's equivalent of the ever-present anxiety about authenticity. That is why Wittgenstein must fail.

To make a mistake with a word requires at least that the word can appear in an inappropriate context and still make sense. If the unusual use of a word, outside an appropriate context, made no sense at all, then the unusual use would not produce a mistake, but only noise. So the possibility of making a linguistic mistake turns on the possibility of using a word meaningfully and incorrectly, at once.[18] At one and the same time both meaningfully and incorrectly. Raindrops can't make mistakes. When a given raindrop is blown away from my house, missing the tin roof, landing inaudibly on the grass, it doesn't make a mistake. It just doesn't make any sound. Can bees make mistakes? Suppose a bee with a head cold, returns from the nectar field and dances his hive off in the wrong direction. Would that be a mistake? It is true that missing out on the nectar is bad for the hive, but not everything that is bad for the hive is a mistake. No bee made a mistake when the hive was built in the garden of Mr. B. Hayter, although when Mr. Hayter blew the hive away with his shotgun, it was not a good day for the hive. So did the bee with a head cold make a mistake, or was the bee just blown off course (immunologically) the way the inaudible raindrop drop was blown off course (meteorologically)? I am not sure this is a question that can be definitively answered, but it must be relevant that the bee is not able to *correct* his mistake. Suppose, misled by the bee with the head cold, the bees head off in the wrong direction, buzz around a bit, and then, quite by accident, run into the original languid nectar field, hot in the afternoon sun. If on returning to the hive, the very same immunologically challenged bee now dances the correct dance, this will be better for the hive, and so the first mistake will, in some sense, be corrected. But I don't feel like saying that the bee *corrected* the mistake. The bee simply went off and did a completely different thing, which, as it happens, proved better for the future of the hive.

Making a mistake and correcting a mistake are linked. I don't want to flat-out deny that anyone could make a mistake unless they were able to correct it. For it is certainly possible that an otherwise competent professor of mathematics might for a while be unable (for reasons of fright, despair, or disease) to correct a mistake that he or she would otherwise have been fully able to spot. And this would be a legitimate case of making a mistake without also, at that time, being able to correct it. Nevertheless, it is almost true that anyone unable to correct a mistake is unable to make a mistake.

To make a mistake requires not only that a word be able to occur, meaningfully, in inappropriate circumstances but also that it be able to be corrected. Both of these require that the word can be weaned from the context of its birth, that it can be *repeated* in different contexts. *Repeating a word in various contexts is repetition within the frame of representation.* Just as the same barstool appears here and, again, there, so the same word appears in this context and, again, in that. This is the first again of this chapter's title: an again trapped in the frame of representation. Correcting a mistake requires being able to do something like cite or quote the mistaken signs and replace them with the correct ones. I suspect that this is one of the reasons why Deleuze and Guattari insist that "the first determination of language, is not the trope or the metaphor, but *indirect discourse*" (Deleuze and Guattari [1980] 1987, 77).[19] And they conclude from this that bees do not have language.

What of A and B? Do they have language? The builder called A could easily make a mistake of the sort that the bee made. Working away at his mysterious project, A notices a place for a slab, but suffering from a head cold, yes, it's going around, he calls for a block. What does he do when B comes over with the block? He could do any number of things. Remembering when I have been rebuilding dry stone walls, there is not always a place for a stone which you thought would fit, I realize that when the block comes, A might take it and try to use it, either succeeding or, if not, then setting the block on the ground and calling for one of the other three types of building stone. Or perhaps A sees B with the block, looks confused, takes the block, tries to use it, either succeeding or not. What A can't do is say: Oh, Oh, I must've made a mistake; sorry B, could I have a slab, please. At this stage, A and B are not that different from ants and bees, but there must be a way to get from ants and bees to Aunt Bea, or else language could not have evolved. The question is how.

This is what I was calling Wittgenstein's first problem, how to enlarge the linguistic lives of A and B so that they could more completely model our own lives. His solution will be to appeal to what he italicizes as the *practice of language* [der *Praxis der Sprache*] (Wittgenstein [1953] 1976, §§51, 21). The practice of language is the institutional network of linguistic action that Wittgenstein can also call "*customs* (uses, institutions)" (Wittgenstein [1953] 1976, §199). Let us imagine that such a complex practice, our very own, has, somehow or other, been built up. Now what? Why is this a fall?

I don't want to underplay the glory of Wittgenstein's (nevertheless inadequate) solution. Who would have thought that you could account for the complexities of our linguistic life without ever appealing to the meaning of a word, at all, but only to the actions of those who use words? Who would have thought that there could be a completely satisfying description of Aunt Bea's complex linguistic life by reference only to actions, hers and others? "Well, I assume he *acts* [er *handelt*] as I have described. Explanations come to an end somewhere" (Wittgenstein [1953] 1976, §1). The relative irrelevance of "the general notion of the meaning of a word" to our understanding of the practice of language is a big surprise (Wittgenstein [1953] 1976, §5). This is a tremendous accomplishment. Wittgenstein thinks of the significance of a word not in terms of the *general notion of meaning* but in terms of the possible and actual uses of the word. "But what is the meaning of the word 'five'?—No such thing was in question here only how the word 'five' is used" (Wittgenstein [1953] 1976, §1).

This is both the glory and the tragedy[20] of Wittgenstein's approach to authentic linguistic action: It is the source both of wonder and of anxiety, for the general notion of the meaning of a word was doing some work. The sounds of raindrops on the tin roof are not free; they obey the laws of physics, willy-nilly. The general notion of the meaning of a word could have performed the same function as the laws of physics but in a different realm, in the normative realm. If there were meanings of words, sitting somewhere in heaven or our heads, then these meanings would nail down the possible significances of our words. Correct use would be determined, willy-nilly, by those meanings. We would only be free to violate those heavenly linguistic norms, in the way we are free to double park; you can, but it's still illegal. The linguistic violations would still be violations, no matter what we said. The general notion of the meaning of a word would have grounded our linguistic practice and *stopped* the *play* of possible meanings. Double negation.

Without the general notion of the meaning of a word, Wittgenstein approaches the practice of language as a groundless activity, held in place by nothing more than that activity itself. Like a game. And yet like a game, language grabs us. One word from one person, the right person, can glorify an entire day, or more. And this is part of the wonder of language, a wonder it shares with life and the world. How can this be? How can just words, just these sounds, make it difficult to speak, my heart is beating so. It is as if there were an unnamable source of energy toward the center of our linguistic practice, as if there were an "intense center at its profoundest depths" (Deleuze and Guattari [1980] 1987, 225). The intense center of a game, basketball or chess, would be the unnamable source of the energy, the life in our play. It is a romantic thought, featuring the importance of the earth, the rough ground (Wittgenstein [1953] 1976, §107).

> The earth is the intense point at the deepest level of the territory or is projected outside it like a focal point, where all the forces draw together in close embrace. The earth is no longer one force among others. . . . The earth has become that close embrace of all forces, those of the earth as well as of other substances, so that the [romantic] artist no longer confronts chaos, but hell and the subterranean, the groundless. (Deleuze and Guattari [1980] 1987, 339)

The territory of language, the territory marked by criteria, is the domain of knowledge. But what gives criteria their strength, the power of knowledge, comes from another place, without ground, the Earth. "And then, without grounds, I shall act" (Wittgenstein [1953] 1976, §211). The turn to practice reveals the groundlessness of our linguistic life. Its wonder.

But if wonder is one result of this turn to practice, anxiety is another. Anxiety about what others might have meant, about what we might have meant. The groundlessness of our life with language sets the problems of authenticity and inauthenticity which are still guiding us toward something animal. Cut free from the general notion of meaning, our words can be taken in any number of different ways. Our words can be repeated in all sorts of circumstances so we can almost always bend them in good or bad directions. Which one is their authentic direction? There is no way to tell. Our linguistic practice is groundless. On the basketball court you pass me the ball, or so you think, and I just walk off the court taking it home. Was this a pass or a gift? What would make it an authentic pass? It is always the same old story, when is a kiss just a kiss? Neither external nor internal criteria will be any help in settling our anxieties about whether some pass, some kiss, was, or was not, authentic. The turn to action, to the practice of language, left language groundless, and so brings us back, this time from the side of language and meaning, to the question of authenticity.

This should not be a surprise. Authenticity is always a question of meaning. What is the meaning of his kiss? Is it an honest expression of affection? Is it an affectation of the European? Or is it simply an unimaginative way of getting between my legs? Authentic linguistic action, Wittgenstein's explicit concern, makes this connection to meaning even more obvious. What did she mean when she said, "I would hate to be alone, tonight: I really hope you can come"? Was this inadvertently lewd? But the lewd use of *come* is not so obscure. Then was it intentionally lewd? But she has never been so blatant before. Unless the curling smile behind her sadness was not simply friendly, but actually mischievous. In a melancholy sort of way. But was it really mischievous? After all, she was pretty sad. On the other hand, her stomach flashed beneath her tiny clinging shirt in what must surely have been a sign of mischievousness. Unless she dressed without thinking. But everybody thinks. Or do they? And so it goes—each interpretation demanding one or another more. These are the endless hermeneutical musings of all who are on their way to love: teenaged, middle-aged, and geriatric. Authenticity requires that we *stop* the *play* of meanings. Double negation. But without the general notion of the meaning of a word, how can we? And if we cannot, how can we ever hope to escape from anxiety to what Wittgenstein really pines for: "peaceful security"? (Wittgenstein [1953] 1976, §607). "Thoughts that are at peace. That's the goal someone who philosophizes yearns for" (Wittgenstein 1980, 43).

Stage 3: Redemption. We will never find peace by returning to the general notion of the meaning of a word. It will not help to interpose, between the word and our use of the word, the meaning of the word, for *however we model the meaning of a word*, either that meaning just *is* the use of the word, in which case we will have made action primary just as Wittgenstein did, or the meaning of the word is different from the use of the word, in which case a gap would remain to be bridged between the meaning of the word and the actual use of the word, and into that gap will rush all of our familiar anxieties about the authenticity of our actions, linguistic and otherwise. So it won't help to return to the general notion of the meaning of a word.

By this time, A and B have arrived at the same place the fifteen-year-old boy in Kleist's story arrived when he woke to self-consciousness and lost his grace, possibly forever. Wittgenstein's move, here, is precisely the same as Herr C.'s: to abolish self-consciousness, to simulate something animal (Wittgenstein 1969, §359). But it will be a *simulation*. Double negation can be no more.

A and B on the original building site had four words each with only one possible use. There was never any possibility that one of those words might have meant something other than the only thing it could be used to do. They couldn't joke. They could barely make a mistake. The complexity of Aunt Bea's linguistic life has given our words many different uses, and so, after the fall into language, there is always a question of whether some use of a word was to be taken this way or that. Mistake has become an ever-present danger. That is where the anxiety slips in, and we begin to lose sleep over the question of authenticity. Since Wittgenstein knows that it wouldn't help the situation to appeal to the general notion of the meaning of a word, he has no choice but to achieve authenticity by *stopping* the *play* of language some other way. But how?

One possibility would simply be to close our eyes to all but one of the possible significances of an action, linguistic or otherwise. This is the dusty road to self-deception and would deliver not authenticity, but only inauthentic authenticity. Wittgenstein knows this. In fact, in one discussion of the peaceful security that he yearns for, he imagines the following exchange.

> "But if you are *certain* [*sicher*], isn't it that you are shutting your eyes in the face of doubt?"—They are shut [Sie sind mir geschlossen]. (Wittgenstein [1953] 1976, p. 224)

The idea is that there are times when we can discover our eyes shut to the anxieties posed by alternative possibilities but to which we haven't actually shut our eyes. They are, so to speak, naturally closed. The way an animal's eyes are closed to anxiety. That is the plan. To work ourselves into the position, not of pretending to be animals, but rather, of enjoying the blindness to anxiety that is characteristic of animals, without pretense. How is this to work? By going home (Wittgenstein [1953] 1976, §116).

Wittgenstein believes (incorrectly) that *when words are in their proper contexts they mean only one thing.* No anxiety. No fear of inauthenticity. When words are used outside their proper contexts, what he calls being used metaphysically, they do not mean anything at all. Outside the proper contexts of their use, words may seem to mean something, but in fact, they do not. That is the difficulty, as Wittgenstein sees it, of philosophy. "My aim is: to teach you to pass from a piece of disguised nonsense to something that is patent nonsense" (Wittgenstein [1953] 1976, §464). Once we realize that the bastard uses of our words, outside contextual wedlock, are completely without meaning, mere noise, the anxieties caused by wondering if those meanings were actually in play evaporate. And with these anxieties gone, we can enjoy a freedom from anxiety so pure it is something animal. "What we do," he says, "is to bring words back from their metaphysical to their everyday use" (Wittgenstein [1953] 1976, §116). Wittgenstein figures the attempted metaphysical use of words as the attempt to walk on frictionless ice: Our words just keep slipping around, seeming to mean this, seeming to mean that, but not really meaning anything, at all (Wittgenstein [1953] 1976, §107). This is what makes the metaphysical use of a word inauthentic, theatrical, it is the attempt to mean some one thing by our words which, there and then, on the ice, cannot be meant.

Wittgenstein wants to return us to the building site, before the fall. To a time when each word could ever mean only one simple thing, when mistakes were barely possible, when humans were only animals. This Kleistian ambition is visible in the opening paragraph of Wittgenstein's book which tells a tale of authentic linguistic action almost unrecognizable as the action of humans. It is a Zombie Shopping Spree (see Cavell 1995).

The tale begins when Wittgenstein imagines giving a helpful person a piece of paper on which appear the marks

Five red apples

The helpful person takes the piece of paper and hands it to a grocer. The grocer then goes to a drawer marked

apples

and takes out a color chart, from somewhere, perhaps his pocket, and on this color chart the word red is "paired," as we would say, with a color sample, like this

blue   [some color sample]
red   [some color sample]
yellow [some color sample]
green [some color sample]

then the grocer takes an apple of more or less the color of the sample directly (not diagonally) opposite the word

red

out of the still open drawer while reciting the cardinal numbers from one to five. He takes out one apple as he recites each cardinal number; he does not, for example, take out two apples when he says two, three for three, and so on. Wittgenstein doesn't mention anything about putting the apples in a bag, but one assumes that the five red apples are being purchased and not just cradled in the grocer's arms. That is the tale of five apples, a tale of linguistic action undisturbed by any anxiety. But it is a tale of linguistic action that is blind, willfully or otherwise, to the possibility of mistake, to other ways of reading the color chart, to other ways of using the cardinal numbers, and so on. There are other possibilities here, and if these two don't notice them, that doesn't make those other possibilities disappear. It just makes the peaceful security of their would-be authentic linguistic action wooden, fake. Eye-catching, perhaps, but a codpiece nonetheless.

It was such a nice idea. Held in place by the friction of their everyday contexts, the semantic play of our words would come to a stop. By itself. Without play, our linguistic life would be fully serious. And this reminds one of the failures of Herr C. in his fencing match with the bear, a bear described as possessing almost total seriousness. Complete seriousness is also a mark of authenticity (Cavell [1969] 1976, 109; Bearn 1998b; Bearn 2000d). Had Wittgenstein's plan worked, then outside its home context, a word would not mean anything at all. Nothing. Just noise. Outside its everyday home, a word would be like military decorations pinned to a La-Z-Boy: completely empty of meaning. Pinned to the recliner, the medals could not mean that the La-Z-Boy served in the Battle of the Bulge. But if so decorating the La-Z-Boy curls the corners of your mouth, even a little, that means that even this bizarre use of military decorations is not without meaning. Even Wittgenstein can get a joke, so even Wittgenstein should know that his attempt to achieve authenticity, complete seriousness, *must fail* (Wittgenstein [1953] 1976, §246). The unusual nonserious significances of a word can never be ruled completely out of play. So the play of our linguistic life will never disappear. And neither will our anxiety about the authenticity of our linguistic life. Wittgenstein was seeking complete and perfect seriousness, but play is ineradicable, in spite of police. Anxiety about the inauthenticity of our own or others' actions is ineradicable.

Wittgenstein had two problems. He was to augment the linguistic lives of A and B so that they could be a model of our own lives. But he was also to accomplish this without enlarging the possible significances of every linguistic utterance to such an extent that we would never be able to escape anxiety, to enjoy authenticity. These two problems cannot be solved together. Suppose, mirabile dictu, Wittgenstein found a way to remove all possible significances of a word except one serious significance. Then he would have returned us to the building site. That seems to have been the point of beginning his book with the Zombie shopping trip, the tale of five apples. But things were never as wonderful as we like to imagine. Life, linguistic and otherwise, was not so very rich on the building site. A and B couldn't joke; they could barely make a mistake; they were indeed more like bees than Aunt Bea. And that is just why Wittgenstein enriched A and B's linguistic practice, to bring it closer to our own. But once it becomes ours, then the possibility of mistake is always real. Even when we are not *aware* of that possibility, even when our eyes are, for some reason, shut to that possibility, the possibility is still afoot. We made love in the summer sun, and I was in bliss. Completely unaware that for the entire week you had just wanted to screw. I felt my whole future life softly folding into your arms, but I never saw you again. It was not what I thought it was. The part I cherished most was fake. So too is Wittgenstein's peace. So too is Wittgenstein's approach to authenticity.

Like Herr C., Wittgenstein would have very much liked not to be human. He knows he is not a god, but he refuses to see that he cannot be an animal either. And so it begins to look as if the jaded have won, after all. It begins to look as if there is no hope of securing the authenticity of any action, linguistic or otherwise. And there isn't. But I promised that although Wittgenstein's project would fail, we would not rush into the arms of the jaded. Now I must explain how. The trick is to find a way to move beyond both authenticity and inauthenticity. The trick is to move beyond the performance of actions, whether authentic or inauthentic, to enjoy the seafoam joy of an actual performance. The trick is to break on through (to the other side).

Again and Again: Deleuze's Two Repetitions

I have been stimulated by the expression "beyond authenticity and inauthenticity" ever since I found it in the last paragraph of some remarks that Derrida improvised at the first Any conference held in Los Angeles in May 1991 (Derrida 1991, 45).[21] The twin fates of Herr C. and Wittgenstein have now brought us to a Derridean moment. If it is not possible to stop the play of linguistic meanings, then we will lose not only authenticity, but also inauthenticity. For not being able to stop the play of language puts us in some Butler's nightmare where nothing means what it means without also meaning something else; where nothing is what it is without also being something else.[22] Moore's the pity. This means that while nothing will be simply authentic, nothing will be simply inauthentic either. We have moved beyond authenticity and inauthenticity. But this Derridean beyond is not the beyond that I am heading toward. In fact, this Derridean beyond is a rather nice example of the ersatz Yes that comes from repeating No. Repetition is the problem. A different repetition will be the solution.

Unless words were repeatable, there would be no meaning. Unless actions were repeatable, it would not be possible to perform actions. Unless territorial markings were repeatable, there would be no territories. So repetition, being able to perform an action, again, is the key to meaning anything, at all, whether authentic or inauthentic. It was repetition that brought us from the more or less causal world of raindrops and bees to Andy's fully linguistic Aunt Bea. Were it not possible for a word to be repeated, we would not be able to assert anything, and so it would not be possible to assert anything true, or false. Or false. That *or false* is the reason this repetition is a force of ruin. Before we turned to Kleist and Wittgenstein, we met this *or false* as the result of thinking about criteria. Criteria make possible knowledge that Morag is limping in response to her painful broken ankle, but they also make it possible for Morag to merely act like she is in pain. And it was at just his point that I lead us off to Kleist's Herr C. and the dream of animality that Wittgenstein shares with Kleist. It is time to pick up the line we were launching toward repetition.

According to Deleuze we will never understand repetition, or difference, so long as we insist on putting these notions in chains, in what he calls "the four iron collars of representation," one of which is identity in the concept (Deleuze [1968] 1994, 262). Thus chained, we will be able to approach the repetition of concepts but never the concept of repetition (xv, 19). Sometimes Deleuze describes his approach to repetition as an alternative to the traditional thought that "only that which is alike differs" (Deleuze [1968] 1994, 116; Deleuze [1969] 1990, 261). This is the thought familiar to Davidsonians and critics of Kuhn, that in order for there to be a disagreement between two persons there must be agreement, so that there can be no radical incommensurability. Deleuze approaches repetition from the other side, "only differences are alike" (Deleuze [1968] 1994, 116; Deleuze [1969] 1990, 261). Deleuze's idea is that if there were no differences there would not be two things to be alike in the first place. But it remains a strange approach. Lets take it from the ground up.

Anyone walking along the railroad tracks, which, in their way, already form a rhizomatic system, will have noticed railroad ties, one after the other, repeating themselves, as to infinity. Collared by identity, this repetition appears as the repetition of railroad ties. But no ties are really identical; there are "little differences, variations and modifications" between any two ties (Deleuze [1968] 1994, xix). The myriad differences between each tie, are dominated by the concept of a tie, but not entirely, and the result is the apparent repetition of ties along the tracks. This repetition is only apparent; because there remain recognizable differences between the particular ties. Real repetition would require not just resemblances and analogies but two different things whose identity was so complete that they shared the identical conceptual representation. "In every case," Deleuze writes, "repetition is difference without a concept" (23).

Repetition, which we might have thought to be a matter of the Same, turns out to be a matter of the different, the obscure: "intoxication, the properly philosophical stupor of the Dionysian Idea" (Deleuze [1968] 1994, 214). Two, which repeat, must be two, so they must be different, but they must repeat, so they must be conceptually identical. Their identity may be representational, but their difference must be *subrepresentational*.[23] And the question now becomes: Are there any real repetitions, at all? Are there any subrepresentational differences without concepts?

This possibility—the possibility of real repetition—is in conflict with what Deleuze calls a certain "vulgarized Leibnizianism" (Deleuze [1968] 1994, 11),[24] for

> if (a) each particular thing can be fully characterized by its *complete concept*, and
>   if (b) each *complete concept* picks out only one thing, and
>   if (c) each thing has only one *complete concept* which picks it out,
>   then (d) the jig is up: in such circumstances there could be no difference without a concept, no real repetition. (See Deleuze [1968] 1994, 11–12)

But everything turns on the existence of complete concepts. I will consider two cases. First, if in some circumstances we are forced to work with incomplete concepts, then there will be, in those circumstances, differences without concepts, repetition. And second, if it turns out that there can be no such thing as a complete concept, at all, then there will be real repetition, tout court, unhedged by special circumstances.

Words provide an example of the first kind of case, where circumstances force us to make do with incomplete concepts. In this vulgar Leibnizian scheme, the comprehension or sense of a concept and the reference of that concept are inversely proportional: The "larger" the sense, the "smaller" the reference (Deleuze [1968] 1994, 12). So, for example, the concept *dog* includes in its reference all dogs, whereas a concept with a larger sense, *cooked dog*, includes far fewer dogs, especially in Pennsylvania. The idea of a complete conceptual representation of a thing is the idea of a concept whose sense is so comprehensive that only one thing can fit in, like a lock that can be turned by one and only key. Clearly, the concept *cooked dog* is not such a lock; it can be opened by many more keys than one, in fact, any parboiled pooch would do. To restrict the reference of a concept to one particular thing, it often seems that its sense would have to become infinite.

Now think about words. The word *rock*, for example, refers to many more than one thing; indeed, it refers to many more kinds of thing than one. The definitions of words are finite, and this means that the concepts they embody cannot be complete concepts; they will not pick out one and only one thing. Words are therefore like locks that can be opened not only by what they are *meant* to be opened by but also by hairpins and hatpins. This is one source of wordplay. The limited control exercised by our intentions over our words makes inadvertent puns possible (Bearn 1995a). Also repetition. Words with finite definitions, referring to more than one particular, bring into existence "true repetition," but it is secondary (Deleuze [1968] 1994, 13). And this is true of all words. Deleuze, again:

> We have here a reason why the comprehension [or sense] of the concept *cannot* extend to infinity: we define a word by only a finite number of words. Nevertheless, speech and writing, from which words are inseparable, give them an existence *hic et nunc*; a genus thereby passes into existence as such; and here again extension is made up for in dispersion, in discreteness, under the sign of a repetition which forms the real power of language speech and writing.
> (Deleuze [1968] 1994, 13)

The secondary repetition that forms the real power of speech and writing is explained by the inadequacy of our concepts, which produces a situation in which every concept and every set of concepts always applies, perfectly, to more than one object: the phenomenon of twinning (Deleuze [1968] 1994, 13). We can only ever talk about twins, ever, and so inauthenticity is always a threat, a threat we can never escape.

We could escape if we could construct a concept which was complete. This is the second kind of case I must consider: the more fundamental issue of the very possibility of complete concepts. For if there can be no complete concepts, not even infinite ones, then we will have produced a reason to believe that there is real repetition, unhedged by circumstances.

"Here, I throw the apple to you." Suppose you wanted to represent this very apple. *Apple* won't do, for it could refer to any apple, at all, fresh, cooked, inflatable, whatever. Take the Leibnizian road of addition. Consider: *Green apple.* But we are just beginning, any green apple, whether a ripe Granny Smith or a still young Delicious with a hard body would satisfy this concept. We could add more concepts: *Tart green apple.* But this gets us no farther. Scientific sophisticates will have been itching to offer some monstrous concept like *tart fleshy green apple trajectory through space-time.* And let us simply stipulate that this monstrous concept picks out no other apple but the one in this room. It still won't be a complete concept. For this ugly concept is still a *universal*, though an especially devious one, so even if—in the actual world—it only picked out our apple, it would still, here and now, represent many different particular apples in other possible worlds.

Of course if we could restrict our concept to the actual world, our problems would be over, but the actual world is simply another particular, though a big one, and if we could represent particulars, we wouldn't be having this problem in the first place.

Infinity won't help, either. We begin with an infinite number of possible particulars from which our concept is to select just one. Now, imagine our infinitely long string of concepts growing. As each new concept is added to our growing string of concepts, we will eliminate some of that infinite number of possible particulars, but the number remaining will always be the same: infinite. It is just as if we began with the infinity of positive integers and tried to reduce them to one integer by subtracting finite numbers of integers. We could perform an infinite number of subtractions and still be left with an infinity of integers.

Finally, even indexicals will be no help, for from at least the time of *The Blue Book*, we have known that indexical definitions presuppose, and cannot ground, verbal ones (Wittgenstein 1933, 1–5). There is no way out. Neither sophisticated space-time trajectories nor infinity nor Mr. Pointer himself will help. There are no complete concepts. The twinning that we saw arrive with the inadequacies of our linguistic concepts is here to stay, and that means that secondary repetition is here to stay. And unless we can find an unusual way out, we will never be able to escape the dark side of twinning, the threat of inauthenticity. The way out is through primary repetition.

In order to move in on the primary sense of repetition, Deleuze asks what explains the existence of secondary repetition. There is an easy answer, but it won't satisfy Deleuze. The easy answer is: The incompleteness or inadequacy of concepts is what explains secondary repetition, difference without a concept. He refers to this as "a nominal definition and a negative explanation of repetition" (Deleuze [1968] 1994, 16). What is left out of such a negative explanation is any positive account for why secondary repetition appears whenever there are incomplete concepts.

Deleuze's answer is surprising. In its primary sense, repetition refers to the swarming differences that escape through the holes in the knotted nets of incomplete concepts. He tells us that every time we find ourselves confronted by a limitation like the inadequacy or incompleteness of our concepts, we should ask what such a situation presupposes. It presupposes a swarm of differences, a pluralism of free, wild or untamed differences, a properly differential and original space and time; all of which persist along-side the simplifications of limitation and opposition. (Deleuze [1968] 1994, 50)[25]

Unless there were swarming differences, secondary repetition would not be explained by the incompleteness of our concepts. So in some sense these swarms of untamed differences are the beating heart of repetition. But they are mysterious. What are they?

Approach this by analogy with a vulgarized kinetic theory of gases. The secondary sense of repetition, the repetition of railroad ties, is like the temperature of a gas. Every morning when I come into the lab, the oxygen is at room temperature. Secondary repetition. But beneath the apparently calm surface of that repeated reading, are the wilder motions of the molecules of which the gas is composed. The temperature of the gas is an easily observed molar effect of the otherwise imperceptible molecular activity of the gas. For precisely analogous reasons Deleuze can speak of secondary repetition as naked, that is perceptible, and primary repetition as clothed, that is imperceptible (Deleuze [1968] 1994, 24).

The reasons can only be analogous, because the swarms of differences that make secondary repetition possible are not just tiny, they are *subrepresentational*. We just saw that no particular can be completely trapped in a language of representation.

> It is impossible to complete the description of an actual occasion by means of concepts. (Whitehead [1925] 1967, 169–70)

Thus every singular particular is neither *one* instance of a concept, nor *many* instances of the same concept. Neither one nor many, they are what Deleuze and Guattari come to call multiplicities, remarking: "A multiplicity is defined not by the elements that compose it in extension [Fregean reference], not by the characteristics that compose it in comprehension [Fregean sense], but by the lines and dimensions that it encompasses in 'intension'" (Deleuze and Guattari [1980] 1987, 245; see Deleuze [1968] 1994, 238). A multiplicity is like a pack of wolves that is defined neither by the wolves that make it up in extension nor by the features that define a wolf in comprehension, but by the variable intensities of the relations between the wolves. The swarms of subrepresentational differences are swarms of intensities, and these swarms of intensities are the positive explanation for the existence of secondary repetition. What are these intensities? They are the sensual singularities that we struggle and fail to capture with our favorite categories; because categories are always made rather for justice and injustice than for becoming beautiful.

> Here we can see why the concept of difference is so important to *Difference and Repetition*. It is because he [Deleuze] wants to distinguish actual differences, defined by characteristics that are ruled by the possibility of negation (*not-kind-hearted*), from pure differences or intensities. (*Becoming hardened is not not-becoming softer and each one of us expresses becoming hardened in a different way—that is, sets it in a different relation to other becomings, including becoming softer.*) (J. Williams, 2003, 9)

We are close to Bergson.

We are convinced that each object has more or less one color, and when such an object is placed in brighter light, we convince ourselves that what we see is qualitatively the same color; the change, we say, only affects the quantitative intensity of that one color. We compare the change in color of the object to an oboe playing one note louder and louder, instead of to an orchestra with more and more instruments joining or leaving the oboe (Bergson [1889] 1960, 35). The supposedly pure color of a wall is already so many different colors. We would not ordinarily say that the yellow wall is also at the same time green. But don't think! Look! (Wittgenstein [1953] 1976, §66). Even a white sheet of paper under different illuminations is different shades of white, even purple (Bergson [1889] 1960, 53). But you have to pay attention to the sheet of paper; you have to look for the changing shades, the becoming-purple. Sensual experience is essentially linked to expression. In order to taste the soup you can't just swallow, you have to reach for it, taste it, hold it in your mouth. Savoring is expressing. Savoring is caressing. And what you caress is not Flavor B75A. You caress sensual singularities. Swarming intensities. Perhaps this is what Bergson meant by intuition (Bergson [1903] 1992).

The true secret of repetition is that it doesn't presuppose the Same, the identity of a concept, which will only open us to the repetition of concepts, repetition of the Same. The true secret of repetition is that there are swarms of pure intensities that, under the condition of incomplete concepts, produce the diversity of what is given as so many almost identical railroad ties. This repetition of the Same, if framed as the repetitious labors of Sisyphus or ourselves, can seem a curse (Deleuze [1968] 1994, 293). The curse of twinning, trapped in a hall of mirrors, never to escape.[26] But if we could find a way to make the swarms of wild intensities *by* which the diverse is given appear *in* the given, in the sensible (56–57), then we might escape from the iron collars of our identities to an "aesthetic of intensities" (244), then we might ride a wild wave of pure intensities, dying the good death, experiencing an ecstasy without excess. Secondary repetition can be a curse, but primary repetition may be its cure (Deleuze [1969] 1990, 287–90).

Derrida's No, Deleuze's Yes

The difference between Derrida and Deleuze is simple and deep: It is the difference between No and Yes, the difference between Derrida's No, which reeks of the thick smell of Schopenhauer, and Deleuze's Yes, blowing in, fresh and salty, off Nietzsche's new seas. It is the difference between a philosophy trapped in the frame of representation and one that breaks on through (to the other side). It is the difference between playing a Derridean game you can never win and Deleuzoid game you can never lose. It is the difference between No and Yes.

The negative bent of Derrida's philosophy is veiled by the importance he gives to play and to the impossibility of distinguishing the serious from the nonserious, but this play and this impossibility are both made possible by an absence, a lack. We all know that words can mean many different things—there is room for semantic play—but one normally thinks that this semantic play is restricted by the central, serious meaning of the word. It is the absence of such a central meaning which, in Derrida's hands, releases the play of language. Derrida: "The absence of [the central signified,] the transcendental signified extends the domain and the play of language infinitely" (Derrida [1967b] 1978a, 280). The fine-grained consequences of this are that the semantic play of our words is unrestricted; the large-grained consequences of this are associated by Derrida with the closure, if not the end, of the history of metaphysics as presence. But at this point I am only interested in drawing attention to the crucial role played by the negative in defense of these consequences. As Derrida put it in 1967: "The *overabundance* of the signifier, its *supplementary* character, is thus the result of finitude, that is to say, the result of a lack which must be *supplemented*" (290). I will be trying to link Derridean play, made possible by a lack, to secondary repetition that can also, if only in part, be explained by a lack.

In Deleuze's scheme, primary repetition is made up of the swarming subrepresentational differences that show up in (secondary) repetition of the Same, and so when Derrida speaks of the "logic that ties repetition to alterity," he begins to sound as if he is moving in on primary repetition. But he is not. That phrase is from the following the passage:

> My [written] communication must be repeatable—iterable—in the absolute absence of the receiver or of any empirically determinable collectivity of receivers. Such iterability (*iter*, again, probably comes for *itara*, *other* in Sanskrit, and everything that follows can be read as the working out of the logic that ties repetition to alterity) structures the mark of writing itself, no matter what particular type of writing is involved. . . . A writing that is not structurally readable—iterable—beyond the death of the addressee [and beyond the death of the sender] would not be writing. (Derrida 1988a, 7)

Iterability is here being introduced to name a specific power of writing, but Derrida quickly generalizes it to cover any significant mark, written or spoken, for when a spoken remark is overheard, it is functioning in the absence of the intended receiver, and when we inadvertently stumble into a pun, our spoken remarks are functioning in the absence of the clarified intentions of the sender (Derrida 1988a, 10).

Derrida will argue that there can be no linguistic action unless the marks employed are iterable. A sign that could not appear in *other* circumstances at *other* times would not be a sign; it would be mere noise. So iterability *broaches* linguistic action. But iterability also *breaches* linguistic action, ruining all hope of ever meaning one single serious thing, thus repeating for *sense* the Deleuzoid argument against ever being able to *refer* to one single particular. This ruination of sense is carried by the "logic that ties repetition to alterity" (Derrida 1988a, 7). It can be demonstrated by subtraction (see Bearn 1995b).

Since words are iterable, they can be used with any number of possible senses, the serious ones more or less discrete and the nonserious ones blurring everything. Suppose we tried to subtract from the possible significances of a mark all serious significances but one, and every possible nonserious signification. What would happen? The resulting mark would either be iterable, or not.

Take the first horn first. If it were iterable, then there and then, it might mean something *other* than what we had intended it to mean. Derrida:

> Iterability alters, contaminating parasitically what it identifies and enables to repeat "itself"; it leaves us no choice but to mean (to say) something that is (already, always, also) other than what we mean (to say), to say something other than what we say *and* would have wanted to say, to understand something other than [what we understand, and so on]. (Derrida 1988a, 62)

This is the logic that ties repetition to alterity, and it is not different from the logic that, in Deleuze, reveals "the essence of that in which every repetition consists: difference without a concept" (Deleuze [1968] 1994, 25). Iterability is another name for secondary repetition; it doesn't break through the frame of representation releasing swarms of intensities; it simply characterizes life within the frame.

According to the second horn, if the result of our subtractive procedures is not iterable, then we will have succeeded in producing a mark with one and only one serious significance. A noniterable sign. But precisely that success would be failure. For a mark that is not iterable means nothing. This is the tragic trajectory of Derrida's approach to linguistic action: Its end (goal) would be its end (death) (Derrida 1988a, 129). That is why Derrida ends one of his early books with the aperçu: "Rising toward the sun of presence, it is the way of Icarus" (Derrida 1967c, 104). I have wandered off again to Derrida's tragic trajectory, but my main concern now is to convince you that there is no primary repetition in Derrida's philosophy.

According to Deleuze, diversity is given. Diversity is a characteristic of the sensible. But diversity is an effect; it is given *by* swarms of differences, the primary sense of repetition (Deleuze [1968] 1994, 222). The concept closest to this in Derrida is différance, the famous différance with an inaudible *a*. Everything seems right. Like Deleuze's swarms, Derrida's différance produces differences. Derrida writes: "Différance is the non-full, non-simple, structured and differentiating origin of differences" (Derrida [1972b] 1982, 11). Again, the swarms were fully affirmative and positive, not merely negative, and Derrida insists that "différance is the name we might give to the 'active,' moving discord of different forces, and of differences of forces, that Nietzsche sets up against the entire system of metaphysical grammar" (18). But something is wrong here. Différance is *non*full, and yet it is affirmative. These are the two sides of différance that Derrida calls, eyeing Bataille, the economical and the noneconomical (19).

The nonfull side of différance is the economical side of différance. It is the "detour which, in the element of the same, always aims at coming back to the pleasure or the presence that has been deferred by, calculation" (Derrida [1972b] 1982, 19). It is this absence, this detour, which links soul and body, good and evil, inside and outside, speech and writing, in mutually supplementary relations (127). In this economical sense, the différance is "the medium in which opposites are opposed" (Derrida [1972a] 1981, 127). This side of différance does not take us any further than iterability, and so it doesn't take us any further than secondary repetition understood negatively by default in the concept. Moreover, this reference to a "medium" makes one think that Derrida may still be in the grip of the Davidsonian thought that Deleuze is trying to overcome, namely, that "only that which is alike differs" (Deleuze [1968] 1994, 116; contrast Derrida 1988a, 146).

The noneconomical side of différance is the affirmative excessive side, the Bataille side, for if it is not possible to mean just one thing, then we are always meaning more, and the nonoriginary origin of this excess can be figured as an explosive fountain—call it dissemination. This noneconomical side overflows the boundaries of the opposites originating from the economical side. The economical side is the side of limitation; the noneconomical, the side of excess, initiating an "expenditure without reserve, the entirely other relationship that apparently interrupts every economy" (Derrida [1972b] 1982, 19).

Neither of these sides of différance is fully affirmative; both of them can be understood in terms of absence, in terms of a lack. Derrida seems to presuppose the traditional picture of concepts as vessels, hoping to be perfectly filled. If there is endless play, it is because the vessels can never be perfectly filled. But the very fact that the vessels of meaning can never be perfectly filled means they can overflow. Indeed, the very idea of excess presupposes that of a finite container. So neither side of difference escapes the negativity of secondary repetition; neither side breaks out of the frame of representation. They only play within it, disseminating unruly significances endlessly. As Deleuze and Guattari say: "Lack or excess, it hardly matters" (Deleuze and Guattari [1980] 1987, 115).

In fact, without mentioning his name, Deleuze and Guattari launch *A Thousand Plateaus* by separating their approach decisively from Derrida's. They separate their book, which they describe as rhizomatic—modeled on crabgrasses and irises, where every root can become a stem and every stem a root—from two different figures of the book as root. The first rejected figure of the book as root is the figure of a book as one root that divides into two and then four, branching into a tree (Deleuze and Guattari [1980] 1987, 5). This is a fine figure for a system in which there is a central signified and a limited amount of play about and around this one fixed root. Like the game of tetherball. But it is the second, rejected figure of the book as root which recalls Derrida.

> This time, the principal root has aborted, or its tip has been destroyed; an immediate, indefinite multiplicity of roots grafts onto it and undergoes a flourishing development. . . . The world has lost its pivot; the subject can no longer even dichotomize, but accedes to a higher unity of ambivalence or overdermination, in an always supplementary dimension to that of its object. (Deleuze and Guattari [1980] 1987, 5–6)

This is a fine figure for the absence of a central signified that "extends the domain and the play of signification infinitely" (Derrida [1967b] 1978a, 280). My own attempt to show that Derrida is unable to find room for the primary sense of repetition is one way of showing why Deleuze and Guattari find it necessary to move beyond this figure of the book to their favorite "vegetal model of thought: the rhizome in opposition to the tree, a rhizome-thought instead of an arborescent-thought" (Deleuze [1968] 1994, xvii). They will even oppose an arborescent-thought that begins, like Derrida's, from the *absence* of a principal root.

But there is, finally, a third way to interpret différance, not economically and not noneconomically, but rather as a placeholder for what may come. We are told *différance* remains a metaphysical name and that what it purports to name is simply and literally unnamable, but Derrida assures us that if we admit this without nostalgia but rather with a certain laughter and dance, then we may see something he calls "Heideggerian *hope*" (Derrida [1972b] 1982, 27), "the yet unnamable glimmer beyond the closure" of metaphysics (Derrida [1967a] 1976, 14). The glimmer of the other of calculation, or quite simply, of the other (see Caputo 1997, 17). This is the other that has entered Derrida's writings from the 1990s on, the messianic "structure of experience" (Derrida [1993] 1994, 168), a messianic structure without a messiah, a messianic structure that forms the desert beneath or beyond Abraham's desert, what Derrida can call a "desert in a desert" (Derrida and Vattimo1998, 19).

> Each time I open my mouth, I am promising something. When I speak to you, I am telling you that I promise to tell you something, to tell you the truth. Even if I lie, the condition of my lie is that I promise to tell you the truth. So the promise is not just one speech act among others; every speech act is fundamentally a promise. This universal structure of the promise, of the expectation for the future, for the coming, and the fact that this expectation of the coming has to do with justice—that is what I call the messianic structure. (Caputo 1997, 22–23)

Iterability's been at it, again, making possible the messianic structure of experience but also, and at the same time, ruining the possibility of any particular messiah ever coming. This messianic structure of experience repeats in large scale the structure of iterability which I initially applied to the use of words. It does not manage to break through the frame of representation, but characterizes one of its features, what Derrida can call its necessarily "despairing" messianic structure (Derrida [1993] 1994, 169).

Derrida invokes life in the desert, but not the way it is invoked by Deleuze and Guattari. In their nomadology, they distinguish two ways of being on the move, two unsedentary forms of life in the desert: the life of the migrant and the life of the nomad. The migrant goes from point to point, from oasis to oasis. There are lines and points, but the points are primary. Nomads too have points, where the yaks spend the winter, where they spend the summer, where we move the sheep during lambing time, and

so on. But the points are subordinated to the lines they draw. For nomads, the

> water point is reached only to be left behind; every point is a relay and exists on
> only as a relay. A path is always between two points, but the in-between has
> taken on all the consistency and enjoys both an autonomy and a direction of its
> own. The life of the nomad is intermezzo. The nomad is not at all the same as
> the migrant; for the migrant goes principally from one point to another, even
> if the second point is uncertain, unforeseen, or not well localized. But the
> nomad goes from point to point only as a consequence and as a factual
> necessity; in principle, points for him are relays along a trajectory. (Deleuze
> and Guattari [1980] 1987, 380)

Derrida's desert in a desert, awaiting a messiah who cannot come, is neither
nomadic nor migratory. It is the life of the Flying Dutchman, Vanderdecken,
plying the seas, longing for a home that will never come. Not a nomad. Not
even a migrant. Only a sedentary soul banished from home. Oedipus wandering in exile.

Iterability broaches and breaches both the fine-grained linguistic action
and the large-grained messianic trajectory of experience. But neither iterability nor even his once favorite inaudible "a" will help Derrida break
through the frame of representation. He has discovered the paradoxical
characteristics of life within the frame of representation, but he has not
broken through to the other side, to the swarms of intensities. Because he is
unable to say Yes, he has not broken through.

Derrida is unable to say Yes, because he thinks Yes must always have a
point. It must always be directed at something *to which* it says Yes. Thus
Derrida insists that each Yes is already doubled: "The 'first' is already,
always, a confirmation: *yes, yes, a yes* which goes from *yes to yes* or which comes
from *yes to yes*" (Derrida 1988b, 126). But what must be repeated must also
be scarred by what it hopes to avoid; that is the lesson of iterability; that is
the lesson of secondary repetition. So it is hardly surprising to find Derrida
writing: "This repetition, which figures the condition of an opening of the
yes, menaces it as well: mechanical repetition, mimeticism, therefore forgetting, simulacrum, fiction, fable. Between the two repetitions [of *yes*], there
is a cut and a contamination, simultaneously" (131). It is this "fatal necessity
of a *contamination*" which makes it impossible for Derrida to say Yes (Derrida

1987c, 10). But the contamination is not necessary, unless we cannot escape the frame of representation. And I shall now try to show how to break on through (to the other side).

Break On Through

We think our inability authentically to mean exactly one thing, to perform exactly one act, is the source of our cares; so we dream of perfectly filled intentions. But would we succeed, we would fail. And there is no escape; we must await a messiah who cannot come. Derrida's philosophy, like Schopenhauer's before him, is a pessimistic philosophy of inevitable failure. It is, indeed, brightened by smiles, but these are the smiles of Estragon, wry smiles, curled by empty repetition (see Derrida [1980] 1987b, 99, 243–44). Smiles curled by an awareness of our futile situation. They do not, like recreational lying, ride laughing lines of escape, lines of flight. They do not break on through (to the other side).

This tragic dimension of Derrida's philosophy shows up most clearly in the "Envois" of *The Post Card*: a series of postcards sent by one lover to another. In an early postcard, we read:

> *5 June* 1977
>
> I would like to write you so simply, so simply, so simply. Without having anything ever catch the eye, excepting yours alone, and what is more while erasing all the traits, even the most inapparent ones, the ones that mark the tone, or the belonging to a genre (the letter for example, or the post card), so that above all the language remains self-evidently secret, as if it were being invented at every step, and as if it were burning immediately, as soon as any third party would set eyes on it (speaking of which, when will you agree that we effectively burn all this ourselves?). It is somewhat in order to "banalize" the cipher of the unique tragedy that I prefer cards, one hundred cards or reproductions in the same envelope, rather than a single "true" letter. While writing "true" letter, I remembered the first (one) coming of (from) you, which said exactly this: "I would have liked to answer right away; but speaking of 'true letters,' you forbade me to write any." I am sending you Plato and Socrates again. (Derrida [1980] 1987b, 11)

The possibility of expressing one's love to one person and one person only is here figured as the possibility of sealing a letter, keeping the eyes of others out. But the iterability of every mark makes this impossible; because as the author of these postcards insists, "letters are always post cards" (Derrida [1980] 1987b, 79).

Whenever I say "I love you," I am using a form of words slurred each Saturday into the alcohol mouths of girls without last names. Do I want them between us? In bed with us? Nor is it just drunken couples I must share my love with; also hiding in my bed is the other love of my life: fresh, hot, white pizza. Whispering sweet love, the bed crumbs full of pizza. So one dreams of saying it so simply, so simply, so simply that it would not be repeatable. One dreams of words that burn to ashes as we use them. But it will never work. There will always be ashes, or I will never have said anything. For the ashes that remain are the work of iterability. They are the other meanings that, as I argued, cannot be subtracted from our assertions without eliminating meaning altogether. And since it is a matter of love, there is an urgency and a poignancy to these postcards that is missing from most of Derrida's writings. Here, above all, one cannot mistake the Schopenhauerian inclination of his thinking.

Why doesn't Derrida realize that in the end it is not so horrible to have pizza in bed with your lover? The pure goal of being with your lover, authentically and absolutely alone, projects an ideal coupling on the cold steel tables of an operating theater. I am more drawn along the line Emmanuel Ax extended in this remark on Yo-Yo Ma: "If he says that Bach, ice-skating, pizza and falling in love with love are related to each other, he means it, and believe me, he'll end up convincing you of it" (Saltzman 1997, 79). Don't clear the couch. Love in the heaps of what we love, old sweaters, favorite books, misplaced pens, dictionaries. Pile it in. Pile it all disorganized in. This is love not surgery. It is love. But Derrida cannot say Yes.

Derrida is connected to Schopenhauer by meaning, by wanting to say, hence by desire. With some rare exceptions, European philosophy has always construed desire as a lack, a painful lack. Plato tells us that when we desire something we must lack it, and that this lack is painful. What we desire, when we desire, is to stop the desire. Pleasure, on this account, is an interruption in the painful endurance of desire (see Schopenhauer [1819] 1969, vol. 1, §57). But the pain will return just as surely as thirst and hunger. If only we could escape desire altogether. The author of the postcards even considers suicide but discovers that act, too, ruined by iterability, by the ashes remaining behind, for there are always ashes (see Derrida [1980] 1987b, 196).

Derrida plays the blues of desire in the key of meaning, of wanting to say. He returns desire and intention to the dehydrated concept of intentional meaning. Or we could say: He returns the "t" to intension. Derrida insists that meaning something is wanting to say, a painfully empty intention seeking completion. So the desire continues to live. Were it completely satisfied, the meaning, the wanting to say, the lack, would disappear. Die. So desire too broaches and breaches linguistic action. The lack at the heart of Derrida's philosophy is desire's lack. This is what makes his philosophy as pessimistic as Schopenhauer's. It doesn't look pessimistic because of the importance of play, but Derrida's play comes from no Yes but only from his particular kind of double negation: Desire (wanting to say) is the first negation, a lack wanting to be filled; the second negation was to have been the filling of that lack. But a double negation is an imitation Yes, and Derrida knows this better than anyone. He taught us all that double negations deliver ersatz affirmations. What broaches breaches. There is a "power of death in the heart of living speech: a power all the more redoubtable because it opens as much as it threatens the possibility of the spoken word" (Derrida [1967a] 1976, 141).

The failure of double negation to find its way to affirmation is the source of what there is of play in Derrida's thought. It extends "the domain and play of signification infinitely" (Derrida [1967b] 1978a, 280). Secondary repetition, iterability, desire itself—all have us trapped in the pain of desire. Is there any way out? Yes. Primary repetition. Yes.

It is not that Deleuze rejects the Derridean discoveries, it is only that he rejects their fatality. There is a problem that iterability raises that I have not yet mentioned: If the domain of signification is extended to infinity, how do we manage to communicate even as well as we do. Derrida's answer is power, or the police (Derrida 1988a, 105). Deleuze and Guattari figure this combination of *both* the infinite play of significances *and* the (subjectivating) power that stabilizes that play, as "a face: the *white wall/black hole* system" (Deleuze and Guattari [1980] 1987, 167). The white wall is the plane where the signifiers play. The black holes police the play. Without the black holes, our every statement would be ineradicably "indeterminate" (167). So far Deleuze and Derrida are together. They separate only over the possibility of breaking through the frame of representation, breaking through the white wall / black hole system. But this is not a little difference. It is difference in-itself.

> Difference is light, aerial and affirmative. To affirm is not to bear but, on the contrary, to discharge and to lighten. It is no longer the negative which produces a phantom of affirmation like an ersatz, but rather a No which results from affirmation, Negation is an epiphenomenon. (Deleuze [1968] 1994, 54)

Difference is affirmative. Saying Yes in both directions. All directions. In Deleuze's philosophy, as we saw, an ersatz negation can be the result of double affirmation, not a No, a swerve. Once again I am walking along railroad tracks. It is awkward. But Yes, I want to walk this direction. And Yes, I want to walk along this awkward track. So I swerve, lope, around the irregularities. I want the view intensified; I want the view from my garden, here. So I plant some bushes, blocking some of the view to intensify the power of the looming mountain. To preserve a friendship, growing deeper, in increasingly awkward circumstances, they swerve from sex, becoming cosmos otherwise (Deleuze and Guattari [1980] 1987, 342–46). Double affirmation delivers negations as epiphenomena.

Derrida's problem was with desire. Thinking of desire for an object or a person, we construe desire in negative terms, as a lack. The problem is with meaning. Thinking of meaning an object by a word, we construe meaning in negative terms, as a lack: as a vessel desiring satisfaction, wanting to be filled with meaning. And then the discovery that these two fillings, of desire and of meaning, cannot be accomplished drapes our lives in black, relieved, if at all, only by Estragon's smile. But it need not be. If we consider desire and meaning as bridges between subjects and objects, we will never escape (Deleuze and Parnet [1977] 1987, 89). But perhaps the identities of all objects and all subjects are, as Deleuze puts it, "only simulated, produced as an optical 'effect' by the more profound game of difference and repetition" (Deleuze [1968] 1994, xix). This more profound game is precisely the swarming intensities, the primary repetition, which provided the only positive explanation for secondary repetition, the very same secondary repetition that is now causing such existential pain. We are all tied up in knots. The knots of our concepts. Representational knots. Untie them. How? Sensually. Caressing sensual singularities.

We know what we have to do; we have to loosen up, disorganize our thoughts, we have to lose our selves, not in god or Nietzsche's early primordial unity; we have to disorganize our thinking and our living so that we can ride the lines that representation has tied in knots. We have to die, not the biological death, but the other death, the good death. Deleuze:

> The other death, however, the other face or aspect of death, refers to the state of free differences when they are no longer subject to the form imposed upon them by an I or an ego, when they assume a shape which excludes *my* own coherence no less than that of any identity whatsoever. (Deleuze [1968] 1994, 113)

By releasing desire from the four iron collars of representation, desire is released from ruination, released from the ruination of having *something* I desire, *something* I want to say. That is what brought the whole tragic story of secondary repetition down on our necks. But what does desire become, thus freed from the idea of a goal, a point? What is pointless desiring? Deleuze, speaking with Parnet, said:

> Desire is therefore not internal to a subject, any more than it tends toward an object: it is strictly immanent to a plane which it does not pre-exist, to a plane which must be constructed, where particles are emitted and fluxes combine. . . . Far from presupposing a subject, desire cannot be attained except at the point where someone is deprived of the power of saying "I". Far from directing itself toward an object, desire can only be reached at the point where someone no longer searches for or grasps an object any more than he grasps himself as a subject. (Deleuze and Parnet [1977] 1987, 89)

To break through the frame of representation, to untie the knots we have gotten in to, we must desire without an object. These desires will be pointless, but they will be pointless in a positive sense. Beyond one and many. Their pointlessness will not consist in their not having a point, nor will it consist in their having many points, as if we were some sort of existential one-man band. Rather, desire's pointlessness will consist in delirious swarms of points. These are the same swarms of intensities which, speaking of the primary, subrepresentational sense of repetition, I have already described as neither one, nor many, but a multiplicity (Deleuze and Guattari [1980] 1987, 245). Good pointlessness, good death, and good repetition were made for each other. But how do we release desire from the iron collars of conceptual representation?

It cannot be done alone. It takes at least two—perhaps not two persons—but it takes two (Deleuze and Guattari [1980] 1987, 243–44). And it must be beautiful. We begin to break on through by contagion, catching it, by touch, from the beauteous particles emitted by something or somebody else, at first slowly, repetitively, breathing beauteous particles deep inside our bodies, particles which take over our organs and cells, disorganizing them, exhaling more joyous particles, becoming-imperceptible as self and as other, camouflaged not by representing something we are not, but because we are surrounded by swarms of beauteous particles (280). Beauty. Although Deleuze and Guattari rarely mention beauty, they do remark, in the first section of *A Thousand Plateaus*, that "nothing is beautiful or loving or political aside from underground stems and aerial roots, adventitious

Figure 4-3. Yayoi Kusama. *Infinity Mirrored Room (Fireflies on the Water)*. 2000. 450.0cm × 450.0cm × 320.0cm. Mixed media. © Yayoi Kusama.

growths and rhizomes" (15). More typically, however, they will speak of the anomalous, and they warn us not to treat the anomalous as what is "outside rules or goes against rules," but rather as designating "the unequal, the coarse, the rough, the cutting edge of deterritorialization" (244). Not simply outside rules, because the outside of rules remains in the grip of the rules, so that it is not really outside, at all.[27] The anomalous is neither clearly within nor clearly without our conceptual categories, and this brings it very close to what Kant defines as free beauty (*pulchritudo vaga*), the wild or untamed play of sensations, untamed by this concept or that, eluding the frame of representation, extending play to infinity (Kant [1790] 1987, §16). Not the infinity of the sublime, infinity up. Not the infinity of dread, infinity down. This is the infinity of joy, infinity out, horizontal, looking out over the salty sea, as far as eyes can see. It needn't be a work of art, but it must be pointless, and it must be beautiful. In its pointlessness, beauty will recover its autonomy, but this time, not by negation (see Deleuze and Guattari [1980] 1987, 347). This time, beauty's autonomy will derive not from its *lack* of connection, but from myriad lines of affirmation, a multiplicity of lines connecting it from here to everywhere, so to no place in particular. That is its autonomy.

Consider a graphic model of a work of art. Start with graph paper. Each of the intersecting lines can be imagined pulling against each other, so putting *tension* on each intersection along two dimensions, x and y. A three-dimensional graph is a space of lines pulling their intersections along three dimensions, a twenty-dimensional graph along twenty dimensions. And an n-dimensional graph is a space of lines putting tension on each intersection along an indeterminate multiplicity of dimensions.[28] This last is a maximally beautiful, maximally intense work of art. It is dense with tension, with lines pulling it in myriad ways, some formal, some political, some pretty, some cute, some pornographic, some aching, some loving, and so on. But it is not as if this were a huge addition that would still leave us with desire as a sum of various lacks, and so it would leave us marooned on an island of despair with Schopenhauer and Derrida. These n-dimensions are not "striated in every direction" (Deleuze and Guattari [1980] 1987, 489). These n-dimensions are neither one nor many. They are a subrepresentational multiplicity. Primary repetition.

This graphic model of a work of art is also a model of a maximally beautiful, maximally intense life. And it allegorizes *within* the sensible, the subrepresentational swarms *by which* the sensible is given (Deleuze [1968] 1994, 56–57). Thus intensity within experience is allegorically connected to the swarms of differences on the other side of representation. The beauty of the anomalous person or thing with whom we break on through the frame of representation will be a more modest version of the same idea, not yet, however, an *n*-dimensional creature or creation. The anomalous will be coarse and rough, because it is not a perfect instance of any type. It is this very coarseness and unpredictability that give the anomalous the power to materialize us beyond identity (see Nancy [2002] 2007). Becoming beautiful. The anomalous is not merely pretty, but attractive, rough, and edgy—the surprising sexual energy of the apparently shy and quiet, the surprising intellectual power of the guy or the girl in leather, something that places the anomalous on the edge, the border line. Something that draws us out, disorganizing our thoughts, lives. Something with which we can form undulating lines of becoming. Racing beyond speed, because beyond the representational mile markers that we left behind when desire became pointless.

The anomalous can be a person, but it needn't be a person. It can be a work of art, a scientific problem, a book, the weather some afternoon, the salty taste of the sea, but in each case it is the roughness, the coarseness, of the anomalous which gives it the power to draw us out to the border lines of our conceptual representations. Like a sorcerer (Deleuze and Guattari [1980] 1987, 246). Drawn to the border lines of our existence, experiencing the delight of riding a sinuous line, slipping away from the categories we normally live within. And as we follow, contributing directions and lines of our own, the vitality of the anomalous will spread not by reproduction but like a virus, by contagion, by touch (241–42). This is a process of intensification, for we will find ourselves pulled in a multiplicity of ways, becoming an *n*-dimensional graph. Drawn out by the anomalous individual, drawing ourselves out further becoming-imperceptible not by representing what we are not, but by disappearing into an *n*-dimensional swarm of intense relations. The beauty of this assemblage will materialize the Kant's formal notion free beauty, playing between the concepts of representation, not within them. "A theater where nothing is fixed, a labyrinth without a thread. (Ariadne has hung herself.)" (56).

Our loves are already like this, and we know it. We all know how ridiculous to say I love you, let me count the ways. And we know, too, how easily we can catch joy from another, like a virus, beginning to move without either one knowing where we are going, but together, and joyful (see Deleuze and Guattari [1980] 1987, 272–73, 278–79). This is what desire can be. Deleuze and Guattari affirm that "becoming is the process of desire," a desire we now know to be pointless, in a positive sense (272). Two bodies caressing, unwrapping themselves, disorganizing themselves, swarming intensities, swarming caresses, seafoam joy. Becoming-beauty, or saying beauty otherwise: *becoming-becoming* (see Deleuze [1968] 1993, 56–57).

From Performing Actions to Actual Performances

Theater as representation. Follow the script. Repeat after me. Secondary repetition, the repetitious repetitions of modern life, casts our lives in the false colors of theatrical lighting (Deleuze [1968] 1994, xix; Deleuze [1969] 1990, 286). When we began, we discovered that money ruins sex and art, not because there are some things you shouldn't sell, but because money is a medium of representation. So deeper than the political and economical problem of money is the problem of representation. The white wall/black hole system. The solution is to break though the frame of representation. But we never believe it. We always think that the solution is to remain within the frame, but to make the performance of our actions authentic. Not just to say "I love you" the way everyone does, but to say it and mean it, really mean it. To mean it. And nothing else. The failed project of Derrida's postcards. But to perform an action of a certain type is to rely on the criteria for being an action of that type, and so there is no escape from acting according to a script, no escape from the threat of inauthenticity. This is where Derrida leaves us: undecidably between authenticity and inauthenticity (Derrida 1991, 45). A Derridean way of finding ourselves beyond authenticity and inauthenticity.

Secondary repetition threatens to inauthenticate our lives. But secondary repetition can also be a Deleuzoid way beyond authenticity and inauthenticity. Taking the walk to our spot, again. Driving past the cows, again. Listening to the slow movement, again. These are ways of discovering the sensual singularities in so-called repetitions. Revealing that the same is not the same; it is different. Only that which differs is alike. Repetition is a technique for finding the anomalous where it is least expected. In the familiar paths of our lives. Take them again. Once more. Another round. Each thing, anomalous.

Releasing our desires from their objects and our selves from their identities, we can experience the seafoam joy of becoming-becoming. Seafoam is the sea becoming foam, not a straight line anywhere, all curves. Curves of bubbles bigger and smaller, whole cities of bubbles conjugating and reconjugating, assembling and reassembling. "It is as if the ground rose to the surface, without ceasing to be ground" (Deleuze [1968] 1994, 28). It is as if the subrepresentational ground rose to the surface of representation without ceasing to be subrepresentational. Sea becoming foam. Becoming becoming. Seafoam joy.

There is another theater. There is another repetition. The theater of representation breathes the musty interior air of iterability. Secondary repetition. But the theater of repetition breathes fresh salty sea air. Primary repetition.

> The theater of repetition is opposed to the theater of representation just as movement is opposed to the concept and to representation which refers it back to the concept. In the theater of repetition, we experience pure forces, dynamic lines in space which act without intermediary upon the spirit, and link it directly with nature and history, with a language which speaks before words, with gestures which develop before organized bodies, with masks before faces, with specters and phantoms before characters—the whole apparatus of repetition as a "terrible power." (Deleuze [1968] 1994, 10)

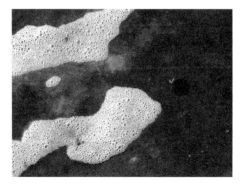

Figure 4-4. Seafoam. Photo by Jessica Morgan.

Actual performances are not the performances of actions because they are an aspect not of the theater of representation but the theater of repetition. Actual performances will be theatrical; yes, there may be makeup, perfume, and rented clothes, but they will not aim at a model or goal, and so they will be beyond inauthenticity no less than they are beyond authenticity. "To break through language in order to touch life" (Artaud [1938] 1968, 13). Breaking through to the other side of representation.

Remember when we played with blocks, we could aim at a model, give our actions a point: This, we told our friends proudly, is the Titanic. Or we could just play, allowing our desires to grow, one block here, another there; let's put a row over here; and the pointless play continues without aiming at a model. Derrida's play is of the first sort. He divides the plane of existence like a board game, and plays continually, never winning through to Yes, never losing it all in No. This was inevitable. According to Derrida, to really win, one would have to mean to throw a seven, and nothing else at all. It would require massive negation. One would have to subtract from the meaning of one's intentional action, every possibility but one: seven. But this is precisely what iterability, secondary repetition, makes impossible. So Derrida tells us that "we must conceive a play in which whoever loses wins, and in which one loses and wins on every turn" (Derrida [1972b] 1982, 20). This is the fate of those who cannot break through from secondary to primary repetition.

Deleuze imagines another game, a game more like just playing with blocks, a divine game in which at every roll of the dice "the whole of chance is affirmed in a necessarily winning throw" (Deleuze [1968] 1994, 283). Complete affirmation. However the blocks are arranged, we play on from there. This divine game is a figure for Deleuze's Yes, a Yes as complete as it is, because it derives from a desire that is as pointless as it is, because it is a beautiful becoming. "That the universe has no purpose, that it has no end to hope for any more than it has causes to be known, this is the certainty necessary to play well" (Deleuze [1962] 1983, 27). But to affirm chance in this way is to play a divine game not a human game, and when Deleuze asks himself what is the human game closest to this divine game, he replies: "As Rimbaud said: look for H, the work of art" (Deleuze [1968] 1994, 282).[29] There is no other existential or aesthetic problem than that of becoming-becoming. Becoming beautiful (see 293).

The difference between performing actions and an actual performance is the difference between No and Yes. It is the difference between playing a Derridean game you can never win and Deleuzoid game you can never lose. It is the difference between a philosophy trapped in the frame of representation and one that breaks on through (to the other side). It is the difference between Derrida's No, which reeks of the thick smell of Schopenhauer, and Deleuze's Yes, blowing in, fresh and salty, off Nietzsche's new seas. An actual performance. Seafoam joy. Yes.

derrida is the reason wittgenstein fails
deleuze is the reason derrida is only a messenger

Keep Everything in Sight at the Same Time

Tender Buttons.

—GERTRUDE STEIN

Words are like tender buttons. They have official uses, well-known uses. They are like mother's milk to us. Are my male nipples, barely rising from my flat chest, therefore useless? Atavistic remnants of some Aristophanic hermaphroditism? We know better. Many uses. Many pleasures. Words too. Many uses. Many pleasures. Pleasures and powers that come with the sensuality of their sounds, the mingling of their meanings, the look of their letters. Tender senses textured. Everything in sight at the same time (Deleuze and Guattari [1980] 1987, 35).

Love and death make us all poets. Seeking the power of words, we fold their sounds into their significations. There is always more. By multiplying, intensifying. Linguistic sense sensualized. "Concept responding to concept the way passionate flesh congests, every note a nipple on the breast" (Gass [1976] 1991, 57). Tender words. And the senses discover their sensuality, redeem themselves. Come alive. Again. Everything in sight at the same time. An erotics of sense and sensation. Come becoming. Come. Yes.

in the parched mouths of philosophers
desire becomes want

Desire without Desires

> . . . sexual passion . . . or some other misfortune.
>
> —PLATO, *Republic*

> Once a rhizome has been obstructed, arborified, it's all over, no desire stirs;
> for it is always by a rhizome that desire moves and produces.
>
> —GILLES DELEUZE AND FÉLIX GUATTARI, *A Thousand Plateaus*

The most persistently negative feature of philosophy is the traditional interpretation of desire as a disturbing lack. It is at least as old as Plato, and it lives on in Kant, Mill, Lacan, and Derrida. Despite the work of Deleuze and Guattari, it shows no signs of losing popularity. And Derrida's featuring the force of such expressions as "wanting to say" or "vouloir dire" shows that this conception of desire may structure semantical as well as existential investigations. It is time to articulate, criticize, and replace the traditional picture of desire as lack. In its place I will sketch an affirmative erotics of desire without desires. Start with Plato.

Plato's Legacy: Picturing Desire as a Lack

Plato's discussion of desire brings into view three features of the traditional picture or representation of desire: (a) the negative interpretation of desire as a lack, (b) the interpretation of satisfaction as external to desire, and (c) the transcendent trajectory of desire, which points it in the direction of immortality and eternity.[1]

In Plato's *Symposium*, Agathon offers the idea that when someone desires something, they will probably lack the thing they desire. Socrates immediately insists that this is far more than merely likely. It is necessary. Lacking *x* is part of what desiring *x* consists in. Plato:

> [Socrates:] "At the time he [i.e., Eros] desires and loves something, does he actually have what he desires and loves at that time, or doesn't he?"
>
> [Agathon:] "He doesn't. At least that wouldn't be likely," he said.
>
> "Instead of what's *likely*," said Socrates, "ask yourself whether its *necessary* that this be so: a thing that desires desires something of which it is in need; otherwise, if it were not in need, it would not desire it. I can't tell you, Agathon, how strongly it strikes me that this is necessary. But how about you?"
>
> "I think so too." (200a–b, italics trans.)

It is not hard at all, it is altogether too easy to picture desire as a lack. The very word *want* says *lack*, or rather *need*. Some dictionaries stack this family of words, nicely enough, in the following way: *lack* is a mere absence, but if we add to this lack desire, we will produce *want*, and if we add to want urgency, we will produce *need*, and if we add to need imperative, we will have produced a *requirement*. This is probably more articulated than we need here, even though it rather nicely raises doubts about the sufficiency of the idea of lack to account for the concept of desire. If lack is only necessary, then what do we add to lack to make it a sufficient condition for desire? Not desire, of course. But if not desire, then what?

Our first reflections on what we want fall into Plato's pattern. I want a new bike. If I had a new bike, I couldn't any longer want it. I would have it. Try it with desire. I desire a new bike. Even before we get to deciding whether I could continue desiring it after I possessed it, the sentence itself, *I desire a new bike*, sounds a bit formal, if not perverse. Unlike mere want, which in the sense of need is an almost objective feature of the world, desire is wet. If I say that I desire a new bike, I feel as if I am probably referring to a specific new bike, not the generic new bike that I want. If my heart is set on a specific bike, then I might desire it. And when the bike comes, I will not simply use the bike as if I merely wanted a bike. When the bike comes, I smile at its gleaming bright frame, stroke the hard smooth bars of its frame, gently squeeze the curved grips of the brakes, inhale the acrid sweet smell of new rubber. Such a person would love their bike. They might have desired it. They might still. But we are in the wet beyond want. In the parched mouths of philosophers desire becomes want.

By the time Socrates extracts Agathon's concession that desire is necessarily a lack, readers of the *Symposium* will already have met the negative picture of desire in the remarkable story Plato puts into the mouth of Aristophanes. I cannot resist telling it.[2] For according to Plato's Aristophanes, people were originally spherical with four arms, four legs, two heads, and two sets of genitalia representing all the combinatorial possibilities of male and female (189e). These remarkable creatures were able to walk around upright as we do, although on four legs. In order to move quickly they had developed a most impressive form of locomotion; the creature was a kind of eight-spoked cartwheel by means of which it was able to pick up amazing speed. So fast and so powerfully did they move, that they soon began to roll up Mount Olympus making an assault on the gods. To stop all this feverish behavior, Zeus cut the creatures in half in order both to slow them down and, at one stroke, double the number of creatures who could serve the gods (190d). After they were cut, Apollo turned our heads around to face the site of the wound and pulled the remaining skin together over the wound at the navel (190e). A bit later, noticing how unhappy they were, Zeus moved their genitals around to the side of the cut so that they could enjoy erotic pleasure copulating within each other and not only on the ground, "like cicadas" (191c). Even here, in this amusing fable, we see a genitalized approach to erotic delight.

As with so many other ecological interventions, Zeus's punitive intervention produced unintended consequences. In particular it produced erotic desire, which had not existed before. Aristophanes: "Since their natural form had been cut in two, each one longed for its own other half, and so they would throw their arms about each other, weaving themselves together, wanting to grow together" (191a). Moreover, since Zeus punished us by taking something away, the picture of desire or love thus invented will naturally be construed in terms of a lack, the lack of an original wholeness or integrity. Love, therefore, "is the name for our pursuit of wholeness, for our desire to be complete" (192e).

Horn in on almost any barroom conversation about love and you will hear Plato's Aristophanes. Looking for my soul mate, the one from whom I was severed. He makes me feel so complete; he's my other half. The familiar worry about whether love follows the magnetic law that opposites attract or the avian law that birds of a feather flock together finds its origin in this Aristophanic situation, because on that account, each lover seeks a lover that is at once same and different, both their original and their opposite number. Even the colloquial expression "my other half" and the ironic "my better half"—even these casual expressions were invented by Plato's Aristophanes. And in this story we can already see the role played by the picture of the self as having an identity, for it is the identity of the original whole that both defines and directs desire. Desire is a specific lack in pursuit of a specific wholeness. In your arms I am, once again, home. Whole. It would be idyllic, if it weren't for the smell of death.

Given the idyllic way the Aristophanic story has entered our minds, it is striking that in the original story desire is *punishment*. Those barroom conversations don't frequently talk about punishment. They don't frequently talk about how horrible it is to be in love. More typically it is the moon-faced one in love whom everyone is happy for, even if the loved one is absent. So it is surprising to hear desire spoken of as the result of punishment, to hear desire spoken of as something we would rather be without, dreaming of a life without the punishment of desire. It is not that we cannot imagine situations in which desire would be painful, when we would indeed feel punished by desire. It is just that only a particularly narrow view of desire would make those painful experiences the central or paradigmatic cases of desire. And Plato's does just that.

Why would Aristophanes want a life without desire? Perhaps it is squeamishness or timidity. Desire can cause pain, so a life without desire is a life without that source of pain. A life without desire. What is that? Long stretches of listlessness? Perhaps it is something like what Heidegger refers to as a pallid lack of mood. "The pallid lack of mood—indifference—which is addicted to nothing and has no urge for anything, and which abandons itself to whatever the day may bring" (Heidegger 1962, 345). However, Heidegger speaks of this moodlessness not as an idyllic dream, but as a "burden," a burden he colors "gray" (134, 345). And so since the picture of desire as lack projects the dream of a life without any desires at all, it comes to seem less and less idyllic, more and more corpsed.

SATISFACTION

In Plato's Aristophanic story, we express our longing for wholeness as desire, as love. Were we not broken, punished, there would be no desire, and were we to find and bond with our other half, we would have overcome punishment, overcome desire, overcome love. This is one of the puzzling consequences of the traditional picture of desire as lack. What desire as lack desires most of all is death. Its own death. It is a state we call satisfaction. Desires are satisfied by filling a lack, and so the traditional picture of satisfaction is not separate from the traditional picture of desire as lack. Satisfaction is the death of desire as lack. We might have thought of this in terms of filling a glass with water. The empty glass is the desire. The filled glass is the satisfied desire. When the glass is filled the glass is still there, filled. But if desire is construed as an absence, then it is like the empty space in the glass that is gone when the glass is filled. So when a desire is satisfied, the desire, pictured as a lack, has completely disappeared. Thus there is a sense in which desire can never be satisfied, for when it is satisfied, it does not exist any more either to be satisfied or not to be satisfied. If Plato's Aristophanes wants to figure desire as punishment, then like punishment, desire cannot be satisfied. It can only stop. Wittgenstein might have diagnosed this as a matter of crossed pictures; we say desire is a lack and then picture it both as an absence and also as a container of an absence and therefore miss the odd result that if desire is a lack, desire cannot be satisfied

Plato's picture of desire as a lack has the paradoxical consequence that lovers cannot embrace. While they are apart, lacking each other, they can desire or love one another. But when they are embracing and the lack has been overcome, their desire, their love must vanish. Lovers can't embrace. And a good thing too, shouts the Aristophanic chorus; love itself was only punishment.

Plato's Socrates is concerned to make it possible for lovers to embrace, to make it possible to have a desire and to satisfy a desire at one and the same time.[3] The trick will be to keep the desire, the lack, present even after it has been satisfied. But the way he has this set up, desire is a lack and satisfaction is the filling of that lack; the way he has this set up, just about his only two moves are these: Either to deny that satisfaction completely fills the lack, in which case the satisfaction is no satisfaction (Lacan), or, alternatively, to permit the satisfaction to be a full satisfaction but to invent a new desire to take the place of the old one, in this way preserving both the satisfaction and new desire just barely distinguishable from the first one that disappeared into its satisfaction. Plato takes the second option, implementing it as follows. He places our more or less continually flowing experience on an existential egg slicer and slices it into thin temporal slices.

Each slice will have the minimal temporal extension necessary to experience a sensation or a thought. This will not be nothing, and the glories of the calculus will incline us, today, to think of these as infinitesimal slices of Chronological time defined by some more or less familiar use of nineteenth-century mathematics. Egg slicer in hand, Plato's Socrates can observe that since we live in the infinitesimal present, the future is always absent, so that when lovers embrace, their love can always continue; because what they lack is not each other, there and then, but each other *in the future*. Plato's Socrates therefore advises Agathon:

> "Whenever you say, *I desire what I already have*, ask yourself whether you don't mean this: *I want the things I have now to be mine in the future as well*." (200d)

Figure 6-1. Egg slicer. Innerhofer Photodes–Stockfood Munich.

And Apollodorus who is reciting the *Symposium*, reciting what he was told by Aristodemus, who taught him the story in the first place, Apollodorus tells us, for once in his own voice:

> According to Aristodemus, Agathon said he would. (200d)

This is a key point in the defense of the picture of desire as lack, for it attempts to make it possible for lovers to embrace in love. And since it is a key point, it is striking that Plato hedges Agathon's agreement here, almost as if Plato were marking this point in particular as weak, a place to return to later and think over again.

The point about the future is indeed oddly artificial. As I am enjoying the hot fresh pizza, it turns out that I do not have one desire for pizza. I have a very large number of sequentially ordered desires for pizza. As I bite into the first slice at time t, my desire for pizza-at-t will have disappeared, leaving me with pizza in my mouth. Plato's move is to say that while my desire for pizza-at-t has died, another desire is at that very moment born to take its place, the desire for pizza-at- $t + 1$. Like a relay race, as one desire dies away, another almost identical desire begins.

Two questions remain. First what does this do to the number of my desires? Do I have one desire for pizza, or do I have however many momentary desires it takes to move from the first mouthful to the last? Strictly speaking, I will have a long line of nonidentical but very similar desires. They are all desires for pizza, or even this pizza at different times. Which times? It is one sign that philosophy is building structures of air that we don't have any access to these structures, and we have no idea how many of these desires it takes to cover one pizza dinner (see Wittgenstein [1953] 1976, §118), We were making it all up just to save the picture of desire as lack. Math will incline us to the thought that there will be an infinity of desires within any finite segment of enjoyable pizza eating, but that sounds like too many. All those however many infinitesimal desires are not a metaphysical discovery, but rather the beginning of a reductio of the Platonic picture. The egg sliced desires are there for only one purpose, to fix problems like that of continuing to desire pizza while you are eating it, problems like that of how to make it possible to embrace your heart's desire. It's a singularly artificial solution and a sure sign that we need to start afresh on the subject of desire, but does it even work in its own terms?

The second question. Does this postulated series of momentary desires even do what it was meant to do, namely make the enjoyment of pizza or our heart's desire possible? In a certain sense it does not, for what it guarantees is that at any time t I will be *dissatisfied* with my present situation, punished by the desire for pizza at $t + 1$. Rather than making satisfaction possible, it seems to make dissatisfaction inevitable. Rather than escaping Zeus's punishment, the multiplication of desires makes that punishment inescapable. Before this multiplication Aristophanes could at least hold out the hope, if it is not fear, that with a little bit of luck you could find and unite with your other half, overcoming desire, overcoming love, overcoming punishment. On the modified multiplied series of desires even this is no longer even possible. Whenever you have your mouth around the hot salty pizza, you are pained by the desire to have your mouth around the same piece of pizza in the next moment. This is bad enough. But if we remember that human experience, unless Aionic, is Chronologically structured, it becomes clear that in every present moment the pain of desire for the future will be upon us. This is a fundamentally nihilistic result. Pictured as lack, desire desires more than anything else its own death, and now it begins to look as if only with our actual death in Chronological time will desire achieve its end. The death of desire. Death, our only escape from Zeus's punishment. When the king of terrors becomes our only hope, things have become bleak indeed. And it sounded so idyllic. Apart from the smell.

DIOTIMA'S ASCENT

As Plato tells the story, Socrates is shown the way out of this nihilistic result by Diotima, a woman from Mantinea. Diotima adds to Socrates' account of the tantalizing momentary satisfaction of desire that when we desire something, what we want is not simply to possess what we currently lack, but to possess only the *good* we lack, not the bad (205e). And furthermore to possess this good *forever*. In Diotima's words: "Everyone wants to have good things forever and ever" (205a). It is a strong claim. If you enjoy the warm endings of long, slow, delicious meals or something, then endless heaps of even delicious food might seem a bit too quantitative to capture what we really desire, but grant that we want to possess good things forever. Diotima's claim won't stop there, for her claim is that we want to possess something good *forever*, and were we to die, we would only possess it until we were parted from it at death. Diotima draws this conclusion for an unusually struggling Socrates: If what we agreed earlier was right, that love wants to possess the good forever, then "it follows from our argument that Love must desire immortality" (207a). It's a rather amazing conclusion: Whatever we want, we also want immortality. And you thought you were just hungry.

Some philosophers may think this is where the action is. Diotima takes herself to have discovered that one presupposition of simply wanting lunch is that we desire a metaphysical miracle. I rather think it reveals the vermilion swamp from which this philosophy grows. Even in its own terms, it fails. Plato's Aristophanes and indeed Diotima herself seem to want to escape from desire forever, but endless pizza and immortality only ensure that we will always be able to silence our momentary little desire for pizza-at-*t*. Borrowing an image from Plato's *Gorgias*, we could consider ourselves immortal leaky containers that we kept full by pouring water in the top at precisely the rate it was dribbling out the bottom. If all Diotima can give us is endless pizza and endless Chronological time, she will not yet have given Aristophanes what he really wanted: to escape the pain of desire, once and for all.

Nevertheless, as Diotima explains how to achieve immortality, she brushes by an idea that gives my own view an intimate connection to the Platonic picture otherwise so foreign. Let's see. According to Diotima, the way to immortality is by reproduction, by "giving birth in beauty whether in body or soul," that is what desire really desires (206b). She is banking on an analogy with the sense in which progeny give parents immortality, but it's a little hard to follow.

As Diotima uses the word, pregnant seems to mean able or eager to create or reproduce, so those who are "pregnant in body" will find themselves, on reaching sexual maturity, yearning for carnal reproduction (208e). She also notices that "whenever pregnant animals or persons draw near to beauty, they become gentle and joyfully disposed and give birth and reproduce, but near ugliness they are foulfaced and draw back in pain," and so she tells us, more than once, that reproduction can only happen with what is beautiful, not with what is ugly (206c–d, 209b). The same thing applies to those who are "pregnant in soul": When they are joined with beauty, they produce the immortal works of the soul: "wisdom and the rest of virtue"

(208e–209a). Moreover, when one joins with a more beautiful thing, one achieves a more perfect immortality, and it is this that motivates Diotima's well-known stepwise ascent to the Beautiful "itself by itself with itself" (211b).

Diotima's ascent is by negation. We subtract from the boy we love everything but the *beauty* of his particular inner thighs, and the movement has started. We are on our way to desiring the tender inner thighs of any boy at all, and even beyond, to the inner thighs of girls and bodies in general. And then we subtract the impurities from those corporeal beauties, and move on through beautiful customs and wisdom, until finally we face a sea of objects of all sorts which are the same insofar as they are beautiful, "a great sea of beauty, and, gazing upon this, he [the lover] gives birth to many gloriously beautiful ideas and theories" (210d). And then, suddenly, out of the corner of our eye, we catch sight of something even more wonderful than a beautiful object. Becoming rhapsodic, Diotima continues:

> "First, it always *is* and neither comes to be nor passes away, neither waxes nor wanes. Second, it is not beautiful this way and ugly that way, nor beautiful at one time and ugly at another, nor beautiful in relation to one thing and ugly in relation to another; nor is it beautiful here but ugly there, as it would be if it were beautiful for some people and ugly for others. Nor will the beautiful appear to him in the guise of a face or hands or anything else that belongs to the body. It will not appear to him as one idea or one kind of knowledge. It is not anywhere in another thing, as in an animal, or in earth, or in heaven, or in anything else, but itself by itself with itself, it is always one in form; and all the other beautiful things share in that, in such a way that when those others come to be or pass away, this does not become the least bit smaller or greater nor suffer any change. So when someone rises by these stages, through loving boys correctly, and begins to see this beauty, he has almost grasped his goal. This is what it is to go aright, or be led by another, into the mystery of Love: one goes always upwards, for the sake of this Beauty, starting out from beautiful things and using them like rising stairs." (210e–211b)

Pause for a moment. There's more to come. Consider what we have caught sight of. It is like nothing we have ever seen. It never changes, never becoming other than it already is. All the changing beautiful things are beautiful by sharing in it, and yet when they change, it never changes nor loses any of its beauty. It is not a beautiful anything at all, and yet it is beautiful in a way that surpasses any beautiful thing. This is the place where Diotima seems to brush by a notion of beauty beyond the representation of any beautiful thing. She is on the verge of breaking through representation altogether, and I would join her there. Yes, I would. But she is held back by her sense that beauty itself is pure being, unmixed and unchanging, not becoming. She has caught sight of a still point of the turning world, a still point without which nothing's beauty could ever blossom or fade. She has not found a becoming beyond representation; she found the condition of representing anything becoming. Nevertheless, even in her own terms she is not quite there. Here Diotima concludes her discussion with Socrates (as recited by Apollodorus):

> "But how would it be, in our view," she said, "if someone got to see the Beautiful itself, absolute, pure, unmixed, not polluted by human flesh or colors or any other great nonsense of mortality, but if he could see the divine Beauty itself in its one form? Do you think it would be a poor life for a human being to look there and behold it by that which he ought, and to be with it? Or haven't you remembered," she said, "that in that life alone, when he looks at Beauty in the only way that Beauty can be seen—only then will it become possible for him to give birth not to images of virtue (because he is in touch with no images), but to true virtue (because he is in touch with true Beauty). The love of the gods belongs to anyone who has given birth to true virtue and nourished it, and if any human being could become immortal, it would be he." (211e–212b)

The Beautiful itself. Giving birth in the Beautiful itself, we would achieve immortality, if any human could. We are familiar enough with Plato's maneuverings for this to sound almost familiar, but it still retains a certain strangeness: "color or any other great nonsense of mortality" (211e).

In spite of the myriad ways I must distance myself from Plato and from his approach to desire, it is possible to describe Diotima's ascent in abstract terms I can fully endorse. And I enjoy the encouragement this gives me. According to Diotima, if we permit ourselves to be drawn by beauty, we will be able to escape Chronological time. So phrased, that is exactly what I feel, though my escape route is different. Diotima suggests that the key to escaping Chronological time is to give birth in Beauty itself which will lure us up and out of Chronological time by negation. Against this, I want singular beauties, anomalous individuals, to lure us or seduce us to the sensuality of the senses, disorganizing us, luring us out of Chronological time by addition, becoming-becoming. Uncanny similarities. Separated only by the manner of escape. Plato up through a second No. Myself out along the diagonal. An affirmative line of flight. A sensuous Yes.

Someone might have thought there were only two ways to become a graceful dancer, unaffected and authentic: either to become an ethereal angel or to become a wooden marionette. But beginning as we do, struggling with inauthenticity and contingency, the way up and the way down could only back themselves, by double negation, into a vermilion corner. The way out is not by negating or subtracting anything, at all; it is out along an Aionic diagonal, Yes.

The difficulty with Plato's approach was articulated by Plato himself in his dialogue *Parmenides*. It is a bit slippery, but let's try. If our destination, the top of the Diotimic staircase, is the Beautiful, "itself by itself with itself" (*Symp* 211b), then there is no way for that Beauty to also be what all earthly beautiful things share when they are beautiful (*Parm* 133c–134e). Suppose the young boy toweling off did share in Beauty itself by itself, then the Beauty he shared in could not be Beauty itself by itself, for it would be shared with the young boy. It would be fleshed. Beauty itself by itself cannot be fleshed and still remain itself by itself. And if the boy does not share in Beauty itself by itself, then in Diotima's own terms, the boy is not really beautiful, and there will be no way to support the Diotimic ascent from fleshed beauty to beauty itself by itself. The Diotimic ascent is impossible. This is the failure of the Platonic project. It could be represented as a failure due to the use of double negation to transcend the earthly. If we begin earthly and polluted, first negation, and try to approach the heavenly by subtraction, second negation, we will never do better than an ersatz heaven. We will never be able, fully and completely, to leave the earthly. For that something unearthly is necessary. And all of a sudden one can understand the trajectory of a book such as Kierkegaard's *Philosophical Fragments* in which Johannes Climacus insists that there is no immanent road to the transcendent, no maieutic method of achieving eternal happiness (Kierkegaard 1844b).

One expression of my difference from Plato is his more or less eliding the distinction between beauty and perfection, beauty and ideality. Better authorities than I tell me that Plato can sometimes speak of sensuous beauty

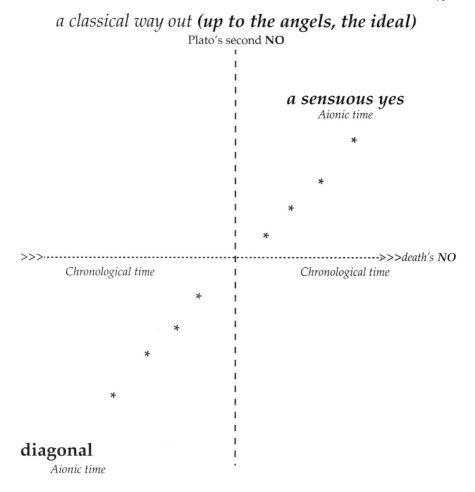

Figure 6-2. Temporal modalities of existence.

(a double lambda kallos) in opposition to the ideals of goodness (*Laws* 727d–e), but that when he does so he doesn't even use the same word that Diotima uses in the ascent passage (a single lambda kalon) (Lawrence 1961a, 544–45). Plato thus keeps perfect beauty separate, sometimes even orthographically separate, from the sensual beauty that is the anomalous irregular beauty with which I will try to break through the plane of representation. Diotima's ascent passage itself, by speaking of beauty pure and absolute and not polluted, projects a notion of perfected beauty and begins the ascent to transcendence. In an imperfect world, perfection must be elsewhere, and if it is elsewhere, then the dilemma just rehearsed is, as Plato's *Parmenides* insists, inevitable.

I have no taste for perfection. Both the beauty of what I characterize as the other side of representation and the beauty of beauteous objects that lure us there are instances of imperfection: the beauty of imperfection. Disorganized and imperfect. We make things beautiful in this sense, a more or less Kantian sense, not by slicing off imperfections but by adding and affirming so that there is no one thing that the beauteous object or life is. By sensualizing our lives we can move beyond representation, not toward the transcendent but toward absolute immanence, not immanence in something or immanence to something, but sheer immanence (Deleuze 1995a, 4). Beyond identity. Indefinite singularities. Not the life of an identifiable representable individual. But an indefinite life. Simply *a* life. "A life is the immanence of immanence, absolute immanence: it is sheer power, utter beatitude" (Deleuze 1995a, 4). Sheer power, utter beatitude, but I am getting ahead of myself. Soon I will articulate the disarticulated goal of an immanent beauty. A way beyond representation without saying No. An affirmative Yes beyond the No's of both conceptual representation and beyond Diotima's attempt to break on through (to the other side) by subtracting pollution, by double negation. Plato's genius is to have sensed that Beauty was beyond representation. His timidity was in presenting this as transcendent rather than as immanent in living life, which he can only construe as the pollutions of color and of flesh (*Symp* 211e–212a). The way to Aionic time, the way to break through (to the other side) is not by negation of what is bad but by affirmation, absolute affirmation. Absolute immanence. "Immanence: A Life . . ." (see Agamben 1996).

The Paradox of Masochism and Its Overcoming

The picture of desire as lack is a very simplified picture of desire. One which, as we have just seen, raises all sorts of difficulties just in its own terms, preeminently those of enjoyment, satisfaction. One of the simplifications that

I have not mentioned is a fairly natural consequence of thinking of desire in terms of punishment. As surprising as it is to be told that Plato's Aristophanes thinks of desire as *punishment*, it is quite familiar to suppose that it makes little or no sense to desire pain. This is the familiar platitude that we like pleasure and dislike pain, and it is a platitude that is consistent with, if it does not actually follow from, the picture of desire as lack. If desire is a painful punishment, then we could not coherently, or sanely, desire pain. Call this the paradox of masochism. The picture of desire as lack can be developed into the idea that where x is an object of your desires, then

    (a) If you lack x, you will feel a kind of pain, and
    (b) If you have x, you will feel a kind of pleasure.

The paradox can then be generated by putting pain in for x, giving us the paradoxical sentences

    (c) If you lack pain, you will feel a kind of pain, and
    (d) If you have pain, you will feel a kind of pleasure.

The plain paradox of masochism, when masochists are in pain, they aren't, and when they aren't, they are.

According to the picture of desire as lack, masochism is impossible. And since evidently masochism does exist, I once thought that it would be possible to generate an argument against the Platonic picture in the following way.

> If we picture desire as lack, then it is not possible to desire pain.
> *But it is possible to desire pain.*
> So: the picture of desire as lack must be false.

I was hoping that the paradox of masochism would raise trouble for the picture of desire as lack in much the way that Russell's paradox raised problems for Frege's attempt to ground arithmetic in a logic of classes. This little argument is valid and sound, but I no longer expect very much from the paradox of masochism because, as Wittgenstein knew, philosophical pictures have many sources and cannot be removed by one little argument, however valid.[4] There are circumstances that seem to force on us the picture of desire as lack—I will mention them soon—and thus there is little chance that the paradox of masochism will do what I once wanted it to do: destroy the picture of desire as lack. Nevertheless, masochism is incompatible with the development of the picture in terms of (a) and (b), above. So if liking pain is a widespread phenomenon, there will be a widespread variety of cases that the picture will capture only with difficulty.

Defenders of the traditional picture will naturally try to accommodate themselves to the possibility of desiring pain by lofting empirical hypotheses that explain away the apparently paradoxical (c) and (d). The crudest response would be to say that those who desire pain are physiologically set up so that what normal people feel as pain, they feel as pleasure. You hear this almost every time someone starts talking about masochism. But there is no reason to believe this except that it saves the picture. So that just begs the question. A more careful accommodation between the picture of desire as lack and the reality of masochism would be to say that when it looks like someone is desiring pain they are really just desiring pleasure but for some reason they require that their pleasure be *delayed by a detour through pain*.

This hypothesis, that those who seem to enjoy pain are actually enjoying pleasure, only delayed, turns out to be a very natural hypothesis. But I don't understand its allure. Some people seem to desire pain, but if desire is a painful lack, that is a paradox. So we say that they are not desiring pain. They are desiring pleasure, delayed. But if they desire the delay and the delay is painful, they are still desiring pain. So the hypothesis of delayed pleasure cannot solve the paradox of masochism. Or if it can it must take another turn, a turn to the idea of desiring something not for what it is in itself but only as a means.

This is an old Athenian spot: We don't want to drink the bitter medicine for itself but only as a means to something else, health. It all goes by so quickly, soon enough we are nodding along saying that we desire the medicine; of course, they tell us, nobody is denying *that*, but we don't really desire *it*, what we really desire is health. And then with barely a thought we say that the same must be true in general whenever it seems that pain is being enjoyed. When it seems that pain is being enjoyed, it isn't. It couldn't be. You can't enjoy pain. What you enjoy is what the pain gives you. Just as in the case of bitter medicine, you don't really desire the bitter taste, you desire health.

It is so hard to know what to say. Do I want the medicine that I voluntarily drink? Or do I not *really* want it but only the health I hope it brings? Why are we so sure of what we really want? It all seems too clean. Wittgenstein would say too smooth, not rough enough. Sometimes it does make sense. Sometimes it does make sense to say that we desire something only as a means. In those cases, when we consider whether, if we could, we would take our health neat, without the bitter medicine, there is no problem. Of course we would take our health neat. In those cases when we thus divide the so-called end from the so-called means, we willingly take the end without the means. And its easy enough to see that this is how things work with bitter medicine. But there is a faded Humean atomization of experience and significance behind all this (Wittgenstein 1986). And anyway it won't work with bitterness, even though it was the analogy between bitterness and pain which brought us to this Athenian spot in the first place.

Medicine is a special case. Outside of medicine there are some bitter things that are enjoyed not only for their causal consequences. There are a number of bitter cordials such as Campari and Suze, which are more popular in France and Italy than in the States. One is even called bitter; its name is Amer Picon. And now it should be obvious that simply because some bitter things like medicine are desired only for their effects, it does not follow that Amer Picon is desired only for its effects. People voluntarily order Amer Picon in lieu of crème de menthe despite the similarities of effect. Even if we don't like bitter medicines, sometimes we enjoy Amer Picon. And why should pain be different from bitterness?

Again we have made things too smooth for ourselves. We have convinced ourselves that what we desire is not the thing we say we desire. We don't desire the fish; what we really desire is what the fish gives us. And now in a kind of hysterical use of the example of bitter medicine, someone will say that there is only one thing we desire. All desire is for pleasure. And once again, all that is solid melts into air. You don't desire the fish or the drink or the hike or wandering in the late summer katydid evening, no. Nobody really desires those things; the only thing anyone can ever really desire is pleasure. Pleasure. It sounds all right, but it is nihilistic. It is nihilistic not only because pleasure, the satisfaction of desire is, once again, desire's death. Existentially, it is a nihilistic story because on this account nothing else matters. Nothing else counts. Only pleasure. All that is solid melts into air. And pleasure is one thing, though it comes in degrees. Pain too. One thing, though it comes in degrees. And what is pain? Unsatisfied desire. Wanting to delay pleasure is wanting the pain of unsatisfied desire. And so we return once again to the paradox of masochism. The detour through delayed pleasure got us nowhere.

Start over. Is there any good reason, any reason apart from the Platonic picture of desire as painful lack, to think that desiring pain or even enjoying pain is in any way at all paradoxical. My own view, inspired by Deleuze and Guattari, is that most people, most normal nonpathological humans, do enjoy pain, and that when we come to see how this can be, we will be one step closer to dismantling the pristine picture of desire as a lack (see Deleuze and Guattari [1980] 1987, 152, 155). Along the way we will see that pleasure is not one thing and doesn't come in degrees; neither is pain one thing nor does pain come in degrees. As natural as it has become, it is all an illusion. A grammatical illusion.

It is a grammatical illusion, in Wittgenstein's sense, to think that pain is what we don't like and that pleasure is what we do like (Wittgenstein [1953] 1976, §110). It is an illusion fostered by the tendency to sublime the logic of our language, the tendency to fabricate one deep underlying essence of pain, in order to offer one simple explanation of the various uses of the word *pain* (§§38, 89). My technique for dispelling the illusion that nobody could *really* enjoy pain will also be borrowed from Wittgenstein. I will simply remind us of those parts of our lives that do not fit the oversimplified account of pain. But I will not go so far as to offer a perspicuous description of our use of the word *pain* (see Cavell 1979, 78–79). My aim here is only to prove that it is not just masochists. We all enjoy pain. And although this simplified way of putting it—we all enjoy pain—will have to be modulated and complicated, it will still work as an opening move against the oversimplified picture of desire as a painful lack. We all enjoy pain. Not every pain, of course. But we all enjoy pain.

Example 1: Loose teeth.

One pain that we all share is the pain of losing our baby teeth, and no doubt almost everyone can remember worrying their loose teeth. What we are not used to admitting is that this activity was both enjoyable and painful. When I have suggested this to others, the suggestion has been immediately dismissed. I have been told that the pain stimulated by wiggling a loose tooth couldn't have been really enjoyable or else we would have felt sad when the tooth fell out. But this is an inconclusive response, for although it is true that we do not regret the loss of our deciduous teeth, this might be because we were trading one pleasure for another, the main course for dessert, or something of the sort. More typically, I have been told that even if such pain is enjoyable, it is not the pain itself which is enjoyable, but what the pain signifies. On this account, children don't really enjoy the pain of the tooth; it is rather that they are looking forward to the cessation of the pain when the tooth falls out, and each moment of pain brings the child that much closer to the loss of the tooth and the disappearance of the pain. It is the empirical hypothesis I mentioned above, the hypothesis of pleasure delayed or detoured through pain. But if this were one of the ways to enjoy pain, we might expect people to report enjoying the experience of being under the drill in the dentist's chair, for in that case too, each moment of pain brings us closer to painlessness. The hypothesis of delayed pleasure loses some of its attractiveness at this point. Perhaps we did really enjoy the pain we caused by worrying our loose teeth.

I can remember, as a teenager, so after my adult teeth had arrived, forcing my thumbnail between my two front teeth and enjoying the slight twinge of pain and the aroma of powdered finger nail, and this means that what I was enjoying could not have been the anticipation of losing my teeth, but the pain itself. However, I do not want to lean too heavily on the accidents of my juvenile behavior. Fortunately there are widespread cases, closer to hand. Athletic cases.

Example #2: Athletics.

Athletes, and those who exercise regularly, speak with pride of enjoying the burn. Often they can be so committed to the pain of a good workout that a painless work out can be experienced as a failure of character. As in the case of loose teeth, when I have reminded people of these facts, their immediate reaction is to deny that what athletes enjoy is the pain itself. Encouraged, no doubt, by their commitment to the fundamental impossibility of enjoying pain, my conversationalists insist that athletes enjoy the burn because it is a means to becoming fit or to winning a victory in athletic competition, which two things are enjoyed for their own sake. The pain is merely a means to these enjoyable ends. The empirical hypothesis of delayed pleasure once again.

If it were true that athletic pain was enjoyable only as a means to fitness or victory, then athletes should be ready to trade long preparation and hard-fought victory for easy and painless victory. They should be ready to trade what is merely a means (like bitter medicine) for the end itself (like health). Who would not? Who would not trade the pain for the gain? But the more one thinks about it, the more the imagined effortless success takes on the melancholy colors of King Midas. While the team was practicing, you would be at home in front of your Satellite TV, with a bowl of chips, a pitcher of beer, and 250 channels of easy pleasure. Nevertheless, when it was time for the 100 meters, you would still be able to speed out ahead of the field. Painless victory. If this seems a pointless, unenviable athletic career, then maybe pain is not entirely extrinsic to our athletic enjoyments. And maybe that is why, growing up in Smallville,[5] the teenage superman did not run track. There is no more interest or pleasure in the idea of Superman winning a race against Earthlings than there is in a race between teenager and a toddler.

If the pain was only enjoyable as a means to an end, we should be able to slice off the pain and keep the end without any loss of pleasure. But fairly obviously the loss of the struggle is also and at the same time the loss of the pleasure. So at least in part, the pain is *constitutive* of what we enjoy when we enjoy athletic victory. This is a first chink in the armor of the paradox of masochism. Here is a pain that is constitutive of our enjoyment.

But how can it be that we enjoy pain? It may help to consider our enjoyment of things that are sweet. If we have a taste for sweets, then we enjoy sweet candies, the icing of chocolate cakes, ripe peaches. But this doesn't mean that we will enjoy anything that comes up to the same level of cloying sweetness as butterscotch candy. There are not many people, even among those who like cake icing, who enjoy putting enough sugar on scrambled eggs to bring them up to the same degree of sweetness as icing. A clean case—though a bit esoteric—is provided by those who enjoy dry, red Bordeaux with the taste of the earth, but who also enjoy the syrupy pleasures of a sweet Sauterne. Such a person would not typically enjoy sugaring the first to bring it up to the sweetness of the second. What they like is not sweetness but the sweet Sauterne. When it is a matter of sweetness, it is not simply a degree of sweetness that we like; rather what we like is icing that is sweet in the manner of icing, or peaches sweet the way peaches can be. It is not the case that if we like sweet icing we will like anything that is as sweet as that; quite the reverse, icing may be the only thing in the world we like that sweet. The conclusion of these confectionary considerations is that it is false to say that sweetness, tout court, is something we like. And if this is true, if sweetness is not always delightful, then maybe pain is not always abhorrent. Perhaps, in the right circumstances, we do enjoy pain, not simply as a means to an end, but for itself. That is why I started with the universal experience of losing teeth. My last example, also universal, will be that of intimate pleasures.

Example #3: Enjoying Intimacy.

Many people enjoy pains when those pains are part of sexual activity. I will grant that few people have taken those pleasures as far as those so strikingly photographed by Robert Mapplethorpe, but I am setting aside this relatively exotic space of intimate pleasures. My suggestion will be that even garden variety sexual enjoyment involves the enjoyment of pain. Scratched backs, pinched nipples, playful nibbling bites; many people enjoy pains when they are associated with sex, or sex with the right person. As in the case of sweet things, this does not mean that they will always enjoy pain or that they will enjoy all pains. It simply means that many people enjoy pains when they are associated with sex. Of course, as common as it is, not every body enjoys having their nipples pinched. Still enough people do enjoy this to make trouble for anyone who would like to squeeze the enjoyment of pain off into the corner of the rare and philosophically irrelevant. But it gets better. There are some enjoyable features of sexual activity that are almost universal. Let's consider climactic sexual events.

Set aside the distinction I have, on and off, been sketching between sex unstructured by genital obsessions and sex that is so structured; set that distinction aside and consider, to the extent that it can be isolated, genital enjoyment itself. Even so constrained, we can enjoy various kinds of genital stimulation, and I want to constrain these even further. Consider simply the climactic moments themselves. And again I am not even sure this kind of isolation of one experience can be accomplished. Actually, I am sure it cannot. But insofar as it can be, concentrating your attention exclusively on the climactic moments, do you not feel that it would be correct to describe these moments as involving some element of hurt or tinge of pain in those moments of intense enjoyment? And isn't it also the case that were we to subtract the tinge of pain from our enjoyment the climactic moments of intimate enjoyment would be essentially changed? If this is so, then pain is not wholly external to the enjoyment of intimate pleasures. But is this so?

Of course, it is a terrible waste to think only of genital excitement, but is it true that the powerful genital sensation of shuddering climax is painful? Sometimes I think that pain is simply intensive sensation. At times like that I scratch my cheek, as I am doing now. Hard. Not hard enough to make it bleed but it's probably red now. I can't see from where I am. And it is tingling warm. I feel as if it is more sensitive to the breeze or gentle fingers now, and there is no doubt that I am enjoying its tingly sensations. It is not that scratches are always good, but scratchings multiply sensations, intensify them. And climactic genital excitement is not unlike that, hypersensitivity of the penis the vagina the anus the clitoris. And this too the result of vigorous rubbing. Everybody gasps.

If these climactic enjoyments are tinged with pain, then since we care a good deal about intimate pleasures, there ought to be an explanation for why or how we have kept this fact from our eyes. One reason is that we have not thought very hard about what pleasure is, and so we have misconstrued what Wittgenstein would have called the grammar of pleasure and pain. In utilitarian theory, where this topic arises naturally, any concern with the nature of pleasure is rather quickly circumvented by speaking of maximizing the satisfaction of desires rather than of pleasure itself. It is easy to think, no doubt partly under the influence of utility theory, that pleasure and pain are like temperature, pleasure being degrees above zero and pain degrees below zero. And if one thought of pleasure and pain in this way, then to enjoy a pain would be as impossible as it appeared to be when we approached from the side of desire as lack, the side of (c) and (d) above. But pains are grammatically very different from pleasures: (Almost) all pleasures have intentional objects and (almost) no pains do. That is to say, when we enjoy something, for example, Jaap ter Linden's recording of Bach Suite #1, there is typically something we are *taking pleasure in*, but when we are in pain, for example, when we close the drawer on our finger, there is something that caused our pain, not something that we are *taking pain in*. When we enjoy pain, the athletic burn for example, then there is something we are enjoying. But that is a paradigm of our problems: How can what you enjoy be pain? Perhaps we should be more radical.

Maybe there is nothing to match what philosophers have meant by pleasure and pain. It would not be the first time. There is nothing to match what many philosophers have meant by art either (e.g., Bearn 1997b). So what is the philosophical way of thinking about pleasure that I want to abolish? It is like the role of monetary value in a market economy.[6] If I am a single-minded financial investor deciding between investing in gold or IBM or Microsoft or Mitsubishi or pork futures, it won't matter to me what in particular these various companies do or what these substances are for; all that matters is how much money I am likely to make from them in the future. Of course, if I don't eat pork and I am a less single-minded investor, I might rather not invest in pork futures. But that would impurify my financial calculations. The particular way of profiteering from these different investments is irrelevant to my quest for profit; all that matters is how much money I will or won't make in the next six months. This is why some people are deaf to concerns about the environment. The power plant is simply a profit machine.

The philosophical way of thinking about pleasure that I would like to abolish thinks of pleasure much as our single-minded investor thinks of the money he will make. On this account whenever I am enjoying something— perhaps it is a late wine conversation in the cooling summer evening—what I am enjoying is the pleasure this activity is giving me. So as between that conversation and something else—perhaps late wine breeze through the windows reading alone—there is only one firm basis on which to decide, namely, which one gives me more pleasure. I may pick the one that gives me less pleasure, but that will be because I have impurified my considerations. I have already called this picture of pleasure nihilistic, and now it should be more clear why. On this account I only ever desire one thing. Not the conversation, not the company, not the cool night air, nothing. Nothing matters except one thing. Pleasure. And on the other side I only ever resist one thing. Pain. So far this is just calling names. Even if I am right about the nihilism of this picture, it might still be true, and so I need to do more to motivate the rejection of this picture of pleasure and pain.

Part of the reason Bergson's work is so attractive is that he convinces by demonstration. And like Wittgenstein, he gives his readers orders.

Try, for example, to clench your fist with increasing force. You will have the impression of a sensation of effort entirely localized in your hand and running up a scale of magnitudes. In reality, what you experience in your hand remains the same, but the sensation which was at first localized there has affected your arm and ascended to the shoulder; finally, the arm stiffens, both legs do the same, the respiration is checked; it is the whole body which is at work. But you fail to notice distinctly all these concomitant movements unless you are warned of them: till then you thought you were dealing with a single state of consciousness which changed in magnitude. (Bergson [1889] 1960, 24–25)

We compare the change in our experiences to an oboe playing one note louder and louder, instead of to an orchestra with more and more instruments joining or leaving the oboe (Bergson [1889] 1960, 35). But we were talking about pleasure and pain. Another demonstration. Bergson has another suggestion.

We shall easily understand this process if, for example, we hold a pin in our right hand and prick our left hand more and more deeply. At first we shall feel as it were a tickling, then a touch, which is succeeded by a prick, then a pain localized at a point, and finally the spreading of this pain over the surrounding zone. And the more we reflect on it, the more clearly we see that we are here dealing with so many qualitatively distinct sensations, so many varieties of a single species. (Bergson [1889] 1960, 42–43)

These observations are devastating to the idea that pain is one thing that varies with intensity. It is not one thing. Neither is pleasure.

The illusion is fostered by the fact that the *cause* of the experience, the pin's pressure on our finger, is continuously increased, and so we think that the experience itself, the intensity of the pain, must also be continuously increased. But don't think. Look (Wittgenstein 1953 [1976], §66). Consider temperature. "Close attention can easily discover specific differences between the different sensations of heat, as also between the sensations of cold. A more intense heat is really another kind of heat" (Bergson [1889] 1960, 47). This is the one that stopped me. Perhaps it was the fact that there are thermometers that made me skeptical of this one. But then, in my shirt sleeves, I stepped outside into the winter air, and there it was, a sharp biting that I almost recognized, but which I had never addressed as a modality of the cold, itself.

Now return to pleasure pain and the paradox of masochism. The paradox can be derived from the familiar expression of being given pleasure, the thought that *whenever we enjoy anything, the thing we enjoy gives us pleasure*. It follows immediately that if I enjoy having my nipples nibbled or if I enjoy the burn of my muscles during exercise, then the burn, although it hurts, *gives me pleasure.* That is an instance of the paradox of masochism. When I am in pain, I am in pleasure. Or worse, when I am in pain, I am not in pain. But there is no paradox of masochism. It was the expression "to give pleasure" that misled us by its apparent similarity to being given a bruise. When we enjoy, for example, sitting at our picnic table, biting into a sun-warmed tomato, sweet salty juice running from the corners of my wet lips, what we enjoy is *not the pleasure it gives us.* What we enjoy is the tomato at the picnic table in the sun and, let me be honest, Mr. Shaw teaching me on the Pentways terrace of my summer childhood how to shake salt on a tomato and eat it like an apple. The paradox of masochism is an artifact of a reductive interpretation of enjoying the tomato as only enjoying pleasure.

Moreover, to say that what we enjoy, in the experience of the tomato, is the *pleasure* raises another question. What do we enjoy in the pleasure? Perhaps we will be told that pleasure just is enjoyable. But if we are going to stop there, why not stop at an earlier stage? Why not stop at the stage where we say that what I enjoy is sitting at our picnic table biting into the tomato and so on. Why explain our enjoyment of a summer glass of cold water in terms of what cold water *gives us?* Why not construe it in terms of cold water. What I enjoy is the cold wet on my mouth running down my chin. That is what I like. We know what to say when we say what it is we like. Perhaps there will be a lot of indexicals, but they point to the crease in her back not to the pleasure that her creased back gives me.

To speak of pleasure as what we enjoy simultaneously saves us the trouble of saying what it is that we are enjoying, our sensual succumbing, and makes our enjoyment look more objective. As if the subjective side of enjoyment was what particular things caused my pleasures and the objective side was the pleasures themselves. But a world of pleasure is a world without the difference between tomato juice in your mouth and water in your mouth; all that differs is the amount of pleasure. Or pain.

And thus the paradox of masochism disappears. It was only an artifact of a nihilistic picture of enjoyment as receiving pleasure from contact with objects. When one enjoys intimate activities with a lover, it is perfectly possible for one dimension of these pleasurable activities to involve activities that, in other circumstances, might be refused. She leans over and bites the side of my chest. And the same goes for loose teeth, sore muscles, and perhaps climactic sexual events as well. Sometimes we will speak of taking pleasure in some activity or we will speak of an activity as painful or pleasurable, and as Wittgenstein insisted in the *Blue Book* and elsewhere, *there is nothing wrong with such locutions.* All that matters is that we not slip into saying that what we enjoy is not his lips on the small of our back but rather the pleasure caused by their contact. The familiar idea that all we ever really enjoy is pleasure is a mistake. A philosophical illusion.

I hope these three classes of examples (loose teeth, athletics, and intimacy) are familiar enough to secure agreement that we do enjoy what are sometimes called pains and that therefore any simplified account that made enjoying painful activities impossible must be mistaken and any simplified account of desire that made desiring such painful activities impossible must similarly be mistaken. What this means is not, as I once had hoped, that the picture of desire as lack is incoherent, but what it does mean is that we need some account of the persistence of that account. In Wittgenstein's terms we need an account of the confidence we place in the picture of desire as lack, a confidence that seems able to survive the difficulty with ever satisfying such a desire which we met while considering Plato and the difficulty with desiring and enjoying pain which we met while considering masochism. It is to the question of the genesis of the picture of desire as lack that I now turn.

The Genealogy of Desire as Lack

In order to understand the genealogy of the picture of desire as lack I will lift Heidegger's account of the "ontological genesis" of things with properties (Heidegger [1927] 1962, 68). I will be using Heidegger's discussion of the practical world of useful work to provide an analogical account of the genesis of the picture of desire as lack.[7] It will take a short while to sketch the Heideggerian source for this analogy.

Modern philosophers working in the shadow of Descartes's skepticism about whether we can know if we are dreaming can find themselves thinking that what really exists are, on one side, subjects disconnected from the world and even their bodies and, on the other side, objects inert and meaningless. The world of things having become, in Whitehead's words, "a dull affair, soundless, scentless, colorless; merely the hurrying of material, end-lessly, meaninglessly" (Whitehead [1925] 1967, 54). The confidence that a meaningful human world is even possible is, from this point of view, only defensible if we can find a way to construct a meaningful world out of this worldless subject and these lifeless things. But so entirely divided from each other, this lifeless world and this worldless life will never be able to come together, and so the dream of a meaningful world, even at the level of physical description has become "a sort of mystic chant over an unintelligi-ble universe" (Whitehead [1938] 1968, 136). In the positivist thirties White-head took this bleak situation as a reductio of the Hume-Newton metaphysics on which it was based, Hume delivering us a closed, in the logical sense, field of perceptions without any interpretive lever, Newton providing an effective interpretive lever in the form of laws of motion and gravitational attraction but with no reason for existence of those laws (135). A mystic chant over an unintelligible universe.

Deleuze's swarming intensities, which we are beginning to become ac-customed to, are not inconsistent with the metaphysic of actual entities which Whitehead developed in place of the reductio he had diagnosed. After all, Deleuze thought *Process and Reality* "one of the greatest books of modern philosophy" (Deleuze [1968] 1994, 284–85), and he judged White-head to stand "provisionally as the last great Anglo-American philosopher before Wittgenstein's disciples spread their misty confusion, sufficiency, and terror" (Deleuze [1988] 1993, 76). But although Whitehead is well aware that there are phenomenological reasons to oppose the lifeless nature of modern philosophy, he devoted his energies to constructing an alternative, an alter-native that Heidegger, had he known of it, would probably have tarred as just more of the metaphysics of presence. Heidegger is a better guide to the gene-alogy of lifeless nature, and it is therefore that story which I will use analogi-cally to account for the genealogy of the picture of desire as lack.

Like so much else in philosophy, this sort of ontological genealogy can sound pretty foreboding, but in this case the central claim is pretty straight-forward. "When I open the door, for instance, I use the latch" (Heidegger [1927] 1962, 67). In my life it is mostly knobs, not latches, but when I open the door, I don't explicitly think about the doorknob, at all. I walk into the other room. The doorknob is invisible and immaterial. Someone will be ready to say that if I don't think about the doorknob explicitly, then I must anyway be thinking about it implicitly, but someone ready to say that, is in the grip of an intellectual picture of human action. There is no reason to say I *must* be thinking about the doorknob unless one thought that if I were not thinking about it *somehow*, I could not be acting at all, as if I were possessed by an other, like a Zombie. So, this thought continues, since I am not a Zombie, I must be thinking about it somehow. Action without intellectual guidance is, according to this picture, impossible. The only question is whether the intellect is mine or, as in the Zombie case, another's. Heidegger is well aware that this picture is sometimes in place. And we all know that it is sometimes out of place, because when describing the motion of the planets, for example, there need be no intellectual guidance to the motions of Venus. Heidegger's insight was to see that this picture is also out of place when describing our most ordinary activities.

Heidegger's story begins with a network of tools mutually interconnected. Needles reaching toward thread and thence to fingers and thimbles, needles reaching through the material they penetrate, pins reaching the materials they fasten ready, and pins also lined up headfirst in her mouth resting behind her teeth, waiting, she herself reaching out to others mumbling lips of conversation, secure beyond eye contact, thread reaching through material and back to the cotton fields it came from and on to the shoulders the completed shirt will rest on, keeping warm, revealing sensual intensity. This is just a cutting from larger network of relations which constitutes the world of the seamstress, which is invoked by the appearance of the word *needle* in *Being and Time* (70). Heidegger has all sorts of names for these relationships, at least four. The "towards-which" (*Wozu*) directed to the future use of the tool, and the for-which (*Wofür*) which is directed toward the future use of the shirt made, and the whereof (*Woraus*) which reaches back to the materials involved and, finally, the deepest of these reachings out is the for-the-sake-of-which (*Worum-willen*) which he introduces this way: "The primary 'towards-which' is a 'for-the-sake-of-which'. But the 'for-the-sake-of' always pertains to the Being of *Dasein* [that is, roughly, a human being], for which, in its Being, that very Being is essentially an *issue*" (84). In this case sewing the shirt is finally reaching toward a deep for-the-sake-of-which, namely, the kind of being that the person who will be wearing the shirt will be living, or the kind of being that the person sewing the shirt is living, and it is precisely here that Heidegger will raise questions of our taking, as Emerson would say, dictation from others rather than manifesting self-reliance in forming the kind of being we are. But that is not our immediate concern with this seamstress.

When she is sewing, and everything is moving smoothly, the pin is there in her mouth with the others she is removing as she sews, and her conversation with her friend is what occupies her peaceful mind, not the dozens of implicit sewing thoughts that the picture of intentional action seems to require. These dozens of acts are not guided by dozens of thoughts. Instead of action guided by explicit or implicit thoughts, we act: When I open the door, for instance, I use the latch. I imagine this as if there were invisible lines reaching from needle to spool to pin to shirt to warmth to cotton to the kind of being she is living. The reach of these invisible lines organizes her sewing world; these lines are energized by her sewing, but there would be no sewing without these lines or others like them, this is Heidegger's point, the needle is not what it is independent of the thread; what makes the thread thread is its position in this loose and changing system of joinings which reaches from the cotton blooming in the warm sun to the way the shirt accentuates her shoulders, and more. It is not as if there were first this inert metal pin-shape and then we added to it further properties and relations; that is the picture of lifeless nature which Heidegger is trying to overcome. Heidegger is not doing a *naturalistic* genealogy of pins which might indeed begin with a lifeless piece of metal. His target is rather what it *means* simply to be a piece of metal, and his claim is that this kind of being, which reaches out nowhere, is a deficient mode of the kind of being of the needle which reaches out. So that rather than trying to build the needle in her hand out of a piece of metal *plus something*, values or functions or norms, we should approach the mere metal sitting there by way of the needle in life. In his terms the being that reaches out, which he calls ready-to-hand, is the origin from which the being that just sits there, which he calls present-at-hand, is derived.

The present-at-hand just sitting there is, according to Heidegger, derived from ready-to-hand smooth living. The method of derivation is negative, in the existential sense of that word which I have been playing with since the first chapter. Yesterday when I was walking to work, I passed underneath some trees just as the dusty soil under them was being kicked up by passing mowers and in the suddenly dusty air, beams of light appeared before my eyes. As the dust settled the beams disappeared and clear vision returned. This is what happens to the seamstress when something disturbs her smooth transparent motions and the sewing breaks down. She pricks herself with a pin going into her mouth or her thread gets tangled and pulling it firm, knots. The whole thing grinds to a stop and she peers at the knot. We are not yet to the stage of mere present-at-hand sitting there because the dumb thread knotted in place disrupts our projects, so it appears as a pain in the neck. And a pain in the neck is ready-to-hand but in the mode of not being the way things are meant to work, the un-ready-to-hand is what Heidegger calls it, and he says that when we stand, momentarily helpless before the knotted thread, the snagged fishing line, the way we stand is a "deficient mode of concern, and as such uncovers the Being-just-present-at-hand-and-no-more of something [still fundamentally] ready-to-hand" (Heidegger [1927] 1962, 73; Dreyfus 1991, 70–71). But we are caught in a web of Heideggerian translations, and the distinctions are about to pile up, between conspicuousness and obtrusiveness and obstinacy, and the distinctions themselves become obtrusive (Heidegger [1927] 1962, 73–74).

The simple thing is that we don't notice or pay attention to the invisible lines reaching between the needle and the thread until the thread breaks. Looking up, we seek the thread the needle was reaching for, and the dust of disturbance has revealed the shafts of light that were there all along. Mechanically inept, car breakdowns drive this point home; the car won't start; it just sits there in the way of our plans, a dumb pile of metal and grease. Mere things. This is how the lifeless world appears, through negation, death. Just as we might have supposed.

And what do you do when the thread knots? When the car just sits there? You think. You plan. Don't yank at the knot; it'll only get worse or break off altogether. Look it over; work at it; rethread the needle; and start back where you broke off. Confronted by what we don't want, confronted by the roughing up of our smooth functioning, we think. That is when the traditional picture of action presupposing thought appears, that is where it applies. When things are functioning smoothly the doorknob is invisible; when it just spins in the slot like the one in the downstairs toilet that should be pushed not turned, it becomes visible as a (broken) knob in the dust of our frustrated actions, and we think: How am I going to get out of this bathroom without yelling. What a place to be trapped. How can I restore the balance the dust obscured. It is the same kind of pattern we met in

Wittgenstein, the pattern of skepticism. When our involvement with things, when our casual acceptance of the world snaps then, suddenly, it seems presumptuous ever to have been so casual, and we try to think our way back to the time of innocence. Double negation, precisely the double negation that again and again I have enlisted Derrida to overpower. *There is no way back.*

We have already met these three stages while discussing Wittgenstein. First is the smooth functioning of our life with thread or cars or finding our way through the house or the woods. The doorknob is invisible, as are the lines reaching out and back constituting our world. Second, during breakdown, the doorknob becomes visible in a frustrating sort of way, and if things fail to return to the comfortable smooth functioning we were enjoying, they will finally sort into a lifeless world and a worldless life, entirely divided from each other. The third stage is the attempt by double negation to return to the state of smooth functioning. But once divided, although you can bridge the gap, what you are left with is only a gap bridged, scar tissue, idealism realism transcendentalism. Once the chasmic gap has opened up, there can be no satisfactory closing it. Each attempt to discover a way to close the gap discovers us squeezing our eyes shut (Wittgenstein [1953] 1976, 224). After the lifeless world has appeared, it won't go away, even if Heidegger is correct to have pointed out that our access to the lifeless world of things is only through the disturbance of our living world, the living world of the seamstress. This is why there is something inevitably disappointing about the claims for the priority of the ready-to-hand over the present-at-hand; once divided, the present-at-hand inevitably gets the upper hand, not because science always wins, but because skepticism always wins; the café nihilist always wins, unless we move off in the other direction. Reaching pointlessness. The way east is to the west (Deleuze and Guattari [1980] 1987, 154).

Heidegger's sensitive description of the everyday world is completely in the grip of goal-directedness. The very concept of needles reaching to thread is goal-directed. Heidegger's is finally a deep and powerful goal-directed description of our lives, for the final "towards-which" is the kind of being of the person sewing. But still it is goal-directed. I am interested in going the other direction.

I share Heidegger's interest in understanding the genealogy of the visibility of my hand, for example. But whereas Heidegger is interested in understanding what happens when my hand is broken, I am interested in what happens when my hand is held. Caressed. I don't want to play the late

Romantic game that Heidegger shares with Wittgenstein, seeking the way back. Of course the seamstress can close off the knotted thread and pick up again and the shirt may be fine, but the knot's there. The cut heals; the scar remains. The other direction. Unlike Heidegger, I am not afraid of the doorknob being visible. I want to feel it. To sensualize the world. As Sartre knew, there can be no caresses for Heidegger, no sensual body. The soft inner thighs that we met while thinking about Plato are not available for Heidegger because his picture of the world is one in which the norm of smooth functioning dematerializes the elements of that world; the world *withdraws* when it is functioning smoothly (Heidegger [1927] 1962, 69). Rather than try fruitlessly to return to a lost origin, I want to move off in the other direction, in the direction of pointless Aionic time. An erotics of desire. But even though facing the other direction, Heidegger's genealogy of the mere thing suggests an analogous genealogy of desire misconceived as lack. Here's how.

You are having a wonderful time; it could be alone. You are climbing up the steep hillside rockslide; the sun is going down, and you're wanting to get into the woods for the night. The climbing is hard for your out-of-shape body. The weight on your back makes you worry about tipping over backwards. Coming out over the ridge at the top, you find the wind rough, strong, and blowy. It is suddenly exciting, almost erotically exciting. The field opening up at the top; the grasses blowing. Looking out over the valley. Only noticing the little yellow blossoms when you get up from resting. A land of dead steel-gray trees all barkless and smooth, branches everywhere, trunks shaping into silhouettes as the sun moves beneath the horizon. You stop to camp in an island of trees, find a good spot, pile up wood, and make a fire circle. Matches? Damn it all! Where are the matches? I thought I remembered to pack them, but hurried with the setting sun and the drive, I must have forgotten them. And now no matches, no fire, no warmth. Angry becoming dejected. Damn! At least there is a bottle of wine. But it's so dark without the fire, getting cold. Why did I have to forget the matches. And thus is born the picture of desire as lack. Born of *ressentiment*.

The picture of desire as lack is born of frustration and *ressentiment*. Before you found out about the missing matches, you were moving continuously over the mountain, losing the trail, finding the trail, enjoying the wind, the flowers, the steel-gray wood, but these were not separable lacks satisfied; you were flowing over the mountain. Like a school of fish.

A school of fish seems to move like a single organism, so it gives the illusion of looking this way and looking that, but it really has no leader. For when fish are schooling, "dominance systems do not exist or they are so weak as to have little or no influence on the dynamics of the school as a whole. There is, moreover, no consistent leadership. When the school turns to the right or left, individuals formerly on the flank assume the lead" (Wilson [1975] 1980, 207–8). Like a school of fish, wandering up and over the rocks to the grassy field can look like it is tracking a goal; it can look like the seamstress. But it is from another world. The movement off to the mountain was the beginning of a caress, caressing a world not a person, but caressing nonetheless. It is not the work world; if anything, it is the play world, but not just any play world. This play world is modeled on the theater of repetition.

As we move up and over the mountain, we are feeling our way out in all directions at once, a school of fish, alert for food or predators. Schooling is a nomadic practice: "Nomadism is a necessary condition for the evolution of schooling" (Wilson [1975] 1980, 208). Schooling can develop when a species is freed from a "territorial existence," when a species is deterritorialized, for "species that spend part or all of their lives feeding in the open water, moving opportunistically from one site to another are the ones with the potential to evolve schooling behavior" (208). This opportunistic wandering school can model the opportunistic wandering over the mountain, not seeking this or that, but alert, hypersensitive to sensual enjoyments, sights, sounds, touchings. Yes. And also tasting stems of grass and peeled black birch bark. Yes. And aromas too. The smells of earth underfoot. Yes, those too. Feeding on sensual joy. There are no lackings here, simply the construction of a plane of joy with nothing more important than any other, so a flat plane. But I am getting ahead of myself.

All of this comes to an end when the matches are discovered missing. It is as if the school came to a halt, around a single stone, a hole hollowing out in the middle of the teeming fish. And so it might. Matchlessness might ruin it all. A great evening heading out for fun can be thrown off balance by the discovery that the movie is sold out. You are all in the car, loose noisy joking on the way to the movie. Not really thinking about what the movie will be like, but still enjoying being together going out. Then it's sold out. So you look around at each other. Pile back in the car. Silently. A hollow pit in your stomach. It aches with absent movie fun. And then focusing on your frustration, you can get stuck, ugh, unable to think about anything but your *not* being able to go to the movie. Sometimes it stays there. It's not much fun, but it goes away. Sometimes you force yourself to go bowling. You must force yourself because you know you are only trying to fill the absence of movie with the presence of bowling. Square peg in a round hole. But when you get there. Without noticing it. You may start moving again. Loose joking as you walk back from your gutter ball to the seats. Moving again.

In the epigraph to this chapter, Deleuze and Guattari suggest that desire dies when the motion of these joy-sensitized particles stops. "Once a rhizome has been obstructed, arborified, it's all over, no desire stirs, for it is always by a rhizome that desire moves and produces" (Deleuze and Guattari [1980] 1987, 14). And it is true that when the school of desires stops and hollows out, it dies. A lifeless lack of movies and matches. "Those who link desire to lack, the long column of crooners of castration, clearly indicate a long resentment, like an interminable bad conscience" (Deleuze and Parnet [1977] 1987, 91). Desire as lack then enters the same hopeless logic of double negation that we've been meeting again and again. The lack, if it needs to be supplemented, can never be fully and finally supplemented, so it is doomed to dissatisfaction. And then the backwash takes away even the great joy of the mountain, for we naturally begin thinking of our enjoyments along the trail as little *successful* versions of the unsuccessful desire for the matches. But with this we are back at the start of the Platonic story, desire pictured as lack, unable to be satisfied, metamorphosing into a long series of desires. And we are back with the triple curse. Desire pictured as lack, satisfaction as external to desire, and the inaccessible ideal of eternal satisfaction. Desire pictured as lack inevitably shatters into unavoidable nihilism.

But why should we make what happens during breakdown, when the matches are forgotten, paradigmatic for the entire account of desire?

An Erotic Picture of Desire without Desires

The picture of desire as lack is most at home when our desires are frustrated, indeed it is only then, when they are frustrated, that our awareness of our desires becomes most explicit and distinct. So it is only natural that we use a picture of desire at its worst to help us understand desire, itself.

And so Aristophanes comes finally into focus. At first the Aristophanic construal of desire as punishment seems a bit surprising, but if it is true that our traditional picture of desire is a picture of desires *arrested*, rhizomes obstructed, then the Aristophanic conception falls easily into place. Desire as lack *is* punishment.

The question now is how to understand desire unfrustrated without making frustrated desire the model of desire, itself. If the traditional model presents desire as fundamentally a desire for its own death, then I want to sketch a picture of desire which fundamentally wants more life, so that desire desires desire. The traditional picture is a picture of punctiform desires, specific desires answering to specific lacks of a person with a specific identity a specific conceptualizable identity (see Bearn 2000a). The erotic picture of desire is not in this way punctiform; our inordinate desires are neither one nor many. As the interesting is that in which we have no particular interest, so the erotic picture of desire is a picture of desire without desires. Without identifiable desires. In place of a hermeneutics of art and desire we need an erotics (cf. Sontag [1966] 1990, 14).

Having identifiable desires goes together with having identifiable enjoyments. But there is room for skepticism even about the existence of identifiable enjoyments. What's your favorite color. In the face of a questionnaire to this effect we can, easily enough, come up with an answer. In fact in the United States 63 percent will say that blue is either their favorite or their second favorite color (Wypijewski [1997] 1999, 15–16, cf. 92). But it is just as we saw with sweet tastes earlier in this chapter. There are blue things that even blue lovers don't often like, corpse blue, for example. We can't really say precisely what we like, any more than we can say precisely what we thought was interesting. No longer intent on destination (Black 2000).

A bit more than ten springs ago, on Cape Cod, I ate mussels for the first time and enjoyed them with Malcolm and Nell. I liked the taste of mussels and wanted to taste them again. But the next time I had them, I wasn't sure I liked them. I wasn't sure they were tasting the way they should. I was fully prepared to like them, if they were tasting the way they had that night on the beach at the Cape, but I just wasn't sure they hadn't gone off. Now without hesitation I say that I enjoy the taste of mussels, but what do I enjoy? What am I tasting? Do I even know what the taste of mussels is? Like the clams New Englanders call steamers, I normally eat mussels outside in a festive hors d'oeuvre kind of way, leaning over a pot of hot mussels, butter or gingered soy sauce at the ready, rushing to eat some before Alice and Cary eat them all up. And always there are the first mussels, harvested from Cape Cod docks, enjoyed by a fire on the beach, Malcolm, the twins, Nell, wine. Always that night. Do I even know what I am enjoying?

Sometimes I am a logic boy; everyone is a logic boy, sometimes. If you really want to decide if you like the taste of mussels, subtract Nell and the beach and that night and the fun of Dionysian eating. And what is left. The taste of salt water. Subtract it. The pieces of sandy grit in your mouth as you chew. Subtract it. Taking off the mussels' little beard. The genital look of the mussels themselves. Subtract it. The taste of gingered soy sauce. Gone. And what is left. Have I ever even tasted what is left? Do I even know if I would like what was left? And then I wonder, do I really enjoy the taste of mussels at all, perhaps it is all that other stuff that goes with it. We're about to meet at the corner of objectivity and subjectivity. Stop. That is a corner laid out within the frame of representation. And our enjoyment is bound to seem subjective.

Don't say our enjoyments are subjective. Don't say that what we enjoy is simply or merely a subjective effect of all those accompaniments and not the enjoyment of the objective mussels themselves. Allow yourself to be drawn by the thought that desires lead us through to the other side, disorganizing our selves and lives. Labyrinthine seductions, the seductions of the labyrinth. Don't let yourself say that what you enjoy when you enjoy mussels is merely a subjective effect. Perhaps what we are running into here is an instance, applied to desire, of Heidegger's observation that while you may find a hammer rusting on the roadside, what it is to be a hammer requires a network of relations linking hammers and nails and wood and the kinds of things hammers are used to make. Heidegger puts it this way: "Taken strictly, there is no such thing as *an* equipment. To the Being of any equipment there always belongs a totality of equipment" (Heidegger [1927] 1962, 68). The difference is only that whereas the totality of equipment is always organized by goals, by in-order-to's, the many plied desires are multiply folded without organization, like the labyrinthine folds of a heap of silk. No longer intent on destination.

In the interviews known as Deleuze's *ABCs* Parnet asks Deleuze about his and Guattari's account of desire. Stivale generously reports part of Deleuze's response:

What they [Deleuze and Guattari] meant to express was: until now, you speak *abstractly* about desire because you extract an object supposed to be the object of desire. Deleuze provides a long explanation to emphasize that one never desires something or someone, but rather always desires an aggregate [un ensemble]. . . . In desiring an object, a dress for example, the desire is not for the object, but for the whole context, the aggregate. . . . So there is no desire, says Deleuze, that does not flow into an assemblage, and for him, desire has always been a constructivism, constructing an assemblage [agencement], an aggregate: "aggregate of skirt, of the sunray, of a street, of a woman, of a vista, of a color, constructing a region." (Deleuze and Parnet 1996, "D as in Desire," my emphasis)

The idea of an object of desire is an acceptable abstraction and helpful when we are out to buy presents for others, or ourselves, but to mistake it for the basic reality of desire would be to commit what Whitehead called the Fallacy of Misplaced Concreteness (see Lawrence 1956, 322–25). The concrete reality of desire is like the concrete reality of my enjoyment of mussels, an assemblage of Malcolm and Nell and their twins Geoffrey and Joseph and our daughter Cary and the sand and the fire at night and frenzied hors d'oeuvres on the Pentways' terrace and Ginger and Ellen growing up in Japan with Nell, and now, since Nell has died, mussels, even loud music and beer sloshed on the terrace, are tinged with what is gone, like prayer.

It is not that it is false to say that one enjoys the taste of mussels; it is simply that it is an abstraction from the concrete reality of desire, desire without desires. We should allow ourselves to be seduced by desire beyond representation, to the other side. But this is not something that happens only passively; we must draw the diagonal between the vertical and the horizontal, the square root of two. The space of representation is a striated space, striated by conceptual distinctions, striated by the identity of things, of persons, of desires, of fears. The space beyond is a smooth space. Deleuze and Guattari pick up the notion of smooth space from Boulez. Here they are introducing the notion.

The striated is that which intertwines fixed and variable elements, produces an order and succession of distinct forms, and organizes horizontal melodic lines and vertical harmonic planes. The smooth is the continuous variation, continuous development of form; it is the fusion of harmony and melody in favor of the production of properly rhythmic values, the pure act of drawing a diagonal across the vertical and the horizontal. (Deleuze and Guattari [1980] 1987, 478)

When we desire without desires we construct a smooth space. This is the fundamentally affirmative erotic picture of desire. Not struggling to plug an identifiable lack but caressing the organized body, making thereby a disorganized body, a smooth space. This notion of a smooth space has something also to do with Riemann's geometrical thinking. In 1854, Riemann argued that "the empirical concepts on which the metric determinations of space are based—the concepts of a rigid body and a light ray—lose their validity in the infinitely small; it is therefore quite likely that the metric relations of space in the infinitely small do not agree with the assumptions of geometry" (Riemann in Torretti 2000, §5; see Deleuze and Guattari [1980] 1987, 482–88). At the most basic level space itself cannot be a sum of bits of measurable space; at the infinitesimal level space itself is beyond representation. Measurable Euclidean or Non-Euclidean spaces are particularizations of a space of intensities. If Chronological time is a representation of what is fundamentally Aionic, so too measurable geometric space is a representation of Riemannian spaces. Extensive continua are representations of what is beyond representation: intensive continua. Intense Matter (Deleuze and Guattari [1980] 1987, 153; see Kant 1781/1787, A166ff./B207).

The musical analogy helps. The striated plane of organization is twoply, both the horizontal melody and the vertical harmonization. The plane of organization, the harmony and the melody, is a plane of transcendence because what is organized must always be "concluded, inferred, induced on the basis of what it organizes. It is like in music where the principle of composition is not given in a directly perceptible, audible, relation with what it provides" (Deleuze and Parnet [1977] 1987, 91). I think of it this way: There is a sea of sounds, musical sounds like the Beatles and nonmusical sounds like putting the silverware in the drawer. A musical key can be pictured as eight stepping-stones selected from this sea of sound, eight tones repeating. A melody is a pattern of jumping from stone to stone, and harmony is a simultaneous jumping on other stones at the same time, but the principle of composition, the key itself, is not directly perceptible; it is only concluded, inferred, induced on the basis of the music it organizes. But around all those carefully selected stepping-stones laps the sea of sounds; the striated plane of organization rises from the smooth plane of immanence. A Cagean Sea. In a large class of cases, the energy of a musical composition comes from the energy of that sea. Modulating from key to key reminds the ear that there is more to sound than the original eight tone stones, but by modulating to a *related* key, the Cagean sea of sound is repressed, once again. Even in "Down by the Bay," a children's song about what is found where the watermelons grow includes a moment, "for if I do," which by stepping off the eight tone stones onto an F natural, reminds us that there is a whole sea of sound. That sea is the smooth plane of immanence.

When desire is at its best, desire is without desires. We are following a specific desire beyond the plane of organization. This is the constructive moment of desire, the disorganization of the body of our lives. The construction of a Body without Organs, a BwO. But it is not that we must remove the organs: "The organs are not the enemies. The enemy is the organism" (Deleuze and Guattari [1980] 1987, 158).

> To the [striated] strata as a whole, the BwO opposes *disarticulation* (or *n* articulations) as the property of the plane of consistency, *experimentation* as the operation on that plane (no signifier, never interpret!), and *nomadism* as the movement (keep moving, even in place, never stop moving, motionless voyage, desubjectification). (Deleuze and Guattari [1980] 1987, 159, my emphasis)

Disarticulation—taking apart, disorganizing, taking what seems to be a simple desire and finding its concrete complexity, beyond enumeration. *Experimentation*—not to be constrained by the organization imposed by ethics, efficiency, custom, and convenience—each of these keeps us from the sea of sound. Experimentation: "Where psychoanalysis says, 'Stop, find yourself again,' we should say instead, 'Let's go farther still, we haven't found our BwO yet, we haven't sufficiently dismantled our self' " (Deleuze and Guattari [1980] 1987, 151). *Nomadism*—schools of fish, not a migrant moving from temporary home to temporary home, a nomad, who occupies by moving, taking possession of the desert not by building a fortress but by moving all the time. Nomads: those who don't move. There is no limit to what might be enlisted as a source of energy, no limit to what might be put to use constructing a pointless plane of immanence. A plane of pointlessness. Pile it in; pile it all disorganized in. Saying Yes. The smooth plane of immanence is an affirmative plane. And so it is a plane of Aion, of pointlessness, not Chronos. Of Aionic intensities.

DOWN BY THE BAY

1. Down by the bay (down by the bay) Where the wa-ter-mel-ons grow, (where the wa-ter-mel-ons grow) Back to my home, (echo) I dare not go (echo) For if I do (echo) My mo-ther will say, (echo) "Did you e-ver see a bear Comb-ing his hair?" "Down by the bay.

2. ... "Did you ever see a bee
   With a sunburned knee?" ...
3. ... "Did you ever see a moose
   Kissing a goose?" ...
4. ... "Did you ever see a whale
   With a polka dot tail?" ...

(Continue by making up own verses)

57

Figure 6-3. "Down by the Bay." In *Wee Sing Silly Songs,* by Pamela Beall and Susan Nipp. Los Angeles: Price/Stern/Sloan 1986.

We are ready to leave the negative picture of desire beyond. The picture of desire as lack presupposed a picture of a self with an identity. It is the specific identity of the self that sets us on the trail of what we want or need or desire. And it was the impossibility of satisfying any desire pictured as a lack, the impossibility of kissing those we love, that set Plato on his trajectory to immortality, that set Wittgenstein on his romantic trajectory to the rough ground. But those trajectories won't reach their target.

The girl from Mantinea, Diotima, tried a way out, eternity, enjoying Beauty itself by itself, but unless we can solve the problem of participation, unless we can answer Derrida's argument that iterability not only broaches but also breaches the classification of any object as falling under a concept, the Mantinean way out won't work. But even so, there is much to learn from the Mantinean account. Beautiful objects lure us beyond representation by luring us beyond identity, beyond the frame of representation. Our desires have always drawn us this way, but we refuse to admit it. We insist on classifying our desires, counting them, weighing them. None of this makes any concrete sense. It can be done, there is no doubt, but concrete desires are swarms of schooling fish. Desire without desires.

Why have we not admitted this. Why have we not seen that even striated desires, even little glimpses of classified beauties, draw our lives from beyond the plane of representation. What are we afraid of. The loss of the self. Heraclitus told us that "it is death for souls to become wet," and so in the parched mouths of philosophers, even Heraclitus, desire becomes want (Heraclitus 500 BCE, #95).[8] In the moist mouths of lovers desire comes alive, alive beyond goals and destinations, alive to sensual intensities that flow on the plane we construct as we follow formless beauty wherever it leads. Caressing disorganizes the body and at the same time sets the sensual intensities moving. Caress his arm, caress the odd-shaped sticks at your feet, caress the smell on his neck, caress the chaos of the family reunion, caress the sounds of the recycling truck, the sounds of the Cagean Sea. Above all caress wrist neck knee hair thigh vein, no longer intent on destination. Caress your way beyond goals. Beyond representation. Becoming-becoming. Becoming-beautiful.

> And when we woke it was like nothing
> Ever dreamt before this: wrist, neck,
> The hollow behind the knee, your hair

Filling my hands, all of it while we turned
And turned until we were unforgivable,
Adamant with bark, as if a wayward god had come

Upon us, bewitching breast to breast, fingers
Still tracing a vein, a thigh
No longer intent on destination

But in the keep of one limb resting on another, breath
Lingering in leaves, at the edge of the road
Where we were once lost, your hand faithful

In its nest, your mouth on my mouth
Caught, our feet tangled, looking for earth

—SOPHIE CABOT BLACK, "The Tree"

first we break the grip of meaning
then we free desire
then we can enjoy beauty

**We classify too much
and enjoy too little**
—KAKUZO OKAKURA, *The Book of Tea,* 1906

SEVEN

Becoming Becoming

> The most beautiful arrangement is a pile of things poured out at random.
>
> —Heraclitus, Fragment 57

It's Not Art

The meaning of the word *aesthetic* has narrowed in the last few centuries. The root meaning of the Greek word from which we get *aesthetic* refers to what we feel or apprehend through the senses, and the meaning of *aesthetic* is still sometimes given as "of or pertaining to sensuous perception."[1] But in the eighteenth century, especially in Germany under the influence of Baumgarten, the word "aesthetic" came to refer to a philosophical investigation, not of our experience in general, but exclusively of our experience of beauty. For a while, Kant objected (Kant 1781, A21n). Soon enough, even Kant came to use *aesthetic* to refer to our experience of beauty. That was in 1790 (Kant 1790). The final narrowing of the scope of the word *aesthetic* had occurred by the time Hegel's lectures on aesthetics were posthumously published in 1835. Hegel opens those lectures this way: "These lectures are devoted to Aesthetics. Their topic is the spacious *realm of the beautiful*; more precisely, their province is *art*, or, rather, *fine art*" (Hegel [1835] 1975, 1). From experience in general, to experience of the beautiful, to the experience of fine art: Today any discussion of aesthetics is naturally thought to concern art.

By now the aesthetic is so closely linked to art that in an interview from 1983, when Foucault defended the viability of what he called "an aesthetics of existence," he put his position this way.

> What strikes me is the fact that in our society, art has become something which is related only to objects and not to individuals, or to life. That art is something which is specialized or which is done by experts who are artists. But couldn't everyone's life become a work of art? Why should the lamp or the house be an art object, but not our life? . . .
>
> From the idea that the self is not given to us, I think there is only one practical consequence: we have to create ourselves as a work of art. (Foucault 1983, 350, 351)

So naturally, as I started approaching my own aesthetics of existence, I thought I was going to have to take an interest in art. I even thought that since I was going to be writing about the aesthetic, I was going to have to take a stand on the nature or essence of art. But then, for no particular reason, it struck me that I might not be interested in art at all. Not interested in some thing's being *art*, at all. The connection between an aesthetics of existence and art should be rejected.

I am drawn, as others are, by shadows of branches on sunny walls, by fingertips, gentle on my neck's nape, by the colors of rusting metal, the aromas of spring thawing earth, and more. Often enough I am also drawn by works of art. But is it really that normal or comprehensible to be drawn simply by the *being art* of works of art? To be interested in art, if it is not to be interested in what art *does*, art's work, is to be interested in objects simply because they are classified as art. And what is it to be interested in any object because of how it is classified? It is to be a collector.

If you collect souvenir spoons, you will perk up whenever there is talk about a special spoon that someone picked up in some town in Switzerland. Perhaps you are interested in rounding out your collection, for when the question is collection, the answer is completion. And completing a collection of spoons of Europe is bringing it closer to perfection. Some spoon

Figure 7-1. Souvenir spoons.

from Athens may not bring your collection all the way to perfection because the spoon might be bent, but just having a spoon from Athens brings your collection closer to perfection. For if completion is the goal, then perfection is the ideal.

If you are collecting souvenir spoons, you will be interested in what makes a certain spoon unusual. Sometimes it will be mistakes or misprints, imperfections, that in virtue of making the object more rare make the object more valuable. More valuable to collectors. And if you are interested in souvenir spoons, you will take an interest in what makes a spoon a *souvenir* spoon. Its being a spoon and having been bought in order to remind one of a vacation in St. Moritz may not be sufficient to make the spoon a souvenir spoon. In addition there will probably have to be some mark on the spoon, a crest perhaps, which indicates that the spoon came from St. Moritz. Collectors end as metaphysicians. Occasionally there will be disputes. Disputes about whether some properly crested spoon is not really from St. Moritz at all, but China. Disputes about whether some even Swiss spoon is just a spoon, not really a *souvenir* spoon at all.

And this too is what it is like to collect a painter's work. You perk up whenever someone mentions that there is an Ellsworth Kelly, American born 1923, on display at some gallery. Sometimes, just as with spoons, you will be more interested in completing your collection than in the singular painting that would accomplish the completing. Supposing there is not much interest in the early student drawings, which, to be honest, are just student drawings, you will still not want your collection to be incomplete on account of missing out on this student work. Collection, completion, perfection. Just as with spoons, you will find yourself interested in metaphysics, in what makes a Kelly a Kelly because, apart from famous forgeries, you will not want to have any work in your collection that is not really Kelly's. So you will become more or less adept at what is called connoisseurship, the ability to make *fine distinctions* between similar works. Collectors end as metaphysicians.

To be interested in *art*, this would be to have an interest like that of the person who collects Kelly's paintings or spoons, but an interest directed not to the work of a specific artist or style or period or medium, certainly not to the specific energy of a singular work, but directed to art as such. To *anything* that counts as art. Curiouser and curiouser. Someone with such an interest might become an art collector, interested in assembling a collection of art. And so, just as with spoons, they will find themselves worrying about whether this singular object is a work of art and not something else, like a snow shovel or a knickknack, a mere *objet d'art*. Collectors become metaphysicians and collectors of art become interested in one specific metaphysical question: What is art? And this series of thoughts cannot but raise the Foucauldian possibility that perhaps aestheticians themselves, no less than auctioneers, are handmaidens of collectors, perhaps aesthetics itself is an archaeological twin of the bourgeois game of art collecting (Dewey [1934] 1989, 14; see Held; Haskell; Warwick).

Collectors are interested in classifications and taxonomies, not singulars. They are interested in completion and perfection, or failing that, in a good example of twelfth-century Iberian sculpture.

> A collector is anxious to acquire specimens to illustrate a period or a school,
> and forgets that a single masterpiece can teach us more than any number of the

mediocre products of a given period or school. We classify too much and enjoy
too little. (Okakura [1906] 1976, 86)

As a consumer of soup, you might be interested in how well a given spoon
can spoon; after all, some spoons spoon better than others, but as a collector
of souvenir spoons you care only about completing and perfecting your collection. And so it is with collectors of art; their interest as collectors is not
in the power of any singular work of art; they are interested in their collection. Completion and perfection. If you collect books you will not be interested in what the books are about. Even if you collect seventeenth-century
philosophy books, your interest in seventeenth-century philosophy could be
as thin as if you were collecting seventeenth-century books bound in red.
Collectors are not, as collectors, interested in the material power of what is
singular. Collectors are interested in the formal properties of what they collect. They say they care about art. They say they love art. But if this is love,
it is tame love, love under control. Fleshless. Sexless.

The power of a singular work of art is never the mere fact that it is an
instance of a certain kind of thing. Not even art. The power of art is the
power of a sensual singularity, not the power of a conceptual description.
Mostly we attend to the things about us just enough to discover their habitual conceptual representations. Even in museums: From across the room
it looks like a Corot, and on coming closer, when the label verifies your
identification, you are done. On to the next painting. Often enough, looking at paintings involves no looking at all. "We classify too much and enjoy
too little," as Okakura said. The sensual singularity of paintings can slow
down our hasty interest in identification and overwhelm us with the inordinate shapeless patterns of paint and the inordinate feelings induced in us by
the painting. The work of a powerful work of art might simply be a strong
statement in service of the Counter Reformation, but it can be so much
more. The power of a powerful work of art is the power to drop us in our
practical tracks, drawing us into pointless enjoyments. (Drop and draw.)
Affectionate attention to the sensual singularity of powerful works of art
exposes us to a power that overwhelms our thin interest in identification.
Absolute power. It comes, as it were, from nowhere and takes over our
thoughts and feelings. Absolute power is what *overflows* certainly, what overflows *certainly*. And in its surprising unpredictability, the power of a sensual

singularity shows the energy of creation, of the radically new. To think power absolutely is to think of power as creation inexplicable in terms of its antecedents, creation ex nihilo.[2] The creative upsurge of the present moment, sweeping us along with it. The procreant urge of the world (Whitman [1855] 1939, 14).

We make this creative power of singular works of art invisible when our paradigm of power is something like the power of an outboard motor. The Evinrude can overpower the drag of a boat with the energy of seventy horses. The big guy can overpower me. And the wiry little wrestler can take him down. There is a dimension of power in which we discriminate degrees of power. This engine is more powerful than that. This pump can pump water thirty feet up a pipe. But along this dimension power is not at all like creation. It is rather a quantity that one thing can have more of than another thing. Along this dimension there is something comparative about the very notion of power.

There remains something comparative even when power is conceived as sublime. What Kant characterizes as the sublime is inadequate as a characterization of the power of a singular work of art. Kant, or anyway Lyotard (1982), presents the sublime, impossibly enough, as what makes the unpresentable present. But the sublime thereby shows itself to be representation's way of thinking the beyond of representation. For Kant the infinite is (mathematically) sublime, but the infinite is characterized in comparative terms: "The infinite, however, is absolutely large (not merely large by comparison). *Compared* with it everything else (of the same kind of magnitude) is small" (Kant [1790] 1987, 111, my emphasis). Although it is easy to miss, this characterization of the incomparable remains frankly comparative. It is simply the comparative power of the Evinrude absolutized. It is not beyond compare. And this gives a glimpse of the inability of what philosophers call the sublime to break through to the other side of representation.

Along a different dimension altogether, power overflows certainly. Power beyond compare. I am not trying to point to a kind of power that is even more powerful than the sublime, more powerful than that *compared to which* everything else is weak. That would get us nowhere. That would repeat the sublime's impossible attempt to hoist itself, by comparison, beyond comparison. So the question is whether it even makes sense to think power in noncomparative terms. To think power absolutely. Pointlessness can help us find the other dimension here. As elsewhere.

When we compare two motors or two pumps, it looks as if we were comparing two things. But there are always three. The third thing is the specific task that you are using to compare the first two things. Covering the racetrack fastest. The distance that water is pumped up the pipe. How much the prints could fetch on the open market. There is always a third thing. *Always a task, a goal, a point.* Goal-directedness brings the everyday comparative conception of power together with the sublime. Compared with the sublimity of an infinite magnitude everything else is small, but we must place each magnitude along a third thing that functions as a scale of magnitude (Kant [1790] 1987, 111). Having a goal or a point, a third thing, that is what defines this dimension, along which we can find a comparative conception of power. Along the other dimension power is pointless, absolute: It is the dimension along which power is creation. I am introducing this feeling of absolute power as a feature of our enjoyment of powerful works of art, and that is fine for a beginning. But I hope to show that when approached with affectionate attention, everything can show itself in this light. Everything.

In some cases, even when a work of art is commissioned for a specific goal, the work itself starts something that won't stop there. Such a work is Maya Lin's memorial to the American soldiers who died in Vietnam: People return from that memorial thinking about that war and the friends and lovers lost, they do, but they find their hearts musing not about war alone but of death and loss and inordinate other things as well, singular, personal, general, philosophical. Once again this a positive sense of pointlessness modeled on the interesting as being of no particular interest. And it is this inordinate pointlessness that gives some works of art their power to overflow certainly. This difference between comparative power measured against a goal and the absolute power of pointlessness is a difference of the same kind as that which Nietzsche drew between power as dreamed of by slaves and as experienced by nobles (see Deleuze [1962] 1983, 10, 80). And in terms now familiar, the difference between the sublime conception of power and an absolute conception of power is the difference between mere double negation and fully affirmative affirmation. Between "there is nothing compared to which the sublime is smaller" and the affirmation beyond constraint of absolute power. It is the difference between merely political and metaphysical power (Spinoza) (Negri [1981] 1991). It is a power beyond compare, luring us beyond categories altogether. I will call it beautiful, and in this way lift it out of the narrow confines of a simple concern with works of art. The category of art is not especially relevant to the aesthetics of existence I am calling life drawing.

Art. It is surprising how rare it is to hear or to use the category of art with reference to a particular work of art. The category of art gets used either to offer empty praise of the particular

Now *that's* art.

or to offer criticism without justification

That's not *art*.

Neither of these uses of the category "art" is likely to draw your attention to the sensual singularity of the work before you. Praising something for falling under the concept "art" doesn't direct our attention in any particular direction because it is a kind of generic praise of the work or object which draws nothing in particular out of it, or us. Except an honorific classification. And criticizing something as *not being art* is equally distant from the particular. It turns us away from the singular work itself. That's not *art*, is a rejection of something. The suggestion is that this particular singular object is not really worth our attention. And the reason? Simply not being art. But that is never the reason. Or that could only be the reason if we cared about the category of art, for instance, if we were collectors. Since most of us are not collectors and most of us are not interested in the category "art," to be turned from a singular object because it is not art is to be turned from an object for a reason that doesn't address the sensual singularity of the work. Neither *denying* that something is art nor *affirming* that it is art directs our attention to what is either bad or good about the singular thing. What we want to know is what the singular work of art is about. And even more: what it does, how it works on us, where it draws us, and so on. Simply to be told that it is or is not art is to refuse to address the singularity of the work at all. It is to content ourselves with being librarians.

There are fairly obvious reasons why we would fall in with this way of speaking, this way of using the category of art. The appeal to the concept of pleasure is our escape from having to reveal what we in fact enjoy about tomatoes or kissing, and in just this way, appeal to the concept of art relieves us of the burden of saying what definite things are enjoyable, or not, about the work in question. It makes disputes easy, and irresolvable. Stand-offs at every turn:

—It is not.
—It is too.

Sometimes these discussions degenerate into aggressive orthography, for example when someone insists that while Duchamp's *Snow Shovel* (1915) on which he has written "En avance du bras cassé" is perhaps, after all, art, but definitely not Capital-A Art. As if you could articulate a conceptual distinction by innovative spelling.

When I was first learning about mid–twentieth-century art, I would often find myself in conversation with grown-ups defending the being-art of a Jackson Pollock such as *Full Fathom Five* (1947), and, later in England, defending a sculpture such as *Equivalent VIII* (1966), whose apparently extravagant purchase by London's Tate Gallery in 1972 set off a dispute in some places smoldering still. These were very unsatisfying discussions because I never had the courage to address the positive qualities of the work directly, and my opponents, the grown-ups, never had the courage to point out anything more than the oddness of the look or the ease with which a "child could have done this." And these discussions almost invariably turned to price, In the wake of the Tate purchase this was inevitable. And the turn to price is a sign that we are in the realm of collecting. Not the realm of the singular object, the nameless or only nameable singular; it doesn't matter which we say. We have lost the sensual grain of the singular (Barthes [1973] 1975, 66).

Let us return to the power of sensual singularities, the power of the singular to elude representation, drawing us along with it, beyond representation. This movement is arrested by the category of art, for even if that category did not exclude everything except art, the category of art would still hide the absolute power of artworks Categorizing singular things as art or as something else makes it impossible to feel the power of the sensual singular to draw us beyond our selves. Not to the sublime, as Lyotard would have it. But to beauty.

Figure 7-2. Jackson Pollack. *Full Fathom Five.* 1947. Digital Image © The Museum of Modern Art/Licensed by SCALA / Art Resource, N.Y.

Figure 7-3. Carl Andre. *Equivalent VIII* 1966. Image © Tate, London 2011. Art © Carl Andre/Licensed by VAGA, New York, N.Y. © 2012 Artists Rights Society (ARS), New York / ADAGP, Paris.

Beauty's Yes

It was only a little patch of snow. Under the pine trees. Spring had ker-neled the snow, sprinkled it with needles, pieces of pinecone, splinters of slate from the forest road, twigs, spots of black dirt, shards of acorns. Nothing was the same shape or size as anything else. And it was scattered randomly. I think the biologists call this stuff litter, forest litter. And it is dictionary litter too: "odds and ends, fragments and leavings lying about, rubbish; a state of confusion or untidiness; a disorderly accumulation of things lying about." I don't know what it was; it wasn't just one thing. It must have been allofit; it always is.

I was enjoying a feeling of floating, waking up still feeling the pleasure of the night before, far friends coming near, eating, poking each other up into laughter. Delight. A mouse by the bed. Somewhere too I was hearing the *Leaves of Grass*, read round the clock just two days before. My old baggy green pants were wet from sitting on a big mossy rock in the midst of some trees, standing and leaning and fallen, also green with moss. The air was cold and damp and so rich with the smells of the spring thaw that you could taste the air with your tongue. I wasn't alone, and that helps. There were friends of Yossi's along the forest road. And Yossi and Kristen too. And Oatmeal. And allofit was good. Yes. And beautiful.

Someone might say it was perfect. You could. You could say perfect with the sound of love in your mouth. And that too is good. Oh Yes. It is. And it is the feeling that matters, not the words. But words feel too, and one of the feelings of perfect is the unforgiving feeling of being poised on a peak, so easy not to be perfect that being perfect itself is a matter of not being in any way imperfect. Double negation. And so thinking, Yes, I will not say perfect; I will say beautiful. Allofit.

It isn't that long ago. Sixty-three days. And I still can't quite remember it. Or I can, and then the words never seem quite right. Some wordings of some experiences never seem right. It's not just a platitude; it's also a feature of what it's like to be drawn to the other side of representation. Noticing the patch of snow under the pine trees and feeling its beauty, I put it to the test. It seems an ungrateful act now. But as my father and coauthor used to say: Don't think. Do the experiment![3] Whatever the reason, I looked down and saw the snow, and put its Yes to the test. Supposing it were true that this scattered randomness, this anomalous arrangement was, as I had hoped, as I felt, an affirmation beyond double negation, then this little patch of snow should say Yes to anything. Picking up a stick, I dropped it, from about a foot or two, onto the patch of snow. It vanished, or it vanished as something foreign. It was just like it had always been there. I tried a pebble. It vanished too, becoming the patch of snow. Another stick, bigger. It too. A few more stones melted right back into the snow. A little nut from a bolt lying in the road vanished too. Excited, I dropped my empty coffee cup, one of those diner mugs, ceramic white and a little thick. It landed heavy and big, like it was from another world, for a moment it maintained its kitchen foreignness and then rolled off onto the road. The patch that had welcomed everything hadn't quite welcomed the mug. But even that didn't stop me.

Almost immediately I decided that the reason the mug seemed not to fit was that it was too big, and that if the bumper of a car had landed on the patch and covered it all, it too would have seemed not to fit. Nor was it just the artificiality of the mug; a boulder the size of a car wouldn't seem to fit either. It was a matter of scale, not a matter of the completeness with which the patch said Yes. The patch of snow was really Yes. The patch of snow passed the test. And it's not just the patch of snow. That's the real beauty of it. The patch of snow is everywhere. Beauty too. Yes.

Two weekends ago I was looking out of Cary's upstairs window, thinking about her coming back home. Looking out the window. I was looking down on a picnic table two floors below me. The table top was a frame. Scattered over the table top in no particular pattern were all the things that had fallen from the tulip poplar overhead. Sticky petals, leaves, threadlike filaments from the stamens, two stones for holding down the table cloth now being washed. It too was Yes. It too was beautiful.

I wonder a bit about the frame, about the fact that the irregular patch of snow no less than the rectangular picnic table framed the littered objects. You could think that the framing detracted from the beauty, as if the beauty of the scattered litter insofar as it needed the frame to exist would be less beautiful, more like an artificial flower. So I go downstairs to my books.

Looking up from Schapiro's discussion of the historical contingency of the prepared ground and the frame, I can quote his description of the frame as "a finding and focusing device placed between the observer and the image" (Schapiro 1969, 7). I like this. It takes nothing away from the beauty of the scattered litter. Affectionate attention too is a frame in this sense: a finding and focusing device. For some others and for me, philosophy itself can be a finding and focusing device.

Philosophiren, says Novalis, ist dephlegmatisiren, vivificiren. (Pater [1873] 1990, 152)

And what draws us in or out, intensifying our lives by compression or connection, is beauty. Beauty's Yes. Beauty's And. And Beauty is both what draws our lives and what our lives, at their best, can become.

Unfortunately none of this will make sense if we insist that beauty is a kind of perfection. For perfection is shackled to conceptual representation, arresting becoming. Perfection draws us away from the patch of snow;

beauty draws us into it. And because people expect beauty to be perfect, they are unable to feel the beauty in a littered patch of snow. Unable to see allofit as beautiful. Life drawing is not a matter of perfection. It's a matter of beauty. Nothing in the world is perfect. Plato's disappointment. But on the other side of this bleak ancient vision everything in the world is beautiful. Allofit. Let it draw you. Nouns becoming verbs.[4]

Beauty Is Not Perfection

One of the gifts Gertrude Stein left for us in her 1917 *Lifting Belly* is this:

> Not pretty.
> Beautiful.
> Yes beautiful.
> Why don't you prettily bow.
> Because it shows thought.
> It does.
> Lifting belly is so strong.

—GERTRUDE STEIN, *Lifting Belly*

In the long poem from which these lines were extracted, lifting belly is the way Stein talks about exciting sensual delight. And she implies that lifting belly is beautiful, not pretty. Prettiness shows thought. Like bowing. To perform a bow one must respect the criteria for bowing. One doesn't bow like that. One bows like this. Lifting belly has no time for respecting criteria. It is rather a "splendid example of carelessness" (Stein [1917] 1995, 3). And in another place Stein reminds us that a "special word for careless is caress" (Stendhal 1989, 76). Lifting belly does not show thought, and so it is not pretty. It is not trapped in the frame of conceptual representation. It has broken through to becoming beautiful. Or we could say becoming becoming, since my favorite way of saying beautiful is becoming.

Listen once again to the title of Stein's poem. *Lifting Belly*. As you begin to hear the French Belle inside the English Belly, it suddenly seems that one of the things Stein's title tells us is that her poem is about arousing beauty.[5] Becoming beautiful. Becoming becoming.

Approached this way, many of the familiar features of beauty disappear. Neither becoming nor beauty is visible to those who categorize, to those devoted to identification. Whether we call it becoming or beauty, it is beyond representation, beyond both authenticity and inauthenticity. And letting ourselves be drawn by delicious sensualities is the way to break through to the other side of representation, to break through to becoming becoming. Not to some other transcendent place but to the exciting sensual singularities that our respect for categories hides. Typically, as Bergson puts it, "We do not see the actual things themselves; in most cases we confine ourselves to reading the labels affixed to them" (Bergson [1900] 1980, 159).

And yet people say that some things are beautiful and others not. And people say of two beautiful things that this one is more beautiful than that. These judgments about beauty disappear when beauty becomes becoming. What calls for these judgments, negative judgments and comparative judgments, is not beauty but perfection. And I would be happy to add that lifting belly is not pretty because what is pretty is also governed by perfection. But lifting belly is becoming beautiful.

I want to distinguish perfection from beauty, but when we turn to the philosophical tradition dominant in Europe, we find just the opposite, namely, that beauty is mostly read as a form of perfection. Elaine Scarry's *On Beauty and Being Just* (1999) is ostensibly concerned with beauty, but she is really writing about perfection. Sometimes she casually runs beauty together with perfection, as when she tells us that the beauty of the gods follows from or is a part of their perfection (Scarry 1999, 71). Sometimes the identification is almost explicit, as when she finally brings beauty and goodness together with the example of a "perfect cube" (94). It is, as you could guess, the link between perfection and proportion, which shoulders the *and* Scarry discovers between beauty and being just. The connection between beauty and proportion surfaced in Plato's *Philebus* long before anything like our modern idea of art and beauty existed: "For measure and proportion manifest themselves in all areas as beauty and virtue" (64e). Alberti, in 1486, tells us that "beauty is that reasoned harmony of all the parts within a body, so that nothing may be added, taken away, or altered, but for the worse," and since Alberti also insisted that "we should follow Socrates' advice, that something that can only be altered for the worse can be held to be perfect," it follows that for Alberti beauty is a kind of perfection (Alberti [1486] 1991, 156 [6.2] and 96 [4.2]).[6] This is a kind of perfection that is as inhospitable to becoming as the beautiful patch of snow is welcoming. Perfect proportioning was still associated with beauty by Shaftesbury in 1711: "The truth or beauty of every figure or statue is measured from the perfection of nature in her just adapting of every limb and proportion to the activity, strength, dexterity, life and vigour of the particular species or animal designed" (Shaftesbury [1711] 1999, 415). And the tradition lives on.

It is therefore quite obviously a simple matter to satisfy oneself that beauty has often been construed as a kind of perfection, even a kind of perfect proportioning where any change would be for the worse. It would be something else, altogether more difficult, to demonstrate that the European tradition has been systematically confused, pointing to perfection and calling it beauty. And in any case the European tradition has not been entirely and completely confused, even in my own terms, about beauty. Heraclitus, two hundred years before Plato, in words that form the epigraph to this chapter, tells us that "the most beautiful arrangement is a pile of things poured out at random" (Fragment 57). In 1625, Bacon insisted that any excellent beauty must have "some strangeness in proportion" (Bacon 1625, 169). And in 1757 Burke used his patriarchal ideas about women to prove that beauty was quite different from perfection: ". . . so far is perfection, considered as such, from being the cause of beauty; that this quality [beauty], where it is highest in the female sex, almost always carries with it an idea of weakness and imperfection" (Burke [1757] 1968,110). Even Kant in 1790 writing of the judgment that a flower possesses what he calls free beauty tells us: "The judgment is based on no perfection of any kind, no intrinsic purposiveness to which the combination in the manifold might refer" (Kant [1790] 1987,76). So it is simply not true that the *entire* European tradition has systematically mistaken perfection for beauty. Although they constitute a minority, there are dissenters from the dominant view that beauty is perfection.

My concern is not, therefore, with the European tradition as a whole. I only want to show that *perfection is not beauty*. But what are we to do? I cannot appeal to authority because the authorities disagree. I cannot address myself to an example of beauty because that is just what is in question. What are we to take as examples of beauty? And why care about a famous word like *beauty* anyway? Famous words always cause trouble. Why not, as my friends advise, replace it with some other less contentious word, like *amazing*. But others, for instance the generation eager to distinguish the sublime from the beautiful, have cared enough about beauty to repress it.[7] So perhaps we should care enough to release it. And yet when neither experts nor examples can be trusted, how are we to proceed in differentiating beauty from perfection?

Try grammar. Ask: How many *beautiful* geraniums could there be in Bodrum? And the answer is probably quite a few, especially in a good year. Now ask: How many *perfect* geraniums could there be? And isn't the answer that, it might turn out that no geranium in Bodrum was perfect, even in a good year? And isn't this why it is so hard to judge vegetables at the farm fairs. You end up with a checklist of criteria and then examine each cucumber to determine how well it measures up. And so too with geraniums. Although the town could be overflowing with *beautiful* geraniums, there might be no geranium that was *perfect*. So beauty seems to be different from perfection.

Perhaps this is too quick. Try to explain it away by saying that the criteria for being a perfect geranium are the same as those for being a beautiful one; it is just that the standards are lower for beauty than they are for perfection. This would save the connection between beauty and perfection, with perfection playing the role of an idealized or *perfected* beauty. One strange thing about this attempt to save the link between perfection and beauty is that it interprets appreciating beauty as rather like judging livestock. Moreover, it seems to imply that the only *really* beautiful geraniums are the *perfect* ones. And then this runs into more trouble because when someone insists on talking about a perfect anything, for example a "perfect cube," there is an inclination to say that of course no actual material cube could ever be perfect. And if the same applies to geraniums, then no actual aromatic geranium could ever be really beautiful. "Oh I know," we might say, "you could *call* them beautiful, but they are not really beautiful." And so the answer to our question—How many beautiful geraniums could there be in Bodrum?—cannot, after all, be quite a few. The correct answer must rather be that *truly speaking* none of the geraniums in Bodrum could possibly be beautiful. And how on earth could that be right? So once again beauty seems not to be a form of perfection.

A second way to see a distinction between perfection and beauty is to turn your attention away from *how many* toward the fact that perfection seems dependent on conceptual categorization in a way that beauty does not. Told that a chair is perfect, we will want to know what kind of chair it is, since a perfect comfy chair is likely to be a bad dinner table chair. Told that a chair is beautiful, we may want to know what kind of chair it is, but the important point is that we don't need to know what kind of chair it is in order to determine whether or not it is beautiful. Perfection lives by respecting and idealizing the criteria for being a cucumber or a geranium. It never leaves the plane of representation. The quest for the perfect cucumber takes dictation from the concept of a cucumber. Enjoying a beautiful cucumber takes dictation from no concepts at all. Beauty delights, beyond identity, in becoming. Breaking through to the other side of representation.

It is not that there isn't along the trajectory of perfection a move beyond ordinary representation. There is. But it doesn't move beyond representation as such. It doesn't break on through (to the other side). Once more, picture the plane of representation as a flat plane of latex, stretched smooth. And once again picture perfection in its different forms—perfect hiking boot or perfect ballet slipper or perfect ski glove or perfect soft ball out-fielder's mitt—as what happens when you poke a pencil into the latex plane thus forming a latex cone which rather than breaking through the plane of representation produces a unique point within the distended plane. Although there is a movement to transcendence along the trajectory of perfection, it is not a movement that will break through the plane of representation because what becomes transcendent along this trajectory is a perfected *chair* or perfected *justice* or perfected *courage*. So when transcendence is approached through perfection, we approach a special form of transcendence that purifies conceptual categories and so transcends the materiality of particulars but does not break on through (to the other side of) representation. Beauty breaks through. Beauty breaks through to sensual singularities that were always there. Always there but hidden behind the types of which we took them to be instances.

A third way to confront the difference between beauty and perfection is to think of the relation each of these concepts bears to planning and to the accidental. Here it is significant that beauty can surprise us. We can be surprised to discover beauty where we didn't expect to find it. The stain on a tablecloth. A cheek bruised in a battering. Laundry heaped on the basement floor. To find something beautiful is to be ready not merely to *accept*, but to *enjoy* the accidental.[8] To make something beautiful is likewise to be ready to enjoy the accidental. By contrast, to make something perfect, for example a perfect cube, requires vast amounts of planning and engineering, high tech metallurgy. It is not that there is a contradiction in the suggestion that a perfect cube was chipped off by accident when the glass broke. The glass might have been made of salt. It is simply that perfection enjoys executing a plan, staying on track, sticking to a point. Beauty enjoys the surprising. The pointless. So once again and for a third time beauty is pulling back from perfection and toward pointlessness. Beyond representation.

If beauty is beyond representation, then it is both beyond negation and beyond comparison. This has two revisionary consequences. First: Everything is beautiful. Second: Nothing is more beautiful than anything else. The reason everything is beautiful is not because when you shave off all the irregularities everything can be made beautiful. Beauty is here now. On the surfaces. In the irregularities. As John Cage discovered, "Beauty is underfoot wherever we take the trouble to look" (Cage [1961] 1973, 98). People resist this. Surely some things are not beautiful. I would rather say that for some things it is easy to delight in their sensual singularity, but for others it is more difficult. But it is always possible, if you take the trouble to look. Think of it this way. It is as if there were angels all over the world all singing precisely the same beautiful song. Nevertheless, some angels are right beside you in your room. and others are outside the window. and others still are in the next town. It is true that you have to listen harder to hear those that are distant than to hear those that are near, but it is not true that the singing of the one is more beautiful than that of the other. Beauty is not in the ear or the eye of the beholder. It is in sensual singularity.

This is the way it is walking in the woods in the fall. You are looking around for a good leaf to take home, and you reject this one and that one and that one too. Finally you settle on the one you think is the best. And then walking the rest of the way home, you're looking down at your feet realizing with some sheepish pleasure that each of the leaves you are walking over is equally as nice as the one you are holding tight by the stem between your fingers. No leaf more beautiful than any other. Sometimes I just let go of the stem and come home empty-handed.

But what about ugly things. Surely, someone will say, ugly things are not beautiful. But it is not so simple. It is an interesting feature of the word *ugly* that although it is easy for people to be ugly, it is more difficult for natural objects to be ugly. This can be quite a surprising revelation. And since it is

easy for natural objects to be beautiful, this already suggests that the opposite of beautiful is not ugly. Ask: What would an ugly oak tree look like?
I am not sure, but I am tempted to say that an ugly oak would be one that
had not grown to have the look, the profile, of a typical oak tree, and the
atypical shape might also, I suspect, have to be in some way unsettling or
creepy. And if this is right, then perhaps what is ugly is an unsettling kind
of imperfection. And if we call a person ugly, don't we mean that their
bodily shape or facial characteristics or complexion has fallen away from an
ideal of perfection. Fallen away from some inevitably racially and culturally
constructed ideal of the perfect body, the perfect body which even the air-
brushed models on the billboards cannot exemplify. Hence the airbrush.

The oppression of perfection, the perfect body, is the oppression of the
impossible ideal of making oneself the perfect instance of a type. In the
dressing room, the models we yearn to look like are all complaining about

Figure 7-4. Quentin Massys. *Grotesque Old Woman* c. 1530. © National Gallery,
London/Art Resource, N.Y.

the size of their lips or the length of their necks or their ears or something. Given the confusion of perfection and beauty, it is easy to understand the political attack on beauty, but this attack is metaphysically misdirected and therefore existentially misleading. Hilda Doolittle was already here.

> do not be beguiled
> by the geometry of perfection
>
>> —HD, "The Flowering of the Rod"[9]

It is perfection that oppresses. Beauty caresses.

Mrs. Dalloway knew. "She would not say of any one in the world now that they were this or were that" (Woolf 1925, 8).[10] Mrs. Dalloway had learned that the best thing, what I am calling beauty, is not visible to those who categorize, to those who hide a singular irregular commonplace behind the idea of being an instance of a type. The frame of representation makes it impossible even to see the world. It makes us blind. "This blindness, this *What What What*" (Lucia 2001, 2). Identification makes sensual singularities invisible. And still they wonder what's wrong with a politics of identity. But if not as an instance of a type, how are we to characterize beautiful things? What is an irregular commonplace?

The European tradition offers only one alternative to description in terms of concepts, and that is the notion of the bare particular. A bare thing. A support for the concepts and universals of description. But if we approached sensual singularities with the notion of a bare particular in hand, beauty would disappear into nothing. For if you can say anything about a bare particular, then what is said must be said in terms of concepts. And so if a bare particular is beyond conceptual representation, it is nothing. A bare particular, cold and dead, given life only by the concepts it exhibits. By itself nothing.

This is all backwards, regimenting experience according to a frame of representation that drains life from the world. That kills change. That reduces becoming to being. To see the other side of representation as a pile of bare particulars is to look at the other side from this side. A nihilistic view. And it is the view from this side that makes the loss of identity seem unsettling rather than exciting. What is obliterated from this nihilistic view of the world is the intensity of what exceeds conceptual categorization. Enjoyment. Excitement. Becoming.

An Irregular Commonplace

> There is no clear division among genera; there is no clear division among species; there are no clear divisions anywhere.
>
> —ALFRED NORTH WHITEHEAD, *Modes of Thought*

All this talk about breaking through the frame of representation courts two misunderstandings. The first is the mistaken idea that I am urging us to leave the earth for some better place, some better transcendent place elsewhere. But I have already underlined that breaking through proceeds along a trajectory that is neither up to an immaterial transcendent (Wittgenstein's platonic "what is higher" [1921] 1961, 6.432) nor down to the earth (Wittgenstein's romantic "rough ground, open to view" [1953] 1976, §§107, 126) but out along a pointless diagonal escaping the habits of practical life, the habits of identification. The incommensurable diagonal square root of 2.

The second misunderstanding I am courting is the charge that whatever I am trying to *say* about the other side of representation must fail because whatever is beyond representation is also beyond *linguistic* representation and so I can only end with mystical silence. This was the official ending of Wittgenstein's *Tractatus*, which relied everywhere on "what is higher" but insisted finally that there is nothing to be said about what is higher (Wittgenstein [1921] 1961, 6.432, 7). As almost always with mystical philosophies, Wittgenstein conceded that although what is higher could not make it into linguistic or indeed any representation, it could nevertheless be made *"manifest"* otherwise (6.522). This second misunderstanding of my emphasis on breaking through the frame of representation is epitomized in Ramsey's reaction to this aspect of the *Tractatus*. Ramsey wrote: "But what we can't say we can't say, and we can't whistle it either" (Ramsey 1929, 134). Ramsey is not alone. I think many of us have thought that if the deep truth of the world is beyond representation, then it is thereby also beyond words. Many of us, certainly myself, have felt superior before such facts as that the Dao De Jing insists that the eternal Dao cannot be talked about and then proceeds to go on for another eighty-one chapters (Lao Tzu c. 550 BCE). I am now embarrassed by these reactions of mine, which seem, like Ramsey's, to presuppose a pinched conception of language. As if the only thing we knew how to do with words was to state the truth and that less serious more theatrical uses of language are set aside for later. Or never. This postponement until later was famously a feature of Austin's discussion of linguistic action, and as Derrida observed, Austin of all people should have known better (see Bearn 1995b).

An old teacher of mine once asked a class in the philosophy of education if they had learned anything relevant to limnology from Basho's famous poem: "An old pond: a frog jumps in—the sound of water" (Sato and Watson 1981).[11] The negative response from the class was not unusual and would not be today. It is easy to use the category of poetry to separate what represents the world, true or false, from whatever else language can do. Something else. In this case what can be communicated is, of course, the event of that splash, but why would you want to convey that event? Naturally. there will be some situations where you will care, for instance if the sound of the frog were a sign that someone was coming or maybe sneaking toward you along the edge of the pond. But then what Basho wrote would not have the absolute power it has. The power of conjuring the silence of an old pond, which I imagine in the cooling close of a hot humid day, and then the watery wet splash that fills the darkening silence of the pond, and then disappears, the world silent again, but rippling with liquid sounds through allofit.

You will say that this is just another representation. And so Ramsey is right, beyond representation is silence. All I want to do now is to point out that the power of Ramsey's reaction may reside in an emaciated view of language. When we say that some experience cannot be put into language, we are most likely thinking that it cannot be put into a flat-footed description of the unitary characteristics of a thing. We are not thinking of Basho or Gertrude Stein or John Cage.

Chances are, we are thinking of language as a collection of something like names for something like objects, so we are thinking, for example, of the word *salt* as a something like a name for something like whatever is sodium chloride. We are not thinking of other examples of what chemists call salts. But neither are we are thinking of saltiness. Saltiness. We are not thinking of the salt of seawater sparkling your face tasted with your tongue on your lips. Nor are we thinking of the salty hot of French fries, the salt of sweat on her neck, collecting in the small of her back, the salt of martini olives wet and sweet with gin in your mouth, warm tomatoes right out of the sunny garden, salty tomato juice spilling out the corners of his mouth. In short we are not thinking of an erotics of salt but only a diagnostics of salt. This is. This isn't. And philosophy's interest in art and even beauty has mostly been diagnostic, not erotic.

Like the intensity provoked by Basho's few words, the sensual excitement of salt can be communicated from one person to another by means of language, by means of language freed from the job of representing the world, true or false. Freed to a certain pointlessness. Freed to a mode of communication almost material, the way a baseball bat communicates motion to a baseball, directly, by means of the material motion of the bat (Derrida 1971, 1).

It turns out that one of the many things that is killed by being approached through a frame of representation is language. There is so much more energy in language than simply one thing standing for another. So much more to language than simply representation. We divide language in two: on the one side its representational powers and on the other side the material tools that flex these powers. But there is always more, as Dick Higgins might have said: There is always something else (see Nietzsche [1901] 1967b, #666). You can feel the materiality of the words on your skin and in your mouth, but so too you can feel the materiality of the meanings, which can move in ways uncontrolled by the contextual and intentional sources of what we say (see Bearn 1995a). Everything happens between the materiality of language and its representational content.

> Everything happens at the boundary between things and propositions. Chrisippus taught: "If you say something, it passes through your lips; so if you say 'chariot,' a chariot passes through your lips." (Deleuze [1969] 1990, 8)

This is more than a (fallacious) joke, for if we tried to correct the reasoning by saying that when you say "chariot," it is the *word chariot* that is in your mouth, that would not be right either. Words don't nestle in the space between our cheeks. Maybe the chariot did pass through your lips, after all. Moreover, we only need to think of the erotic use of language during intimacy to remind ourselves that there is a strong sense in which talking about something all by itself takes it into your mouth.

There is more than one kind of sensuality. Or is there? I have so far been counting on the familiarity of a material form of sensuality, but there is also another form. I am tempted to call it immaterial sensuality, but since the reason I want the word *sensuality* at all is because it feels good on the skin, perhaps I should say that there is only material sensuality and that while some sensuality is carnal or corporeal there is also another material sensuality: a sensuality of semantic sense. Since semantic sense is so often thought of in immaterial terms you can understand my temptation to speak of an immaterial sensuality. But also my hesitation. Why not think of this other sensuality simply as a sensuality of sense and enjoy the extra play we are giving the word sense. Or maybe we should fold it all in together as sensuality. What were we trying to prove anyway by naming sensuality into types?

We already know about the delirious pointlessness of carnal caressing. We know, Sartre taught us, that the hand must arrest its functionality in order to caress without caring about the grasping capabilities of the hand. We know, Gertrude Stein taught us, that caress is a special word for careless (Stendhal [1989] 1995, 76). And when people write as unusually as Gertrude Stein, or her admirer John Cage, even their defenders can say that it is the carnal sensuality in the sound of the words that matters, but they forget the way we are also turned on as the senses of the words brush lightly against each other. Kissing. How do words feel each other. By means of their senses.

Consider the hand. The hand's ability to caress; to give and receive the excitement of the caress is not unrelated to the power of the hand to type or to grasp a gearshift or to slap or to do any of the rest of the genuinely innumerable things a hand can do. To focus on some few of the functional goals we might have for the hand is to reduce enormously the things a hand can do carefully or carelessly. Words too. When we focus on some few of the representational things that a word can do, we reduce enormously what the word can do carefully no less than what it can do carelessly.

Austin was proud of increasing the number of things that words can do, but he focused on official language. Even his interest in perlocutionary acts and sequels (which are what we intentionally or unintentionally *effect by* saying what we do) was governed by identifiable acts (Austin 1976, 122, 118; but see Cavell 2005a). Deleuze extends the Austinian analysis to include an unidentifiable performative stuttering.

This is what happens when the stuttering no longer affects preexisting words, but itself introduces the words it affects; these words no longer exist independently of the stutter, which selects and links them together through itself. It is no longer the character who stutters in his speech, it is the writer who becomes a *stutterer in language*. He makes the language as such stutter: an affective and intensive language, and no longer an affectation of the one who speaks. (Deleuze [1993] 1997, 107)

This is an other aspect of sensuality, a sensuality of semantic sense. It is the "pure sheet of jouissance," which Barthes calls the "*bruissement*" of language, *bruissement* from *bruit*, the word for noise (Barthes 1984, 94; see Barthes [1973] 1975). He describes this *bruissement* as what happens when language is denatured, becoming a sumptuous moving tissue of sounds which *irregularizes* the sounds and rhythms of language, a kind of corporeal sensuality (Barthes 1984, 94). Barthes's denatured is Deleuze's minorized (Deleuze [1993] 1997, 109). Thinking ahead to Gertrude Stein, I have added irregularize (Stein 1946). But more is irregularized than the sounds and rhythms of language. The *bruissement* of language *irregularizes* as well the senses of words. This pure sheet of jouissance involves no proper functioning sense, but, and Barthes says this is the difficult thing to understand, neither does this irregularization get rid of sense altogether (Barthes 1984, 94–95).[12] And although Barthes does not quite speak of this as a *beautiful bruissement*, he does explicitly set aside perfection when he tells us that what sounds in the *bruissement* of language is precisely the sound of what when it is functioning perfectly makes no sound (94). If it ain't broke, break it. Break it out. Free the beautiful. Free the becoming.

Barthes's leading example of the *bruissement* of language came to him during a scene in a movie about China where he saw in a village street children standing with their backs to a wall reading out loud from different books (Barthes 1984, 95).

A pure sheet of jouissance. Jouissance. The semantic space of jouissance famously includes the climactic sexual event English calls coming. Becoming. Barthes discusses jouissance when, in another place, he distinguishes texts of *pleasure* from texts of *jouissance*. A text of pleasure plugs a recognizable lack. It is satisfying and fulfilling, and "it is linked to a comfortable practice of reading" (Barthes [1973] 1975, 14). In contrast, a text of jouissance discomforts our practice of reading and in the space thus opened excites us incomprehensibly beyond. Barthes:

> Texts of jouissance: the text imposes a state of loss, the text that discomforts (perhaps to the point of a certain boredom), unsettles the reader's historical, cultural, psychological assumptions, the consistency of his tastes, values, memories, brings to a crisis his relation with language. (Barthes [1973] 1975, 14)

In the movie about China this is complicated once again, and Barthes points this out, because he does not understand Chinese, but you can imagine it in your own language. Imagine it. In addition to the corporeal sensuality would there not also be a sensuality of sense. Would there not be that other sensuality communicated to us by familiar words appearing in unpredictably unfamiliar contexts brushing arms against other words that normally have nothing to do with them. Thinking about all those children reading from different books reminds me of Cage's *Where are we going? What are we doing?* from 1961 (Cage [1961] 1973, 194–259). Cage's piece is four different simultaneous lectures. In the published version of this work the words of each lecture are separated and legible but Cage warns us that "this is a dubious advantage, for I had wanted to say that our experiences, gotten as they are all at once, pass beyond our understanding" (194). Beyond our understanding, following a diagonal right to a material sensuality of sense no less than of the body. I am reminded also of *Thanks: A Simultaneity for People* by Jackson Mac Low. Mac Low might have told us simply to make any noise we wanted, for any length of time, but his articulated directions contribute to focusing our attention and to overpowering our easy confidence in rules, directions, syntax, semantics, and so on. Cage's use of chance operations is relevant here too, for they *force* control out of our intentional hands, making possible a material sensuality of the body and of sense. Sensuality. But what I really like about the Mac Low piece is the powerful Yes in its title. *Thanks.*

The detailed instructions in a Cage score like *26′ 1.1499″ for a String Player* (1954) introduce a new syntax. Deleuze and Guattari admired Cage for exciting what was hidden within art, hidden "underneath aims and objects," so exciting or liberating pointless becomings (Deleuze and Guattari [1972] 1992, 370–71). A pure plane of jouissance. The tools of this liberation include a new syntax.

THANKS

a simultaneity for people

Any person in a room may begin the action by making any vocal
utterance. Other people in the room may make utterances or be silent at any
time after the beginning.

Utterances may be in any language or **none**. They may be (1) sentences,
(2) clauses, (3) phrases, (4) phrase fragments, (5) groups of unrelated words,
(6) single words (among which may be names of letters), (7) polysyllabic word
fragments, (8) syllables, (9) phones (included or not within phonemes of any
languages), or (10) any other sounds produced in the mouth, throat or chest.

Any utterance may be repeated any number of times or not at all.
After a person makes an utterance and repeats it or not he should become silent
and remain so for any duration. After the silence he may make any utterance,
repeat it or not, again become silent, etc.

People may continue to make utterances or not until no one wants to
make an utterance or until a predetermined time limit is reached.

All utterances are free in all respects.

Non-vocal sounds may be produced and repeated or not in place of
utterances.

Anyone may submit any or all elements of this simultaneity to
chance regulation by any methods.

Jackson Mac Low
December 1960 - February 1961
New York City

Figure 7-5. Jackson Mac Low. *Thanks: A Simultaneity for People* December
1960–February 1961. Courtesy of Anne Tardos.

The rhythmic structure. 3;7;2;5;11. is that of
34' 46.776" for a pianist and for the other part
already written for a pianist. All of these pieces
may be played alone or in combination, and in whole
or in part, the title to be appropriately changed
to indicate time in minutes and seconds and the
instrumentalists involved. The present part may be
played on any 4-stringed instrument or(using parts
indicated by dotted lines) any combination of 2 or more.

The notation is in space, the amount equalling a
second given at the top of the page. Vibrato is
notated graphically. ⌢ or V are the conventional
symbols for bowing. H indicates hair of bow, W,
col legno. B indicates bridge (extreme ponticello);
BN is closer to bridge than normal; NB is closer to
normal than bridge, etc., F indicating extreme sul tasto.
Below these notations is an area where bowing pressure
is indicated graphically, the top being least, the bottom
most pressure (i.e. pianissimo, fortissimo). The 4
strings (e.g. violin EADG) are the lower large areas, the
points of stopping these being indicated. These strings
are in a continual state of changing "tune" indicated
by the words, decrease and increase, i.e. tension. Slides
are indicated by angles and curves, harmonics by 3 lines
connected vertically by dots. Vertical lines connecting
two separate events indicate legato. 4 pizzicatti are
distinguished: ., the normal; ┬ , stopped against finger-
board; x against fingernail; ↳ slide following pluck.
A dotted horizontal line indicates saltando. Manner of
breaking triple and quadruple stops is indicated by arrows.
If no indication is given, the player is free to break
as he chooses. The lowest area is devoted to noises on
the box, sounds other than those produced on the strings.
These may issue from entirely other sources, e.g. percussion
instruments, whistles, radios, etc. Only high and low are
indicated.

The 5 pieces (pg. 34 through 58) were written in 1953 in
NYC and are variously dedicated. The time was originally
indicated in terms of ritardandi and accelerandi, metronome
values given at structural points. Vertical lines
accompanied by the actual seconds have been added (1955).
The triple stop at the end of pg. 33 is the triple stop at
the beginning of pg. 34. The other pages were written at
Stony Point, N.Y., August-September 1955 with assistance
from David Tudor which is gratefully acknowledged. The
whole constitutes a fragment of an unfinished work for
many activities and may be performed with any of those to
be written or otherwise calculated.

Figure 7-6. John Cage. *26' 1.1499" for a String Player* © 1960 by Henmar Press Inc.
Used by permission of C. F. Peters Corporation.

It is a syntactic line, syntax being constituted by the curves, rings, bends, and
deviations of this dynamic line as it passes through the points, from the double
viewpoint of disjunctions and connections. It is no longer the formal or
superficial syntax that governs the equilibriums of language, but a syntax in
the process of becoming, a creation of syntax that gives birth to a foreign

>   language within language, a grammar of disequilibrium. (Deleuze [1993b]
>   1997, 112)

It is this new syntax that denatures, minorizes, or irregularizes language,
liberating sumptuous material sensualities involving the body and sense.

The second misunderstanding that I have courted is that if what is beautiful is beyond representation, it must also be beyond words, so there will
be no way to communicate the enjoyment of beauty. This misunderstanding is easy enough to fall for, because when we think of communication, we
think of regular communication of representations of the world. We do not
think of communicating sensual delight. But the examples of Cage and
Mac Low and the scene from the movie described by Barthes show us that,
against Ramsey, we can communicate the enjoyment of beauty. We can.
And this discovery contributes also the resolution, already provided, of the
difficulty of characterizing beautiful things without employing conceptual representations. The solution was to turn *from* the notion that beneath
conceptual description there are bare particulars about which you could
say nothing, and turn *toward* the notion of an irregular commonplace.

In 1946 Gertrude Stein was asked what an irregular commonplace was,
and this is what she said.

>   Anything is the answer. Or anything is an answer. But back to the question.
>   Anything is at once both typical and unique. And so anything is what "every-
>   body knows and nobody knows," an irregular commonplace, and Miss Stein is
>   always writing the portrait of that, and of anything. (Stein 1946)

Anything is at once both typical and unique. This is the key to there being
nothing that is not beautiful. Everything is an irregular commonplace. Pick
up a car crushed bottle cap from the road. It is that. It is a crushed bottle
cap, but it is more than that. There are so many of its features that are not
necessary for being a bottle cap. The eagle indicating that it came from
America's oldest brewery and the way it has been crushed flatter than usual
by the car tires and the pattern of rust. Put it in your mouth and it is altogether otherwise all over again. Rusty metallic tastes mingling with newly
felt shapes and textures. Each one singular. "I am inclined to believe that
there is no such thing as repetition" (Stein 1936c, 288). When you stop to
think of it, there is enormously more to anything than what it takes to be
the thing that it is. Its identity. And what really does it matter that you can

Figure 7-7. Yuengling beer bottle cap.

identify this as a bottle cap? Is that about the irregular commonplace in your mouth, or is it about you the identifier?

> Chorus: I am I because my little dog knows me.
> Chorus: That does not prove anything about you it only proves something about the dog.

> —GERTRUDE STEIN, *The Geographical History of America*

And so it is with identification generally. To identify this as a bottle cap proves something about me, but nothing in particular about the bottle cap. What is an irregular commonplace.

> Anything, as I was saying, that comes before the normal mind in the normal life can be identified by a name, and that aspect of it which has to do with our habitual practical purposes is obviously and clearly seen. But that same anything contains or involves a great many other aspects and qualities that everybody knows are there, even though everybody keeps his mind pretty well fixed on the single practical aspect and is only vaguely aware of the others, and strictly speaking does not know them. (Stein 1946)

So it is our practical purposive habitual lives that blind us to the irregularity of the commonplace and that make us only see anything's being typical and not its being unique, that is, atypical. But everything is an irregular commonplace. And so everything is already ripe for sensual enjoyment. Beautiful. Not perfect. Not pretty. Beautiful (Stein [1917] 1995, 4). Everything is beautiful, and nothing is more beautiful than anything else. Everything is an irregular commonplace. Everything can open out into a pure sheet of jouissance. Becoming becoming.

Becoming Becoming

Deleuze did use the word *beauty*. He once described *A Thousand Plateaus* as a "very beautiful book," and years before he had used the same word to describe Sartre's *Critique* (Deleuze 1995b and 1964b). Again, beauty surfaces early in *A Thousand Plateaus*, but Deleuze and Guattari don't work it very hard in the rest of the book (Deleuze and Guattari [1980] 1987, 15). They do, however, write a great deal about becoming.

Becoming defies common sense and good sense (Deleuze [1969] 1990, 1–3). Alice finds a box under the little glass table. It is marked "eat me," and inside of the box is a cake. She eats it and proceeds to become taller. We want to know how tall she is at any given time, and for common sense this has a definite answer. A few seconds after she eats the cake, she is a few inches taller, and a while later a bit taller still. This is what it means to become taller. Soon enough, Alice's head will hit the roof, and she will imagine writing letters to her feet. Someone who has common sense is someone who knows what's what. Who knows what anything is. Who is a master of identity (3). The flounder in Disney's *Little Mermaid*: This is this, and that is that. That's common sense. Common sense tells us that at any moment Alice will be a definite height. But this is just as if we had taken an egg slicer to her becoming taller, turning becoming into a succession of slices of being. And this kills the becoming twice over. Once within each slice of being which no longer becomes and a second time between the slices which simply succeed each other like the slices of an egg. The becoming has been removed, not completely to be sure; it is still possible by subtraction to determine the difference between the slices, and this will represent how much has changed from slice to slice. And this is good enough for ordinary work, and it is good enough by means of the calculus for science and for physics. But it is not good enough for metaphysics. If there is becoming, then the world cannot be conceptually represented.

Why this fear of becoming? This fear needs to be understood twice. Once intellectually and once existentially. Intellectually, becoming is inaccessible to conceptual thinking because if Alice is really becoming at a given moment, then her height at that moment is both h and not-h, and this is contradictory. Becoming forces a choice either to give up the possibility of a representational account of the world, or with an egg slicer, to give up becoming. And philosophers, although there are well-known exceptions, mostly give up becoming and cling to their commonsensical representations. Common sense is a dreadful liability when doing philosophy.[13] It constrains thinking. Intellectually, it is *common sense* that turns us against becoming.

Existentially, it is *good sense* that turns us against becoming. It is good sense not to put your faith in things that can break, or die. And so philosophers from forever have been telling us that it is a sign of good sense to direct our desires and our loves toward the unchanging, toward the transcendent, toward the transcendent autonomy of god, or of human freedom, or of art. Good sense sets what we care about, the direction of our lives, away from what changes, what fades, what can die (Deleuze [1969] 1990, 3). This is good sense, and it turns us away from becoming. Good sense no less than common sense makes it difficult to do philosophy. Giving a point or definite direction to your life, no less than insisting that the things of this world have a definite identity, is one sure way to kill becoming. And beauty. For becoming is my favorite way of saying beauty.

Becoming. If becoming is beyond representation, then we must remain close to the insight of Deleuze and Guattari that "what is real is the becoming itself, the block of becoming, not the supposedly fixed terms through which that which becomes passes" (Deleuze and Guattari [1980] 1987, 238). And when a sweater becomes you, something of the same sort is going on. When you wear a famous actress's sweater you become that actress in the sense of imitating or aping her, but the sweater doesn't become you. You don't move into the middle space between concepts where becoming occurs. When the sweater becomes you, your identity disappears into new folds of an irregularized you. That is why when the sweater becomes you, your friends are amazed not at your imitating someone else so much as they are amazed that you are no longer quite who you were and yet there you are, more intense, and in the flesh. This is more or less what Deleuze and Guattari mean by becoming imperceptible.

> Animal elegance, the camouflage fish, the clandestine: this fish is crisscrossed by abstract lines that resemble nothing, that do not even follow its organic divisions; but thus disorganized, disarticulated, it works with the lines of a rock, sand, and plants, becoming imperceptible. (Deleuze and Guattari [1980] 1987, 280)

And since Deleuze and Guattari insist that "*movement* has an essential relation to the imperceptible," they as much as tell us that becoming-imperceptible is becoming becoming (Deleuze and Guattari [1980] 1987, 280, my emphasis). Becoming beautiful.

And how do you become becoming. Not by copying. Not by purifying and isolating. You do it in two stages, *first* by breaking the spell of representational concepts and *second* by caressing the sensual singularity with all your senses. Seeking intensity. Our great good fortune is that becoming is everywhere. Everything becomes. That stick, that pen, that rubber band, that bottle, that wall, that roof. Everything is becoming. So everything is beautiful, and the trick is to feel it, to let the sensual power of the singular thing draw you away into sensual enjoyments beyond subject and object, affectionately alert to the irregularity of every commonplace. A pure plane of jouissance. But how.

We can approach sensuous delight in two steps. Drop and draw. First, drop your habits of practical life, dividing the world into the relevant and the irrelevant. Second, let yourself be drawn into it. These two steps should be familiar. They are all over the place. Here is Debord's drop and draw:

> In a dérive one or more persons during a certain period *drop* their usual motives for movement and action, their relations, their work and leisure activities, and let themselves be *drawn* by the attractions of the terrain and the encounters they find there. (Debord 1958, 50, my emphasis)

Deleuze and Guattari appeal to the same two steps when they tell us how to make ourselves bodies without organs. First, the organized body must be disorganized, we have to drop the whole of our normal fantasies, significations, and subjectifications (Deleuze and Guattari [1980] 1987, 1951). Second, this disorganized body will be drawn by sensual singularities into "a joy that implies no lack or impossibility and is not measured by pleasure since it is what distributes intensities of pleasure and prevents them from being suffused with anxiety, shame, and guilt" (Deleuze and Guattari [1980] 1987, 155).

And here is Keith Johnstone who acts, directs, and more importantly teaches improvisation. He has developed a large number of techniques for reawakening the "intensity of the world," the very intensity whose loss is so often an unintended side effect of adultification (Johnstone [1979] 1992, 13). Here is one of his techniques, it's another drop and draw:

> I've since found tricks that can make the world blaze up again in about fifteen seconds, and the effects last for hours. For example, if I have a group of students who are feeling fairly safe and comfortable with each other, I get them to pace about the room shouting out the wrong name for everything their eyes light on. Maybe there's time to shout out ten wrong names before I stop them. Then I ask whether other people look larger or smaller—almost everyone sees people as different sizes, mostly as smaller. "Do the outlines looker sharper or more blurred?" I ask, and everyone agrees that the outlines are many times sharper. "What about colors?" Everyone agrees there's far more color, and that the colors are more intense. (Johnstone [1979] 1992, 13)

Using the wrong words drops the normal representational frame that we take with us when we approach the world, and according to Johnstone, this has the effect of drawing us into a heightened sensual experience of the world. Johnstone's discussion of mask work in the theater fits the same model: Wearing the mask drops your normal identity, and your body can then be drawn into new expressivities. The two phases of sensual design are the two phases of an aesthetics of existence. Drop and Draw.

First, break the spell of the representation. Turn the chair upside down. Then let yourself be drawn into the sensual plane of the chair. Not just with your eyes. Touch it. Slap it. Taste it with your tongue. Open your mouth. We know that our mouths are amazing sensory organs and yet we restrict them to food and sex. When we were children, we put everything in our mouths, and we should continue to do so. And the more senses we loose on the singular object, the more we will enjoy beauty beyond representation.

An irregular commonplace. Beyond truth and falsity. Becoming becoming. Taste it.

Throughout the tradition of European philosophy, every effort has been made to get you to take the world out of your mouth, to use a little common sense and a little good sense to find a way either to settle into the insipid platitudes of the grown-ups or to seek an escapist transcendence along lines of perfection. Beauty beyond representation is uncombed, irregular, and unruly, and so from Plato on they have sought to control it. To fit it into the safe box of goodness to get our minds out of his thighs or hers and on up to beauty itself by itself. But it wasn't beauty. It was the old dream of perfection. Pretty, perhaps, but not beautiful.

Beauty is altogether otherwise. A *bruissement* of the world. A pure plane of jouissance. Listen. Taste the sounds with your whole body. Feel the joy in your mouth. Hypersensual experience is the experience of a beauty that knows no contrary and admits of no degrees. An absolute power beyond comparison. Lifting belly is so strong. This is beauty, which by its sensual allure draws us out beyond identity, beyond the safe pleasantness of pretending you know who you are and what you stand for out into the theatrical intensities of desire deliriously becoming becoming. Don't stop. On the other side of representational identification is a joy that comes from giving up the fruitless search for a home. When you have no home, you are never lost. Right here. Right now. There is no better place. Give up perfection. Taste it now. Drink it. Open your body. Yes. Caress Yes.

Stone soup. A life.

"pleasure" and "art"
keep us from enjoying sensual life.

it's not the pleasure we enjoy,
it's the beer, tickling its thick cold down my throat

it's not the pain we enjoy,
it's the shiver of her nails on my back.

Refusing Beauty; or, The Bruise

> Caution seldom goes far enough.
>
> —WALT WHITMAN, *Leaves of Grass*

Barthes tells us that one of the surprising things about speech is that there is no erasing. There is only going forward. There is only Yes (Barthes 1984, 93). This is a feature of speech that derives from speech's being in time. Not its being in space. We can move back and forth in space but not in time (Bergson [1889] 1960, 154–55). In time, that is in *concrete becoming* as opposed to mathematical abstract time, in concrete becoming, we can only go forward; we can only build on the past which is never lost. Ever (Bergson [1889] 1960, chap. 2). We think of our moving through time as if we were a boat moving across a lake leaving the past behind us like the wake of a boat. But the universe leaves no wake. The past is not left behind us. There is no place for the past to be but here. Now. It is not lost. It is here with us. There are ghosts everywhere.

We think the past is preserved because we can remember it. But it is otherwise. We can remember the past only because the past is never lost. Our mistake is of a piece with the illusion that we can explain how memory is possible because representations of the past are stored in the brain. But this will never do. In order for the brain to explain the preservation of the past and the possibility of memory, the past of the brain *itself* needs to be preserved. And how are we to explain that? Does the brain have a tinier brain in which the brain's past is preserved? No. It will never work. The brain can't solve the problem of the preservation of the past because the brain *has* that problem (Bergson [1896] 1991, 151). Memory doesn't explain the preservation of the past; the preservation of the past explains memory. Concrete becoming preserves everything *subrepresentationally,* and this, not some organ in your skull, is the condition of the possibility of memory. Becoming never erases, never goes back. In becoming there is only Yes.

So let's keep on thinking about a disturbing bit you might have noticed on a recent page. The battered bruise. A cheek bruised in a battering. Here is the passage, once again.

> We can be surprised to discover beauty where we didn't expect to find it. The
> stain on a tablecloth. A cheek bruised in a battering. Laundry heaped on the
> basement floor.

The beautiful bruise on a battered cheek raises the question, which I have been skirting since beginning: Are there or should there be moral limitations to our enjoyment of everything's irregularity, everything's beauty? In particular, the beautiful bruise raises a question like this: How can you say that the bruise on her cheek is beautiful when she received it in the midst of a fight with her alcoholic lover? The objection to enjoying the bruise or even to describing it as beautiful seems to be that our moral characterization of the *cause* of some effect must also apply to *effect* of that cause. Thus, if we are required to say that battering is bad, then we are also required to say that the bruises that result from that battering are bad. And then it seems impossible for the bruises to be beautiful because while the beautiful is good, the battering and the bruises that result from the battering are bad. So the cheek bruised in a battering could not possibly be beautiful. But this series of thoughts starts off on the wrong foot. The fundamental prejudice of philosophers: How could anything originate out of its opposite? (Nietzsche [1886] 1966, §2).

It is not in general true that the properties of whatever *causes* an effect must also be properties of the *effect* of that cause. In the eighteenth century

Dr. Johnson mocked this principle by saying that it amounted to the ridiculous claim that whoever "drives fat oxen should himself be fat."[1] In any case it is obvious enough that there are properties of boiling water that are not properties of hard-boiled eggs even though the boiling of the one is the cause of the hardening of the other. So it is not in general true that the properties of a cause must be inherited by the effects of that cause.

But the opposition to enjoying the beauty of the bruise is so strong that the argument will not stop here. Granting that in general it is not true that effects inherit the properties of their causes, beauty's refusers will say that the principle does nevertheless hold in the special case of moral properties. But this special version of the inheritance principle fares no better. Effects do not inherit the moral properties of their causes. If they did, then nothing good could ever have bad consequences and nothing bad could ever have good consequences. But it is easy enough to imagine a family whose child dies in an accident on a newly frozen pond and that, nevertheless, at long last, the family finds that this accident has brought the survivors closer together. Remember the old Nietzschean tag that "What does not destroy me, makes me stronger" (Nietzsche [1888a] 1982, 467). This is a familiar feature of even such ordinary experiences as getting over homesickness. Good can come out of struggle. Frederick Douglass.

Beauty's refusers will continue to object that this is not enough to save the beauty of the bruise, for although it is sad that the little girl fell through the thin ice to her death, it wasn't immoral. It was just unfortunate. And so it might still be true that effects inherit moral properties from their causes. But this will never do. If good can come from the little girl's accidentally falling through the ice, good could also come from the little girl's having been strangled.

—"Strangled? Is that beautiful too?"
—All in good time. All in good time.

For now I only want to point out that even if the girl had been strangled, the family might still, in the same way and at long last, come together as it never had before.

I picked the battered girl because I wanted to make the bruise's beauty as difficult as possible to see.[2] And so I should also make it clear that I am talking about the bruise being beautiful; I am not talking about enjoying *what the bruise means*. I am talking about the bruise. So I am not particularly interested in cases where we can enjoy or take pride in a bruise that shows how tough you are or what a dangerous mountain biker you are. I am not talking about our reaction to something instantiating the concept of a bruise. I am not talking about what the bruise means, whether that is something relatively good, like that you are tough, or relatively bad, like that your lover is cruel. I am talking about something that escapes concepts, something Gertrude Stein would call an irregular commonplace (Stein 1946). Thinking about my own white skin, I am talking about the nameless colors fading in and out of purple, and as time passes, becoming yellows and greens and browns. Nameless shades and shadows of irregular textures dissolving colors. Skin losing the look of skin.

It was Scarry once again whose *Beauty and Being Just* (1999) by not explicitly discriminating beauty and perfection, and by way of the cheap pleasures of counterexamples, made me think about the beauty of things that were imperfect. Broken. So I was put in mind of some remarks that are preserved in a little essay by the fourteenth-century Japanese essayist Kenko:

> Somebody once remarked that thin silk was not satisfactory as a scroll wrapping because it was so easily torn. Ton'a replied, "It is only after the silk wrapper has frayed at the top and bottom, and the mother-of-pearl has fallen from the roller that a scroll looks beautiful." This opinion demonstrated the excellent taste of the man. People often say that a set of books looks ugly if all the volumes are not in the same format, but I was impressed to hear the Abbot Koyu say, "It is typical of the unintelligent man to insist on assembling complete sets of everything. Imperfect sets are better." (Kenko [1330] 1998, §82)

Almost two years ago I was talking with Sunny Bavaro when I thought: If frayed silk can be beautiful, why not skin? And thankful as ever for her support, that is when I started thinking about bruises. Unless the first time was that same fall when I read this amazing sentence caught from an interview with the painter Francis Bacon:

> Another thing that made me think about the human cry was a book that I bought when I was very young from a bookshop in Paris, a second-hand book which had beautiful hand-colored plates of diseases of the mouth, beautiful

plates of the mouth open and of the examination of the inside of the mouth; they fascinated me, and I was obsessed by them. (Sylvester [1987] 1999, 35)

Beautiful plates of diseases of the mouth. Frayed silk. Imperfect sets of books. These all confirm my confidence that I am not alone in having no doubt that the bruised cheek on the battered girl was beautiful. But my defense of the beauty of the bruise by separating the bruise from its immoral cause cannot be the end of my story. Because the end of my story is not crusty conceptual separation. It is liquid sensual connection.

The strangling too. I have tried to make attractive the idea that everything was beautiful, that everything was an irregular commonplace. And I am as attracted as ever to that idea, so I cannot avoid the consequence that *the battering itself*, like everything else, is beautiful. And once again it will be important to address ourselves to the sensual singularity of the battering and not what the battering means. The question is whether or not it is possible to say that the battering was beautiful without also being required to think that the battering was a morally good thing. Is it possible to receive the battering without receiving it *as a battering*, as an instance of the type battering. To Whitehead's difficulties with the problem of simple location we should add the difficulties here confronted of what might be called simple identification. Both would be examples of the Fallacy of Misplaced Concreteness, the fallacy of mistaking an abstraction for a concrete singularity (Whitehead [1925] 1967, 48–51; Austin 1953; Lawrence 1956, 311ff.).

Simplifying enormously: There are two factors that together can make a specific battering immoral. On the one hand, there is some sort of moral attitude or theory that gives us to feel or to think that battering is bad. On the other hand, there is the identification of the event as an instance of battering. It is only the second that is relevant to the beauty of the battering, and it brings us back again to the problem of being an instance of a type. Simple identification. The problem is not that the event is not a battering. The problem is that it is not *simply* a battering. And neither is it simply both a battering and beautiful. It is beyond concepts and so it is neither one thing nor many. "It is impossible to complete the description of an actual occasion by means of concepts" (Whitehead [1925] 1967, 169–70). This impossibility is one motivation for Whitehead's criticism of traditional educational methods as being over involved with the merely intellectual. He thought that education like thinking itself was easily rutted in familiar abstractions and that part of waking to freedom and power would be strengthening "habits of concrete appreciation" which would reveal actual events in what he calls the "depth" of their individuality (Whitehead 1925 [1967], 198–99). Identification is violation.

The way to see the beauty in the battering will be to discover the sensual irregularity that we hide from ourselves by simply identifying the actual event as an instance of the general type battering. Simple identification. Everything has so many more aspects than simply those that are necessary and sufficient for being an instance of the kind we take it to be. It's Bergson's insight once more: "We do not see the actual things themselves; in most cases we confine ourselves to reading the labels affixed to them" (Bergson [1900] 1980, 159). As you take the sandwich out of the plastic sandwich bag, it catches the light *this* way and makes *these* noises and gives off *these* odors, none of which is either necessary or sufficient for being a plastic bag. And so too every battering will have innumerable other *aspects*, and only a very few of these will even be relevant to its counting as a battering. It's Gertrude Stein again. And in this context, knowing that aspect was a semi-technical term in Whitehead's work, it suddenly makes sense that Whitehead was, with Picasso and Stein herself, one of only three "first class geniuses" that the author of Alice Toklas's *Autobiography* ever met (Stein 1933, 5; Lawrence 1956, 326–27). Reciting Stein:

> Anything, as I was saying, that comes before the normal mind in the normal life can be identified by name, and that aspect of it which has to do with our habitual practical purposes is obviously and clearly seen. But that same anything contains or involves a great many other aspects and qualities that everybody knows are there, even though everybody keeps his mind pretty well fixed on the single practical aspect and is only vaguely aware of the others, and strictly speaking does not know them. (Stein 1946)

The battering's being a battering fits smoothly into practical and moral life; it does. Nevertheless, any battering will also contain or involve a great many other aspects that everybody knows are there even though everybody keeps their mind focused pretty exclusively on the single aspect that mostly matters to most of us most of the time, namely, that the battering is bad. But identification is violation.

What happens when, freeing sensual enjoyment, we attend to the innumerable other aspects. When we attend to these other aspects, the battering will not of course become good. But I think that is behind some of the shock I see in the faces of my friends when I tell them that the battering itself is beautiful. They think I am saying that the battering is morally good. I am not. Even for those with only moral vision, there can be something defiant about the bruise's beauty, the intentions of the batterer are thwarted by enjoying the bruise's beauty since it was no part of the intentions of the batterer to produce beauty on his batterer's face. But even that little bit of positive moral reversal is not what I am after. I am indeed saying that the battering can be sensually enjoyed, but I am not saying that it fits under the heading good in some crooked moral practice or moral theory.

For so long beauty has been associated with goodness. In the *Republic* Socrates insists that goodness produces beauty: "Fine words, harmony, grace, and rhythm follow . . . the sort of fine and good character that has developed in accordance with an intelligent plan" (Plato [c. 380 BCE] 1997, 400d see Nehamas 1999b and 1982). According to Aristotle, if you are really ugly, you can't even hope for happiness, because "we do not altogether have the character of happiness if we look utterly repulsive" (Aristotle [340 BCE] 1985, 1.8, 1099b2–6). The connection between beauty and moral goodness is quite obviously still with us in the drawings that animate Disney movies.[3] So it is easy to slip into thinking that to enjoy the beauty of the battering is to find the battering morally good. But *attending affectionately* to sensual experience does not make what we experience fall under the concept of the morally good. Sensual attention is the beginning of breaking through to the other side of representation: beyond good and evil no less than beyond truth and falsity. The beauty of an actual occasion will be invisible to one who can't break the spell of its meaning.

Return to the battering. The battering will produce sounds: hands hitting faces, yelling, screaming, chairs falling over, sobbing, and so on. Late last summer when I was talking about this with friends I would slap my bare knee with both my hands fairly loudly fairly fast more or less arrhythmically. And that would be my rapid fire demonstration that a battering could be beautiful. QED.

Perhaps it is no surprise that Spinoza shares something like this account of the battering, since for Spinoza "no action, considered in itself, is good or evil" (Spinoza 1677, IVP59D). Nevertheless, given the bruise I am considering, it is still amazing to find that he actually discusses battering. "The act of beating, insofar as it is considered physically, and insofar as we attend only to the fact that the man raises his arm, closes his fist, and moves his whole arm forcefully up and down, is a virtue" (IVP59S). The beating is a virtue in that it "expresses a power of my body; it expresses what my body can do in a certain relation" (Deleuze [1970] 1988, 35). So my own rapid-fire QED puts us near that master of the QED, Spinoza himself.

Going a little more slowly, consider just the sound of a slap. There is a nice sound when the baseball slaps hard into the first baseman's mitt. When Steve Reich composed *Clapping Music* in 1972, he drew our attention to regular rhythmic irregularities of hands clapping (Reich 1972). And we can attend to those sounds also during a battering. If the one is beautiful, so too is the other. Screams too. The score for Yoko Ono's *Voice Piece for Soprano* (1961) reads

Scream
    1. against the wind
    2. against the wall
    3. against the sky. (Ono [1961] 1999)[4]

And if these screams can be beautiful, why not the screams of an actual battering? And by now you will have figured out the trick. What differentiates the actual beating from these staged sounds is that when staged we turn our loving ears loose on more than the identification and significance of what is happening. And so we enjoy beauty. And there is no reason we couldn't attend in this way to the battering. We might not like to. We might refuse to. We might like to live in a moral universe as neat and tidy as Plato's, or Disney's. But we don't. Burtynsky (Pauli 2003).

Someone refusing beauty might insist that it is not possible to decontextualize the sounds, to strip the sounds off the battering, and enjoy their beauty. But this is in two ways confused. In the first place it is those who would refuse beauty that have to slam the door on the sounds of the battering and focus only on the logical fact that it is a battering. Logical fact because the sensual reality of the battering is simply not relevant to its being immoral. All that counts is the logical fact that this is a battering and that batterings are immoral. It's as if beauty's refusers have no sensations but only intellections. So it is beauty's refusers who would confine the morality of the battering in decontextual prison. But we already know that contextual lockup is never secure (Derrida 1971). So whether or not it is impossible to refuse beauty, it is not possible to lock up the immoral battering without the sounds of the battering leaking in.

In the second place, the way to see the beauty in the battering is precisely not to strip the sounds off the battering and attend just to those. To open yourself to the pointless colors and forms of the battering requires seeing more of the singular event than simply its identity, its meaning. It requires attending to more, not less. So the Derridean discovery that sensual and conceptual doors are never shut tight is one aspect of the open possibility of enjoying the sensual sounds even of a battering. It turns out that those who refuse beauty are doing just that: refusing something that is there. Thus revealing the repressive spirit of morality. It is beautiful, but you shouldn't enjoy it. The enjoyment itself is immoral. Like the little dog, this little enjoyment takes us behind the curtain. The cover is blown. Pay no attention to the man behind the curtain.

Discovering the beauty in the bruise pulls the curtain from the illusion that there is any unity to what matters, to what is *important* (Whitehead [1938] 1968, 11ff.). Beauty matters, and goodness matters, and so we build a comforting fantasy where beauty is a consequence of the good and perhaps goodness is a consequence of beauty too. But the drunken battering that produced our beautiful little bruise can bring it all down. Even the movies recognize the existence of something that the Wicked Witch of the West refers to as beautiful wickedness.

> Oh, what a world! What a world! Who would have thought a good little girl like you could destroy my beautiful wickedness.[5]

Behind the curtain is the blunt truth that what is important does not form a unitary whole. We are misleadingly near the insistence of political theorists such as Charles Taylor who say that the fundamental problem with much moral thinking is that it doesn't recognize a genuinely irreducible diversity of goods (Taylor 1982, 129–44). But I am after more than this. Taylor argues that there are incommensurable goods and that any attempt to reduce them to some combination of formal and utilitarian considerations is bound to betray our experience of moral life. And this is true. But that is not what is behind the curtain.

Taylor's discovery of the incommensurable diversity of goods is a discovery within the frame of representation. You might have thought that there was only one thing that mattered, for example material well-being, but Taylor insists that there are other things that matter. Other things whose accomplishment may not be compatible with material well-being. This is Taylor's list: integrity, charity, liberty, and rationality. Moral codes or systems always take a representation of the human world for granted, and so they and their justifications live within the frame of representation. Whitehead tells us this too. "The point is that moral codes are relevant to presuppositions respecting the systematic character of the relevant universe. When the presuppositions do not apply, that special code is a vacuous statement of abstract irrelevancies" (Whitehead 1938 [1968], 13). And the diversity of goods defended by Taylor does not break the frame of representation.

A sign of this failure to break through, and a sign also of disruptive power of beauty, is that in the midst of Taylor's discussion of incommensurable goods, he insists that a certain "we" would be "rightly alarmed" by anyone who did not concede that moral considerations should silence aesthetic considerations, for example, concerning Mozart or flowers (Taylor 1982, 137). Intriguingly, it is precisely music that is singled out by Whitehead as making moral considerations retreat to irrelevance, precisely music that silences the voice of morality. "The retreat of morals in the presence of music, and of dancing, and the general gaiety of the theatre, is a fact very interesting to philosophers and very puzzling to the official censors" (Whitehead [1938] 1968, 13). The reason for this is that sensual attention such as is required for the enjoyment of music is a rough edge that can begin breaking though. "Music is never tragic, music is joy" (Deleuze and Guattari [1980] 1987, 299).

Someone will say that on the contrary music can be tragic and that even Whitehead's own leading example, *Carmen*, might be an example of tragic music. Perhaps. But what is never tragic is delighting in the sensuality of sounds. Sensual enjoyment is always Yes. And this delight is an expression of the rough edge of deterritorialization, the first rough excitement of becoming becoming. Breaking through always starts rough. Smooth and to the point presupposes representation. That is why Whitehead insists that to acquire learning we must "grasp the topic in the rough" (Whitehead [1938] 1968, 6). That is why Tournier's twins Jean-Paul are so attracted to tides.

> The tide is a clock run mad, suffering from a hundred parasitic influences—the rotation of the earth, the existence of submerged continents, the viscosity of the water and so on—that defy reason and overset it. What is true one year is no longer so the year after, what goes for Paimpol won't go for Saint-Cast or Mont-Saint-Michel. It is the typical example of an astronomical system of mathematical regularity, intelligible to the marrow, being suddenly warped, dislocated and fractured, and, while still continuing to function, doing so in an atmosphere of turbulence, and troubled waters, with jumps, distortions and alterations. I am convinced that it was this irrational element—the appearance of life, freedom, and personality it gives—that attracted Jean. (Tournier 1975, 128)

And it is the irrational element that is the source also of sensual delight. What doesn't fit. Not this or that. An irregular commonplace. What Tournier calls "something or other" (Tournier 1975, 128). It is the something or other that initiates becoming becoming.

It is precisely this something or other that draws us to the beauty of the bruise. Those who refuse beauty simply think that it would be immoral to forget or otherwise set aside that the source of the sounds was a battering. Morality here keeps us from enjoying the sounds. Of course. But it is worse. Morality here keeps us from even being aware of the sonic sensuality of our experience. How? By focusing our attention on what type an instance is an instance of, and thus making the irregular commonplace disappear. But that means it makes the thing itself disappear. Morality makes us blind.

It is not just morality in the usual sense that blinds us. A fine sense of the contextually appropriate, the ideal equally of the very polite and the very pragmatic, a fine sense of the contextually appropriate is able to make sensual singularities disappear whether the context is moral or aesthetic. Just this morning I realized this is what many people do with certain sorts of even old avant-garde music. Take, for example, Henry Cowell's 1939 *Pulse* for six percussionists, scored for three Korean dragon's mouths, three woodblocks, three Chinese tom-toms, three drums, three rice bowls, three tem-

Figure 8-1. Edward Burtynsky. *Nickel Tailings No. 34*, Sudbury Ontario, 1996. Photo(s) © Edward Burtynsky, courtesy Nicholas Metivier, Toronto / Howard Greenberg & Bryce Wolkowitz. New York.

ple gongs, three cymbals, three gongs, three pipes, and three brake drums.[6] Three brake drums. If we don't ourselves, at least we can imagine others who would recoil from this description, saying that it couldn't be worth listening to. How can you make music by beating on automobile parts? Its just like the bruise and the battering. Refusing to experience the irregular commonplace. Refusing to see past being an instance of a type. Refusing to feel the universe on your skin. Refusing beauty.

Let's end with a photograph. A photograph by Edward Burtynsky of poisonous nickel tailings running off through a field in Sudbury, Ontario. A field polluted past death. Being confronted with this striking photograph is as unsettling as being told that the bruise is beautiful. I was forcing the bruise *on you*, so it didn't have the same effect on me as this photograph. Burtynsky is doing this polluted field *to me*, and it leaves my judgment unsure. Is this or is this not beautiful? But we have been too busy judging beauty. The point is not to judge but to enjoy. To excite. To set in motion. Becoming becoming.

Like the beautiful bruise, Burtynsky's photographs reveal that what matters is not all of one piece. In the face of these photographs of poisonous creeks we feel both the beauty and the poison and don't know whether to judge them good or bad. Feigning philosophy, someone will say both. But what we really need is a way to approach ethical life without double negation. A way to approach moral life with more than a No to evil. With more than simply: Get off my back. And here the beauty of poisoned fields might help us to an ethics without respect. An ethics of affection. "Where mere morality obtains, only the forbidden and the forbidding or else the compulsive and barren sense of duty operate. Over against this, the aesthetic metaphor and the aesthetic mode offer excitement, allurement, inspiration" (Lawrence 1961a, 553). Let's see.

hate needs categories,
affection doesn't.

An Ethics of Affection

Man is but a speck.

—BENEDICT DE SPINOZA, *Tractatus Theologico-Politicus*

Either ethics makes no sense at all, or this is what it means and has nothing else to say: not to be unworthy of what happens to us.

—GILLES DELEUZE, *Logic of Sense*

The relation of most ethical theory to the anguish of existence is like the relation of dusting to architecture. It's good to dust. And since dust always returns there is always more good to be done by dusting. But good dusters presuppose furnished structures, and there is no connection between being able to polish a table and being able to design it, between dusting a house and designing a building open on all sides to life. Ethics navigates through life within the frame of representation. But only by being drawn to life, only by being drawn to the other side of representation, can we live our lives in the seafoam joy of becoming becoming.

We expect ethical considerations to generalize. So ethical considerations can present themselves in terms of what some *types of being* owe to other *types of being*. This is the logical structure of the demand to respect other people, for example. And it is the logical structure of considerations affecting the distribution of goods of all sorts, like access to medicine and to food, education, shelter, a living wage, a reliable voting apparatus, and more. These are worthy ideals, but the ethical machine works only on instances of types—for example, instances of the type sentient creature or the type person. Ethical machinery is therefore blind to sensual singularities, and if these are what draw us to becoming becoming, then ethics and life drawing will find themselves in conflict. And so it is. The ethical machine cannot digest sensual singularities. Refusing beauty. It spits them out.

Not an Ethics of Human Rights

Good as these ethical ideals are, if they are taken to be foundational, or normative for living, then there will be no room for life drawing. So take a deep breath. I will be spending a few pages in an attempt to show that ethical theory, whether grounded on human rights or on mutual respect, cannot ground itself; it begs the question. Then by means of the surrealism of the Césaires, I will return to characterizing the ethical dimensions of life drawing. It is not a matter of obeying this rule or this principle, or even of treating all members of the same type the same way; it is rather a mode of existence that aims to be affected by as much of one's surroundings as possible and to affect as much of one's surroundings as possible (Spinoza [1677] 1994, IVP38). Hardly an ethics of the traditional sort, this is not a systematic way of making decisions; it is simply another way of saying becoming becoming. It is not an ethics but an aesthetics of existence, and so if it were not so cute, we might spell this ethics of affection one letter differently: An Aethics of Affection.

   Let us approach the difficulty of grounding ethical theory by means of a real ethical problem. Antiblack racism in the United States of America. There are many structural and psychological dimensions of antiblack racism, but let's focus on the fact that many schools in predominantly black neighborhoods are not funded at the same dollar/student level as schools in predominantly white neighborhoods. This inequity would be justified if black schools and white schools, although both instances of the type school, were nevertheless *not* both instances of some other type. And not just some other ad hoc type but some other relevant type. In the United States many people think that one relevant type that differentiates many black and white schools is being in a community that generates substantial income from property taxes. These people think that being in a community that generates substantial income from property taxes is what earns you the right to have more money spent on your education. The property tax type in question separates, but only roughly, predominantly black schools from predominantly white schools. The connection between these two types of school and the property-tax type is only made by the accident of the history of slavery and its aftermath in the United States. Given the history of U.S. slavery and its aftermath, the connection is predictable, but the connection is not necessary. The property-tax type is not essentially related to any racial distinctions, and so it is not essentially related to the distinction between schools that are predominantly white and schools that are predominantly black. This can make the property-tax type in question seem neutral, color blind in the rhetoric of one side of this debate. This neutrality is simply another way of saying that the two types, black and white schools and property-tax revenues, are accidentally connected. And if the type is neutral on matters of race, how can it be, so the argument goes, that it perpetuates antiblack racism? The answer is that given the racist history of the United States, a color-blind type might nevertheless mirror and preserve the racist divisions in the society. It is familiar ground.

And then the typical ethical move. Find a type that *includes* both black and white Americans, and then argue that if these two racial types belong together in this category, then the same dollar/student investment must be made both in predominantly white schools and in predominantly black schools. There are really two moves here. First, finding a category that includes black and white Americans. There are an enormous number of such categories: American, North American, alive at this moment, not from Mars, never saw a living dinosaur, under forty-five feet tall, and so on, through even more Goodmanesque types. It is the second move that does the work. Ethicists must find a category that not only includes black and white Americans but also has the consequence that being included in this category earns one the right to have more or less equal resources invested in one's education. We are often urged to care equally about all humans, and if this were correct and included caring about education, then we should make equal per student investments in predominantly white and predominantly black schools. Or so it seems.

But it is not really clear why one is obligated to care equally about every human being. It is not in general true that, as a *matter of fact*, I care equally about all instances of a given type. For instance I do not care equally about all poisonous snakes or dogs. No one objects if I care much more about the poisonous snake that I have just stepped on than I do about just any poisonous snake. And I care more about my own dog, Islay, than I care about just any dog, no matter how cute. Nor is it a matter of my own personal involvement; if I discover that dolphins in some part of the world are suffering from a fatal viral infection, I would care more about them than I would care about just any old dolphin. I play favorites.

Some will be tempted to work against my actual favoritism by arguing that since I do care about some members of a given type, I am therefore *obligated* to care equally about any member of that type. We are often told that since the deaths caused by an earthquake or hurricane or something are human deaths, we should care about those dead people because not to do so would be *inconsistent* with caring about the people in our own families. But it is not true. I like apples and care about apple harvests insofar as that affects my ability to buy relatively inexpensive apples. So I will care if there is a bad harvest in Vermont but not if there is a bad harvest in France; my apples don't come from France. If the world harvest is so bad that I can no longer afford Vermont apples, then I will be concerned. Otherwise not. Our caring is under no obligation to treat all members of the category apple the same way.

In fact, our caring mostly begins from particular individuals, not from classes and categories. That is why when they are trying to get us to care about hunger in other parts of the world, they show us pictures and tell us stories about individual persons. These particular stories attract our attention, and then, safely hooked on a particular, they nudge us into caring more generally about the whole devastated town or island or something.

It is not generally true that if I *do* care about a member of a given class, then I *ought* to care equally, or at all, about every member of that class. And this can be shown even without recourse to any of the irrelevant but infinite classes that, logically speaking, every instance is a member of. No. There is no way around it. Ethicists must provide an argument for their assumption that there is something special about the type Human Being, or whatever concept they use to put black and white humans in one class, some special feature that supports the obligation either to care equally about every member of the class, period, or to care equally about every member of that class on the condition that I care at all about any single member of it. And the usual list of putative obligation-supporting features can include being rational or being free or being sentient or being able to feel pain or being made in the image of god. And in each of these cases it becomes possible that the class of those possessing that obligation-bearing feature either excludes some humans or includes some nonhumans. Utilitarians are famously tempted to go in both of these directions, toward infanticide and toward veganism. But if it is not generally true that I should care equally about every member of a class, then what is it about being rational or being free or being sentient that turns the trick?

The moral tradition is strangely silent on this issue. Modern moralists, if not ancient and medieval ones, generally assume that their racist opponent is already committed to some general Enlightenment principle such as that all men are created equal. This cuts down on work, for in that case all the defender of difference needs to do is point out that men of African descent are no less men than those of European. And the argument is over. Although in fact it never really began.

One way to feel this is to ask yourself how you would urge an all-men-are-created-equal person to remove the sexism and begin believing that all human beings were created equal, not just the men. The difficulty is that along an enormous number of dimensions human beings are obviously not equal. All human beings are, however, human beings, and, tautologous or not, that might do the trick. But we have just seen that there is no obligation to treat every member of a class equally, so that won't do, no matter how we resolve the difficult question of whether grounding moral obligation on biology would affect the modality of moral judgments. Perhaps the most direct move against the sexist version of the Enlightenment principle would be to say that there are no morally significant differences between human beings. But apart from being false that just helps itself to the prize. It is precisely the moral equality of all humans, not just the men, that we are trying to justify.

God might seem to help here because we could say that while there are indeed morally significant differences between those deserving of punishment and those not, it is nevertheless true that at birth or conception or quickening, or something, god puts different but morally equal souls in each human body. Set aside every question about how we could ever have grounds for such a claim, let alone know it. Suppose it is true. It still turns out that the appeal to god raises what we could call Euthyphro questions, namely does god put morally equal souls in each human body because humans are morally equal (which makes moral considerations primary) or are humans morally equal because god just happens to put morally equal souls in each human body (which makes happenstance and arbitrary power primary). Nothing prevents moralists from opting for the second, but if they do so, they must forfeit their faith that moral values have more metaphysical weight than raw power. And since many moralists have turned to morality to escape the brutality of raw power, this is unlikely to be a popular option. So likely as not they will follow the Platonic Socrates for whom gods are imagined to take dictation from morality and not the other way round. And in that case we still haven't begun. We haven't begun our defense of the moral equality of all human beings, not just the men. We could go on and consider defending the moral equality of humans on the basis of humans being free or sentient or able to feel pain. But in each case the result will be the same. Whether or not we find that it is not *true* that all humans possess the property in question, we will find that the *moral* status of the property in question, its mysterious ability, all by itself, to obligate us, is still undefended. A question begged, a loose thread.

So let us simply *assume* that all humans are morally equal and see what happens. There are still some surprises. There is something particularly odd about the appeal to Enlightenment values—Enlightenment values like moral equality and human dignity, for example—to defend an appreciation or respect for the differences between people. The general argument is meant to show, somewhat paradoxically, that we should respect difference because we are not different. Eighteenth-century universalism and twenty-first-century multiculturalism make an exceedingly odd couple. Nevertheless, nobody says anything because moralists of today are just as afraid of rejecting the Enlightenment as those of an earlier period were of rejecting god. But first I must show that Enlightenment ideals are the problem. They are the problem because they are racist. This proceeds in two stages.

It is by now well known that many of the heroes of the Enlightenment, Hume and Kant for example, were racists who firmly believed that their racism was not incompatible with their universalism (Eze 1997). But it continues to be widely believed that the racism of these Enlightenment philosophers does not pollute their universalist moral philosophy. You can hear people saying that it was, for example, Kant, the little man, who was a racist but the moral philosophy that this racist man wrote is not intrinsically racist. So they tell us that we are free to help ourselves to Enlightenment notions such as human rights and the moral dignity of human beings without fear that we are appealing to deeply flawed notions. But in the first instance what this self-congratulatory attitude masks is that universalism is itself tinged with a certain species of racism. The racism for example of "The Brotherhood" in Ellison's *Invisible Man*. Almost out of nowhere a member of the Brotherhood jumps down the throat of the novel's central figure: "'Why do you fellows always talk in terms of race!' he snapped, his eyes blazing" (Ellison [1952] 1980, 292).

Sartre's figure of the "Democrat" also shows that Enlightenment ideals produce a certain kind of racism. Here is Sartre in 1946.

> For a Jew, conscious and proud of being Jewish, there may not be much difference between the anti-Semite and the democrat. The former wishes to destroy him as a man and leave nothing in him but the Jew, the pariah, the untouchable; the latter wishes to destroy him as a Jew and leave nothing in him but the man, the abstract and universal subject of the rights of man and the rights of the citizen.
>
> Thus there may be detected in the most liberal democrat a tinge of anti-Semitism; he is hostile to the Jew to the extent that the latter thinks of himself as a Jew. (Sartre [1946] 1995, 57)

And this is not an accident. The universal subject of human rights is not discovered by attending to differences between cultures, races, sexes. It is constructed precisely by subtracting everything that makes us different, that makes us particular, and by placing a moral halo on the remainder. It is not an accident that the subject of human rights is hollow. There would be no universal subject unless every particular difference—cultural, racial, sexual—were suppressed. And this is the key to why the ideals of the Enlightenment are much more than simply tinged with racism. They are the real thing. Let's see.

The universal subject of human rights is an impossible notion. The subject of human rights cannot be completely hollowed out, and yet it must be hollowed out. It cannot be completely hollowed out because were the universal subject really empty, it could house nothing, not even universal human rights. And yet it must be hollowed out, deprived of every particularity, if it is to avoid the parochialism and traditionalism that are the enemies of Enlightenment. This paradox was invisible to the heroes of the Enlightenment because their own particularity was invisible to them. It is easy to be blind to the contingency of your own cultural racial and sexual lives, especially so if you find yourself in a position of relative power, like educated white European males. So the invisible substance at the heart of an otherwise empty universalism will be provided, more than likely, by the particular attitudes of educated white European males. And so we arrive by way of Enlightenment universalism and moral equality, and by way of the tinge of racism Sartre discerned in the liberal democrat, at the real thing. The privileging of educated white European males. Racism itself. Eighteenth-century universalism and twenty-first-century multiculturalism do indeed make an odd couple.

When difference is defended because we are not importantly different, then difference survives as style. As entertainment. As tourism. The Enlightenment gives non-European cultures a backhanded compliment. Since the invisible particular substance of the supposedly merely formal universalism is provided by privileged European values, this means that other cultural, racial, sexual configurations can indeed be defended and respected, but only as entertainment. Not as genuine alternatives to European privilege. No doubt some still visit other cultures to make contact with the primitive. The primitive in that sense shared both by logicians and anthropologists, the raw and the originary. This sort of tourist is not content with the Disney version of the indigenous cultures of the Yucatan on sale in the lobby of the beachfront hotel. This sort of tourist seeks out the minor religious ceremony in the surrounding villages because it is there that they think they may find the real, the authentic, the raw, the originary. And what originated from this originary primitive? The universal human subject quietly humming the racist anthems of European Enlightenment. This originary other is, of course, no threat to the Enlightenment because it was discovered by looking backward and serves only to reveal the rough beginnings of what we can be thankful was smoothed out by Kant and Locke and Rousseau. It is no more a threat to the racist ideals of the Enlightenment than the much more frequent tourist who is satisfied by the trinkets in the lobby. Yes it is true, as the Enlightenment taught, that since we are not *importantly* different we can take an interest in difference but that interest by its very genesis could not be *important*. Is it any wonder that the liberating interest in multiculturalism finds it difficult not to succumb to the trite, to the kitsch?

As I write, the second Bush president is leading the second U.S. war against Iraq. And the currently favored retroactive justification for starting that war is that the United States is thereby bringing democracy to Iraq. This is a particularly clear case of the invisible substance concealed in the hollow of the universal human subject. The particular ideals of democracy are thought universal and good whereas the particular ideals of Islamic republics, for example, are thought to be merely and divisively particular. The United States is doing Iraq a favor by attempting to bring democracy to Iraq, but it would be no kind of favor to reinvent the United States as an Islamic republic. And yet both are particular political ideals. Nor is there any way out through an appeal to religious freedom. Religious freedom is the bone often tossed by secular democrats to religious fundamentalists. But religious freedom means nothing unless religion is already half dead. When the religious dream of a religious republic, the idea of mere religious freedom stinks of secularism. Disney religion.

The racism at the heart of the Enlightenment shows itself in the interest taken in Disney differences. Differences shackled to the frame of representation, a Eurocentric frame of representation. And it has been the burden of these few pages to show that this is a necessary consequence of the paradox of the universal subject. The universal subject must be empty, but it can't be empty and still do any work. So it must be filled with invisible content. The privileged position of educated white European males of the eighteenth century.

We started down this trail of discovery because we were trying to argue that school funding in predominantly white and predominantly black neighborhoods ought to be at roughly the same dollar/student level. We thought to show that this inequity was unjustifiable because blacks and whites were (a) both included in one class and (b) that that class demanded equal dollar/student funding of schools in both black and white neighborhoods. We failed three times over. First of all, by means of a brief discussion of apple harvests, we failed to find an argument that showed a connection between being included in the same class and deserving equal concern. In the light of this first result we showed secondly that demonstrating that blacks and whites were equally human beings or equally rational or equally sentient or something was not enough, all by itself, to justify equal dollar/student funding levels. In addition we would have to show that it was inconsistent to admit that blacks and whites were both rational or something and then persist in accepting unequal educational funding. What was missing was a connection between being rational and equal educational funding. Third, we just gave the critic of antiblack racism the prize by supposing that there were universal human rights including, improbably enough, a universal human right to relatively equal educational funding in predominantly black and predominantly white neighborhoods (UN Resolution 1948, art. 26). Further examination of the universal subject of human rights showed it to be fundamentally and unavoidably racist. And thus we return to the beginning once again seeking a basis for our opposition to antiblack racism.

Another Dead End: Respect and Self-Respect

> Respect commands us to keep our distance, to touch and tamper neither with the law, which is respectable, nor—therefore—with the untouchable.
>
> —JACQUES DERRIDA, *On Touching*

It can seem plausible that a nonracist ethical theory could be built on respect, mutual respect, and self-respect. Yet standing in the way of an ethics of mutual respect is Kojève's reconstruction of Hegel's dialectic of the master and the slave. Kojève warns us that "a liberation without a bloody fight, therefore, is metaphysically impossible" (Kojève [1933–39] 1980, 56). In an era when the attractiveness of relations of mutual respect has become trite, it comes as something of a shock to be told that the heart of respect is violence. But Kojève is right. The heart of respect is violence, and so the very idea of mutual respect is not destined to produce peace. Only stalemate.

Start with chain saws.[1] I never really became comfortable with chain saws. They are dangerous and can be lethal, so when I was told to respect their power and the ease with which in the hands of a novice they can jump and buck, I did what I was told. I gave the chain saw at hand a wide berth. After that first day I never picked up another one. A very wide berth indeed.

In its social use, respect is what we owe to those of higher status. Respect your elders. You can't wear that to the inauguration. Dignity is the word that Kant's translators, for example, use to name that in humans which is deserving of respect. And it is significant that dignity belongs to honorable offices of high rank and also to persons holding those offices or ranks. We are so used to the ideal of mutual respect that this hierarchical or asymmetrical heart of respect is difficult to hear. But you can hear the asymmetrical hierarchy in respect if you remember the word *respectable*. And you can hear the same asymmetry in dignity if you remember the word *dignitary*. Not every one is a dignitary; only those of high office seated at the head table. And these dignitaries are not completely unlike chain saws, for one of the things attendant on occupying exalted positions is that you are thereby able to exercise the powers of office. You are deserving of respect not for being a human but for being a powerful human. The difference from chain saws is only that in this case the power derives from social conventions and not mechanical inventions.

The expressions of respect that are appropriate with dignitaries also bear some resemblance to those that would be appropriate with chain saws. In each case it is a question of giving the target of respect a wide berth. Sometimes dignitaries, precisely like chain saws, are literally given space. Geometrical space. Some expressions of respect for dignitaries are different. There are various ritualized ways of marking one's inferiority before the exalted dignitary. Bowing. Lowering one's head. Not turning one's back on the dignitary. In general to show respect is to be courteous, to treat as one would the members of a court. Perhaps even by making a curtsy to the monarch. In North America from the European settlement until roughly the middle of the eighteenth century the main function of manners was "to enforce hierarchical social relations" (Thornton 2001). The violence, such as it is, of this system is a function of the power of the dignitaries, but it is also a part of the hierarchical social arrangement itself. And given this asymmetrical hierarchy, the notions of respect and dignity are entirely unproblematic. What happens when we remove the hierarchy and assume that all humans or persons or something are dignitaries?

Some or most of those who write about respect do not think of it this way. They think of there being two kinds of respect, depending on what the target of respect is. If the target of our respect is something the target could lose, that is one kind of respect. It is sometimes called evaluative respect (Dillon 1997, 229).[2] If the target of our respect is something the target could not lose, then that is another kind of respect. This is sometimes called recognition respect, and its target includes "dignity, the form of status worth all persons have simply in virtue of being persons" (229). It is a bit dramatic to distinguish two kinds of an attitude simply because the attitude can take different targets. Are there two kinds of obeying the law, one for laws that change from state to state and one for those that persist all around the country? In any case for my purposes this difference between the targets of respect is not as important as the commonalities of expression which are shared by the two kinds of respect. In the case of persons, to respect their dignity is once again to give them space. Leeway. But why? What is this dignity that we cannot lose, this dignity that we have simply because we are persons? The dignity of persons is sometimes derived from or grounded in three things: equality, agency, and individuality. Thus recognition respect for persons actually divides into three, one kind for each of the grounds of personhood (229). But we have already considered how enormously difficult it is to come up with a way of showing the moral equality of humans or persons without begging the question. And we will have a similar difficulty demonstrating that since each person is an individual they are therefore deserving of respect. There might, however, be a connection between agency and respect.

Perhaps not surprisingly our discussion of chain saws and what Feinberg calls the "raw pre-moral idea" of respect gives us an idea of what we are looking for in the concept of agency that might link it to respect (Feinberg 1973, 1). Power. We are looking for a kind of power that all persons have to the same degree and one that they could not possibly lose. What kind of power will this be? The question almost answers itself: freedom of the will.

Freedom of the will can give persons power, but can it deliver the required asymmetrical hierarchy? Can it give us a category of underlings beneath and equally beneath all persons? In a court setting lower orders are easy to come by. They are the courtiers who are not dignitaries and are without dignity. But if dignity is generalized so that even the lowest courtier has the same dignity as the highest dignitary, then we will need to find a class that is categorically beneath every person. In a Kantian framework this is easy. The generalized underling is nature. For Kant the spontaneity of reason makes every person a law giver of nature. In virtue of our spontaneity we stand outside of nature giving it laws almost as if we were god or at least a monarch. And so this power, this spontaneous power of rational beings, is literally supernatural. In Kant's ethics the connection to monarchy is if anything more explicit, since each rational being is to think of itself as the lawgiver of a kingdom. The spontaneity of reason, the freedom of the will, makes each of us monarchs of nature standing above the natural laws to which the lower orders of being must submit. The spontaneity of reason makes all rational beings stand above nature, and to the same extent. We have found our universal underling: nature.

Perhaps we do not stand outside of nature. Perhaps we are not free. Perhaps reason is not supernaturally spontaneous. That is not my concern now. If we did stand outside nature, then this picture of all persons having dignity would be quite right. Moreover, approaching dignity from beyond biology would not threaten the modality of moral judgments in the way that any broadly naturalistic approach threatens to. So let us suppose this supernatural picture of human spontaneity is fine. What then?

Well, then, the relation between every person or human being or rational being or something will be like the relation in an earlier age between the monarchs of different realms. Each of them would be safe and in absolute control of the land within their borders. And so long as France and England don't trespass on each other's territories, all will be well. And so too with individuals. If each individual is a monarch of his or her domain, then so long as no other individual monarch trespasses, all will be well. But in that case there is no need to invoke notions of respect or mutual respect at all. And this reveals another feature of respect that is easy to miss. Not only is respect an asymmetrical or hierarchical relation, it is also, in its normative dimension, a specialist in saying No. Saying No to what is disrespectful. And so as with what Nietzsche calls slave morality, it does not begin with a triumphant affirmation of itself but by saying No to what is outside, different, disrespectful, dirty (Nietzsche [1887] 1967a, I.10). The origin of respect is in disrespect. Trespass. And its color? Vermilion. The color of worms.

Let us therefore imagine something disrespectful. What in face of the affront of trespass does respect enjoin. It demands withdrawal. It demands that the affronting one withdraw. The asymmetrical nature of respect demands that the monarch trespassing withdraw. And if the monarch does not withdraw? Then we are on the verge of violence, for the one trespassed against will be justified in feeling morally permitted to force the invading monarch back to his or her proper realm. It is shocking to our notion of mutual respect to find Kojève insisting that there is no way from monarchical domination of master over slave to liberation except through a bloody fight. We are even told that such a fight is metaphysically necessary (Kojève [1933–39] 1980, 56). But now this metaphysical necessity can seem logical. Respect is an asymmetrical relation. Mutual respect is a symmetrical relation. So the very category of mutual respect is contradictory.[3] Of course, it is possible for there to be a fraudulent appearance of mutual respect, which, as in the case of peace between monarchs, is inevitably mediated by the threat of violence. But really, and without fraudulence, to move from an asymmetrical relation to a symmetrical one will only be possible if we overpower those benefiting from the asymmetry. Kojève's bloody fight.

Insofar as the contradictory notion of mutual respect makes any sense it is as stalemate. Violence stalemated. The monarchical version of such a stalemate was official doctrine in the United States during the cold war. It was called mutually assured destruction. MAD. To the extent that the USSR and the United States avoided direct assaults on each other this was because each knew that if either of them trespassed on the other then in the ensuing nuclear war both parties could be mutually assured of their destruction. Mutual respect between monarchs, which is saved from contradiction by modeling itself on MAD, is a good thing. It is better than nuclear war. And each government during the cold war contented itself, violently enough, with fighting the other around the edges. But it is extraordinary that there are philosophers who would make relations of mutual respect the ideal of human relations. It is slave morality at its most pure. Double negation. A bad thing, mutual death, must be stopped. Backing into an ersatz affirmation.

The situation is not significantly altered when we transpose these monarchical reflections into a more individualistic key. Here there are territorial issues involving the body but also involving the objects of desire. A trivial example. If two persons deserving of equal respect come together to a door. Who goes first? If only one of the persons were deserving of respect, then of course all would be well and that person would go through first. And this is why asymmetrical relations like white supremacy and patriarchy make the world safe for respect. They decide who gets to go first. The white men go first or patronize their inferiors by making a show of letting them go ahead. By now this is old news. But if two persons *equally* deserving of respect approach the door together, one must give way to the other, thus reaffirming the asymmetrical logic of respect. How does this not produce violence? White supremacy and patriarchy are still able to do their work hiding respect's violence. But racism and sexism can only smooth things over so long, only until the asymmetrical privilege of white men comes under threat.

One place where many feel this threat concerns our leading example itself. Education. Here the perceived threat to white supremacy is called affirmative action. It used to be called desegregation. And here the weapons are really drawn. Real weapons. Mutually assured destruction is what the paradoxical notion of mutual respect becomes in reality. By and large it doesn't exist between individuals in contemporary society because the asymmetrical structures of society—white supremacy and patriarchy, for example—make a safe space for the asymmetrical relations of respect. There may be places within society where mutually assured destruction does stalemate violence. And then with the trenches dug in the earth we can for a time rest in peace. But in our asymmetrical society these stalemates are intrinsically unstable. The basic point is that those who model their lives on respect can pick either of two ideals around which to organize their lives: either the ideal of keeping or acquiring an asymmetrical privilege or the ideal of the cold war, stalemated violence. It is a bleak picture.

Nor will things be helped if we appeal to the notion not of respect but of self-respect. These do not necessarily go together. It is possible to imagine a setup where only a few persons are deserving of respect and the rest are obligated to pay obeisance to them. In such a setup none of those paying obeisance would have self-respect. Perhaps certain traditional societies are in fact like this. I don't know. But what is self-respect? To have self-respect is to think of yourself as deserving of the respect of others, to think of yourself as deserving deference. If I permit myself to be used as sex toy by the neighbors, then my friends will ask me in outraged tones: Have you no self-respect? If I had had self-respect, I would not have permitted others to treat me in this way. Self-respect adds to the violence built into respect from the start because someone with self-respect will force others to defer to them, to treat them with respect. Two persons with self-respect may even think that stalemated violence is *itself* an affront to their dignity. They are, after all, being forced by threat not to exercise their self-respect by forcing others to respect them. In certain depictions of street gangs, respect and self-respect are the twin engines of gang warfare. And still people think respect is a good thing (see Ripp 2001).

In Defense: Rights and Respect

I have argued that human rights are racist and that the notion of mutual respect is self-contradictory and that a culture of self-respect will never be able to deliver peace but only ever an unstable stalemated violence. But even if these criticisms were defensible, we would not be able to assess the power of these familiar ethical ideals without determining what if anything the notions of human rights and respect were good for. Both positively—what they encourage—and negatively—what they discourage.

Positively, these two notions, which have taken on such weight in the last two hundred years, can function to make industrial capitalism run. Both the notion of rights and that of respect presuppose a firm distinction between what is mine and what is not. And this contributes to the easy acceptance of the rhetoric of rights and respect by cultural formations devoted to private property. The self that possesses rights and enjoys respect can be pictured as a "simple defensive castle with my experience inside, insulated abruptly from a not mine and not me domain outside" (Brumbaugh 1982, 34).[4] Unless the defenders of rights and respect invoke some such identifiable isolable self they will be unable to answer simple questions such as *who* possesses rights or *who* is deserving of respect. In *Science and the Modern World* Whitehead briefly turned to the ethics of industrial capitalism and discusses it in terms I find congenial.

> The doctrine of minds, as independent substances, leads directly not merely to private worlds of experience, but also to private worlds of morals. The moral intuitions can be held to apply only to the strictly private world of psychological experience. Accordingly self-respect, and the making the most of your own individual opportunities, together constituted the efficient morality of the leaders among the industrialists of that period [the nineteenth century]. The western world is now suffering from the limited moral outlook of the three previous generations. (Whitehead [1925] 1967, 195–96)

This limited moral outlook enforced a respectful distance between subjects, including corporate subjects, and it permitted those subjects, within that protected domain, to maximize their benefits, however construed. The cultural formation that guaranteed that my dignity, my private sphere, would not be trespassed against by others out to maximize their own benefits must, on this picture, be seen as an external constraint on the acquisitiveness of the internal self, corporate or otherwise (Brumbaugh 1982, 34). Nice perhaps as protection but properly minimized so as to give maximal play to the subject of rights deserving respect. The minimal state.

If the self is conceived as a simple defensive castle, then the rhetoric of rights and respect are its defensive walls. They protect the space within by obliging others *not* to violate my rights and *not* to trespass beyond a respectful distance. The positive work accomplished by rights and respect in defense of industrial capitalism is in fact negative. Negative, not because of the injustices that dog postindustrial capitalism but because the force of the appeal either to rights or to respect is to stop something bad, to arrest a violation. The positive value of rights and respect is no other than the double negation from which I have been trying to escape ever since we began. Trying to escape from double negation to a genuine affirmation.

Being defensive, the rhetoric of rights and respect will be very important to those who are otherwise powerless to stop their exploitation. When you find yourself helplessly pinned to a wall by an enemy made feverish by hatreds (religious, racist, sexist, patriotic), then there is no other line of defense than defense. And here an appeal to rights and to respect may be a force for good, one of the few defenses available to the powerless subjects of exploitation and abuse. Often, as in the case of lynching, it is a useful defense only for others and only after some time. But it remains a defense of some power, and some significant victories. Some indeed involving criticism of the unequal dollar/student funding of schools in predominantly white and predominantly black neighborhoods, a living struggle. In contrast, when exercised by the powerful, the language of rights and respect can do enormous damage. Powerful defensive weapons in the hands of the powerful simply increase anxiety and danger. When a powerless individual sits down or stands up for her rights, that is courageous and moving. But when a powerful person or nation or corporation asserts their rights against those less powerful, it is not courageous and it is not moving. It's a mugging.

I am not sure how to preserve the good accomplished by the rhetoric of rights and respect as exercised by the powerless without at the same time opening the doors to aggressive violence accomplished by the powerful. And the universalist rhetoric, which is inevitably part of the appeal to rights and respect, makes it very unlikely that you could save the good and exclude the evil. The universalist rhetoric makes it very unlikely that you could say: You powerless can demand respect and assert your rights, but you over there, you powerful ones, you are not allowed to. The crux of the problem is the notion that each subject, whether biological or national or corporate, is a simple defensive castle. And this problem is established by habits of categorization and identification. This is a pear. This is not. This is a person. This is not. This is me. This is not. This yearning for being, being identified as this or that, is an expression of anxiety in the face of becoming. Clutching desperately to identifiable particulars, the excitement of becoming slips inevitably through our fingers. Our existential thirst languishing unslaked.

Perhaps the way to avoid the bad consequences of a universalized appeal to rights and respect is to avoid appeal to those notions at all. Perhaps we should imagine what a genuinely affirmative ethics might look like, an ethics powered not by double negation but by affirmation.

Perhaps a genuinely affirmative ethics would be an ethics of affection.
Perhaps.

The Surrealist Anticolonialism of Aimé and Suzanne Césaire

> We have been taught either to ignore our differences, or to view them as causes
> for separation and suspicion rather than as forces for change. Without
> community there is no liberation, only the most vulnerable and temporary
> armistice between an individual and her oppression. But community must not
> mean a shedding of our differences, nor the pathetic pretense that these
> differences do not exist.
>
> —AUDRE LORDE, *Arsenal*

Racism is just one example of the kind of hateful attitude that divides
groups of people from one another. The general difficulty may come into
focus by appeal to the following diagram:

The difficulty begins as hate between persons mediated by the types
they represent, mediated by their being instances of different types, whether
those types are racial, sexual, political, national, religious, or something

one inclusive category	human nature, dignity, rights,
(Type #1) **vs.** (Type #2) **vs.** (Type #3)	racism sexism and other hatreds
| | | | | | | | | | | | | | | | | | | | | | |	individual identifiable persons many instances of types

the frame of representation

[[[[[swarming sub-personal multiplicities, beyond one and many, becoming becoming]]]]]

Figure 9-1. The frame of representation.

else. Suppose we are dealing with racism and white supremacy. In that case individual persons will hate or fear or resent other persons *as instances of racial types*. So it is easy to think that we could overpower racism by moving up to some more inclusive category that would include blacks and whites without prejudice. But the move up to the more inclusive category never works. Ever. Either it fails because the racists find that even though blacks and whites are both human or rational or persons, blacks are nevertheless hateful for some other reason, like being lazy or shiftless or smelly or something. But if the move up succeeds, it still fails because by moving up into the Enlightenment, you activate the racism of Ellison's Brotherhood, the racism of Sartre's Democrat, and racism period, privileging educated white European males.

There may seem to be hope. We have only to reverse direction. To drop to the level of the identifiable individual is to drop into a Hobbesian universe, but the aggressive competitiveness of such a universe can seem reason enough to move back up. Perhaps the concept of person can be so freighted with ethical requirements that it becomes inconsistent to admit that someone is a person and then to treat them abusively. It is tempting, but the job of finding all those ethical requirements in the concept of personhood looks impossible. That is, it looks impossible unless all this talk of personhood is simply a cover story for arbitrarily freighting whatever inclusive category with whatever ethical requirements we would have signed up for anyway. And that is the question-begging argument I have been refusing throughout this discussion. So perhaps after all it is just as hopeless as it looks. But it isn't. There is no need to yo-yo back and forth between the Enlightenment's universal subject of human rights and the Hobbesian individual.

When we were reversing direction, going down from the one inclusive category, we stopped too early. We stopped at identifiable individual persons. We ought to have gone down beneath the level of the particular person to the swarming sensual singularities that seethe subpersonally, subrepresentationally. Precisely this turn both from the Enlightenment and from Hobbes was taken by Aimé Césaire in his 1957 letter withdrawing from the French Communist Party.

Césaire recognized that the then current practice of French Communism was guilty of the same Enlightenment racism depicted by Ellison and described by Sartre. Césaire describes this Enlightenment racism as it appears under cover of Assimilationism.

> *Assimilationism*—The term refers to the tendency to consider everyone—the natives of the colonies and the French of the metropolitan state—as belonging to a single "family," as "kinsmen," and hence as being equal and having equal rights and duties. Assimilation, beheld in theory, appears to its exponents as a *condition of equality*; to the assimilated, who see it in practice, it appears as the imposition upon them of the colony-holding country's values. (A. Césaire 1957, 10n)

Césaire describes his turn from these Enlightenment ideas as a Copernican revolution (A. Césaire 1957, 12). And since we have for so long staked the hope of liberation on the Enlightenment, on personhood, on respect, and on rights, this is indeed a complete turning around. As if around the axis of our real need. But if this is to succeed, it requires both an evasion of abstract universalist communion and of particularist separation. This is how Césaire puts it:

> I am not going to entomb myself in some straight particularism. But I don't intend either to become lost in a fleshless universalism. There are two paths to doom: by segregation, by walling yourself up in the particular; or by dilution, by thinning off into the emptinesses of the "universal."
>
> I have a different idea of the universal. It is of a universal rich with all that is particular, rich with all the particulars there are, the deepening of each particular, the coexistence of them all. (A. Césaire 1957, 15)

This "different idea of the universal" may be another way of describing what I have been pointing to with the words "beyond representation." It is sensed sensually by letting yourself be drawn through to the other side of representation. Exciting becoming becoming. Césaire's different idea of the universal is beyond both one and many, beyond both the type and the instance. It is drawn to life by swarming sensual singularities. And it is beautiful.

I owe to Robin D. G. Kelley the idea that Césaire's Copernican Revolution, Césaire's escape from the racism of the Enlightenment, was through surrealism (Kelley 2000). In particular it was surrealism's breaking through representation to the marvelous that was the inspiration not for his resigning from the French Communist Party but for the positive suggestion of a different surrealist idea of the universal. And Kelley's essay also sent me to this passage from 1941 written by Suzanne Césaire:

> And this is the domain of the strange, the Marvelous, and the fantastic, a domain scorned by people of certain inclinations. Here is the freed image, dazzling and beautiful, with a beauty that could not be more unexpected and overwhelming. Here are the poet, the painter, and the artist, presiding over the metamorphoses and the inversions of the world under the sign of hallucination and madness. . . . Here at last the world of nature and things makes direct contact with the human being who is again in the fullest sense spontaneous and natural. Here at last is the true communion and the true knowledge, chance mastered and recognized, the mystery now a friend and helpful. (S. Césaire 1941, 137)

The Césaires point to a way beyond universalism and particularism, which excites marvelous beauty. Convulsive beauty. For as André Breton announced: "Convulsive beauty will be veiled-erotic, fixed-explosive, magic-circumstantial, or it will not be" (Breton [1937] 1987, 19). Becoming convulsed by beauty, becoming becoming, is where we will find an ethics neither of rights nor or respect. An ethics of affection. A fully affirmative ethics no longer shackled to the demand that it oppose evil. An affectionate ethics. An aesthetics of existence.

Amor Fati

The mark of an ethics of double negation is the importance of *ressentiment*; an ethics of self-respect, for example, will make a home for *ressentiment* as a responsible expression of having been disrespected. The mark of an ethics of affirmation is its commitment to the love of fate. *Amor fati.* Here is Nietzsche making a new year's resolution in January 1882:

> I want to learn more and more to see as beautiful what is necessary in things; then I shall be one of those who make things beautiful. *Amor fati:* let that be my love henceforth! I do not want to wage war against what is ugly. I do not want to accuse; I do not even want to accuse those who accuse. *Looking away*

shall be my only negation. And all in all and on the whole: some day I wish to be only a Yes-sayer. (Nietzsche [1882] 1974, #276)

With Nietzsche I am never alone. Contemporary moralists are not too critical of the notions of respect or human rights, nor are they inclined to put beauty at the center of their reflections, contenting themselves rather to squabble over the right and good. But then there is Nietzsche. An affirmative ethics is precisely the ethics that in turning from rights and respect we were turning toward. And Nietzsche tells us that the mark of such an affirmative ethics is the love of fate, and he just about says that to live the love of fate is to live a life for which there is only beauty. Only waltzing. So an affirmative ethics counsels us to become beautiful to become becoming. And the way to achieve this is by love. By affection. With Nietzsche I am never alone.

Written during the last months of Nietzsche's authorship, *Ecce Homo* is itself an expression of the love of fate. Between the preface and "Why I Am So Wise" Nietzsche inserts an account of the genesis of the book. He lists three books that he has completed in the last few months and concludes: *"How could I not be grateful to my whole life?*—and so I tell my life to myself" (Nietzsche [1888c] 1967a, 221). And it is our good fortune that this expression of the love of fate is also a how-to book. Its full title is *Ecce Homo: How One Becomes What One Is*. But what does that mean?

I once worried about whether this made any sense at all. I am already what I am, and so what sense could it make to become what I already am? I was sure that one of the conditions of becoming something was that you were not already that something. So I was not particularly happy with the notion of becoming what one is. But now I like thinking that Nietzsche is telling us to animate or to excite what we are. I like thinking that he is telling us how to induce a becoming in what we took for being. Or in other words how to induce becoming becoming.

Nehamas interprets becoming what one is in superficially similar terms, but on examination the similarities disappear. Here is Nehamas:

> To become what one is, we can see, is not to reach a specific new state and to stop becoming—it is not to reach a state at all. It is to identify oneself with all of one's actions, to see that everything one does (what one becomes) is what one is. In the ideal case it is also to fit all this into a coherent whole and to want

to be everything that one is: it is to give style to one's character; to be, we might say, becoming. (Nehamas 1985, 191)

On this account to become what one is consists in making something out of your life. The material that we begin with is everything we have ever suffered or accomplished, and the love of fate will mean that none of this is discarded. What we make out of this material is described both as giving style to one's character and also as constructing a character that is becoming, that is beautiful. And of course, I am charmed by the double sense of becoming that Nehamas invokes, but I fear I do not share his sense of beauty.

Nehamas describes becoming what you are as an act of self-creation, so what he means by constructing a character with style or becoming or beauty shows up also in his discussion of self-creation.

> The self-creation Nietzsche has in mind involves accepting everything that we have done and, in the ideal case, blending it into a *perfectly coherent whole*. (Nehamas 1985, 188–89, my emphasis)

And by perfectly Nehamas really means perfectly. Here he is again.

> In the limiting case this desire [to affirm the world as it is] presupposes that I have assembled all that I have done and all that has led to it into a whole so unified that nothing can be removed without that whole crumbling down. Being, for Nietzsche, is that which one does not *want* to be otherwise. (Nehamas 1985, 191)

It is a conception of beauty familiar from the tradition, and as Nehamas's own words reveal, it is a conception of beauty modeled on perfection. In fact, this is a form of beauty which, far from being becoming, must in fact never change, for any change would be decline, decay, degeneration. Thus, on this account to become what you are is first of all to accept everything that you have done or suffered as material from which secondly you create a self, a style of character as close to a single perfectly coherent whole as you can manage. If this activity of self-creation never stops, it will be because perfection is inaccessible. In the ideal case one would not induce a becoming at all but rather stop becoming and enter a state of being. Perfect being.

I do not want to measure the distance between Nehamas's interpretation and Nietzsche's texts. The aspect of his interpretation that I want most to avoid is the perfection of the single coherent style that we must give to our character in order to become who we are. And Nehamas is right. Nietzsche can write like that (Nietzsche [1882] 1974, #290). But I want to see what happens if we approach becoming what one is not as creating a perfectly coherent character, or more likely failing to, but rather as inducing a becoming in what we had taken for being. Or in other words to induce becoming becoming.

One way to look at this is as giving style to one's life in a sense rather different from the one articulated by Nehamas. Here, for example, are Deleuze and Parnet:

> I should like to say what a style is. It belongs to people of whom you normally say, "They have no style." This is not a signifying structure, nor a reflected organization, nor a spontaneous inspiration, nor an orchestration, nor a little piece of music. It is an assemblage, an assemblage of enunciation. A style is managing to stammer in your own language. It is difficult because there has to be a need for such stammering. Not being a stammerer in one's speech, but being a stammerer of language itself. Being like a foreigner in one's own language. Constructing a line of flight. (Deleuze and Parnet [1977] 1987, 4)

And if becoming what one is sets the task of giving style to our lives, then this will mean to make our lives stammer, not to stammer out some weak attempt at perfection but to make our living itself stammer, or shimmer. On Nehamas's interpretation it would be easier to give style to your life if you did or suffered fewer things. If only one thing ever happened to you, then it would be easier to attain a perfectly coherent unity. Less would be more. But on Deleuze's reading of style, more is more. More shimmers more. Perfect coherence is perfect being, and so it could never change, never stammer, never shimmer. Thus to achieve style as Deleuze imagines it is not to organize, least of all to organize coherently or perfectly, but to disorganize. To let loose a rhizomatic *and*.

> The tree is filiation, but the rhizome is alliance, uniquely alliance. The tree imposes the verb "to be," but the fabric of the rhizome is the conjunction, "and, and, and," This conjunction carries enough force to shake and uproot the verb "to be." Where are you going? Where are you coming from? What are

you heading for? These are totally useless questions. (Deleuze and Guattari [1980] 1987, 25)

To become what one is one must learn the art of wandering. Wanting to get somewhere, having a goal, a direction, a sense, raises obstacles and *ressentiment*. But "the land is flat from on high and when we wander" (Stein 1936a, 101). Of course, the land is flat from on high. The way of transcendence, as against god we are always in the wrong, flattens even more effectively than an airplane. But wandering flattens by way of immanence. Like sauntering.

> Some, however, would derive the word [sauntering] from *sans terre*, without land or a home, which, therefore, in the good sense, will mean, having no particular home, but equally at home everywhere. For this is the secret of successful sauntering. (Thoreau [1862] 1984, 93)

When we free ourselves to saunter and to wander where our feet take us, then there is no struggle to climb the hill. If we climb, we climb. If we don't, we don't. And in this sense the land is flat. A flat plane of immanence. A pure sheet of jouissance. Life's *bruissement*. Stone soup.

In *Ecce Homo* when Nietzsche finds that it is finally time to provide a "real answer to the question, *how one becomes what one is*," he says quite curtly: "To become what one is, one must not have the faintest notion *what one is*" (Nietzsche [1888c] 1967a , II.9). And this echoes on in Deleuze and Guattari's rhizomatic wandering, completely unconcerned with where you are going, where you are coming from, where you are heading (Deleuze and Guattari [1980] 1987, 25). But it's pretty strange advice. What is Nietzsche trying to avoid?

Nietzsche is trying to avoid what he calls the "average" (Nietzsche [1888c] 1967a, II.9). And I think this is a place where Nietzsche is strongly influenced by Emerson. Nietzsche admired the spirit he found in Emerson: "His spirit always finds reasons for being satisfied, even grateful" (Nietzsche [1888a] 1982, 9.13). I suspect that Nietzsche's aversion to the average is animated by the same spirit that breathes in Emerson's aversion to conformity. "Society is everywhere in conspiracy against the manhood of every one of its members. . . . The virtue most in request is conformity. Self-reliance is its aversion" (Emerson [1841] 1983, 261). Nietzsche's counsel not to know what you are becoming is of a piece with Emerson's famous dismissal of consistency. "A foolish consistency is the hobgoblin of little minds, adored by little statesmen and philosophers and divines" (263). What little philosophers adore is a foolish consistency, a superficial consistency, which makes these little philosophers worry whether what they are saying or doing today is consistent with what they said or did yesterday. That is the way of the vermilion worm. Rather, "Speak what you think now in hard words and tomorrow speak what tomorrow thinks in hard words again" (263). Do so and Emerson assures us that there will be a deeper consistency in our lives because "no man can violate his nature" (264). So by giving up every idea of the kind of life you want to live and living intensely now you will in the end have given a singular shape to your life. A wiser deeper consistency that we could never enjoy if we consciously aimed at consistency, let alone conformity.

In Nietzsche's how-to book the advice and predictions are similar. Give up any conscious idea that you are aiming to make your life an instance of this or that idea. Just "play" (Nietzsche [1888c] 1967a, II.9). And what will happen, for Nietzsche no less than for Emerson, is that "the organizing 'idea' that is destined to rule keeps growing deep down—it begins to command; slowly it leads us *back* from side roads and wrong roads; it prepares *single* qualities and fitnesses that will one day prove indispensable as a means toward a whole" (II.9). By giving up a concern with morality and indeed giving up a concern with goals of any sort, by living pointlessly, a deeper consistency will be discovered.

If this deeper organizing idea is interpreted as what makes life a perfectly coherent whole, then we have Nehamas's interpretation of how one becomes what one is. And you can certainly hear it murmuring in the passage just cited. But I hope you can also feel the rhythm of another becoming. Another becoming that will draw Nietzsche away from Emerson. The difference can be introduced as a difference between two kinds of play. Playing with something can teach us where there is play in the object, and where there isn't. So where the fingers of a hand can move and where they can't shows us what its skeletal structure is. This is playing with a point, playing as a technique of discovery. And what is discovered is precisely where play is impossible. "Play constituted on the basis of a fundamental immobility and a reassuring certitude which is itself beyond the reach of play" (Derrida 1966, 279). This is what Emerson expects from his dismissal of a foolish consistency. Throw away every prior conception of who you are or where you came from or what you want to be and then you will discover your essence.

But what if there were a kind of playing unrestricted by the fundamental immobility that is beyond the reach of play. From a restricted to a generalized play. What if playing played for no point but play itself. What would that mean for how one becomes what one is? At least it would mean that one would not be playing at becoming while dreaming of being, of essence, of a perfectly coherent whole. It would be playing at keeping becoming in play. And here it would be essential to induce becoming even in those life events that look as fixed as death. Terrible accidents, for example. Or being severely abused.

But Nietzsche's how-to doesn't at first look like it would have that effect at all. What does he tell us about *amor fati*.

> My formula for greatness in a human being is *amor fati:* that one wants nothing to be different, not forward, not backward, not in all eternity. Not merely bear what is necessary, still less conceal it—all idealism is mendaciousness in the face of what is necessary—but *love* it. (Nietzsche [1888c] 1967a , II.10)

Something happens to us. We would rather it had not happened to us. It might be something terrible. We could bear it or conceal it or love it.

BEARING IT

"The weight-bearing spirit takes upon itself all these heaviest things: like a camel hurrying laden into the desert, thus it hurries into its desert" (Nietzsche [1883–85] 1980, I.1). There are so many stories here, so many ways we may bear what happened to us. So many ways we may be hurrying into our own deserts. In each of them, we live our lives as if centered around our injury. How we live out that centering is of course enormously various. Nietzsche's desert metaphors tell us that the liquid shimmer of delight will be missing from living the camel in your desert. Or the turtle, anywhere. In the face of suffering pull in your arms, your feet, your head, even your tail. Bear it. Don't even move. Hold your breath. Bear your suffering in a state of desensitization. Turn off all feeling. And by feeling nothing suffer nothing.

> This state of emotional apathy, of not suffering any feeling, excitement or enthusiasm, not experiencing either affection or anger, can be very successfully masked. If feeling is repressed it is often possible to build up a kind of mechanized, robot personality. . . . Many practically useful types of personality are basically [of this] schizoid [type]. Hard workers, compulsively unselfish folk, efficient organizers, highly intellectual people, may all accomplish valuable results, but it is often possible to detect unfeeling callousness behind their good works, and a lack of sensitiveness to other people's feelings in the way they over-ride individuals in their devotion to causes. (Guntrip 1952, 37–38)

How many of us, when suffering, have not some time or other hidden our lonely lives in a frenzy of activity. Loveless. Lifeless. People lose there lives when they bear their suffering off into their own deserts. Some die.

CONCEALING IT

We would rather it hadn't. But it did. Something terribly painful happened to us. If we haven't the strength to bear it, we can at least conceal it. All idealism is mendaciousness in the face of what is necessary. Idealism conceals what happens to us behind life-denying ideas that crawl, cold and dank, out of the swamps of *ressentiment* (Nietzsche [1887] 1967a, I.10). We met this at the very beginning. Those who are injured by the strong may, out of *ressentiment*, create ideals that deny value and importance to whatever it was that injured them. It might be the aggressive, the strong. It might be an accident. It might be nature itself. And idealism is a way of denying or concealing these awful truths. That is its mendacity.

The preface of *Ecce Homo* makes it clear that Nietzsche is no inventor of new ideals. He will not invent otherworldly transcendent ideals with which to conceal the awful truths of our earthly lives.

> *Overthrowing idols* (my word for "ideals")—that comes closer to being part of my craft. One has deprived reality of its value, its meaning, its truthfulness, to precisely the extent to which one has mendaciously invented an ideal world.
>
> The "true world" and the "apparent world"—that means: the mendaciously invented world and reality. (Nietzsche [1888a] 1982, Preface #2)

Transcendence works in familiar ways. Transcendent moral ideas are used to climb up over whatever it is that has violated us. Violent people. Violent nature. Ideals are noble-indignation stilts (Nietzsche [1887] 1967a, III.26). The indignance of the injured may not be able to overpower the aggressors physically, but their indignation already overpowers them metaphysically and morally. The mendaciousness of idealism consists precisely in its transcendence.

But how did the true world become a fable? How did the moral universe become a fable? It was only recently that I began to feel the power of Copernicus to destabilize the moral universe. If the earth were at the precise center of a finite universe, then it would make sense to think that the universe or its creator cared about how humans behaved. But when the earth and humans occupy a minor bit of a minor solar system adrift in an unbounded void, then the supposition that the universe or its creator cares especially about human life stops making any sense at all. The universe and the position of the earth in it show that in the unlikely event that the universe had an intelligent creator that creator really doesn't care very much about earthlings. Earth is in the back of the closet buried under a pile of asteroids. And yet today even without that metaphysical backing, without even a taste for metaphysics, moralists will tell us that murder is absolutely wrong. As if the universe cared. And often these same moralists, who are sure that murder is absolutely immoral, also believe in abortion or war or the death penalty. But, so they tell us in slick patronizing words, these aren't really murder. They are simply the taking of lives. More air! More air!

> "You shall not steal! You shall not kill!"—such words were once called holy; in their presence people bowed their knees and their heads and removed their shoes.
>
> But I ask you: Where have there ever been better thieves and killers in the world than such holy words have been?
>
> Is there not in all life itself—stealing and killing? And when such words were called holy was not *truth* itself—killed?
>
> Or was it a sermon of death that called holy that which contradicted and opposed all life?—Oh my brothers, shatter, shatter the old law-tables! (Nietzsche [1883–85] 1980, III.12.10)

Wounded. You wish you weren't. You wish you were healthy. But you aren't. You're sick. You're getting old. Your shoulder has never been the same since you fell. Tennis is almost beyond you. The only friends that could lift your spirits don't care to, anymore. And your father's dead. The awful truth is that everyone faces this future. Most worse.

> My formula for greatness in a human being is *amor fati:* that one wants
> nothing to be different, not forward, not backward, not in all eternity. Not
> merely bear what is necessary, still less conceal it—all idealism is menda-
> ciousness in the face of what is necessary—but *love* it. (Nietzsche [1888c]
> 1967a, II.10)

And if we are not *to bear* our sufferings, or *to conceal* them by menda-ciously shrinking them to the merely apparent or the merely temporal, then what is it *to love* them, to live the love of fate? How does one become what one is?

At first it doesn't look that attractive. To want nothing different? If the light bulb goes out, do I not replace it? If the car needs gas, do I not fill it? If I need water, do I not drink? How could Nietzsche think that not filling an empty tank was the mark of greatness in a human being. But if Nietz-sche wants to be only a Yes-sayer, if he wants to live the love of fate, isn't this what he is wishing for?

No. When *amor fati* is interpreted as not raising a finger, no matter what happens, then the love of fate begins to stink of the swamp; it begins to smell of the denial of this world. When *amor fati* is interpreted in this way, it begins to smell to Nietzsche of Christian idealism. Zarathustra spends a brief moment rejecting just this interpretation of the love of fate; it is an interpretation he attributes to "the pious."

> "Let the world be! Do not raise a finger against it!"
>
> "Let him who wants to slaughter and kill and harass and swindle the people:
> do not raise even a finger against it! Thus they will yet learn to renounce the
> world."
>
> "And your own reason—you shall yourself choke and throttle; for it is
> reason of this world—Thus you shall yourself learn to renounce the world."
> (Nietzsche [1883–85] 1980, III.12.15)

So interpreted, the love of fate is an expression of an ascetic world-denying, turn-the-other-cheek attitude. So interpreted, *amor fati* is not a way of saying Yes to life at all. It is a way of saying No. It is in fact the very concealing strategy of idealism that Nietzsche already set aside. So we are at an impasse. If we are not to bear it and not to conceal it, how are we to live the love of fate as an affirmation, as saying Yes?

A terrible accident has cut short my career. Changed my life forever. I am finally home from the hospital. My visiting friends are all smiling. They tell me how well I look. How lucky I was. How I might not have survived at all. I smile back, but all I want is for them to leave. To leave me alone. Their alert, upbeat faces, even their sneakers revolt me. I am thankful they don't really mean it when they say they will drop by next week. I don't want to see anyone. Ever again. Least of all that insipid woman who assures me that everything will be fine and always manages to leave with a god bless you.

Sometimes people in such situations can think of nothing else but the accident. Brooding on their misfortune. If only I had left earlier or taken a different route or never met him in the first place. This person is not bearing suffering. They are being crushed by it. They may never recover. Living out the rest of their lives wishing they had not survived. Or drunk. It happens.

Nietzsche's how-to book won't save everybody. But how could it save anyone without turning back into the camel or idealism? How does one become what one is? The answer only became clear to me two weeks ago when I read a brilliant interpretation of Deleuze's ethical position in *The Logic of Sense* (Stankovic 2005). Our problem is to find out how one becomes what one is, and *The Logic of Sense* begins with a discussion of becoming. I seem always to be coming back to this, to Alice getting taller. So I can be brief. If we take an egg slicer to becoming, we can reduce it to a series of segments of unchanging being. At every discrete unchanging moment Alice will be a definite height. And that is fine; it is the only way becoming can be worked consistently into the frame of representation. But genuine becoming will have been entirely removed, replaced by the difference between beings. Genuine becoming is precisely what is not represented by thin slices of being. If Alice were genuinely becoming at time t, then at time t Alice would have to be both $4\frac{1}{2}$ feet tall and not $4\frac{1}{2}$ feet tall. Becoming is essentially inconsistent, essentially unrepresentable. That is why becoming is beyond representation. We've been here before.

How do wounds occur. A knife cuts skin. One body. A knife. Cuts another body. Mine. Egg-sliced, we are presented with two states of my body. Uncut and cut. No becoming in sight. Egg-slice becoming as fine as you like, you will never find becoming anywhere. Every time we think we have caught it, it slips through our clutching conceptual grasp. Where is it? "The stoics distinguish between two kinds of thing" (Deleuze [1969] 1990, 4). On the one hand, bodies and states of affairs and, on the other hand, becomings. In this context Deleuze calls becomings incorporeal events that "play only on the surface, like mist over a prairie (even less than a mist, since a mist is after all a body)" (5).

> Mixtures [of bodies] in general determine the quantitative and qualitative
> states of affairs: the dimensions of an ensemble—the red of iron, the green
> of a tree. But what we mean by "to grow," "to diminish," "to become red," "to
> become green," "to cut," and "to be cut," etc., is something entirely different.
> These are no longer states of affairs—mixtures deep inside bodies—but
> incorporeal events at the surface which are the results of these mixtures. The
> tree "greens." (Deleuze [1969] 1990, 6)

How do wounds occur? Deleuze and Guattari have taught me to think of it this way. The incorporeal event, becoming-cut, condenses as my wounded finger, and once it is condensed, then conceptual representation can work its own magical illusions on my wound (Deleuze and Guattari [1991] 1994, 159). How do I deal with it? Bear it. Conceal it. And this is where our injured person finds himself or herself, wanting to be left alone to escape all that insipid good feeling. This was our impasse. And now it seems as if we were at an impasse because we were trying to understand how one becomes what one is while remaining within the frame of representation. We should have broken through being to becoming. That is how one becomes what one is. One takes what one is, wounded, and induces within it becoming. But how?

It is all a mater of releasing the incorporeal event. Deleuze insists that we do this by willing the event. The becoming-cut. The becoming-injured. The becoming-rejected.

> What does it mean to will the event? Is it to accept war, wounds, and death
> when they occur? [No.] It is highly probable that resignation is only one more

figure of ressentiment since ressentiment has many figures. (Deleuze [1969] 1990, 149)

Resignation is just bearing what happens to me, turning into a camel or a turtle. And what does it mean to will the event without *ressentiment*? We are told that it requires a kind of leaping in place because we do not will something different from being wounded. We will something *in* our being wounded, the becoming-wounded that condensed as my wound. Here, in a passage only made clear to me by Stankovic (2005), is Deleuze's more complete account.

> It wills now not exactly what occurs, but something *in* that which occurs, something yet to come which would be consistent with what occurs, in accordance with the laws of an obscure, humorous conformity: the Event. It is in this sense that the *Amor fati* is one with the struggle of free men. (Deleuze [1969] 1990, 149)

Willing the event is releasing something in what has already been condensed or actualized—for example, my wound. So to will the event is not actualizing anything; it is rather to counteractualize, to release from being wounded something that escapes being wounded (Deleuze [1969] 1990, 150). My becoming-wounded. Having started off with a defense of pointlessness, I was thrilled that when Stankovic was explaining this he emphasized that counteractualization must be pointless. Here he is:

> Counter-actualization is not teleological action if by telos we understand an object, e.g. an actual world, that comes about. . . . To counter-actualize means to counter-actualize the present actual world such that the constantly othering or constantly differing world, is always in the process of coming about. (Stankovic 2005, 8–9)

To counteractualize is to become becoming. To become beautiful. That is the meaning of *amor fati*. That is how one becomes what one is. By becoming becoming.

"There is no other ethic than the *amor fati* of philosophy" (Deleuze and Guattari [1991] 1994, 159). This has rather striking consequences.

> Either ethics makes no sense at all, or this is what it means and has nothing else to say: not to be unworthy of what happens to us. To grasp whatever

happens to us as unjust and unwarranted (it is always someone else's fault) is, on the contrary, what renders our sores repugnant—veritable ressentiment, resentment of the event. There is no other ill will. What is really immoral is the use of moral notions like just or unjust, merit or fault. (Deleuze [1969] 1990, 149)

It is easy enough to see how thinking of your injuries as undeserved can breed *ressentiment*, indignance, ill will. So let's start with a good thing. You and a beautiful smiling Yes, have fallen in love. It's amazing. It's dizzying. The world itself, etherealized. Standing in fat drops of summer rain, soaked to your naked souls, dripping liquid desire. That can happen. But now what? How do you become worthy of your good fortune? Not by letting it condense into a state of affairs. Not by primping your appearance so that when you walk down the street together they all say what a perfect couple; you look so perfect together. Not like that. Not by settling into the frame of representation as a perfect couple. Not static perfection. Not pretty. Beautiful. You become worthy of your falling in love with the beautiful smiling Yes by inducing together further becomings. "One never comes; one is always coming" (Stankovic 2005, 9). Becoming beautiful. Becoming becoming.

Oddly enough, what Deleuze has to say about academic writing helps us understand what it is like to be worthy of the good things that happen to one.

My ideal, when I write about an author, would be to write nothing that could cause him sadness, or if he is dead, that might make him weep in his grave. Think of the author you are writing about. Think of him so hard that he can no longer be an object, and equally so that you cannot identify with him. Avoid the double shame of the scholar and the familiar. Give back to an author a little of the joy, the energy, the life of love and politics that he knew how to give and invent. So many dead writers must have wept over what has been written about them. (Deleuze and Parnet [1977] 1987, 119)

The shame of the scholar: turning your love of the beautiful Yes into an object to be displayed. The shame of the familiar: letting your readiness to gasp, your readiness to be surprised by the beautiful Yes, fade and vanish into the expected the unsurprising. Familiar as family. Not that. You must *love* your fate. And you must especially love your fate when you have been lucky enough to share it with a beautiful Yes. And you must love it too when you are unlucky enough to be wounded.

Confined to a wheelchair, resenting your inability to walk—this turns your injury into an object, an object ripe for *ressentiment* and indignance. I don't deserve this. It is always somebody else's fault. Willing the event is discovering in your injury your becoming-wounded. This becoming beyond representation is a window to anywhere, to allofit. It can condense as your crippled life, your broken body. But it is more. Not pole-vaulting. But still inordinately more. The infinity of integers above one hundred does not include sixty-three, but there are still an infinity. Not pole-vaulting. But still inordinately more. Willing the event without *ressentiment* is loving fate. It is not resenting your confinement to a chair. It is living life on wheels. Wheeling life.

How does one become what one is? Hard enough not to lose the beautiful Yes to being. It is harder still to find *in* your being wounded a way to becoming becoming. *Amor fati.* To become what one is one must want nothing different. Not to bear our wounds. Nor yet to conceal them. But to love *in* our being wounded our becoming-wounded, the incorporeal event that is a line of flight. Breaking through to the other side of representation doesn't take legs. You can do it sitting down. You can do it blind. But it is hard. Very hard. And some never will. Even the lucky ones.

> One must never have spared oneself, one must have acquired hardness as a habit to be cheerful and in good spirits in the midst of nothing but hard truths. (Nietzsche [1888c] 1967a, III.3)

The Contours of a Post-Copernican Ethics

It is remarkable that ethics is still pre-Copernican. In the years since 1543 physicists and astronomers have become so accustomed to the displacement of the Earth from the center of the universe, so removed from the life-and-death struggle of Giordano Bruno, that they sometimes casually say that it doesn't matter any more, that depending on your frame of reference, any point at all can be treated as the center of the universe. But ethicists still work as if the Earth were at the universe's center. How does this show itself? In the struggle to defend unconditional judgments about the moral value of actions or people or states of affairs. If a pre-Copernican ethicist thinks it's wrong to kill your neighbor, then it is not wrong because he might have given you a ride to the store tomorrow. It is not wrong because you like him. It is not wrong because you can't stand the sight of blood. It is not wrong because it is illegal. It is not wrong because you don't want to be that kind of neighbor. All these might be true, but they are not why it is wrong. It is unconditionally wrong to kill your neighbor. And pre-Copernican astronomy allegorizes the morally unconditional. There is nothing more central to the universe than the treatment of people, the people who live at its center. On the Earth. Ethics is still pre-Copernican. But man is but a speck (Spinoza [1670] 1951, 202).

A post-Copernican ethics will be an ethics without desert. Or let us say that in a post-Copernican ethics nobody will deserve anything just because of the type they are an instance of. Not persons. Not dogs. Not dolphins. And this scares people. They are afraid that if it is not built into the nature of things or at least the nature of concepts that it is wrong to kill your neighbor, then there will be nothing to prevent us from killing whomever, whenever we like. This is a familiar concern, but I confess I find it confused.

Those worried about indiscriminate killing seem to think, oddly enough, that it is moral philosophy that keeps us from killing each other. But first of all moral philosophy has often been used not to stop killing, but to justify it. Just-war theory and the doctrine of double effect are perhaps minor players, but bioethics has industrialized the use of moral argument to justify killing. Bioethics is a killing machine (Badiou [1998] 2001, 35–36). So first of all it seems false that moral philosophy is a great bulwark against killing. Moreover, even if we leave the bioethicists in their medical offices and just consider killing your neighbor, does it really seem that the reason you don't kill your neighbor is because of moral philosophy? Do you really want to kill him, buy the gun, sneak next door, and then think—Oh oh, Kant says in chapter 2 that we should treat persons as ends in themselves—and then do you suddenly and against your inclination rein yourself in? Moralists concerned that ethics without desert would let loose violation on humanity not only seem unaware of the role of moral philosophy in justifying racism, justifying war, and justifying killing; they also seem to think that humans are just itching to kill each other. Maybe they are. Maybe they are. And even supposing they were as eager as you like to kill others, how likely is it that moral philosophy would stop them? Personally, I rather think that even in the genocidal twentieth century, most people were not itching to kill their neighbors. But even if they were, it is very likely that some racist moral argument helped them to the belief that their killing spree was justified.

A post-Copernican ethics will be an ethics without desert, without transcendent criteria of right and wrong. But it will still be an existential aesthetics, a mode of existence. It is just that the criteria that would be used to guide our life will be immanent. Not transcendent. And the contours of the post-Copernican ethics that I am sketching will direct us toward becoming beautiful, becoming becoming. And this raises another worry for moralists. They fear that if everything is beautiful, even corpses, then nothing will prevent someone from becoming becoming by committing genocide. Once again this is confused because transcendent moral criteria do not prevent genocide. And perhaps the path to beauty through murder is not as successful as the path through affection. That is what I want to argue.

The point of these worries of the moralists is not after all to prevent genocide. They know both the complicity of moral philosophy in the genocide of Native Americans and the impotence of moral philosophy in the face of any real genocide—Armenian, Jewish, Cambodian, Tutsi. There have been many mass killings in spite of transcendent moral criteria. No. The point of these worries is not to stop genocide but to demand that a post-Copernican ethics be able, theoretically, to set itself against mass killing. Even if practically it, like every previous ethics, will more than likely find itself impotent when the shooting begins. And I am eager to meet those demands, eager to show that an ethics of affection is not a killing machine.

Let us start with Deleuze and Guattari's discussion of the kind of immanent criteria that could be appealed to by what I am calling a post-Copernican ethics, or rather a post-Copernican mode of existence.[5]

> There is not the slightest reason for thinking that modes of existence need transcendent values by which they could be compared, selected, and judged, relative to one another. On the contrary, there are only immanent criteria. A possibility of life is evaluated through itself in the movements it lays out and the intensities it creates on a plane of immanence: what is not laid out or created is rejected. A mode of existence is good or bad, noble or vulgar, complete or empty, independently of Good and Evil or any transcendent value: there are never any criteria other than the tenor of existence, the intensification of life. (Deleuze and Guattari [1991] 1994, 74)

There are never any criteria other than the *tenor of existence*, the *intensification of life*. We already saw this in action in Nietzsche's explanation of how one becomes what one is. A life of indignation is a life with being-injured at its center. The way to love fate is to release from your being-injured the inordinate multiplicities of becoming-injured. This will induce intensities of becoming where once there was only condensed lifeless being. A wire is tensed when it is pulled from different directions, and difference is the key that releases intensities. Becoming is beyond representation because when something becomes taller, it is at one and the same time both $4\frac{1}{2}$ feet tall and not $4\frac{1}{2}$ feet tall. So difference is also built into becoming. And so too intensity. Becoming intense is becoming becoming.

The philosopher who made the contours of a post-Copernican ethics visible, more even than Nietzsche, was Spinoza. And Spinoza's ethics was officially an ethics of affection. Here is Spinoza showing how important affection is to his ethics:

> Whatever so disposes the human body that it can be affected in a great many ways, or renders it capable of affecting external bodies in a great many ways, is useful to man; the more it renders the body capable of being affected in a great many ways, or of affecting other bodies, the more useful it is; on the other hand, what renders the body less capable of these things is harmful. (Spinoza [1677] 1994, IVP38)[6]

Spinoza's affectionate ethics projects a powerful intense existence. Power is what we really mean by freedom. There is no reason to believe in anything like a faculty of the will that might or might not be disconnected from the natural causal order. Nietzsche, not to mention Spinoza,[7] was here too: "The 'unfree will' is mythology; in real life it is only a matter of *strong* and *weak* wills" (Nietzsche [1886] 1966, #21). It is only a matter of power. What sorts of things make you feel powerful? What sorts make you feel weak? Remember our indignant injured person. He or she will feel weak so long as they do not release the becoming-injured from the being injured, from their being-injured, *god damn it*. The love of fate is a recipe for feeling powerful, a recipe for leading an intense life. Becoming becoming.

The intensity of living is the immanent criterion that Yes-sayers need in order to be critical of the boy kicking his grandmother in the shins. Life is simply more intensely enjoyable if you permit yourself to be affected by more things. The more things, the more people, the more tastes, the more styles, the more smiles you allow yourself to be affected by, the more powerful you will be. Not just olives but garlic too. *Not just, but also.* And life is more intense if you learn to affect more things. Not just your friends but strangers on the street too. The homeless. The poor. *Not just, but also. Not just, but also* is the key to intensifying your life. The rhizomatic *and*. And that is why Spinoza's proposition is so important to a post-Copernican ethics.

Does saying Yes mean saying Yes to measles and sickness?[8] No. Spinoza thought we should model what is bad on what makes us sick (Deleuze [1970] 1988, 30–43). Of course, you steer away from things that make you weak. *Ressentiment*, measles, indignation, and holding a grudge all make you weak. And so does dropping a heavy stone on a toad. Eric and I were so surprised at the way it squirted when the stone hit. Its insides disgorging through its mouth. And it just lay there. Dead. Our frantic energy stopped cold. Weakened. Unnerved. An ethics of affirmation steers away from *ressentiment*, measles, and cruelty. Where is affection heading. Pointlessness. Pointless intensities. Becoming beautiful.

The way to become beautiful is to become becoming. The way to break through the frame of representation is by affection, and the paradigm of this affection is the love of fate. Without affection there is no becoming. Without affection for irregularity, affection for otherness, affection for differences, there could be no becoming beautiful. Hate needs categories. Affection doesn't. There is no becoming within the plane of representation. And there is no racism *except* within the plane of representation. Typological thinking is a greenhouse for racist behavior. Affection is its aversion. That is why I am so inspired by the Césaires, Aimé and Suzanne. There is no need for respect. There is no need for rights. The Césaires had a different idea of the universal. They embraced the marvelous beyond representation. They were intimating the contours of a post-Copernican ethics of affection. Affection. Intensity. Convulsive beauty. Becoming.

Cadenza

> These little things—nutrition, place, climate, recreation, the whole casuistry of selfishness—are inconceivably more important than everything one has taken to be important so far. Precisely here one must begin to *relearn*.
>
> —FRIEDRICH NIETZSCHE, *Ecce Homo: How One Becomes What One Is*

The words *life drawing* evoke art classes with which we are familiar, easels scattering around a naked model, and something less clear, the intimation of a different practice, ceding control, letting your life be drawn by sensual singulars beyond representation, into beauty, becoming becoming. Wittgensteinians deny it, but you can feel those senses entangling like lovers' limbs. And the happy discovery of those befriended senses glows even warmer for having been there, all along, quietly waiting for our affectionate attention. It's enough to give you hope.

We all know how easy it is to try too much: Anxious we will lose the essential, we squeeze so hard it all escapes through our fingers.[1] It becomes difficult even to choose the adjective for what we enjoy. In face of the allure of pleasure, the tastes and textures we enjoy disappear. The reprimanding moralists were right about that, anyway: Seeking simply pleasure slights the very things we enjoy. So we turn from pleasure to fulfillment, earnestly working to achieve some goal we think important. Fulfilling our desire for financial security. Leading a fulfilling life as a physician. Fulfilling our dreams for our families. Who doesn't sometimes succumb to thinking of their life in terms of hurdles to hurdle? Even if we don't always follow through, we always begin by intending to focus our attention on what must be accomplished in order to achieve the goals we seek. The final victory brought closer by means of several intermediate achievements. And the world shrinks.

When we give our lives a purpose, a point, when we set our sights on fulfilling goals, then it is only this purpose that lights the world. Where its light doesn't reach, the world falls back into darkness. It has its advantages, of course. If you want to accomplish something, then you would do well to focus your complete attention on what your sought-for accomplishment requires. But then the entire world falls into two categories: either relevant to my purpose or irrelevant. Tasks present themselves either as work or as squandered energy. With a little luck, you will succeed. But what, here, is fulfillment? Everything is beautiful. Everything is textured flesh. But with your eye on achievement, with your eye on fulfillment, you won't feel it. With fulfillment as your goal, fulfillment is reduced to simply crossing a line, getting the job, making the deal. It is as if the flesh of fulfillment had been reduced to a conceptual representation of itself, a conceptual certainty with nothing overflowing certainly, no taste of desire without desires. The round peg is pounded into its round hole, and we are done. Now what?

Mostly we conceive our lives in terms of a fulfillment we lack, a success we seek, and when fulfillment is ours, it's over. Then what? Another success? Seek it. Achieve it. Here is your degree. Here is your long-awaited letter of promotion. Then what? A life can be lived this way, leaping from achievement to achievement, never slipping into the warm thick of liquid corporeality, the Cagean Sea. Give up fulfillment. Give up your goals. Give up your fantasy of meaning. That is the first movement, to drop your goals, but it is only a beginning. Blank pointlessness, the negative mode of pointlessness, and existential anxiety reveal themselves when we move no farther than the first movement. Becoming arrested. It feels awful. It feels awful, and when the morning light plays through the forest leaves, drawing our gaze up from the ground, we refuse. Restoring our downturned gaze, we refuse the dappled bright.

You could stop there. Some do. But there can be more. Even with your eyes turned from the wood morning yellows, it is hard to avoid lichen greens flashing on the forest floor. Listen to their shapes with your eyes. Always and all ways things draw our attention. Let them. Fulfillment rewards our refusals, but a life fulfilled is not enough. Drop your aching for fulfillment, and enjoy being drawn into the lichen's moist dry. Release your affections from their instrumental yearnings. Release your attention from its methodical approach to achievement, and you are ready for the second movement. Something is drawing your attention. Don't turn back to your work. Attend affectionately, and you will enjoy being drawn. Once more, you will find yourself beginning moving, beginning becoming. It cannot be done alone, because affectionate attention follows. Let it happen. Let yourself be drawn into the lichen's singularly textured colors. And let yourself be drawn beyond the lichen, to even more. Everything is an irregular commonplace, a sensual singularity, but only to those who, freed from instrumental worries, are free also to open their hearts in all directions at once. Attend affectionately and follow. Follow a wayward line of pure enjoyment.

But Life Drawing can be dangerous. As you are drawn away from your organized life, aimed at fulfilling your favorite goals, you risk falling apart altogether. That is the challenge of Life Drawing: wandering aimlessly, without identity, yet not shattering to the floor in a million pieces. How are we wanderers to manage? Keep everything in sight at the same time.

We are drawing out our lives, long and slow, making and maintaining connections. Nothing rejected. The old tired carrot flavors the soup. When painting with oils, there can be erasings, but when drawing with ink, there is only Yes. And . . . And . . . And. Life Drawing, too, is without erasure. Attending affectionately is never done. There is no line to cross, no end to our becoming drawn here and there. Don't resist. Draw out the wayward lines, long and slow, enjoying the intensities of connection. The intensive lines of pure enjoyment break only when we resist becoming. When we try to preserve what once was, when we aim to achieve what is not. Continuing becoming is becoming otherwise. Difference without a concept. Continue. The more we allow our attentions affectionately to be drawn by sensual singulars, the more we will be drawn to allofit, an immanent immense.

Nor need we give up our gardens or enjoying the late summer harvest. The heat of the sun ripens the summer tomatoes, but that is not the point, purpose, or meaning of sunlight. The greater part of the sun's warming rays are, from the gardener's point of view, squandered. And yet the tomatoes ripen. The sun has a power beyond comparison. And so it is with your friend who doesn't ache to fulfill a dominating goal, whose attentions move affectionately among mycological explorations, and midwinter truffles, chocolate dark and cardamom rich, who can tumble through evenings of couch cozy films, and yet while the careerists toss in their sleepless nights, casually hurdles the hurdles that have shrunk their worlds. Always and all ways things draw our attention, and as we turn affectionately in their direction, our lives intensify, enjoying becoming, so that the windfallen apples are even sweeter. Attending affectionately to what happens to draw your attention—rust, sticks, green weathered copper—attending affectionately to what happens to draw your attention emboldens and strengthens our living. Life Drawing is not plotting and planning but being ready to receive, ready to receive the gifts of wandering, ready for enjoying.

In the art class, nothing draws your attention so much as the model's penis or the model's breasts. You could shut down, dismissing the erotic atmosphere as invisible to your focused professional eyes, but that is not the only way. Perhaps as you attend to shadows cast by breast and penis along the curving lines of their thighs and shoulders, the sexual energy continues otherwise. As your fingers scratch the charcoal over paper, the charcoal sounds share the intensity of a generalized eroticism. Even your face tingles to the shrill sounds of charcoal drawing. It is enough to give you hope. As you let yourself be affected by more and more, you will become powerful, not more powerful than this or that, but powerful beyond any particular task. Power overflowing certainly. When we drop our aching for perfection, for fulfillment, we release ourselves to movement, to becoming becoming. Life Drawing. Becoming beautiful.

better and more beautiful than being is becoming

1. Michelle De Mooy emphasized this to me while imagining a house without organs.

2. Barbara Flanagan asked me this on a beach going out to Nappatree Point in Watch Hill, Rhode Island.

3. As I remember, I discovered it by accident in 1977 while paging through the 1970 issue of an amazing publication called: *Source: music of the avant garde.*

4. Alvin Lucier's first recording of the piece is available online at: http://ubu.artmob.ca/sound/source/Lucier-Alvin_Sitting.mp3.

It is also for sale in a more recent recording of his at: http://www.lovely.com/titles/cd1013.html.

1. YES AND NO

1. I owe this way of generalizing the possibility of tragedy to the writing and conversation of Michael Mendelson. These considerations are not unrelated to Derrida's use of the ever-present possibility of play in his various discussions of iterability.

2. David Hawkes pointed me to a use of worms parallel to Nietzsche's: Blake's use of worms to mock Christian virtues in the *Marriage of Heaven and Hell*: "The cut worm forgives the plow" (Blake 1977, 183). Nietzsche discusses swamps and worms at a number of different places, for instance:

> It is on such soil, on swampy ground, that every weed, every poisonous plant grows, always so small, so hidden, so false, so saccharine. Here the worms of vengefulness and rancor swarm, here the air stinks of secrets and concealment; here the web of the most malicious of all conspiracies is being spun constantly—the conspiracy of the suffering against the well-constituted and victorious, here the aspect of the victorious is *hated*.

And what lying is employed to disguise that this hatred is hatred. (Nietzsche [1887] 1967a, 3.14)

3. In 1973, Deleuze and Guattari offered the following criticism of the "Mouvement pour la Libération des Femmes," an activist French group:

> In this sense, wouldn't the highest aim of the M.L.F. be the machinic and revolutionary construction of the non-oedipal woman, instead of the confused exaltation of mothering and castration? (Deleuze and Guattari 1973a, 102–3.)

In 1980, they wrote:

> It is, of course, indispensable for women to conduct a molar politics, with a view to winning back their own organism, their own history, their own subjectivity: "we as women . . ." makes its appearance as the subject of enunciation. But it is dangerous to confine oneself to such a subject, which does not function without drying up a spring or stopping a flow. The song of life is often intoned by the driest of women, moved by *ressentiment*, the will to power and cold mothering. . . . [But] it is no more adequate to say that each sex contains the other and must develop the opposite pole in itself. Bisexuality is no better a concept than the separateness of the sexes. It is as deplorable to miniaturize, internalize the binary machine as it is to exacerbate it; it does not extricate us from it. It is thus necessary to conceive of a molecular women's politics that slips into molar confrontations, and passes under or through them. (Deleuze and Guattari [1980] 1987, 276)

4. The failure of double negation to attain what in the first paragraph of this section I called "joy" recalls Derrida's logic of the supplement, which if it is needed, that is, if there is something to be supplemented at all, cannot be completely or fully supplemented because any supplement could never be more than supplemental (see Derrida [1967a] 1976).

5. Nietzsche's *Die fröhliche Wissenschaft* was originally published in 1882. In 1887, it was republished in an expanded edition with a new subtitle: *la gaya scienza*. In the introduction to his translation of this book Walter Kaufmann draws attention to the fact that the *Oxford English Dictionary* entry for "gay" includes: "*The gay science*: a rendering of *gai saber*, the Provençal name for the art of poetry," and the *OED* dates this use of the English expression to the first half of the nineteenth century. *La gaya scienza* thus refers to the art of the troubadours, and it is this which puts me in mind of medieval knights and courtly love. Courtly love, itself, was a term invented in 1883 (Bowden 1997, ix).

6. "Nothing more can be said, and no more has ever been said: to become worthy of what happens to us, and thus to will and release the event, to become

the offspring of one's own events, and thereby to be reborn, to have one more birth, and to break with one's carnal birth—to become the offspring of one's events and not of one's actions, for the action is itself produced by the offspring of the event" (Deleuze [1969] 1990, 149–50).

7. In a second phase of Nietzsche's genealogy of morals, *ressentiment* changes direction, becoming bad conscience and guilt. Self-contempt. (Nietzsche [1887] 1967a, 3.15).

8. For more on the metaphysics of language see Nietzsche (1888a) 1982, 3.5, but also Whitehead (1929) 1978, xiii, 158.

9. The only sympathetic reader of Nietzsche I ever studied with, Jay Ogilvy, made sure that I would never forget the "soul as subjective multiplicity."

10. "Professor Deleuze has suggested the following note as an explanation of the term: '*Haecceitas* is a term frequently used in the school of Duns Scotus, in order to designate the individuation of beings. Deleuze uses it in a more special sense: in the sense of an individuation which is not that of an object, nor of a person, but rather of an event (wind, river, day or even hour of the day)' " (Deleuze and Parnet [1977] 1987, 151n9).

11. Danger is written over the door of where I want to take us, but philosophy, especially moral philosophy, sets itself against danger: hiding behind moral goodness. Squeamishness is morality's strongest supporter. If we were willing to risk danger, we might be able to enjoy so much more than being good. "For believe me: the secret for harvesting from existence the greatest fruitfulness and the greatest enjoyment [*Genuss*] is—*to live dangerously!*" (Nietzsche [1882] 1974, 4.283).

12. I owe this striking fact to my colleague Michael Mendelson, who, if I understand him properly, is taking the dark road philosophy has never explored: inescapable horror. I am more traditional than he is (see Mendelson 2000b).

13. In a passage from the 1886 preface to *The Gay Science* republished in *Nietzsche contra Wagner* (1888d) Nietzsche writes of a "second dangerous innocence in joy, more childlike and yet a hundred times more subtle than one has ever been before" (Nietzsche 1888d, epilog #2). I think this *second* innocence is a double negation and too close to Christianity.

14. Deleuze (1968) 1994, chap. 3, and the 1971 conclusion to Deleuze (1964a) 1973a both address the issue of an alternative image of thought . . . alternative to the resentful, orthodox image of thought at work in most of philosophy. Also see Deleuze and Guattari (1991) 1994.

15. This brings the aims of thought together with what Whitehead characterized as God's aims: "In this function, as in every other, God is the organ of novelty, aiming at intensification" (Whitehead [1929] 1978, 67).

16. Here I think of Daniel W. Smith's brief footnote about Deleuze and Wittgenstein in D. W. Smith 1997, 178n30.

17. In Whitehead ([1929] 1978) propositions are more fundamentally lures for feeling aiming at intensity than conceptual representations aiming at truth.

18. I find this confirmed by reading around in Simon Blackburn's *Oxford Dictionary of Philosophy*. For it is when he drops the mask of truth and objectivity that his dictionary comes to life and proves itself to have been written, not by a librarian, but a philosopher (see Blackburn, 1994).

19. Deleuze and Guattari (1980) 1987, 243ff.

20. See in particular D. W. Smith 1996 and Deleuze 1964a. And Heraclitus's Fragment #93: "The Lord whose oracle is that at Delphi neither speaks nor conceals, but indicates [sometimes translated as 'gives a sign']" (K. Freeman 1948, 31).

21. This gesture in the direction of a conception of the event is due to Deleuze. It is different from the adjacent characterizations of events due to Derrida and Lyotard. At this stage, the differences can be put this way. For Derrida there can be no event; everything we can experience can be again, is structured by iterability (Derrida 1967c, 50). For Lyotard, this is not true; significance is a function of phrasing phrases, but between one phrase and another there is an empty gap of nothingness, and confrontation with this nothing is Lyotard's event (Lyotard [1983] 1988, #100). The event I have just heisted from Deleuze is an event that is not nothing but not conceptualizable either. It is a pure sensual singularity: a haecceity (Deleuze and Guattari [1980] 1987, 260–65).

22. In the preface to the *Structure of Scientific Revolutions* (1962) Kuhn recalls discussions with Cavell.

23. In Christianity the return is always a second innocence, which, to be pure, needs supernatural help. The innocence I am describing needs no such help.

24. Whitehead ([1929] 1978, 68): "The argument, so far as it is valid, elicits a contradiction from the two premises: (i) that in becoming something (*res vera*) becomes, and (ii) that every act of becoming is divisible into earlier and later sections which are themselves acts of becoming."

25. Thanks to Alison Freeman for pointing to the pointlessness in the middle of this description of rhizomes.

26. *Pais paizon* means "a child playing" and these are the words that appear in Heraclitus Fragment 52.

27. Casals's recording (1936–39) of this piece doesn't bring out the wondrous repetition of this G as much as Ma does. Casals moves the G back into the bass line.

2. LEARNING TO SWIM

1. This is the same language Derrida uses when he is discussing iterability, but Derrida never finds his way to a positive conception of pointlessness (see Derrida 1977, 62).

2. "These brambles are only snippets from a jungle, of course" (Nathaniel Lawrence, personal communication, December 1985).

3. Thompson Clarke, in unpublished writings on skepticism, makes memorable use of this Sophoclean figure.

4. Nietzsche is close to this distinction between two kinds of pointlessness when, in his notes, he distinguishes two kinds of nihilism: positive and negative.

> Nihilism. It is *ambiguous.*
> A. Nihilism as a sign of increased power of the spirit: as *active* nihilism.
> B. Nihilism as decline and recession of the power of the spirit: as *passive* nihilism. (Nietzsche [1901] 1967b, #22)

5. Deleuze and Guattari praise Cage as an exemplar of the "authentic modernity" of art in the same breath that they describe that authenticity as consisting in "liberating what was present in art from its beginnings, but was hidden underneath *aims* and *objects,* even if aesthetic" (Deleuze and Guattari [1972] 1992, 371, my emphasis).

3. *ANDANTE VIVACE*

Beethoven used this tempo marking, *Andante Vivace,* in his *Duo for soprano and tenor, with piano,* Opus 82 #5. Its date is uncertain. It is sometimes given as 1809.

1. In the body of this chapter, parenthetical numbers will refer to the pages of *Slowness* (Kundera [1995] 1997).

2. In Michel Tournier's *Gemini,* the hand is praised for being amazingly able to form a fine simulation of the sexual organs of both sexes, and the length of the arm hangs the hand at just the right place (Tournier 1975).

3. *Vivacious* feels like a word more at home modifying women than men. Supposing my sense of this is correct, I am not sure why it is so. It might be the patriarchal attitude that men are not vivacious, they are serious. The warriors, not the child rearers. I seem to be pushing an ideal for everyone that patriarchy restricts to women.

4. According to *The Grove Dictionary,* "In the 18th century *vivace* often meant something much slower [than it does today]. The Anonymous *A Short Explication* (1724) put it between *largo* and *allegro*; [and] Leopold Mozart (1756) said *vivace* and *spiritoso* meant 'that one should play with understanding and intellect . . . they are the median between quick and slow.'" The *Grove* directed me to an article by Charles Cudworth that concerns itself only with the tempi indicated by English musicians, but restricting itself to that domain, it concludes authoritatively: "'Vivace' meant 'lively', but not necessarily 'fast', to eighteenth-century English musicians" (Cudworth 1965, 195).

5. My colleague Michael Raposa elaborates the religious significance of boredom, positive and negative, in his *Boredom and the Religious Imagination*, a work of love (Raposa 1999). He brought *Walden* into his reflections on boredom, and I will too.

6. *The Unbearable Lightness of Being* tells us that "kitsch is the absolute denial of shit, in both the literal and figurative senses of the world; kitsch excludes everything from its purview which is essentially unacceptable to human existence" (Kundera 1984, 248). It is not as if kitsch excludes evil—evil is there—what it excludes is *"moral ambiguity"* (Mendelson 2004). In its supreme confidence, everything is easy; there are no difficult problems, certainly no insoluble problems. *Slowness* makes the connection to kitsch more or less explicit by linking the dancer concept to the "grand march" (17). *The Unbearable Lightness of Being* puts the most extended discussion of kitsch in a section called "The Grand March," an example of totalitarian kitsch, the May Day Parade. There is American kitsch too, of course, and multicultural diversity kitsch.

7. Terri Mastrobuono and Camilla Schade presented *Parallel Lives*, a version of *The Kathy and Mo Show*, which after being improvised in 1980 became an off-Broadway success in the middle 1980s (Gaffney and Najimy 1998).

8. This is one possible reading of Kierkegaard's *Either/Or*, namely that the editor of that book, Victor Eremita, is trying to escape the inevitable failure of the project of becoming a self, by vanishing from the stage of society, retiring, a hermit, victorious over the public. I owe this interpretive gambit to Melissa Blackman.

9. Unless this is the ersatz No that derives from double affirmation. I think that if the publicity of the event is what seems important, then this will be fast rather than slow ecstasy. Everything, as always, depends on everything else.

10. See the concluding discussion of Bearn 1997a, where this poem by Wallace Stevens is also invoked. But at that time I did not see that intensity was the ideal, not authenticity, so I did not then assert a positive role for theater.

11. "Withdraw into yourself and look. And if you do not find yourself beautiful yet, act as does the creator of a statue that is to be made beautiful: he cuts away here, he smooths there, he makes this line lighter, this other purer, until a lovely face has grown upon his work. So do you also: cut away all that is excessive, straighten all that is crooked, bring light to all that is overcast, labour to make all one glow of beauty and never cease chiseling your statue, until there shall shine out on you from it the godlike splendour of virtue, until you shall see the perfect goodness surely established in the stainless shrine" (Plotinus [c. 300 CE] 1949 1.6.9). Also see Socrates on sculpting the soul in Diogenes Laertius [c. 225 CE], 1995, 1:165.

12. Sex on the sidewalk. This is hurried and scary, and that is a lot of its power. Fast and fun. But doesn't it need representation? Doesn't it need the thrill of breaking a code? Doesn't it need the code? Don't you need to know

you are on the sidewalk? Will it turn out that the intensity of the fast requires representation but that the intensity of the slow does not? Not so fast. Did Socrates know where he was when he was lost in thought, outside of Agathon's, before the Symposium? Did you know where you were when she crushed you hungry against the brick wall, in the shadows?

4. AGAIN AND AGAIN

1. Thanks to Mark McKenna for jogging my memory and for introducing me, telephonically, to Jim Calder, a member of the now disbanded Luftkugel, who kindly spoke with me on the phone today, fleshing out my memory of that exciting night (phone conversation, January 27, 1999).

2. I am using the word *actual* to indicate what Whitehead would have meant by the word, namely, the final realities of which the world is composed (Whitehead [1929] 1978, 180). A more beautiful way to say it is becoming.

3. February 9, 1999, the night's end, daybreak.

4. "The plight of the actor is always with us" (Davidson 1982, 270).

5. Listening to these words of double negation in a song written by my oldest friend, Eric Tamm, sung by one of his more recent friends, Janis Weiss, one of the Skeptics.

6. Deleuze and Guattari discuss this Kleist story in *A Thousand Plateaus* ([1980] 1987, 268), and they like the bear.

7. Leaping is not dancing. Leaping is ruined by the necessity of pushing off the earth, so it comes back down and is not a pure leap, which would be flight, but even so it will be scarred by the pushing off. Dancing, in contrast, has made its peace with the earth (EPPA spring 1999, talk with Walter Brogan and Margie Haas).

8. Michael Raposa always reminds me that there is a nondirected awareness, call it a pointless awareness, that is a part of some martial arts. Hypersensitivity in the service not of sensual delight but of self-defense. I do not think that this pointless awareness has anything to do with Kleist's serious bear.

9. There is a tremendous amount of positive pointlessness in the *practice* of archery described by Herrigel, even if it is often *described* in terms of double negation. Herrigel tells us that his master once told him that he would succeed "by letting go of yourself, leaving yourself and everything yours behind you so decisively that nothing more is left of you but a purposeless tension" (Herrigel [1948] 1999, 47). Linking purposelessness and tension is precisely what I am trying to do, so it is perhaps right to take my project as separating some of the practices of Zen archery from the thoughts of double negation to which even Herr H.'s master can succumb.

10. This "true" is a sign that we are still trapped within the frame of representation.

308 Notes to pages 117–132

11. Often these boundaries are the same for animals as they are for humans. Haraway tells an amazing story about the struggle the American Museum of Natural History had in acquiring for each of its naturalistic dioramas the appropriate ideal family, one male, one female (maybe two), a baby, no aged animals, no disease, every specimen, *perfect*. It took two years to find, and kill, an appropriate bull elephant: very large, of course; it had to have symmetrical tusks, and it had to be shot while facing the gun, for the proper male is not cowardly, but brave (Haraway 1989, 40–41).

12. Two kinds of becoming-animal, representationally and nonrepresentationally (Deleuze and Parnet [1977] 1987, 53). Two kinds of theater (Artaud [1938] 1968).

13. I don't know whether nonhuman animals experience the right kind of anxiety. That is an empirical question.

14. I learned this when *The Claim of Reason* (1979) was still fresh, sitting in on a seminar Norton Batkin was teaching on the *Investigations*.

15. Urination can mark territory only by separating itself from the simple function of urination. The smell becomes autonomous. A signature. (See "1837: Of the Refrain," in Deleuze and Guattari [1980] 1987, 316–17.)

16. According to Cavell, the philosopher's concern about whether we can know anything at all is a "response which expresses a natural experience of a creature complicated enough or burdened enough to possess language at all" (Cavell 1979, 140).

17. There are Derridean arguments for the necessity of supernatural help if we are ever to return to Eden.

18. I am thinking of numberless times that my colleague Mark Bickhard has pressed this point against various incautious causal reductions of meaning.

19. The main reason they privilege indirect discourse is, however, that when we talk we just repeat what we have been told to say: "Language , always goes from saying to saying" (Deleuze and Guattari [1980] 1987, 76, and see 79). Also see the importance Deleuze gives to "free indirect discourse" in a number of places, for example, Deleuze 1991.

20. "Plenitude is the end (goal), but were it attained, it would be the end (death)" (Derrida 1988a, 129).

21. The conclusion of this chapter draws throughout on Bearn 2000c.

22. Rather than remaining content with the Kantian settlement with skepticism, Deleuze asks what must being be like, what must things as they are in themselves be like if secondary repetition is possible. This means that rather than turning to a kind of skepticism, even of a Kantian variety, I will be following Deleuze in trying to determine what features of the world as it is in itself would explain our epistemological limitations. And in Deleuze's hands this reveals a rather unusual account of being. Deleuze:

Being (what Plato calls the Idea) "corresponds" to the essence of the problem or the question as such. . . . Being is also non-being, *but non-being is not the being of the negative;* it is the being of the problematic, the being of problem and question. For this reason, non-being should rather be written (non)-being or, better still, ?-being. In this sense it turns out that the infinitive, the *esse*, designates less a proposition than the interrogation to which the proposition is supposed to respond. This (non)-being is the differential element in which affirmation, as multiple affirmation, finds the principle of its genesis. (Deleuze [1968] 1994, 64)

A few pages later, Deleuze links these thoughts to Eros: "Why is it that Eros holds both the secret of questions and answers, and the secret of an insistence in all our existence?" (Deleuze [1968] 1994, 85). This is why I will be trying to make sense of breaking through (to the other side) of representation.

23. "It is here that we find the lived reality of a sub-representative domain." (Deleuze [1968] 1994, 69). In 1968 and 1969 Deleuze sometimes called this domain *sense*.

Sense is what is expressed by a proposition, but what is this *expressed*? It cannot be reduced either to the object designated or to the lived state of the speaker. Indeed, we must distinguish sense and signification in the following manner: signification refers only to the concepts and the manner in which they relate to objects conditioned by a given field of representation; whereas sense is like the Idea which is developed in the sub-representative determinations." (Deleuze [1968] 1994, 154–55; see Deleuze [1969] 1990, 12–22, and Deleuze and Guattari [1980] 1987, 219)

24. Why vulgar? My colleague Michael Mendelson suggests that it might be vulgar because in full-fledged Leibnizian metaphysics, the reflection of each monad in every other may mean that there is, at bottom, only one complete concept.

25. There are two ethics, one representational and familiar, which makes justice and racism possible, and another beyond representation and unfamiliar, which opens us to delicious delight, an ethics of affection.

26. The second epigraph to Derrida's *Speech and Phenomena* (1967c) is a passage from Husserl's *Ideas* I, §100: "A name on being mentioned reminds us of the Dresden gallery and of our last visit there: we wander through rooms and stop in front of a painting by Teniers which represents a gallery of paintings. Let us further suppose that the paintings of this gallery would represent in their turn paintings, which, on their part, exhibited readable inscriptions and so forth."

27. This is a point familiar to readers of Derrida. At Derrida (1967b) 1978a, 36, this problem is attributed to the "unsurpassable, unique, and imperial grandeur of the order of reason." At Derrida (1972b) 1982, xiv, Derrida suggests that this problem requires that we approach the outside of reason "obliquely." Derrida's suggestion is adjacent to Deleuze's advocacy of the diagonal, for example at Deleuze and Guattari (1980) 1987, 295: "Free the line, free the diagonal." But the distinction between Derrida and Deleuze is the distance between the impossibility (Derrida) and the possibility (Deleuze) of riding a diagonal through the frame of representation. As always, it is the difference between No and Yes.

28. *"Flat multiplicities of n-dimensions* are asignifying and asubjective" (Deleuze and Guattari [1980] 1987, 9).

29. Rimbaud, *Illuminations* c. 1875 includes a prose poem titled *H*:

All monstrosities violate the atrocious gestures of Hortense. Her solitude is an erotic mechanics, her languor, loving's dynamics. Under the surveillance of a certain childhood, she has been, in numerous ages, the ardent hygiene of the races. Her door is open to misery. There, the morality of actual beings is disembodied by her passion or her action—Oh terrible shudder of young lovers on the bloody soil and near brilliant hydrogen! Find Hortense.

6. DESIRE WITHOUT DESIRES

1. I can no longer remember the specific circumstances of John Hare's encouragement of the following contentious reading of the *Symposium*, and I know he would find a number of things to correct in my presentation, but at that time my respect and love for him gave weight to his passing remarks. Roslyn Weiss, leaving my office on a laugh, also helped me write for and against Plato in this way.

2. Thinking of a white clapboard church and Dennis Washburn reading these texts aloud on September 12, 1981. "I do."

3. This may remind one of the difficulty that confronted Wittgenstein of a word's being used meaningfully and at the same time being misused.

4. Michael Mendelson helped me see this limitation of the earlier version of these considerations. Even Frege's project was not halted by Russell's paradox, which was a puzzle to solve; it was halted by Gödel.

5. Sure that Plainville was too obvious, Steve Goldman looked a little into this and came up with Smallville. Now, to make sure no one ever wonders again, there is a TV show.

6. Remember: Why do we think that money ruins sex, and why don't we think it ruins everything?

7. Conversation with Michael Mendelson was the place these thoughts were first uttered; e-mail with Paul Standish is where they first found the keyboard.

8. Michael Mendelson suggested to me that the very notion of liquidity makes trouble for identity: one thing running into another. If you are interested in identification, you should first get the distilled water, clean the lab bench, and dry it off. Heraclitus may also have been worried about how water extinguishes fire.

7. BECOMING BECOMING

1. This definition and this brief history of the use of "aesthetic" are drawn from the *Oxford English Dictionary*.

2. The creative energy of absolute power is close to what the tradition called creation ex nihilo, for if there is genuine novelty, it can't come from something, else it would not be genuine, so it must somehow come from nothing.

3. This advice is not that different from Wittgenstein's: Don't think, look! (Wittgenstein [1953] 1976, §66).

4. Sunny Bavaro proposed this as a motto for the Lehigh Humanities Center, rendered into Latin by Barbara Pavlock: *E. nominibus in verba*.

5. Jose Pitti pointed to the belle in belly during a conversation in the Humanities Center in the early morning of June 15, 2005.

6. The notes and glossary of the MIT Press edition of Alberti 1486 made it possible to telegraph these remarks.

7. I am suspicious of the eighteenth-century division of the beautiful from the sublime. The explosive power of Diotima's beauty is turned into dainty little fragile things, and so a place had to be found for the power once attributed to beauty. It was given to the sublime, but that too was tamed either as a benevolent deity, or human reason, or simply mathematical infinity. Last Wednesday, Nick Sawicki pointed out that the mere fact that mountain climbing became a pastime in that century is a sign that even mountains and waterfalls had lost their power really to terrify us. Neither the eighteenth century's beautiful nor its sublime retains the power of Diotima's beauty, the power to overflow certainly.

8. When I was friends with Wittgenstein I could have said that it was important to accept the accidental, for in Wittgenstein it is always a question of accepting our life on the rough ground. But the shift from accepting to enjoying the accidental is allofit.

9. Seth Moglen sent me these lines in rebuttal of Elaine Scarry after Scarry's visit to Lehigh University in the Fall of 2001.

10. Paul Standish cautions me that Mrs. Dalloway's aversion to saying of anyone that they were this or that, might be a Deleuzoid Yes, but it might also be a descent into affectlessness.

11. Nathaniel Lawrence told this story to his classes at Williams. Cf. Brumbaugh 1982, 80.

12. This is neither the conceptual content, to which McDowell thinks experience is restricted, nor the motor intentional form of nonconceptual content defended, for example, by Dreyfus and Kelly (McDowell 1994; Kelly 2001; Dreyfus 2007).

13. Although I can't put my finger on the passage, I feel sure I read this counter-Russellian vision of philosophy in either *Difference and Repetition* or *The Logic of Sense* (Deleuze [1968] 1994; Deleuze [1969] 1990).

8. REFUSING BEAUTY; OR, THE BRUISE

1. Simon Blackburn used this point to destroy an attempt I once made to reconstruct a Whiteheadian argument from a general characterization of the cosmos to a characterization of the cause of that cosmos. I found the quoted passage in *Brewer's Dictionary of Phrase and Fable*, which I have consulted ever since my family sent me off to boarding school, with four different dictionaries.

2. Or so I thought until Rick Matthews asked me without hesitation whether a battered baby would have been more difficult. He's right, of course.

3. *Shrek* proves the rule by exception.

4. Sonic Youth, *SYR 4*, 1999, disk A, track 5, performed by Coco Hayley Gordon Moore.

5. Alex Doty's essay on the *Wizard of Oz* made this sentence visible to me (Doty 2000, chap. 2).

6. Thanks to Drew Francis for telling me about this piece and for recounting how he once performed it.

9. AN ETHICS OF AFFECTION

1. Feinberg 1973 gave me courage to lead with chain saws. He too finds violence, danger, and fear at the heart of respect. I was directed to Feinberg by my generous colleague Robin Dillon.

2. In the passages cited in this paragraph Dillon is discussing kinds of self-respect, and I have perhaps rashly taken the liberty of sharing her distinction with the category of respect.

3. My friend Michael Mendelson gave me the word *asymmetrical* and so paved the way for the word *contradictory*.

4. Brumbaugh emphasizes *simple* to make sure we are imagining Chepstow Castle in Wales and not, for example, the complex Beaumaris Castle on the Island of Angelsey, in which, Brumbaugh tells us, "every part of the castle is outside every other part" (Brumbaugh 1982, 31).

5. Thanks once again to the thorough and insightful work of Daniel W. Smith. This time to "The Place of Ethics in Deleuze's Philosophy" (D. W. Smith 1998).

6. This passage also suggests an attractive philosophy of education.

7. Here is Nietzsche in an 1881 postcard to Overbeck written flush with his discovery of Spinoza: "I am utterly amazed, utterly enchanted. . . . Not only is his over-all tendency like mine—making knowledge *the most powerful emotion*—but I recognize myself in five main points of his theory:. . . he denies free will—; goals—; the moral order of the world—; unegoistical actions—; and evil—" (Nietzsche 1982, 92, translation altered).

8. A question from Steve Goldman.

CADENZA

1. Cavell cites the following sentence from Emerson's essay "Experience" as an epigraph to Cavell 1990c: "I take this evanescence and lubricity of all objects, which lets them slip through our fingers then when we clutch hardest, to be the most unhandsome part of our condition."

Adorno, T. W. (1951) 1984. *Minima Moralia: Reflections from Damaged Life*. London: Verso.

Agamben, G. 1996. "Absolute Immanence." In Agamben 1999.

———. 1999. *Potentialities*. Stanford: Stanford University Press.

Alberti. (1486) 1991. *On the Art of Building, in 10 Books*. Translated by J. Rykwert, N. Leach, and R. Tavernor. Cambridge, Mass.: MIT Press.

Alston, A. 2004. "Beyond Nationalism but Not without It." Cited from *Anarchist People of Color*. http://www.anarchistpanther.net/writings/writing4.html.

Ammons, A. R. 1981. *A Coast of Trees*. New York: W. W. Norton.

Ariew, R., and D. Garber. 1989. *G. W. Leibniz: Philosophical Essays*. Indianapolis: Hackett.

Aristotle. (340 BCE) 1985. *Nicomachean Ethics*. Translated by T. Irwin. Indianapolis: Hackett. I use the Bekker page numbers.

Artaud, A. (1938) 1968. *The Theater and Its Double*. Translated by M. C. Richards. New York: Grove.

Austin, J. L. 1953. "How to Talk: Some Simple Ways." Reprinted in Austin 1979.

———. 1956. "A Plea for Excuses." In Austin 1979.

———. 1962. *Sense and Sensibilia*. New York: Oxford University Press. This book was reconstructed by G. J. Warnock from Austin's lecture notes, some of which date from 1947. The last revision of those notes was made in 1958 for lectures Austin delivered at Berkeley.

———. 1976. *How to Do Things with Words*. The William James Lectures Delivered at Harvard University in 1955. 2nd ed. Edited by J. O. Urmson and M. Sbisà. Oxford: Oxford University Press.

———. 1979. *Philosophical Papers*. 3rd ed. New York: Oxford University Press.

Bacon, F. (1625) n.d. *The Essayes or Counsels, Civill and Morall*. Mount Vernon, N.Y.: Peter Pauper Press.

Badiou, A. (1998) 2001. *Ethics—An Essay on the Understanding of Evil.* New York: Verso.

Baker, G. 1988. "The Reception of the Private Language Argument." In Baker 2004.

———. 2004. *Wittgenstein's Method: Neglected Aspects.* Oxford: Blackwell.

Barthes, R. (1973) 1975. *The Pleasure of the Text.* New York: Hill and Wang.

———. 1984. *Le bruissement de la langue: Essais critiques* IV. Paris: Seuil.

Basho. (c. 1690) 1977. *The Narrow Road to the Deep North.* Middlesex Eng.: Penguin Books.

Battcock, G. 1981. *Breaking the Sound Barrier.* New York: Dutton.

Bearn, G. C. F. 1992. "The Formal Syntax of Modernism: Carnap and Le Corbusier." *British Journal of Aesthetics* 32 (3): 227–41.

———. 1993. "Wittgenstein and the Uncanny." *Soundings* 76 (1): 29–58.

———. 1995a. "The Possibility of Puns: A Defense of Derrida." *Philosophy and Literature* 19 (2).

———. 1995b. "Derrida Dry: Iterating Iterability Analytically." *Diacritics* 25 (3): 3–25.

———. 1997a. *Waking to Wonder: Wittgenstein's Existential Investigations.* Albany: State University of New York Press.

———. 1997b. "Aestheticide: Architecture and the Death of Art." *Journal of Aesthetic Education* 31 (1): 87–94.

———. 1998a. "Kitsch." In *The Encyclopedia of Aesthetics*, edited by Michael Kelly, 64–70. New York: Oxford University Press.

———. 1998b. "Sounding Serious: Cavell and Derrida." *Representations* 63 (Summer): 65–92.

———. 2000a. "Differentiating Derrida and Deleuze." *Continental Philosophy Review* 33 (4): 441–65.

———. 2000b. "Individuation without Identity: A Deleuzian Aesthetics of Existence." In *Mapping Jewish Identities*, edited by Laurence J. Silberstein. New York: New York University Press.

———. 2000c. "Pointlessness and the University of Beauty." In *Lyotard: Just Education*, edited by Pradeep Dhillon and Paul Standish. New York: Routledge.

———. 2000d. "Staging Authenticity: A Critique of Cavell's Modernism." *Philosophy and Literature* 24 (2): 294–311.

———. 2010. "The Enormous Danger." In Day and Krebs 2010, 338–56.

Beauvoir, S. de. (1949) 1980. *The Second Sex.* New York: Alfred A. Knopf.

Benjamin, W. (1936) 1968. "The Work of Art in the Age of Mechanical Reproduction." In *Illuminations*, edited by H. Arendt. New York: Harcourt Brace and World.

Bergson, H. (1889) 1960. *Time and Free Will: An Essay on the Immediate Date of Consciousness.* Translated by F. L. Pogson. New York: Harper and Row.

———. (1896) 1991. *Matter and Memory.* New York: Zone Books.

———. (1900) 1980. *Laughter*. Baltimore: Johns Hopkins University Press.

———. (1903) 1992. "An Introduction to Metaphysics." In Bergson, *The Creative Mind*, 159–200. New York: Carol Publishing Group, 1992.

Bickhard, M. H. Unpublished. "The Whole Person."

Black, Sophie Cabot. 2000. "The Tree." *Atlantic Monthly*, June.

Blackburn, S. W. 1994. *The Oxford Dictionary of Philosophy*. New York: Oxford University Press.

Blake, W. 1977. *William Blake: The Complete Poems*. Edited by Alicia Ostriker. New York: Penguin Books.

———. (1790) 1994. *The Marriage of Heaven and Hell: In Full Color*. New York: Dover.

Bohm, D. (1980) 1982. *Wholeness and the Implicate Order*. London: Routledge.

Bois, Y.-A., and R. E. Krauss. 1997. *Formless: A User's Guide*. New York: Zone Books.

Boulez, P. (1963) 1971. *Boulez on Music Today*. Cambridge, Mass.: Harvard University Press.

Bowden, B. (1971) 1997. "Introduction to the Second Edition" of *The Comedy of Eros*, translated by Norman R. Shapiro. Urbana: University of Illinois Press.

Breton, A. (1937) 1987. *Mad Love*. Translated by Mary Ann Caws. Lincoln: University of Nebraska Press, 1987.

Brown, N. O. (1959) 1985. *Life against Death*. Hanover, N.H.: Wesleyan University Press.

———. 1966. *Love's Body*. Berkeley: University of California Press.

Brumbaugh, R. S. 1982. *Whitehead, Process Philosophy, and Education*. Albany: State University of New York Press.

Burke, E. (1757) 1968. *A Philosophical Enquiry into the Origin of Our Ideas of the Sublime and the Beautiful*. Edited by James T. Boulton. Notre Dame, Ind.: University of Notre Dame Press.

Cage, J. (1961) 1973. *Silence*. Hanover, N.H.: Wesleyan University Press and the University Press of New England.

Camus, A. (1942a) 1991. *The Myth of Sisyphus*. New York: Vintage International.

———. (1942b) 1988. *The Stranger*. Translated by Matthew Ward. New York: Vintage International.

———. (1956) 1971. *The Fall*. Translated by Justin O'Brien. Middlesex, Eng.: Penguin Books.

Caputo, J. D. 1997. *Deconstruction in a Nutshell: A Conversation with Jacques Derrida*. New York: Fordham University Press.

Carroll, L. 1895. "What the Tortoise Said to Achilles." *Mind* 4 (14): 278–80. Reprint 1995. *Mind* 104 (416): 691–93.

Cavell, S. (1964) 1984. "Existentialism and Analytic Philosophy." Reprinted with long introductory note in Cavell 1984, 195–233.

———. (1969) 1976. *Must We Mean What We Say? A Book of Essays.* Cambridge: Cambridge University Press.

———. 1979. *The Claim of Reason.* New York: Oxford University Press.

———. 1981. *The Senses of Walden: An Expanded Edition.* San Francisco: North Point Press.

———. 1984. *Themes Out of School: Effects and Causes.* San Francisco: North Point Press.

———. (1987) 1990a. "Psychoanalysis and Cinema: Moments of *Letter from an Unknown Woman.*" In Cavell 1990b, 81–113.

———. 1989. *This New Yet Unapproachable America: Lectures after Emerson after Wittgenstein.* Albuquerque, N.M.: Living Batch Press.

———. 1990b. *Contesting Tears: The Hollywood Melodrama of the Unknown Woman.* Chicago: University of Chicago Press.

———. 1990c. *Conditions Handsome and Unhandsome: The Constitution of Emersonian Perfectionism.* Carus Lectures, 1988. Chicago: University of Chicago Press.

———. 1994. *A Pitch of Philosophy: Autobiographical Excercises.* Cambridge, Mass.: Harvard University Press.

———. 1995. *Philosophical Passages: Wittgenstein, Emerson, Austin, Derrida.* Cambridge, Mass.: Blackwell.

———. 2005a. "Performative and Passionate Utterances." In Cavell 2005b.

———. 2005b. *Philosophy the Day after Tomorrow.* Cambridge, Mass.: Belknap Press of Harvard University Press.

Césaire, A. (1950) 2000. *Discourse on Colonialism.* Translated by Joan Pinkham. New York: Monthly Review Press.

———. 1957. *Letter to Maurice Thorez.* Paris: Editions Présence africaine.

Césaire, S. 1941. "The Domain of the Marvelous." Reprinted and translated in Rosemont 1998, 137.

Clarke, T. 1972. "The Legacy of Skepticism." *Journal of Philosophy* 69 (20): 754–69.

Cowell, H. (1939) 1971. *Pulse.* New York: Music for Percussion

Cudworth, C. 1965. "The Meaning of 'Vivace' in Eighteenth-Century England." *Fontis Artis Musicae (FAM)* 12:194–95.

Cummings, E. E., 1991. *E. E. Cummings: The Complete Poems, 1904–1962.* Edited by George J. Firmage. New York: Liveright.

Curd, P., and R. D. McKirahan Jr., eds. 1996. *A Presocratics Reader.* Indianapolis: Hackett.

Curley, E., ed. and trans. 1994. *A Spinoza Reader: The Ethics and Other Works.* Princeton: Princeton University Press.

Davidson, D. 1982. "Communication and Convention." Reprinted in Davidson 1984.

———. 1984. *Inquiries into Truth and Interpretation.* New York: Oxford University Press.

Day, W., and V. Krebs, eds. 2010. *Seeing Wittgenstein Anew*. New York: Cambridge University Press.

Debord, G. 1958. "Theory of the Dérive." Reprinted in Knabb 1995.

———. (1967) 1995. *The Society of the Spectacle*. Translated by Donald Nicholson-Smith. New York: Zone Books.

Deleuze, G. (1962) 1983. *Nietzsche and Philosophy*. New York: Columbia University Press.

———. 1963. "The Mystery of Ariadne According to Nietzsche." In Deleuze (1993) 1997, 99–106.

———. (1964a) 1973. *Proust and Signs*. London: Allen Lane, Penguin Press.

———. 1964b. "He Was My Teacher." In Deleuze 2004.

———. (1966) 1991. *Bergsonism*. Translated by Hugh Tomlinson and Barbara Habberjam. New York: Zone Books.

———. 1967a. "La Méthode de Dramatisation." *Bulletin de la Société française de Philosophie* 61 (3): 89–118.

———. 1967b. "Mysticism and Masochism." In Deleuze 2004, 131–34.

———. (1968) 1994. *Difference and Repetition*. London: Athlone.

———. (1969) 1990. *Logic of Sense*. New York: Columbia University Press.

———. (1970) 1988. *Spinoza: Practical Philosophy*. San Francisco: City Lights Books.

———. 1972. "How Do We Recognize Structuralism?" In Deleuze 2004, 170–92.

———. (1973) 1995. "Letter to a Harsh Critic." Also called "I Have Nothing to Admit." In *Negotiations*. New York: Columbia University Press.

———. (1988) 1993a. *The Fold: Leibniz and the Baroque*. Translated by Tom Conley. London: Athlone Press.

———. 1991. "Preface: A New Stylistics." In Deleuze 2006, 366–71.

———. (1993b) 1997. *Essays Critical and Clinical*. Minneapolis: University of Minnesota Press.

———. 1995a. "Immanence: " Life . . ." *Theory Culture and Society* 14 (2): 3–7.

———. 1995b. *Le Novel Observateur*, November 16–22, 50–51.

———. 2004. *Desert Islands and Other Texts, 1953–1974*. New York: Semiotext(e).

———. 2006. *Two Regimes of Madness: Texts and Interviews, 1975–1995*. Edited by David Lapoujade. New York: Semiotext(e).

Deleuze, G., and F. Guattari. (1972) 1992. *Anti-Oedipus: Capitalism and Schizophrenia*. Minneapolis: University of Minnesota Press.

———. 1973a. "Balance-Sheet Program for Desiring Machines." In Guattari 2009, 90–115.

———. 1973b. "On Capitalism and Desire." In Deleuze 2004, 262–73.

———. (1980) 1987. *A Thousand Plateaus: Capitalism and Schizophrenia*. Minneapolis: University of Minnesota Press.

———. (1991) 1994. *What Is Philosophy?* London: Verso.

Deleuze, G., and C. Parnet. (1977) 1987. *Dialogues*. New York: Columbia University Press.

———. (1996) 2000. *The ABCs of Gilles Deleuze*, with Claire Parnet, directed by Pierre-André Boutang, filmed 1988–89. English Overview (not a transcription and translation) by Charles Stivale with special thanks to John Morton, May 3, 2000. http://www.langlab.wayne.edu/CStivale/D-G/ABC1.html.

Denon, V. (1777) 1914. *Point de lendemain Paris*. Bibliothèque des Curieux. This edition includes a facsimile of the title page of the first appearance of the story in *Mélanges Littéraires ou Journal des Dames*. This was a subscription publication and the issue with *Point de lendemain* in it was volume 2 from June 1777. At that time, the story was credited to "M.D.G.O.D.R."

Derrida, J. 1966. "Structure, Sign, and Play in the Discourse of the Human Sciences." Reprinted in Derrida 1967b, 278–93.

———. (1967a) 1976. *Of Grammatology*. Baltimore: Johns Hopkins University Press.

———. (1967b) 1978a. *Writing and Difference*. Chicago: University of Chicago Press.

———. (1967c) 1973. *Speech and Phenomena*. Evanston, Ill.: Northwestern University Press.

———. 1968. "Plato's Pharmacy." In Derrida (1972a) 1981.

———. 1971. "Signature Event Context." In Derrida 1988, 1–23.

———. (1972a) 1981. *Dissemination*. Chicago: University of Chicago Press.

———. (1972b) 1982. *Margins of Philosophy*. Chicago: University of Chicago Press.

———. 1972c. "Tympan." In Derrida (1972b) 1982, ix–xxix.

———. 1977. "Limited Inc a b c . . ." In Derrida 1988, 29–110.

———. (1978b) 1987a. *Truth in Painting*. Translated by G. Bennington and Ian McLeod. Chicago: University of Chicago Press, 1987.

———. (1980) 1987b. *The Post Card: From Socrates to Freud and Beyond*. Chicago: University of Chicago Press.

———. 1987c. *Of Spirit: Heidegger and the Question*. Chicago: University of Chicago Press.

———. 1988a. *Limited Inc*. Evanston, Ill.: Northwestern University Press.

———. 1988b. "A Number of Yes (Nombre de oui)." *Qui Parle* 2 (2): 118–33.

———. (1989) 1992. "Force of Law: The Mystical Foundation of Authority.'" In *Deconstruction and the Possibility of Justice*, edited by Drucilla Cornell et al. New York: Routledge.

———. 1991. "Summary of Impromptu Remarks." In *Anyone*, edited by Cynthia Davidson. New York: Rizzoli International.

———. (1993) 1994. *Specters of Marx*. New York: Routledge.

———. (2000) 2005. *On Touching—Jean-Luc Nancy*. Stanford: Stanford University Press.

Derrida J., and G. Vattimo, eds. 1998. *Religion*. Stanford: Stanford University Press.

Dewey, J. (1934) 1989. *Art as Experience*. Carbondale: Southern Illinois University Press.

Dillon, R. S. 1997. "Self-Respect: Moral, Emotional, Political." *Ethics* 107 (2): 226–49.

Diogenes Laertius. (c. 225 CE) 1995. *Lives of Eminent Philosophers*. Translated by R. D. Hicks. Loeb Library, vol. 185. Cambridge, Mass.: Harvard University Press.

Dreyfus, H. 1991. *Being-in-the-World: A Commentary on Heidegger's Being and Time, Division I*. Cambridge, Mass.: MIT Press.

———. 2005. "Overcoming the Myth of the Mental: How Philosophers Can Profit from the Phenomenology of Everyday Expertise." *Proceedings and Addresses of the American Philosophical Association* 79 (2): 47–65.

———. 2007. "Reply to McDowell." *Inquiry* 50 (4): 371–77.

Dreyfus, H., and S. Dreyfus. 1999. "The Challenge of Merleau-Ponty's Phenomenology of Embodiment for Cognitive Science." In Weiss and Haber 1999.

Doty, A. 2000. *Flaming Classics: Queering the Film Canon*. New York: Routledge.

DuBois, W. E. B. (1903) 1990. *The Souls of Black Folk*. New York: Vintage/ Library of America.

Dummett, M. A. E. (1973) 1981. *Frege: Philosophy of Language*. Cambridge, Mass.: Harvard University Press.

Eco, U. 1986. *Faith in Fakes: Essays*. London: Secker and Warburg.

Ellison, R. (1952) 1980. *Invisible Man*. New York: Vintage International.

Emerson, R. W. [1841] 1983. "Self-Reliance." In *Ralph Waldo Emerson: Essays and Lectures*. New York: Library of America.

Eze, E. C. 1997. *Race and Enlightenment: A Reader*. Oxford: Basil Blackwell.

Feinberg, J. 1973. "Some Conjectures about the Concept of Respect." *Journal of Social Philosophy* 4 (2): 1–3.

Foucault, M. 1983. "On the Genealogy of Ethics: An Overview of Work in Progress." In Rabinow 1984, 340–72.

Freeman, A. 1998. "Solitude, Self-Sufficiency, and Pointlessness." *Lehigh Review* 6:139–48.

———. 1999. "Light without Heat." *Lehigh Review* 7:41–52.

Freeman, E., and W. Sellars, eds. 1971. *Basic Issues in the Philosophy of Time*. La Salle, Ill.: Open Court.

Freeman, K. 1948. *Ancilla to the Pre-Socratic Philosophers: A Complete Translation of the Fragments in Diels, Fragmente der Vorsokratiker*. Cambridge, Mass.: Harvard University Press.

Frege, G. (1918) 1968. "The Thought: Logical Inquiry." In *Essays on Frege*, edited by E. D. Klemke, 507–35. Urbana: University of Illinois Press.

Freud, S. 1924. "The Economic Problem in Masochism." In Riviere 1948.

Gaffney, M., and K. Najimy. 1998. *Parallel Lives—Based on The Kathy and Mo Show.* Dramatists Play Service.

Gardner, H. 1972. *The New Oxford Book of English Verse: 1250–1950.* New York: Oxford University Press.

Gass, W. (1976) 1991. *On Being Blue: A Philosophical Inquiry.* Boston: David R. Godine.

Gautier, T. (1835) 1981. *Mademoiselle de Maupin.* The preface to this volume is dated May 1834. New York: Penguin.

Genosko, G. 2001. *Deleuze and Guattari: Critical Assessments of Leading Philosophers.* Vol. 1: *Deleuze.* New York: Routledge.

George, Bobby. 2000. "Undistance Beauty: The Beauty of And." Unpublished.

Glendinning, S. 1998. *On Being with Others: Heidegger-Derrida-Wittgenstein.* London: Routledge.

Grice, H. P. 1989. *Studies in the Way of Words.* Cambridge, Mass.: Harvard University Press.

Guattari, F. 2009. *Chaosophy.* Edited by Sylvère Lotringer. New York: Semiotext(e).

Guntrip, H. 1952. "The Schizoid Personality and the External World." In Guntrip 1969.

———. 1969. *Schizoid Phenomena, Object-Relations and the Self.* New York: International Universities Press.

Haraway, D. J. 1989. *Primate Visions: Gender, Race, and Nature in the World of Modern Science.* New York: Routledge.

Haskell, F. 1963. *Patrons and Painters: A Study in the Relations between Italian Art and Society in the Age of the Baroque.* New York: Knopf.

HD. 1983. *Collected Poems.* Edited by Louis L. Martz. New York: New Directions.

Hegel, G. W. F. (1807) 1977. *The Phenomenology of Spirit.* Translated by A. V. Miller. New York: Oxford University Press.

———. (1817) 1991. *The Encyclopedia Logic.* Translated by T. F. Geraets, W. A. Suchung, and H. S. Harris. Indianapolis: Hackett, 1991. The first edition of this book was published in 1817; it was revised significantly in 1827, and again, but much less for the third edition of 1830, which was the text for this translation.

———. (1835) 1975. *Aesthetics: Lectures on Fine Art.* Translated by T. M. Knox. 2 vols. Oxford: Clarendon Press.

Heidegger, M. (1927) 1962. *Being and Time.* Translated by J. Macquarrie and E. Robinson. New York: Harper and Row.

———. (1959) 1966. *Discourse on Thinking.* A translation of *Gelassenheit.* New York: Harper Torchbooks.

———. 1971. "The Origin of the Work of Art." Written in 1936. In *Poetry, Language, Thought*, translated by A. Hofstadter. New York: Harper.

Held, J. 1963. "The Early Appreciation of Drawings." In *Studies in Western Art: Acts of the 20th International Congress on the History of Art 1961*. Princeton: Princeton University Press.

Heraclitus. 500 BCE. Fragments. In Curd and McKirahan 1996.

Herrigel, E. (1948) 1999. *Zen in the Art of Archery*. New York: Vintage.

Higgins, Dick 1968. "Boredom and Danger." In Battcock 1981, 20–27.

———. 1984. *Horizons, the Poetics and Theory of the Intermedia*. Carbondale: Southern Illinois University Press.

Ives, C. 1920. *Essays before a Sonata*. In Ives 1962.

———. 1962. *Essays before a Sonata, The Majority, and Other Writings*. Edited by Howard Boatwright. New York: W. W. Norton.

Johnstone, K. (1979) 1992. *Impro: Improvisation and the Theatre*. New York: Routledge.

Kant, I. (1764) 1991. *Observations on the Feeling of the Beautiful and the Sublime*. Translated by J. T. Goldthwaite. Berkeley: University of California Press.

———. (1781/1787) 1996. *Critique of Pure Reason*. Translated by W. S. Pluhar. Indianapolis: Hackett.

———. (1785) 1956. *The Groundwork of the Metaphysic of Morals*. Translated by H. J. Paton. New York: Harper Torchbooks.

———. (1790) 1987. *Critique of Judgment*. Translated by W. S. Pluhar. Indianapolis: Hackett.

Kaufman, E., and K. J. Heller. 1998. *Deleuze and Guattari: New Mappings in Politics, Philosophy, and Culture*. Minneapolis: University of Minnesota Press.

Kawakami, K. (1992) 1995. *101 Unuseless Japanese Inventions: The Art of Chindogu*. New York: W. W. Norton.

Kelley, Robin D. G. 2000. "A Poetics of Anticolonialism." In Césaire (1950) 2000, 7–28.

Kelly, S. 2001. "The Non-conceptual Content of Perceptual Experience." *Philosophy and Phenomenological Research* 62 (3): 601–8.

Kenko. [1330] 1998. *Essays in Idleness: The Tsurezuregusa*. Written in 1330. Translated by Donald Keene. 2nd ed. New York: Columbia University Press, 1998.

Kenny, A. 1980. Review of S. Cavell, *The Claim of Reason. Times Literary Supplement*, April 18.

Kierkegaard, S. (1843) 1987. *Either/Or: A Fragment of Life*. Edited and translated by Howard V. Hong and Edna H. Hong. Princeton: Princeton University Press.

Klavier, F., ed. 2004. *Representations of the Dead*. Madison: University of Wisconsin Press.

Kleist, H. von. 1801. "Letter to Wilhelmine von Zenge, Berlin, 22 March 1801." In Kleist 1997.

———. (1810) 1982. "On the Marionette Theater." Translated by Christian-Albrecht Gollub. In *German Romantic Criticism*, edited by A. Leslie Willson. New York: Continuum.

———. 1997. *Selected Writings*. Edited and translated by David Constantine. Indianapolis: Hackett.

Knabb, K. 1995. *Situationist International: Anthology*. Berkeley, Calif.: Bureau of Public Secrets.

Kojève, A. (1933–39) 1980. *Introduction to the Reading of Hegel: Lectures on the Phenomenology of Spirit*. Written 1933–39. Ithaca, N.Y.: Cornell University Press.

Kripke, S. 1982. *Wittgenstein on Rules and Private Language: An Elementary Exposition*. Cambridge, Mass.: Harvard University Press.

Kuhn, T. S. (1962) 1970. *The Structure of Scientific Revolutions*. Chicago: University of Chicago Press.

Kundera, M. 1984. *The Unbearable Lightness of Being*. Translated M. H. Heim. New York: Harper Perennial.

———. (1995) 1997. *Slowness*. Translated from the French by Linda Asher. New York: Harper Perennial.

Lao Tzu. (c. 550 BCE) 1989. *Tao Te Ching (Dao De Jing)*. Translated by John C. H. Wu. Boston: Shambhala. References will be to the eighty-one relatively brief chapters.

Lawrence, N. 1956. *Whitehead's Philosophical Development*. Berkeley: University of California Press.

———. 1961a. "The Vision of Beauty and the Temporality of the Deity in Whitehead's Philosophy." *Journal of Philosophy* 58 (19): 543–53.

———. 1961b. "Time, Value, and the Self." In Leclerc 1961, 145–66.

———. 1969. "Time Represented as Space." In Freeman and Sellars 1971, 123–32.

Laclos, C. de. (1782) 1961. *Les liaisons dangereuses*. Baltimore: Penguin.

Leclerc, I., ed. 1961. *The Relevance of Whitehead*. New York: Macmillan.

Leibniz, G. 1715/1716. "From the Letters to Clarke (1715–16)." In Ariew and Garber 1989, 320–46.

Locke, J. (1689) 1979. *An Essay concerning Human Understanding*. Edited by P. N. Nidditch. Oxford: Oxford University Press.

Long, A. A., and D. N. Sedley. 1987. *The Hellenistic Philosophers*. Vol. 1: *Translations of the Principal Sources with Philosophical Commentary*. Cambridge: Cambridge University Press. References will be to section number and passage letter, e.g., 21.B.

Lorde, A. *Arsenal #4* as cited in Alston 2004.

Lucia, J. 2001. "Both Ways." A collection of poems. Unpublished.

Lucier, A. 1980. *Chambers: Scores by Alvin Lucier.* Edited with interviews with the composer by Douglas Simon. Middletown, Conn.: Wesleyan University Press.

Lyotard, J.-F. 1982. "Presenting the Unpresentable: The Sublime." Translated by Lisa Liebmann. *Artforum* 20 (8): 64–69.

———. (1983) 1988. *The Differend: Phrases in Dispute.* Minneapolis: University of Minnesota Press, 1988.

———. (1988) 1990. *Heidegger and "the Jews."* Minneapolis: University of Minnesota Press.

———. 1991. "Critical Reflections." *Artforum* 24 (8): 92–93.

———. (1993) 1997. *Postmodern Fables.* Minneapolis: University of Minnesota Press.

———. 1995. "Sight Unseen." Typescript of "Les Yeux Fermés" in a translation by Patricia Dailey. Presented as a lecture at Lehigh University on September 11.

Mackie, J. L. 1964. "Self-Refutation—A Formal Analysis." *Philosophical Quarterly* 14 (56): 193–203.

Marx, K. (1867) 1977. *Capital: A Critique of Political Economy*, vol. 1. Moscow: Progress Publishers.

McDowell, J. 1994. *Mind and World.* Cambridge, Mass.: Harvard University Press.

McMahon, M. 1997. "Beauty—Machinic Repetition in the Age of Art." In Genosko 2001.

Mendelson, M. 1995. "Beyond the Revolutions of Matter: Mind, Body, and Pre-Established Harmony in Earlier Leibniz." *Studia Leibniziana* 27 (1): 31–66.

———. 2000a. "The City of Luck, the Plain of Gray, and the Alleys of Loss: Foray into the Landscape of Moral Horror." *Soundings* 81 (1): 231–49.

———. 2000b. "Distance: Nightmare Reflections on Moral Geometry." Unpublished.

———. 2001. "The Body in the Next Room: Death as Differend." In Klavier 2004.

———. 2004. "Moral Horror: Tableaux in Philosophical Gothic." Unpublished.

Merleau-Ponty, M. 1945. *The Phenomenology of Perception.* London: Routledge and Kegan Paul, 1962.

———. 1968. *The Visible and the Invisible.* Written in 1961. Evanston, Ill.: Northwestern Univerisity Press.

Mill, J. S. (1859) 1976. *On Liberty.* Edited with an introduction by Gertrude Himmelfarb. New York: Penguin Books.

Miller, A. 1990. *John Cage: I Have Nothing to Say and I'm Saying it.* Video. The Music Project for Television Inc. and American Masters, USA.

Milner, M. (1950) 1990. *On Not Being Able to Paint*. Madison, Conn.: International Universities Press.

Morrison, J. 1967. "Break On Through (To The Other Side)." Recording: The Doors.

Mounce, H. O. 1981. "Review [of *The Claim of Reason* by S. Cavell]." *Philosophical Quarterly* 31 (124): 280–82.

Mulvey, L. 1975. "Visual Pleasure and Narrative Cinema." Reprinted in Mulvey 1989.

———. 1989. *Visual and Other Pleasures*. London: Macmillan.

Nancy, J.-L. (2002) 2007. *Listening*. New York: Fordham University Press.

Negri, A. (1981) 1991. *The Savage Anomaly: The Power of Spinoza's Metaphysics and Politics*. Translated by Michael Hardt. Minneapolis: University of Minnesota Press.

Nehamas, A. 1982. "Plato on Imitation and Poetry in *Republic* X." Reprinted in Nehamas 1999a.

———. 1985. *Nietzsche: Life as Literature*. Cambridge, Mass.: Harvard University Press.

———. 1988. "Plato and Mass Media." Reprinted in Nehamas 1999a.

———. 1998. *The Art of Living: Socratic Reflections from Plato to Foucault*. Berkeley: University of California Press.

———. 1999a. *Virtues of Authenticity: Essays on Plato and Socrates*. Princeton: Princeton University Press.

———. 1999b. "Culture, Art, and Poetry in *The Republic*." Columbia Core Curriculum Coursewide Lecture Fall 1999. http://www.college.columbia.edu/core/lectures/fall1999/index.php.

Nietzsche, F. (1873) 1962. *Philosophy in the Tragic Age of the Greeks*. Written in 1873. Translated by Marianne Cowan. Chicago: Henry Regnery.

———. (1874) 1995. "Schopenhauer as Educator." In Nietzsche 1995.

———. (1878) 1996. *Human, All-Too-Human*. New York: Cambridge University Press, 1996. In 1886 this was reprinted in two volumes each with a new preface. Volume 1 was the old *Human, All-Too-Human*, and volume 2 included both *Mixed Opinions and Maxims* (1879) and *The Wanderer and His Shadow* (1880).

———. 1880. *The Wanderer and His Shadow*. In Nietzsche (1878) 1996.

———. (1881) 1982. *Daybreak: Thoughts on the Prejudices of Morality*. Translated by R. J. Hollingdale. New York: Cambridge University Press.

———. (1882) 1974. *The Gay Science*. Second expanded edition published in 1887. The expanded edition was translated by W. Kaufmann. New York: Vintage Books.

———. (1883–85) 1980. *Thus Spoke Zarathustra*. Translated by R. J. Hollingdale. New York: Penguin Books.

———. (1886) 1966. *Beyond Good and Evil.* Translated with commentary by W. Kaufmann. New York: Vintage Books.

———. (1887) 1967a. *On the Genealogy of Morals: A Polemic.* Translated by W. Kaufmann and R. J. Hollingdale. In *On the Genealogy of Morals and Ecce Homo.* New York: Vintage Books.

———. (1888a) 1982. *Twilight of the Idols.* Written in 1888. In Nietzsche 1982.

———. (1888b) 1982. *The Antichrist.* Written in 1888. In Nietzsche 1982.

———. (1888c) 1967a. *Ecce Homo: How One Becomes What One Is.* Written in 1888. Translated by W. Kaufmann. In *On The Genealogy of Morals and Ecce Homo.* New York: Vintage Books.

———. (1888d) 1982. *Nietzsche contra Wagner.* Written in 1888. In Nietzsche 1982.

———. (1891) 1984. *Dithyrambs of Dionysus.* Translated by R. J. Hollingdale. Redding Ridge, Conn.: Black Swan Books.

———. (1901) 1967b. *The Will to Power.* New York: Vintage Press.

———. 1982. *The Portable Nietzsche.* Selected and translated by Walter Kaufman. New York: Penguin Books.

———. 1995. *Unfashionable Observations.* Translated by Richard T. Gray. Stanford: Stanford University Press.

Nowinski, J. 1970. *Baron Dominique Vivant Denon (1747–1825).* Rutherford, N.J.: Fairleigh Dickinson University Press.

Okakura, K. (1906) 1976. *The Book of Tea.* With foreword and biographical sketch by Elise Grilli. Rutland, Vt.: Charles E. Tuttle.

Olafson, F. A. 1987. *Heidegger and the Philosophy of Mind.* New Haven: Yale University Press.

Ono, Y. (1961) 1999. *Voice Piece for Soprano.* Recording: Sonic Youth, *Goodbye 20th Century (SYR 4)*, disk 1. Performed by Coco Hayley Gordon Moore.

O'Sullivan, S. 2001. "The Aesthetics of Affect: Thinking Art beyond Representation." *Angelaki* 6 (3): 125–35.

Pater, W. (1873) 1990. *Studies in the History of the Renaissance.* Now known as *The Renaissance.* I cite the edition of Adam Phillips. Oxford: Oxford University Press.

Patton, P. 1996. *Deleuze: A Critical Reader.* Edited by P. Patton. Oxford: Blackwell.

Pauli, L. 2003. *Manufactured Landscapes: The Photographs of Edward Burtynsky.* New Haven: National Gallery of Canada in association with Yale University Press.

Pedretti, C. 1980. *Leonardo da Vinci: Nature Studies from the Royal Library at Windsor Castle.* New York: Johnson Reprint Corp.

Piercey, R. 1996. "The Spinoza-Intoxicated Man: Deleuze on Expression." *Man and World* 29: 269–81.

Plato. (c. 380 BCE) 1997. *Plato: Complete Works.* Edited by John M. Cooper. Indianapolis: Hackett.

Plotinus. (c. 300 CE) 1949. *The Ethical Treatises, Being the Treatises of the First [-Sixth] Ennead with Porphyry's Life of Plotinus, and the Preller-Ritter Extracts Forming a Conspectus of the Plotinian System.* Translated from the Greek by Stephen Mackenna. Boston: C. T. Branford.

Polanyi, M. 1966. *The Tacit Dimension.* The Terry Lectures 1962. Garden City, N.Y.: Doubleday.

Potter, K. H. 1963. *Presuppositions of India's Philosophies.* Englewood Cliffs, N.J.: Prentice-Hall.

Pound, E. (1934) 1987. *A B C of Reading.* New York: New Directions.

Rabinow, P. 1984. *The Foucault Reader.* New York: Pantheon Books.

Ramsey, F. P. 1929. "General Propositions and Causality." In Ramsey 1978.

———. 1978. *Foundations: Essays in Philosophy, Logic, Mathematics, and Economics.* Edited by D. H. Mellor. Atlantic Highlands, N.J.: Humanities Press.

Raposa, M. 1999. *Boredom and the Religious Imagination.* Charlottesville: University of Virginia Press.

Reich, S. (1972) 1980. *Clapping Music.* London: Universal Edition.

Rimbaud, A. 1957. *Illuminations.* New York: New Directions.

Ripp, A. 2001. *Gang Tapes.* Santa Monica, Calif.: Lions Gate Home Entertainment..

Riviere, J. 1948. *Collected Papers [of Sigmund Freud].* London: Hogarth Press.

Rosemont, P. 1998. *Surrealist Women: An International Anthology.* Austin: University of Texas Press.

Rosset, C. 1993. *Joyful Cruelty: Toward a Philosophy of the Real.* Translated by David F. Bell. New York: Oxford University Press.

Russell, B. A. W. 1905. "On Denoting." In Russell 1956, 39–56.

———. 1956. *Logic and Knowledge: Essays, 1901–1950.* Edited by R. C. Marsh. London: George Allen and Unwin.

Saltzman, M. 1997. "Yo-Yo Ma." *New York Times,* Sunday, September 7, 1997, sec. 2, Arts and Leisure, 79.

Sato, H., and B. Watson. 1981. *From the Country of Eight Islands.* Garden City, N.Y.: Anchor Books.

Sartre, J-P. (1937) 1999. *The Transcendence of the Ego.* New York: Hill and Wang.

———. (1938) 1964. *Nausea.* Translated by Lloyd Alexander. New York: New Directions.

———. (1943) 1992. *Being and Nothingness: An Essay on Phenomenological Ontology.* Translated by Hazel E. Barnes. New York: Washington Square Press.

———. (1946) 1995. *Anti-Semite and Jew.* Translated by G. J. Becker. Preface by Michael Walzer. New York: Schocken Books.

Scarry, E. 1999. *On Beauty and Being Just.* Princeton: Princeton University Press.

Schapiro, M. 1969. "On Some Problems in the Semiotics of Visual Art: Field and Vehicle in Image-Signs." Reprinted in Schapiro 1994, 1–32.

———. 1994. *Theory and Philosophy of Art: Style, Artist, and Society.* In *Selected Papers* vol. 4. New York: George Braziller.

Schopenhauer, A. (1819) 1969. *The World as Will and Representation.* Translated by E. F. J. Payne. New York: Dover Publications. This book is in two volumes. The second volume consists of fifty new chapters that Schopenhauer added to the second edition in 1844.

Searle, J. (1969) 1970. *Speech Acts: An Essay in the Philosophy of Language.* Cambridge: Cambridge University Press.

———. 1994. "Literary Theory and Its Discontents." *New Literary History* 25 (3): 637–67.

Shaftesbury, Third Earl of. (1711) 1999. *Charcteristics of Men, Manners, Opinions, Times.* Edited by L. E. Klein. Cambridge: Cambridge University Press.

Shirley, S. 2002. *Spinoza: The Complete Works.* Edited by M. L. Morgan. Translated by Samuel Shirley. Indianapolis: Hackett.

Smith, D. W. 1996. "Deleuze's Theory of Sensation: Overcoming the Kantian Duality." In Patton 1996.

———. 1997. "A Life of Pure Immanence: Deleuze's Critique et Clinique Project." *Philosophy Today* 41, supplement.

———. 1998. "The Place of Ethics in Deleuze's Philosophy." In Kaufmann and Heller 1998, 251–69.

Smith, O. F. 1998. *Fluxus: The History of an Attitude.* San Diego: San Diego State University Press.

Sonic Youth. 1999. *SYR 4: Goodbye 20th Century.* Two audio disks recorded and mixed March–August.

Sontag, S. (1966) 1990. *Against Interpretation and Other Essays.* New York: Anchor Books Doubleday.

Spinoza, B. 1661–76. *The Letters.* In Shirley 2002.

———. (1670) 1951. *Tractatus Theologico-Politicus.* Translated by R. H. M. Elwes. New York: Dover.

———. (1677) 1994. *Ethics.* In *A Spinoza Reader: The Ethics and Other Works,* edited and translated by E. Curley. Princeton: Princeton University Press. References to the *Ethics* will be given using the standard abbreviations, where, for example, IIIP15C refers to corollary to the fifteenth proposition in part 3. See Curley 1994, xxv, for details.

Stankovic, S. 2005. Unpublished. "Overcoming Morality: Ethics as Creative Activity." Presented at the international conference on Gilles Deleuze, Jean-François Lyotard, and Aesthetics: "Sensorium: Philosophy and Aesthetics" at the University of Melbourne, Melbourne Australia, June 22–24.

Stein, G. (1914) 1991. *Tender Buttons.* Los Angeles: Sun and Moon Press.

———. (1917) 1995. *Lifting Belly.* Tallahassee, Fla.: Naiad Press.

———. 1933. *The Autobiography of Alice B. Toklas.* In Van Vechten (1946) 1990.

———. (1936a) 1973. *The Geographical History of America; or, The Relation of Human Nature to the Human Mind.* Baltimore: Johns Hopkins University Press.

———. 1936b. "What Are Masterpieces and Why Are There So Few of Them." In Stimpson and Chessman 1998, 355–63.

———. 1936c. "Portraits and Repetition." In Stimpson and Chessman 1998, 287–312.

———. 1946. "Gertrude Stein Talking: A Transatlantic Interview." I cite from a web page of Alan Filreis: http://www.english.upenn.edu/~afilreis/88/stein-interview.html. It is also available in Sutherland (1951) 1971, 180–203.

Steinberg, L. 1972. *Other Criteria: Confrontations with Twentieth Century Art.* New York: Oxford University Press.

Stendhal, R. (1989) 1995. *Gertrude Stein: In Words and Pictures.* London: Thames and Hudson.

Stevens, W. 1972. *The Palm at the End of the Mind.* Edited by Holly Stevens. New York: Vintage.

Stimpson, C. R., and H. Chessman, eds. 1998. *Gertrude Stein: Writings, 1932–1946.* New York: Library of America.

Stolnitz, J. 1961. "'Beauty': Some Stages in the History of an Idea." *Journal of the History of Ideas* 22 (2): 185–204.

Sutherland, D. (1951) 1971. *Gertrude Stein: A Biography of Her Work.* New Haven, Conn.: Greenwood Press.

Sylvester, D. (1987) 1999. *Interviews with Francis Bacon.* This is a reprinting of the third edition of a book whose first edition was called *The Brutality of Fact.* New York: Thames and Hudson.

Taylor, C. 1982. "The Diversity of Goods." In Williams and Sen 1982.

Thoreau, H. D. (1854) 1985. *Walden.* New York: Penguin Books.

———. (1862) 1984. "Walking." In H. D. Thoreau, *The Natural History Essays.* Salt Lake City: Peregrine Smith Books.

Thornton, T. P. 2001. "Book Review [of C. Dallett Hemphill, *Bowing to Necessities: A History of Manners in America, 1620–1860*]." *American Historical Review* 106 (3): 969–70.

Torretti, R. 2000. "Geometry: Nineteenth Century." *Stanford Encyclopedia of Philosophy.* http://plato.stanford.edu/entries/geometry-19th/.

Tournier, M. (1967) 1997. *Friday.* Baltimore: Johns Hopkins University Press.

———. 1975. *Gemini.* A translation of *Les Météores.* Baltimore: Johns Hopkins University Press, 1998.

Uexküll, J. von. (1934) 1992. "A Stroll through the Worlds of Animals and Men: A Picture Book of Invisible Worlds." Translated by Claire H. Schiller. *Semiotica* 89 (4): 319–91.

UN Resolution. 1948. "Universal Declaration of Human Rights." United Nations Resolution 217 A *(III).* Adopted by the General Assembly of the United Nations on December 10, 1948. Accessed on August 1, 2005, from: http://www.un.org/Overview/rights.html.

Vaneigem, R. (1979) 1983. *The Book of Pleasures.* London: Pending Press.

Van Vechten, C. (1946) 1990. *Selected Writings of Gertrude Stein.* New York: Vintage Books.

Viera, R. 2000. *Four Outsider Artists: The End Is a New Beginning: H. Kox, Mr. Imagination, Charlie Lucas, Lonie Holley.* November 29, 2000– February 25, 2001. Bethlehem, Penn.: Zoellner Arts Center, Lehigh University.

Warwick, G. 2000. *The Arts of Collecting: Padre Sebastiano Resta and the Market for Drawings in Early Modern Europe.* Cambridge: Cambridge University Press.

Weiss, G., and H. F. Haber. 1999. *Perspectives on Embodiment: The Intersections of Nature and Culture.* New York: Routledge.

Whitehead, A. N. (1925) 1967. *Science and the Modern World.* New York: Free Press.

———. (1926) 1996. *Religion in the Making.* New York: Fordham University Press.

———. 1927. "Universities and Their Function." In Whitehead 1949, 91–101.

———. (1929) 1978. *Process and Reality.* Corrected edition. Edited by D. R. Griffin and D. W. Sherburne. New York: Free Press.

———. (1938) 1968. *Modes of Thought.* New York: Free Press.

———. 1949. *The Aims of Education.* New York: Mentor.

Whitman, W. (1855) 1939. *Leaves of Grass, Reproduced from the First Edition (1855).* Introduction by Joseph Furness. New York: Published for the Facsimile Text Society by Columbia University Press.

Wilde, O. 1889. "The Decay of Lying." In Wilde 1990.

———. 1891. "The Soul of Man under Socialism." In Wilde 1990.

———. 1990. *The Works of Oscar Wilde.* Leicester, Eng.: Blitz Editions.

Williams, B. A. O. 1973. "Critique of Utilitarianism." In Williams and Smart 1973, 75–150.

———. 1981. *Moral Luck.* Cambridge: Cambridge University Press.

Williams, B. A. O., and A. Sen, eds. 1982. *Utilitarianism and Beyond.* Cambridge: Cambridge University Press.

Williams, B. A. O., and J. J. C. Smart. 1973. *Utilitarianism: For and Against.* Cambridge: Cambridge University Press.

Williams, J. 2003. *Gilles Deleuze's Difference and Repetition: A Critical Introduction and Guide.* Edinburgh: Edinburgh University Press.

Wilson, E. O. (1975) 1980. *Sociobiology: The Abridged Edition.* Cambridge, Mass.: Belknap Press of Harvard University Press.

Wittgenstein, L. (1921) 1961. *Tractatus Logico-Philosophicus.* Translated by D. F. Pears and B. F. McGuinness. London: Routledge and Kegan Paul. Citations will be by proposition number, not by page.

———. 1933. "Philosophy." This is a chapter from *The Big Typescript* that was published in German and English in Wittgenstein 1993, 158–99.

———. (1953) 1976. *Philosophical Investigations.* 3rd edition 1967. Oxford: B. Blackwell, 1976. Part I of this book was more or less complete by 1945 will be referred to by section number, using the sign "§." Part 2 was finished by 1949 and will be referred to by page number, using the sign "p."

———. 1969. *On Certainty.* New York: Harper Torchbooks. These are notes of Wittgenstein's that were written between roughly December 1949 and his death on April 29, 1951.

———. 1980. *Culture and Value.* Translated by Peter Winch. Chicago: University of Chicago Press. This is a collection of remarks written by Wittgenstein in notebooks dating from 1914 to 1951. The Chicago edition makes the date of each remark plain.

———. 1986. *Wittgenstein: Conversations, 1949–1951.* By O. K. Bouwsma. Edited by J. L. Craft and R. E. Hustwit. Indianapolis: Hackett.

———. 1993. *Philosophical Occasions: 1912–1951.* Edited by James Klagge and Alfred Nordmann. Indianapolis: Hackett.

Wolf, N. (1991) 1992. *The Beauty Myth.* New York: Anchor Books.

Woolf, V. 1925. *Mrs. Dalloway.* New York: Harcourt.

Wypijewski, J. (1997) 1999. *Painting by Numbers: Komar and Melamid's Scientific Guide to Art.* Berkeley: University of California Press.

Young, La Monte. (1963) 1970. *An Anthology of Chance Operations.* Edited by L. M. Young and J. M. Low. 2nd ed. New York: Heiner Friedrich, 1970.